Experiencing William James

EXPERIENCING WILLIAM JAMES

BELIEF IN A PLURALISTIC WORLD

James Campbell

UNIVERSITY OF VIRGINIA PRESS
Charlottesville and London

University of Virginia Press
© 2017 by the Rector and Visitors of the University of Virginia
All rights reserved
Printed in the United States of America on acid-free paper

First published 2017

9 8 7 6 5 4 3 2 1

Library of Congress Cataloging-in-Publication Data
Names: Campbell, James, 1948– author.
Title: Experiencing William James : belief in a pluralistic world / James Campbell.
Description: Charlottesville : University of Virginia Press, 2017. | Includes bibliographical references and index.
Identifiers: LCCN 2017022071 | ISBN 9780813940472 (cloth : alk. paper) | ISBN 9780813940489 (pbk. : alk. paper) | ISBN 9780813940496 (e-book)
Subjects: LCSH: James, William, 1842–1910.
Classification: LCC B945.J24 C28 2017 | DDC 191—dc23
LC record available at https://lccn.loc.gov/2017022071

Cover art: William James by Alexander Robertson James, collotype on paper, date unknown. (National Portrait Gallery, Smithsonian Institution; gift of Alexander R. James)

For John J. McDermott—
who made this book, and so much more, possible

Contents

	Preface	ix
	Abbreviations for Works by William James	xiii
1.	Preliminary Considerations	1
2.	Psychology and Philosophy	25
3.	Rationality and Belief	79
4.	Pragmatism	111
5.	Radical Empiricism and Pluralism	160
6.	Ethics and Social Thought	200
7.	Religion	240
	Afterword	285
	Notes	289
	Works Cited	357
	Index	375

Preface

IN THIS VOLUME, I undertake an overall examination of the thought of the American philosopher and psychologist William James (1842–1910). I believe that such an examination is a worthwhile endeavor because, while he has long been recognized as a central figure in the American philosophic tradition and his ideas continue to play a significant role in contemporary thinking, his thought has been approached over the years in anything but a comprehensive fashion. For the most part, commentators have enthusiastically (if not always carefully) explored pieces of his thought or aspects of his vision, but these pieces and aspects have often suffered because of their isolated nature and their divorce from their context. While this simpler version of James may make the task of commentators easier—whether their aim is to make his thought initially more understandable or to eliminate him as a philosophically unprepared if well-meaning amateur—a more complex version of James offers a richer and more defensible perspective. Thus, a fuller and more complete presentation of his thought is necessary. The present is also an auspicious time to undertake such an overall project because we are the fortunate beneficiaries of the nineteen-volume critical edition of his writings from Harvard University Press and the twelve-volume critical edition of his correspondence from the University of Virginia Press to make more thorough research possible.

My own study of James suffered initially from the input of sincere but misguided philosophy professors. These teachers either wanted to make his position more understandable, for example by discounting all of its psychological themes, or saw him as a philosophical lightweight whose ideas were either mistaken (as in the case of the will to believe), too vague to be of use in contemporary philosophical discourse (as in his presentation of the stream of consciousness), or simply not philosophy at all (as in his interest in the meaning of religious experience). I was thus warned off from studying James's work and urged to pursue "real" philosophy of the sort found primarily in the work of Charles Sanders Peirce, or to a lesser extent in that of John Dewey. Still, I continued to find many themes in James's work valuable, like his openness to outside perspectives, his attempts to address philosophic problems directly and free from the constraints of tradition, and his willingness to use analogies as a form of philosophical argument. These and other values drew me to engage with his ideas further. Additional study of the history of philosophy in America around the turn of the twentieth century also made clearer to me that the kind of philosophy that developed in the emerging American university was not the only philosophy possible.

This volume presents my ideas on James's thinking, especially as he participates in and advances the pragmatic spirit that I believe is at the core of American philosophy. This volume is also the third piece of my projected four-volume study of American Pragmatism, in which the themes of natural place, experience, possibility and community provide the organizational framework for examining the thought of Benjamin Franklin, Ralph Waldo Emerson, James, and John Dewey. My intention in the present volume is to explore the central strands of James's thought, especially how his own role in the pragmatic tradition highlights the complex task of individuals who must navigate a world of nearly limitless possibilities directed by hopes that reach beyond adequate evidence. Hence my subtitle: *Belief in a Pluralistic World*.

I have not been able to discuss all of the intricacies of James's thought in this volume, but I have tried to take careful note of his presentations of his own ideas, with less concern for his critiques of the ideas of others. To tell just his story, I believe, is a sufficiently complex and demanding task. I have included, primarily in the notes, my sense of the relevant secondary material. With some of the criticisms presented there, I am in general agreement; with some, I am not. Developing a broad understanding of the meaning of James's work, however, is only possible within the context of this larger background. While this volume may have at times an historical feel, it is not intended primarily as a study of the past. James is not an exclusively historical figure, although understanding his ideas requires a familiarity with his contexts and problems. It is thus necessary to explore the historical context in which his ideas emerged, and the reactions that they received over the last century, to develop a better feel for the long process of the development of Pragmatism and to be able to help direct its future.

The focus of my writing over the years has been on the branch of pragmatic social thinking that developed at the University of Chicago around the turn of the twentieth century, especially on the thought of John Dewey, James Hayden Tufts, and George Herbert Mead. I have found this work to be of great historical interest in understanding the development of philosophy in America, but also of great present value as we attempt to address our ongoing social problems. At the same time, I have continued an interest in the thought of William James. Among the essays that I have published on his ideas over the years are "William James and the Ethics of Fulfillment" (1981), "Ayer and Pragmatism" (1992), and "A Study of Human Nature Entitled *The Varieties of Religious Experience*" (2003). With this volume, I have expanded and integrated these fragments into a full consideration of his position in American thought.

I am indebted to a large number of people with whom I have studied and worked over the years, and from whom I have learned a great deal about James and American philosophy. I have also been assisted in this project by the ongoing support of The University of Toledo and by a summer stipend from the National Endowment for the Humanities.

Abbreviations for Works by William James

C	*The Correspondence of William James*
ECR	*Essays, Comments, and Reviews*
EP	*Essays in Philosophy*
EPR	*Essays in Psychical Research*
EPs	*Essays in Psychology*
ERE	*Essays in Radical Empiricism*
ERM	*Essays in Religion and Morality*
MEN	*Manuscript Essays and Notes*
ML	*Manuscript Lectures*
MT	*The Meaning of Truth*
P	*Pragmatism: A New Name for Some Old Ways of Thinking*
PBC	*Psychology: Briefer Course*
PP	*The Principles of Psychology*
PU	*A Pluralistic Universe*
SPP	*Some Problems of Philosophy*
TT	*Talks to Teachers on Psychology and to Students on Some of Life's Ideals*
VRE	*The Varieties of Religious Experience: A Study in Human Nature*
WB	*The Will to Believe and Other Essays in Popular Philosophy*
WWJ	*The Writings of William James: A Comprehensive Edition*

Experiencing William James

CHAPTER 1

Preliminary Considerations

This chapter undertakes three tasks. The first is to take an initial look at the importance of James's thought, and to lay out a general overview of his place in the American philosophical tradition through a brief survey of the secondary literature. Next is a biographical sketch that grounds his ideas in the particulars of his experience. In this way, the James who grew up in a nineteenth-century world of wealth and comfort and travel, and who flourished during a Harvard teaching career of nearly thirty-five years, will be matched up with the author of such timeless volumes as *The Principles of Psychology* (1890), *The Will to Believe* (1897), *The Varieties of Religious Experience* (1902), and *Pragmatism* (1907). Finally, I explore his general vision of the contemporary intellectual world to get a sense of his understanding of the crisis that developments in nineteenth-century science had brought to Western thought, especially with regard to the meaning of human existence. This crisis will serve as a backdrop for the rest of this study.

The Importance of James's Thought

William James became a major figure in American intellectual history, especially in philosophy and psychology, in the 1880s and continues to be one to the present day. To get an initial sense of who he was, and of what his ideas were, we can consider a series of five appreciations. We can begin with Josiah Royce, who writes that James was one of only three "representative American philosophers"—the other two being Jonathan Edwards (1703–58) and Ralph Waldo Emerson (1803–82). What makes each of these American thinkers "representative," Royce continues, was that each "thinks for himself, fruitfully, with true independence, and with successful inventiveness, about problems of philosophy," and "gives utterance to philosophical ideas which are characteristic of some stage and of some aspect of the spiritual life of his own people." In describing James, John Dewey remarks that "long after 'pragmatism' in any sense save as a application of his Welt-Anschauung [way of looking at the world] shall have passed into a not unhappy oblivion, the fundamental idea of an open universe in which uncertainty, choice, hypotheses, novelties and possibilities are naturalized" will continue to be associated with his name. Dewey continues that the more we study James "in his historic setting," the more "original and daring" we will see his understanding of the open universe. For Alfred North Whitehead, James, along with Plato, Aristotle, and Leibniz, was one of the four great philosophical assemblers whose work must precede systematization. He saw the essence of James's greatness to be "his marvellous sensitivity to the ideas of the present. He knew the world in which he lived, by travel, by personal relations with its leading men, by the variety of his own studies." Of course James systematized, "but above all he assembled," and "his intellectual life was one protest against the dismissal of experience in the interest of system." Next, Robert C. Pollock writes that we must expect that original philosophers like James, who challenge the familiar and seek "to situate knowledge in the wider context of actual existence," will of necessity throw "well-tested concepts out of alignment" and create "new difficulties." As a result, there will emerge a host of inconsistencies, ambiguities, and fallacies that will take time to sort out. As Pollock reminds us, however, "the warrant for his thought does not lie in its ability to defend itself against all comers, but rather in its power to enlighten us regarding something of importance to all who care to see life in the round."[1]

Finally, John J. McDermott writes that James's relevance "lies in his ability to offer philosophical insight of the kind which refuses to be localized by any strictly circumscribed method or doctrine." McDermott continues that "James's thought is the vestibule to the thought and values of the twentieth century." Among the many breakthroughs to which James provides entry, McDermott lists "the directions of modern physics, psychoanalysis and depth psychology, modern art, and the emphasis on relations rather than on objects or substances." Perhaps most central for McDermott is that "James is a process philosopher, by which we mean that he assesses the journey, the flow, to be more important than the outcome or the product." He further notes that the golden age of American philosophy would be "inconceivable without James as an originating force." McDermott notes, moreover, that there is much more to James than what might appear in any narrow presentation of the author of *Pragmatism*. It is inadequate to speak of James as a pragmatist—or any other "-ist"—McDermott writes at one point: "He was a genius of his own kind, who gave to philosophy, largely by virtue of his personal qualities, a perspective and a context wholly novel in implication." In a similar fashion, he rejects a slightly broader version of this attempt to box James in. He writes: "Unfortunately, James has been approached, in the main, from primarily two vantage points: his doctrine of the 'Will to Believe' and his 'Pragmatism.' While both of these concerns in James are intriguing and carry important philosophical implications, they are subject to grave distortions if seen apart from his insight into the meaning of relations as formulated in his psychology and metaphysics." McDermott indicates that "although a pragmatic epistemology is an important strand in James's philosophy, it does not occupy the center of his vision." At the center of James's vision—his "most important philosophical contention"—is his analysis of "the status of relations and the philosophical implications of that contention, which he subsequently referred to as radical empiricism." Looking out from this relational core, Pragmatism is most accurately understood as "a methodological application of his radical empiricism."[2]

Regardless of tributes like these, for some James was simply too catholic or liberal a thinker to be properly characterized a philosopher. Clearly, he did not fit well into any traditional philosophic harness. At his death in 1910 the *Philosophical Review* offered this backhanded compliment: "No philosopher of the English speaking world has been more widely read by persons not interested in technical philosophy."[3] James's friend Charles Sanders Peirce noted "his almost unexampled incapacity for mathematical thought, combined with intense hatred for logic—probably for its pedantry, its insistence on minute exactitude."[4] Another friend, Oliver Wendell Holmes Jr., saw in James a shortage of "continuously sustained logical thought." For Holmes, James demonstrated the mind of "the Irishman . . . great keenness in seeing into the corners of the human heart but impatience of and incapacity for the sustained continuous thinking that makes a philosopher." James was to his mind "a great psychologist—not a great philosopher."[5] For James Seth, William James represented "a confusion of the functions of philosophy and poetry or religion," because he demands that "philosophy shall match the concreteness and livingness of life or experience, shall reproduce reality in all its concrete 'thickness.'" For Seth, however, philosophy should be more concerned with reasons and more aligned with science. He continues that James "would assimilate philosophy rather to the intuitional and emotional apprehension of poetry and religion than to the conceptual apprehension of science." Seth further found in James over time "a growing and almost morbid dread of the 'academic,' the 'pedantic,' . . . a supreme contempt for the professorial tribe as such." He thus characterized James as a "popular essayist in philosophy" who aims at "interest and surprise" and "picturesque effect," and whose writings produce "a brilliant literary effort rather than a substantial contribution to philosophical discussion."[6] Finally, to round out this initial survey of some of James's contemporaries on the question of whether he should be considered a philosopher, we can note Ferdinand Canning Scott Schiller's description of him as "not, strictly speaking, a professional philosopher at all." James was, for Schiller, one of a long stream of glorious amateurs—a stream that included Descartes, Berkeley, Schopenhauer, Mill, and Spencer—"who have stirred philosophy and stimulated thought." James became a philosopher "from the love of it, from personal interest in its problems, and not because he thought he could make a living by cataloguing the varieties of philosophic opinion, and speculating about the sense of the abstruse abstractions in which defunct philosophers have hidden away their esoteric doctrines." Schiller sees in James's amateur status further value: freed from "the dull mechanical routine of academic philosophy," he could approach philosophic problems freshly and personally, unhampered by "the nerveless and half-hearted efforts of 'dispassionate' research."[7]

Over the last century, during which philosophy has become ever more narrow and professionalized, some later commentators have continued to question James's status as a philosopher. Boyd Henry Bode, for example, notes that "to his contemporaries, he was a personality that did not seem to fit into any of the existing classifications." Among professional philosophers "it was the fashion to say that he was not really a philosopher at all, but a brilliant psychologist with an unfortunate habit of going on philosophic binges."[8] For others, the question of whether James was a philosopher is less important than whether he offered a philosophical system. Donald Cary Williams writes that in terms of theory, "it is vain to look to him for a girdered system, engineered to the last rivet," because his "mind was like a studio crammed with raw materials and debris, many half-hewn blocks of exciting design, and a dozen unmistakable masterpieces." Instead of an ordered philosophy, we find philosophical pluralism, or as Williams puts it, "the intensity, the incessancy, the plethora of his thought were enough to make three or four philosophies—and they did." William Ernest Hocking also rejects the idea that James offered a unified philosophical system, suggesting rather that "in him idealism, realism, pragmatism and mysticism coexisted without achieving a final consistency."[9]

Still, these questionings of James as a philosopher must be read in the context of a rethinking—strongly influenced by James himself—of the nature of philosophy. Max Carl Otto describes him as "a seasoned scholar, not an amateur, in philosophy," who hated the inherited "mustiness" of the discipline and "preferred his butterflies flying." If we follow James and take as our subject matter "the fullness of experience in all its wealth of detail and complexity of interrelation," and pursue it to "the remotest crannies and the widest vistas" that it reveals, Otto believes that we will recognize that his goal was "to feel and know and chronicle each particular in its sovereign singularity and all the particulars in their lawful togetherness."[10] For his part, Horace Meyer Kallen points to James's great influence "as the initiator of a sort of sanitary engineering of the philosophic discipline, an opening up of the sealed chambers of the mind which rest upon the dominant logic of illation [inference] to the cleansing and the health-restoring fresh air of perceptual experience, scientific method, and practical action." By opening up philosophy, John Evan Turner writes, "James has effectually destroyed the pestilent tradition that Philosophy is a specialised culture wholly aloof from the interests and concerns of everyday life. . . . James, once for all, has unlocked the study door and thrown away the key." Or, as Lewis Mumford puts it, James "divested philosophy of its high hat and its painful white collar, and by the mere force of his presence made it human again." For Wendell T. Bush, James's "'real' message" was that "a fact can not be extinguished by an argument, and that no argument can create a single fact, though its toil be distributed through two semesters and many syllogisms." Since these facts belong to everyone, not just to academics, William James Earle indicates that "James addresses himself to the people, not especially to other philosophers."[11]

Continuing on with the theme that James was a different kind of philosopher, we can consider the position of his student and later colleague at Harvard, George Santayana. Santayana writes that "there is a sense in which James was not a philosopher at all," if we are thinking of philosophy as "a consolation and sanctuary in a life which would have been unsatisfying without it . . . an edifice to go and live in for good." Santayana continues that philosophy for James was "rather like a maze in which he happened to find himself wandering, and what he was looking for was the way out." He remained wary of theories and abstractions, yet open to particulars and especially to individuals. Perhaps because he began his teaching career feeling "a little in the professor's chair as a military man might feel when obliged to read the prayers at a funeral," James "kept his mind and heart wide open to all that might seem, to polite minds, odd, personal, or visionary in religion and philosophy." Santayana writes further of James's openness to "sentimentalists, mystics, spiritualists, wizards, cranks, quacks, and imposters—for it is hard to draw the line, and James was not willing to draw it prematurely." It was important to him that "the intellectual cripples and the moral hunchbacks not . . . be jeered at; perhaps they might turn out to be the heroes of the play. Who could tell what heavenly influences might not pierce to these sensitive half-flayed creatures, which are lost on the thick-skinned, the sane, and the duly goggled?" As a result, James "became the friend and helper of those groping, nervous, half-educated, spiritually disinherited, passionately hungry individuals of which America is full." In the process, he became "their spokesman and representative before the learned world; and he made it a chief part of his vocation to recast what the learned world has to offer, so that as far as possible it might serve the needs and interests of these people."[12]

In commentaries on American thought, there are frequent references to James—as there are to Benjamin Franklin, Ralph Waldo Emerson, and John Dewey—as "America's philosopher." Royce presents James as "our national philosopher" and "a prophet of the nation that is to be," in whom "certain characteristic aspects of our national civilization have found their voice." Henry Bamford Parkes notes that "no other thinker has been so deeply or so characteristically American in his intellectual preconceptions and habits of thought, or has reflected so clearly both the virtues and the deficiencies of the American mind." Parkes is especially keen to emphasize James's connection with the American past, from which he acquired his "distrust of abstract theory . . . partly from the suspicion of dogmas and intellectual absolutes that had always been characteristic of the Anglo-Saxon mentality, and partly from the added emphasis on practical utility the Americans had acquired during the pioneering experience." For Parkes, however, James's value also transcends the past. He points to James's "faith in individualism and in freedom, and the realization that every person and every event were in some way unique and could never be wholly explained by general laws," and his "vision of the universe not as a cosmic order in which everything had its appointed place but as the scene of a battle between good and evil in which nothing was predetermined and the future was always uncertain." Parkes continues that "James was most deeply an American when he saw life as an adventure in which there was no ideal harmony and in which struggle and insecurity were the ultimate realities."[13]

Santayana notes that James "had a knack for drawing, and rather the temperament of the artist; but the unlovely secrets of nature and the troubles of man preoccupied him, and he chose medicine for his profession." This comment might suggest to some an early end of the artistic in James's work, but others have made art central to their understanding of James. Jacques Barzun, for example, writes that "the mind is natively not a scientist but an artist," and, in James's case, the mind is "artist first and last." For him, Barzun continues, "art was an extension and clarification of the fluid, fugitive deliverances of experience."[14] In a similar fashion, Dickinson Sergeant Miller writes that "the artist's special task is not that of the man of science, to penetrate into the component parts of things and show how these parts build and rebuild themselves into varied forms; nor is it to point out the component parts of processes and disengage causes and effects." On the contrary, the unique task of the artist is "to catch a unique fact; to catch a 'peculiar effect'; to render a scene or a feeling in its distinction, its individuality." This is what James did repeatedly, Miller continues, and what makes him unique. "To minds of rationalist grain it is always a little odd and puzzling that he should keep telling how systems of philosophy feel, how they are haughty, remote, austere, like a temple; of their dryness, of their grandeur, of their beauty, of their neatness and cleanness, of their straight-laced appearance, of their deadness, toughness, tenderness, thickness, thinness, of every sort of picturable or appreciable quality." In a related fashion, Dewey emphasizes James's skill as a writer, his "power of literary expression." Pointing to James's "picturesqueness of reference" and "brilliant accuracy of characterization," Dewey praises "his sense for the concrete, and for the varied aspects of the world." For Dewey, this ability was not the result of James being "a philosopher who by taking pains acquired a literary gift." Rather

James "was an artist who gave philosophic expression to the artist's sense of the unique, and to his love of the individual."[15]

While there are occasional suggestions that James was not a particularly good writer—as in the comment by Paul Carus that James "seems to be in the habit of sometimes saying what he does not mean and then blam[ing] the world for misunderstanding him"[16]—most commentators salute him for the quality of his writing and its facility for presenting his philosophic vision. McDermott, for example, notes that "few philosophers have written with the verve and elegance of William James," and Williams recognizes "the sorcery of his phrases."[17] Edwin Björkman points to one of the potential costs of James's writing, when he indicates that "his passion for clearness, on the platform as well as in print," caused many to "think him less deep than he is: the plainness of his style seems sadly lacking in profundity when compared with the veiled and oracular utterances of other philosophers." Schiller writes, however, that James was able to show that "it is possible for philosophy to be profound without pedantry, to interest without debauching, to penetrate directly to the heart and mind of all live thinking without commending itself to the vices of the professionals by cultivating an oracular obscurity and enwrapping itself in the pretentious trappings of technicality." Schiller continues in the same vein that "there is a real danger that professed philosophers should come to believe that nothing can be profound but what is obscurely put, and that they should consequently pass over too-lightly the lucidity which seems to reveal the depths of philosophic problems even to the uninitiated."[18]

Van Wyck Brooks notes that James, "with his suspicion of absolutes and dogmas, continued the line that had run through Emerson and Whitman from Benjamin Franklin and others a century before, believing that, since 'morality, compassion and generosity,' as Jefferson said, are 'innate elements of the human constitution,' men could dispense with authority and be trusted with freedom."[19] While the importance of Emerson and Whitman was clear to James, that of Franklin (1706–90) was not. In "The Moral Philosopher and the Moral Life," for example, he writes of the need to "get beyond the coarser and more commonplace moral maxims, the Decalogies and Poor Richard's Almanacs" (*WB* 143). Yet the affiliations of James and Franklin run deep, especially if we look beyond the *Almanac* and the *Autobiography* and search for Franklin's larger moral vision. There we find a rejection of religious morality, especially in its defense of outdated customs, and a call for individual service to advance the common good and to expand human happiness. In this context, even virtues like industry and frugality that are often presented as signs of Franklin's Puritanism or proto-capitalism function more as aspects of a larger Pragmatic morality.[20]

Ralph Waldo Emerson is a figure who is sadly neglected today, especially among American philosophers who have moved away from his adopted role of public sage. Now the model for philosophers is far too often a figure like W. V. O. Quine: a brilliant mathematical philosopher talking to other philosophers abstractly about the intricacies of science. (Richard Rorty provides another model for philosophers, but one that ultimately abandons the label of "philosopher.") In his day, Emerson was a world-famous thinker and writer, and a friend of the James family.[21] In such writings as *Nature* (1836), "The American Scholar" (1837), and "The Divinity School Address" (1838), he urged us all to recognize the fullness of reality, and called on all teachers and preachers to offer their followers the richness of life, of experience, rather than the shell of words, doctrines, or formal ceremonies. As he puts it, if "foregoing generations beheld God and nature face to face," then we too should enjoy "an original relation to the universe." We must recognize the mistake of speaking "of the revelation as somewhat long ago given and done, as if God were dead." For Emerson, "it is a mischievous notion that we are come late into nature; that the world was finished a long time ago. As the world was plastic and fluid in the hands of God, so it is ever to so much of his attributes as we bring to it."[22] Because of his own championing of similar themes, James—from nearby Cambridge—was an easy choice to speak at the Emerson centenary celebration in Concord on 25 May 1903.

In preparation for this fifteen-minute address, James reread Emerson's collected works;[23] the address that he gave contains a statement of his own take on Transcendentalism. He notes that, for Emerson, "the effulgence of the Universal Reason" was present in "the individual fact," and that the "Cosmic Intellect" is to be found "in mortal men and passing hours." He continues:

> Each of us is an angle of its eternal vision, and the only way to be true to our Maker is to be loyal to ourselves.... If the individual open thus directly into the Absolute, it follows that there is something in each and all of us, even the lowliest, that ought not to consent to borrowing traditions and living at second hand. "If

John was perfect, why are you and I alive?" writes Emerson. "As long as any man exists, there is some need of him; let him fight for his own." This faith that in a life at first hand there is something sacred is perhaps the most characteristic note in Emerson's writings.

James emphasizes the centrality of Emerson's "non-conformist persuasion": his belief that, because "the world is still new and untried," we must all find our own way. "In seeing freshly, and not in hearing of what others saw, shall a man find what truth is." He continues that Emerson's proclamation of "the sovereignty of the living individual"—"The present man is the aboriginal reality, the Institution is derivative"—explained his powerful effect on his audience and would continue to be recognized as "the soul of his message" (ERM 111–12). His "revelation" is of the power of the individual, the particular, the novel, the personal. "The point of any pen can be an epitome of reality," James writes, "the commonest person's act, if genuinely actuated, can lay hold on eternity" (ERM 115; cf. VRE 34–36).[24]

John Dewey, seventeen years James's junior, points to the influence that James's work had on him—especially *The Principles of Psychology*, rather than *The Will to Believe* or *A Pluralistic Universe*, or even *Pragmatism*—asserting that "the *Principles of Psychology* is the greatest among the great works of James."[25] In 1903 Dewey wrote to James indicating the centrality of *The Principles* to the developing school of philosophers at the University of Chicago. Of their cooperative volume, *Studies in Logical Theory*, Dewey writes "so far as I am concerned your Psychology is the spiritual progenitor" of Chicago Pragmatism (C 10:215).[26] In later years, Dewey praised James for developing a "biological conception of the *psyche*," informed by the advances of modern science, that "worked its way more and more into all my ideas and acted as a ferment to transform old beliefs." James, he remarks, "had a profound sense, in origin artistic and moral, perhaps, rather than 'scientific,' of the difference between the categories of the living and of the mechanical," and he was able "to think of life in terms of life in action." In this way, James demonstrated how "experience is intimately connected with nature instead of existing in a separate world," and how the universe "which is still in some respects indeterminate and in the making ... implicates all who share in it, whether by acting or believing, in its own perils." Dewey further notes that, as a result, this open universe presents us with philosophical and religious problems that "are not susceptible of decisive evidence one way or the other." In his philosophical work, Dewey continues, James's attempt to present the fullness of the human situation never lost its precedence over his stance as a "professional philosopher." In consequence, James's work "owes so little to dialectics and to tradition." In contrast to the narrowing trends in philosophy, James's "many-sidedness" made him "the most significant intellectual figure the United States has produced."[27]

James's Life and Intellectual Development

Pollock reminds us that philosophical works can be interpreted satisfactorily only when we understand their larger context. "It is necessary," he writes, "to view every such work in its historical setting, while taking into account whatever can render the thought of the philosopher comprehensible, such as the tendencies and crucial issues of the period under consideration, the state of knowledge and the new intellectual atmosphere in which old problems were set." He urges us, further, to widen our analytical perspective, and ultimately to embrace the "whole cultural evolution as the proper field wherein the philosopher's work can be objectified and evaluated." While I hope to present such a perspective in the course of this volume, I recognize as well that no philosopher can be understood without some clear sense of relevant personal aspects. "The biographical details of the life of a major thinker," McDermott writes, are "always of some assistance in enabling us to grasp the issues, the responses, and the omissions found in the work." In the consideration of a figure like James, he continues, "the details are of paramount importance, for his life and his work were entwined in an unusually intimate way."[28]

We can begin with a brief consideration of his paternal grandfather, William James of Albany, New York (1771–1832).[29] This William James was born in County Cavan, Ireland, and raised Presbyterian in the Anglican-dominated country. After the American War of Independence ended in 1783, the eighteen-year-old emigrated to America, working initially as a clerk in New York City. As the years went on, his efforts met with great economic success. Continuing to expand his sights and his field of operations, he became a merchant, a salt extractor, and a land speculator in the area around Syracuse. Later still, he was an investor in the Erie Canal, which ran from Albany past Syracuse to Buffalo. Through these efforts James became enormously wealthy,[30] and at his death in 1832, he left an estate of $3 million to a family consisting of his third wife and ten surviving children.

William's second son by his third wife, and our William's father, was Henry James (1811–1882).[31] He is usually referred to as Henry the Elder to distinguish him from his son—and William's younger brother—Henry the novelist. The elder Henry grew up amid the comforts made possible by his father's great wealth. At the age of thirteen, he was badly injured when a science experiment led by his tutor went awry. The project involved hot air balloons, one of which ignited a barn, and Henry was severely burned attempting to put the fire out. The burns led to painful treatments over the next few years, including a pair of above-the-knee amputations that cost him most of his right leg. He enrolled as an advanced student at Union College in Schenectady in 1828, and although he demonstrated less interest in academic work than in drinking and gambling, he left with his degree in 1830. Henry then entered a period of searching, cushioned by family wealth. After his father's death, when Henry was twenty-one, he lived under a severely restricted inheritance until the will was broken four years later; thereafter, he received an annual income of $10,000.[32] At the age of twenty-three, Henry had a religious conversion and entered Princeton Theological Seminary, but, repelled by its Calvinist theology, he turned against a planned career in the pulpit. Influenced by Transcendentalism, however, and by his friendship with Emerson and others, Henry began a life as a lecturer and writer of religious and social tracts.[33]

At the age of twenty-nine, Henry married Mary Robertson Walsh on 28 July 1840, and the couple had five children over the next eight years: our William (1842–1910), Henry (1843–1916), Garth Wilkinson (1845–1883), Robertson (1846–1910), and Alice (1848–1892). The three younger James children are often overlooked in accounts of the family, as they were in the family itself,[34] because life in the James family was organized around the education of the two elder boys. The family bounced around the Northeast, and back and forth to Europe, as Henry searched for the proper form of schooling for the two. During one of these trips, Henry had a serious episode that, under the influence of the thought of Emanuel Swedenborg (1688–1772), he interpreted as a "vastation." Henry describes his experience as follows:

Preliminary Considerations

> One day... towards the close of May [1844], having eaten a comfortable dinner, I remained sitting at the table after the family had dispersed, idly gazing at the embers in the grate, thinking of nothing, and feeling only the exhilaration incident to a good digestion, when suddenly—in a lightning-flash as it were—"fear came upon me, and trembling, which made all my bones to shake" [*Job*, 4:14]. To all appearances it was a perfectly insane and abject terror, without ostensible cause, and only to be accounted for, to my perplexed imagination, by some damnèd shape squatting invisible to me within the precincts of the room, and raying out from his fetid personality influences fatal to life. The thing had not lasted ten seconds before I felt myself a wreck, that is, reduced from a state of firm, vigorous, joyful manhood to one of almost helpless infancy. The only self-control I was capable of exerting was to keep my seat. (*ERM* 30–31)[35]

As the result of this experience, Henry's work became more mystical. William later wrote that his father's worldview had two central themes. The first was the belief that "the individual man, as such, is nothing, but owes all he is and has to the race nature he inherits, and to the society into which he is born." The second was the refusal to believe that "the great and loving Creator, who has all the being and the power, and has brought us as far as *this*, should not bring us *through*, and *out*, into the most triumphant harmony" (*ERM* 7). Over the years, with his mind concentrated on higher things, Henry and Mary's money slowly disappeared. When they died, eleven months apart, in 1882, the total estate that passed on to their five children amounted to only about $95,000.[36]

Our William James was born in a hotel in New York City on 11 January 1842, and he spent much of his young life traveling in the family's pursuit of languages and culture.[37] A rough chronology of these years runs as follows. From 1843 to 1845 the family was in Europe. The following decade they were back in the United States, mostly in New York City. In 1855 they all returned to Europe for three years, staying in England, France, and Switzerland. The family returned to the United States to live in Newport, Rhode Island, in 1858–59, while William studied painting with William Morris Hunt. The following year they were in Switzerland and Germany. In 1860–61 William was back studying with Hunt in Newport.[38] The family finally settled there as well, living in Newport (1861–64), Boston (1864–66), and Cambridge (from 1866 onward), and sharing the life of the New England social elite. William entered the Lawrence Scientific School, attached to Harvard, in 1861 to study chemistry. He found there not the standard classical education, full of lectures and memorization, but rather laboratory work (which he eventually came to find tedious).[39] William did not graduate from Lawrence, but instead moved on to the Harvard Medical School in February 1864. He graduated from the Medical School at the age of twenty-seven, after time off in Brazil on a research expedition with Louis Agassiz (1865–66)[40] and in Europe to study and recover his health (1867–68)—in June 1869,[41] intending never to practice as a physician.[42]

The defining events in the American experience in the middle of the nineteenth century were those related to the Civil War: the efforts of Southern slave holders to expand the range of slavery, the growing abolitionist movement, the secession of most of the slave states after the election of Abraham Lincoln in 1860, the fighting between 1861 and 1865, and the period of Reconstruction that lasted until 1876. The impact of the Civil War on the members of James's cohort who were killed or wounded, and on their families, was incalculable. In addition, the war's impact on those whose participation saved them from a life of ill health and indecision, and on those—James, for example—whose nonparticipation rendered them far worse, was profound. Neither William nor his brother Henry served in the war. William had briefly enlisted as a ninety-day volunteer in the Rhode Island militia in April of 1861, but his father "bought him out." William agreed to the deal as long as he was allowed to study science at Lawrence. The younger brothers, "Wilky" and Bob, both served—at great personal cost.[43]

The story of James's life in the years between 1869 and 1873 is the story of a series of overlapping crises related to what he was to do with his life—what career he should follow. He went into a tailspin after his final medical examinations in mid-1869 and "touched bottom" in early 1870.[44] As a young man, James suffered from ongoing bouts of depression and periods of collapse. He had eyes that he could not use, a digestive system that he could not control, and a back that he could not trust. His breakdown may have led to some time spent in a psychiatric institution to deal with depression.[45] For a number of years, young James lived at home in a rudderless, half-wrecked state, reading and reviewing books when he felt able.[46] William had been receiving conflicting directions from his father, who undercut him in each chosen career—art, chemistry, medicine—not because the father objected to the specific content of the choice, but because he objected to what he perceived as the narrowing effects of any career.[47]

James was one victim of the epidemic of neurasthenia that swept America in the late nineteenth century. This disease, or better this condition, consisted of a cluster of psychological problems—indecision, anxiety, feelings of worthlessness—combined with such physiological symptoms as indigestion, back pain, and eye strain, all of which may have been psychosomatic. Interpretations of such problems in our time are usually chemical and call for drug therapies, but in James's day the dominant interpretation was genetic. Some people, usually the economically comfortable and often women, were simply born with "weak nervous systems," and they could not produce enough nerve force to deal with the constant pressures and endless distractions of the modern world. The problem of nerve force bankruptcy was exacerbated by the rush and hurry of American life. Writing in this vein in mid-1866, based upon his own experience, medical student James tells a correspondent that "each man's constitution limits him to a certain amount of emotion & action and . . . if he insists on going under a higher pressure than normal for 3 months, for instance, he will pay for it by passing the next 3 mos. below par" (C 4:140; cf. 552).[48]

Perhaps the most striking point in this dark period was James's own undated vastation. He describes the incident, which he presents as that of a French correspondent who was "in a bad nervous condition," as follows:

> Whilst in this state of philosophic pessimism and general depression of spirits about my prospects, I went one evening into a dressing-room in the twilight to procure some article that was there; when suddenly there fell upon me without any warning, just as if it came out of the darkness, a horrible fear of my own existence. Simultaneously there arose in my mind the image of an epileptic patient whom I had seen in the asylum, a black-haired youth with greenish skin, entirely idiotic, who used to sit all day on one of the benches, or rather shelves against the wall, with his knees drawn up against his chin, and the coarse gray undershirt, which was his only garment, drawn over them inclosing his entire figure. He sat there like a sort of sculptured Egyptian cat or Peruvian mummy, moving nothing but his black eyes and

> looking absolutely non-human. This image and my fear entered into a species of combination with each other. *That shape am I*, I felt, potentially. Nothing that I possess can defend me against that fate, if the hour for it should strike for me as it struck for him. (*VRE* 134)⁴⁹

Informed by this powerful experience and the reports of others, he later writes that "the sanest and best of us are of one clay with lunatics and prison-inmates" (*ERM* 62/*VRE* 46;⁵⁰ cf. *VRE* 28). Some light began to appear in James's life, thanks to his chance reading of Charles Renouvier's *Essays*, from which James adopted the definition of free will as "'the sustaining of a thought *because I choose to* when I might have other thoughts.'" He writes that his "first act of free will shall be to believe in free will," a belief that he hoped would enable him to "posit life (the real, the good) in the self-governing *resistance* of the ego to the world," and that would enable him to continue "doing and suffering and creating" without the guarantees of an overall optimism (*WWJ* 7–8).⁵¹

James was eventually hired by Charles William Eliot, a family friend and his former chemistry teacher at Lawrence, and by then the president of Harvard, to teach anatomy and physiology. As the thirty-year-old William writes—apparently without irony—to his brother Henry, on 24 November 1872, "it is a noble thing for one's spirits to have some responsible work to do" (*C* 1:178).⁵² He began teaching the second half of the introductory course on comparative anatomy and physiology in the Department of Natural History in the spring of 1873, drawing on his studies at Lawrence and the Harvard Medical School, and his biological fieldwork in Brazil. During this period when he was establishing himself as an instructor, James also spent time with a circle of friends in what was playfully called "the Metaphysical Club." This club of Harvard men—including Chauncey Wright, Charles Sanders Peirce, and Oliver Wendell Holmes Jr.—pondered a series of general issues related to the nature of science, with a greater concern for how it works than for how it can benefit humanity.⁵³ In 1875 he began to teach courses in psychology, and four years later, in philosophy. As he later wrote: "I drifted into psychology and philosophy from a sort of fatality. I never had any philosophic instruction, the first lecture on psychology I ever heard being the first I ever gave" (*C* 10:590). In 1878 William married Alice Howe Gibbens (1849–1922).⁵⁴ Together, they had five children: Henry (1879–1947), William (1882–1961), Herman (1884–1885), Margaret Mary (1887–1947), and Alexander Robertson (1890–1946).

James remained a professor at Harvard for more than thirty-three years,[55] during which time he rose to both national and international fame, both as a lecturer and writer. His major published works include *The Principles of Psychology*, discussed in chapter 2; *The Will to Believe*, discussed in chapter 3; *The Varieties of Religious Experience*, discussed in chapter 7; and *Pragmatism*, discussed in chapter 4. The last three of these volumes originated on the podium, as did much of James's other published work. Over the years he also carried on inquiries in psychical research. He served as the president of the American Psychological Association (1894 and 1904), and of the American Philosophical Association (1906).[56] Throughout his life, in addition to his writing style, James was known for his active life and electric personality. His sister, Alice, wrote that he was *"just like a blob of mercury"* who "would lend life and charm to a tread-mill." His brother Henry similarly wrote that William had made "philosophy more interesting & living than any one has *ever* made it before."[57]

Despite his fame in Europe and North America, however, William's story continues to be full of self-doubt and ill health. We need to remember that James was never really cured.[58] His accounting of his own personal condition presents a lifelong record of minor imbalances and discomforts, with occasional moments of extraordinary vigor and triumph and others of abject collapse, during which he characterizes his body as "trash" (C 3:150; cf. 153; C 4:200). He undertook numerous experiments on himself—primarily for science rather than therapeutic purposes—with cannabis indica, chloroform, nitrous oxide, and mescal,[59] but he also attempted all sorts of treatments for his real or perceived bodily ills. Among these treatments were: "galvanization" or electrical treatments, visits to a mind curer and to a magnetic healer, Fletcherizing or extended chewing, and injections of dubious value.[60] He did, however, have a bad heart, a condition made worse by a pair of misadventures while hiking.[61] After threatening to do so for a number of years, James retired from Harvard in January 1907 with a Carnegie pension.[62] He hoped that without classroom responsibilities he would be able to complete "a general treatise on philosophy" on which he has been working for a number of years, all the while fearing that "the Angel of Death" would overtake him before he was able to get his "thoughts on to paper" (C 10:409–

10).⁶³ In November 1909 he wrote of his worsening condition, although not without the spark of his appreciation of immediate experience:

> I don't think *death* ought to have any terrors for one who has a positive life-record behind him; and when one's mind has once given up the *claim* on life (which is kept up mainly by one's vanity, I think) the prospect of death is gentle. Meanwhile (however shrunk and crippled one may be) the mere fact of being still part of this real world—the wonderful apparition, as Emerson calls it, has a zest which neutralizes a good many other things. I never admired nature more than I did this summer. The great thing is to live *in* the passing day, and not look farther! (C 12:360–61)

James died at the age of sixty-eight on 26 August 1910 in Chocorua, New Hampshire, dissatisfied, as are all creative minds, with what he had accomplished. He left behind an unfinished volume, *Some Problems of Philosophy* (published in 1911), that was an initial attempt to present years of metaphysical speculations as a systematic unit, but the presentation of his "system" still remained beyond him. He describes his volume as follows: "Say it is fragmentary and unrevised.... Call it 'A beginning of an introduction to philosophy.' Say that I hoped by it to round out my system, which is now too much like an arch built only on one side" (*SPP* 5).⁶⁴ Other posthumous publications continued through 1920, and the republication of James's work has gone on unabated, culminating with the nineteen volumes of the critical edition (1974–88) and the twelve volumes of his correspondence (1992–2004).

James's Vision

A survey of James's thought reveals that there is a center to his work. From the depths of his personal despair and his initial steps in academia, through his frequent challenges to "science" and "Idealism" in defense of freedom and personal choice, he rejects any overarching system that diminishes the place for individuals. His vision is that of a deeply sensitive descriptive psychologist, rooted in evolutionary thought, who is also a prescriptive philosopher cognizant of the needs and longings of the individual live creature who daily faces a natural world found to be insufficient in meaning.

Everyone who reads James recognizes that there is something especially attractive about his style.⁶⁵ Maybe it has something to do with his previously mentioned artistic sensibility, or with the platform style of his writing—his frequent use of first- and second-person pronouns, his homey inclusions of squirrels and dogs, his reliance on metaphor and analogy, and his replacement of philosophical jargon with living phrases like "tender-minded" and "tough-minded"—or with his dispensing with obligatory detailed surveys of the history of philosophy. What he offers us is an immediate encounter with important philosophical issues presented in a new way. This approach is continuous with his larger sense that "philosophic study means the habit of always seeing an alternative, of not taking the usual for granted, of making conventionalities fluid again, of imagining foreign states of mind" (*EP* 4). The "usual" and "conventional" often meant for him the "scientific," and James fought hard to resist the hegemony of science. "Religious thinking, ethical thinking, poetical thinking, teleological, emotional, sentimental thinking, what one might call the personal view of life to distinguish it from the impersonal and mechanical, and the romantic view of life to distinguish it from the rationalistic view," he writes in 1896, "have been and even still are, outside of well-drilled scientific circles, the dominant forms of thought" (*EPR* 134–35).

In the intervening years philosophical style has changed greatly, as we have moved away from the personal and romantic, the broadly human, and toward the precise and the narrow. It is now quite acceptable for philosophers to be dense and uninteresting to a broader public since they seldom seek a public audience anyway. To be more sympathetic to the shift from James's day to our own—to the professionalization of academic philosophy—we must remember that to even understand his position, we need accurate sources, precise and complete formulations, and a grasp of his larger philosophic vision.⁶⁶ We need to combine aspects of his style with aspects of serious scholarship, to balance the dual interests of the appreciation of a living philosophy and the requirements of careful study.

James was particularly cognizant of our situation as active creatures in a partially welcoming natural world. We are, on the one hand, gifted with powers to convert our environment into a home. Our world is in part malleable. He continues that our studies of history indicate that "all great periods of revival, of expansion of the human mind," presented to those who were then active validation for the belief that "'the inmost nature of the reality is congenial to *powers* which you possess'" (*WB* 73). Ultimately, however, we recognize that as natural creatures we are in over our heads, and none of our efforts can prevent inevitable decay and death. As James continues, "the *last* word everywhere, according to purely naturalistic science, is the word of Death, the death-sentence passed by Nature on plant and beast, and man and tribe, and earth and sun, and everything that she has made" (*ERM* 127). Our recognition that our aims will go unfulfilled leaves us seeking explanations that are not to be found. "Witness the attempts to overcome the 'problem of evil,' the 'mystery of pain,'" he writes. Yet, "there is no 'problem of good'" (*WB* 70; cf. *EP* 34).[67] In our attempts to make some sense of this dual reality, we need an understanding of existence that can incorporate and balance both our powers and our extinction. This kind of realism recognizes that we need to take an active part in the physical and intellectual ordering of our world, but with a pragmatic realization that our powers are limited and faith is necessary. McDermott writes that "belief for James was an energizing, a probe, a sally forth with risk acknowledged." Life for James, he continues, "is a series of grapplings, context by context, more or less resolving, more or less enriching."[68]

Although James was very broadly educated and cultured, he was not particularly strong as an historian of philosophy, and it is possible to criticize him for his idiosyncratic presentations. McDermott, for example, points to James's occasional polemics that render "other views in a simplistic manner or out of context." At the same time, he criticizes James's overly generous approach to the philosophic work of other thinkers. He remarks, for example, on "James's propensity to take seriously, in public terms, virtually everyone he has read," and continues that "James's justly praised tolerance of other thinkers and his catholicity of interest often do him a disservice. He is notorious at failing to sort out the thinker and thoughts that have staying power from those he just happens upon."[69] At the present time, we all have the resources to be better historians than he was, and some of us have the interest. Philosophy for him was a pragmatic project rather than an historical one, and philosophic materials from the Greek tradition; from medievalism; from modern explorations into logic, mathematics, and language; and from non-Western philosophy, drew his interest only as they functioned to advance his interests. James was more familiar with the modern period of philosophy, especially from Locke through Hegel, although, as we shall see in chapter 5, he was not necessarily sympathetic to its main foci.

In a letter in mid-1904 James sketches out his perspective for a correspondent as follows: "My philosophy is what I call a radical empiricism, a pluralism, a 'tychism,' which represents order as being gradually won and always in the making. It is theistic, but not *essentially* so. It rejects all doctrines of the Absolute. It is finitist.... I fear that you may find my system too *bottomless* & romantic. I am sure that, be it in the end judged true or false, it is essential to the evolution of clearness in philosophic thought that *some* one should defend a pluralistic empiricism *radically*" (C 10:410). Considering these themes in reverse order, we can begin with finitism as the rejection of the Absolute. Theism is the belief that no purely materialist account of existence can be completely adequate; any full account must allow for more. Tychism is James's acceptance, following Peirce, of the fundamental role of spontaneity or emergence or fortuitism in existence.[70] James's pluralism demands an initial respect for the multiplicity of explanations and perspectives that introduce us to a fuller picture of our existence. Radical empiricism is the position that the inherited tradition of empiricism was itself inadequately empirical, and that a more fundamental analysis of experience was necessary. To round out this presentation of his *Weltanschauung*, we should probably add fallibilism. He presents his recognition of our own tendency to err and the need to respect the contributions of others in a letter to Hugo Münsterberg a few years later as follows: "Do your best; and I'll do my best; and the next generation will do better than either of us and keep whatever either of us may have contributed to the good" (C 11:242). These themes will be developed more carefully as we proceed.

I would like to finish up this initial discussion of James's vision with some further emphasis upon his unique sensitivity to aspects of the human condition. What was driving his philosophic inquiries was not the series of small issues that too often fascinate academic philosophers, but the big question of the place of human existence within the cosmos. If we assume the centrality of the facts of science, as one side of him did, are we led of necessity to its interpretations of determinism and pessimism? Or are we still able to preserve a world of possibility and hope? This tension, and his ongoing attempts at resolution, run throughout his intellectual work. In these attempts, we find his deep sensitivity to aspects of experience.[71] As part of this sensitivity, James the physician is also extremely open to the peculiarities of individuals, to the uniqueness of each person.[72]

James writes that "there were times when Leibnitzes with their heads buried in monstrous wigs could compose Theodicies, and when stall-fed officials of an established church could prove by the valves in the heart and the round ligament of the hip-joint the existence of a 'Moral and Intelligent Contriver of the World.'" Those times, however, had passed, and thinkers in James's day, with their "evolutionary theories and ... mechanical philosophies" (*WB* 42–43), found their answers elsewhere. "Science has made such glorious leaps in the last three hundred years, and extended our knowledge of nature so enormously both in general and in detail," he writes, that it is understandable if on occasion "the worshippers of science lose their head" (*WB* 49) and forget the central importance of fallibility. He writes that, while "philosophic men of science are prompt to admit that all science is but an hypothesis, and at most a probable one," others believe that the finality has been reached. As James notes, "the anti-religious popular scientific professors always speak of religion as if science had made it far more than improbable—namely, impossible" (*ECR* 355).[73] This "lack of scientific imagination" (*WB* 49)—which he calls elsewhere "the puritanism of science" (*ERM* 81)—hampers the recognition that so far we have grasped only handfuls of the universe. As he puts it, "our science is a drop, our ignorance a sea ... the world of our present natural knowledge *is* enveloped in a larger world of *some* sort of whose residual properties we at present can frame no positive idea" (*WB* 50). He continues that both science and religion would benefit from "the liveliest possible state of fermentation" (*WB* 8), and as we shall see in chapter 4, the aim of *Pragmatism* was to carry this process forward.[74]

James was, for example, acutely sensitive to one of the major intellectual issues of the nineteenth century: Pessimism. This doctrine—derived, as he saw it, from the pretensions of science—maintained that nature, and thus we, are part of a monstrous mechanical system that is trapped in a downward spiral toward extinction.[75] Pessimism thus offered a fundamental challenge to our most cherished values of freedom and permanence. The former claim of determinism was rampant in pre-Heisenberg understandings of natural science that incorporated strict orderliness, and thus predetermination, into their presentation of natural order. While this deterministic theme was a powerful one in James's day, it is now recognized to have been grounded on an inadequate understanding of regularity. The latter of these claims—related to entropy, Kelvin's second law of thermodynamics—seems to be true. Even if the end is still untold eons away, we humans are already in a kind of death spiral: nature is a system of finite energy, and we are on a slow decline toward extinction. Still, as we become more comfortable with the fundamental temporality of our existence, admitting it is no longer devastating. If our natural system is finite and bounded, all that we build and cherish will admittedly someday come to an end. Our literature and art will someday be forgotten; our history itself will vanish. In the face of this harsh ultimate reality, however, and without ultimate guarantees, we have to live and grow our food and raise our children. History is what we do with the time remaining. A third pessimistic theme, however, combines the prior two—determinism and eventual extinction—to extract all value from even present experience. In the hands of such a writer as Henry Adams (1838–1918),[76] this kind of pessimism could have devastating effects on individuals' spirits. If we are part of an evolutionary struggle without any purpose, if without cosmic values there are no values at all, there would seem to be no reason to go on.

To this extreme form of pessimism James protests. In *The Varieties*, he writes that for the naturalist like Adams, "mankind is in a position similar to that of a set of people living on a frozen lake, surrounded by cliffs over which there is no escape, yet knowing that little by little the ice is melting, and the inevitable day drawing near when the last film of it will disappear, and to be drowned ignominiously will be the human creature's portion." For such an individual, he continues, "the merrier the skating, the warmer and more sparkling the sun by day, and the ruddier the bonfires at night, the more poignant the sadness with which one must take in the meaning of the total situation" (*VRE* 120; cf. 387–88). Writing to Adams just two months before his own death, James interprets this evidence differently. "Tho' the *ultimate* state of the universe may be its vital and psychical extinction," he writes, "there is nothing in physics to interfere with the hypothesis that the *penultimate* state might be the millennium—in other words a state in which a minimum of difference of energy level might have its exchanges so skillfully *canalisés* [channeled] that a maximum of happy and virtuous consciousness would be the only result" (C 12:556). Thus, for James, recognizing the long-term workings of nature as predicted by science need not prove the end of values.

This is the sense in which McDermott calls James a "post-Copernican" figure. "James faces up to the paradox bequeathed to man by the Copernican revolution," he writes. "Post-Copernican man, no longer the center of the universe by virtue of his planetary setting, has had to affirm his centrality and dignity by the humanizing of all entities and events, including the cosmos itself." Thus, the loss of a given position in existence is not a negative factor, but a positive one. "With James," McDermott continues, "the philosophical enterprise begins anew, for if one is imbued with his viewpoint, nothing is seen in quite the same way again." In particular, James understood what it meant to live in the shadow of Copernicus, in a universe without a center. McDermott continues that James "knew from the first, that if human life were to maintain itself in its most significant and creative aspects, it would have to build itself into the apparently limitless and awesome dimensions of space." Thus, James, whose tentative and open-ended mode of thinking "provided such a scandal to tradition philosophy," can offer us "a plausible and fruitful point of departure" in our search for a workable contemporary cosmology. He recognized, McDermott continues, that our existence makes possible only "intelligibility without a principle of total meaning, and the experience of continuity without the knowledge of finality."[77] In the pages that follow, readers can determine how well James's thought helps them to create an intelligible yet finite life.

CHAPTER 2

Psychology and Philosophy

This chapter begins where James began in academia: deeply engaged with physiological psychology as the latest tool devised to answer the fundamental questions of human existence. Viewing humans as natural creatures, he brought a Darwinian perspective to what in America had previously been largely the armchair endeavor of understanding the soul. He moved early in his academic life within a predisciplinary world in which psychology was the method of philosophical advance, deciding only later that philosophical inquiry that aimed to be "vision" rather than "science" was more likely to answer our important personal questions. A central source in this chapter is James's 1890 masterpiece, *The Principles of Psychology*, especially his examinations of the stream of thought, habit, and the self. Next, there is a consideration of the broad theme of human action that focuses on his discussion of energy and will. This chapter closes with a consideration of what James believes we can learn through a careful study of the fringe areas of psychology.

Psycholophy

As we saw in chapter 1, James's only earned academic degree was the MD. He joined the faculty at Harvard to teach anatomy and physiology in 1873, and over the years, he moved into psychology and then into philosophy. Regardless of his shifting academic titles, however, it is better to consider him a hybrid, a "psycholopher."[1] Part of my evidence here is the fact that philosophy and psychology had not yet separated into the academic disciplines with which we are familiar. They are easier to distinguish now that they have their own departments and journals, but they were less distinguishable around the turn of the twentieth century.[2] We must remember, for example, that James, John Dewey, and Josiah Royce all served as presidents of both the American Psychological Association, founded in 1892, and the American Philosophical Association, founded in 1902, during the first decade of their existence.[3] Further evidence for seeing James as a psycholopher, rather than either a psychologist or a philosopher, is the fact that throughout his academic career—as the old-time denominational college was being supplanted by the new university—both branches of psycholophy were still attempting to separate themselves from the common enemies of the heavy hand of theology and the somewhat lighter hand of commonsense realism. As part of this process of separation, the "new" psychology incorporated the data of comparative physiology, and left behind pastoral aspirations and any role for souls. For its part, the "new" philosophy, largely idealistic in nature, sought a complete system of knowledge within a rational, rather than a theological, order.[4] Eventually, the challenges of Pragmatism and Realism, and the professional triumph of Realism in its various guises, left us with the philosophical scene with which we are now familiar.[5]

We are moving with James through a terrain—consciousness, soul, the self—that has always been difficult. In Western thought there have been several well marked-out trails to follow, especially the religious trail that emphasizes the pursuit of grace and salvation, and the philosophical trail taken by such figures as Plato, John Locke, and Edmund Husserl that emphasizes the clarification of ideas. Emerging within philosophy in James's day was the new trail of physiological psychology. This "new" approach was growing in Europe and America, replacing a psychology that saw itself as mental philosophy. Psychology textbooks that had been full of speculative armchair discussions of perception, memory, imagination, intelligence, feeling, moral will, and so on were now being challenged by textbooks of a new sort that stressed comparative anatomy and physiology, and emphasized the results of laboratory experimentation.[6] In 1900 James describes the contemporary situation as one of "transition and confusion in psychology." Competing in the current mix were the various approaches to the soul and to "distinct ready-made faculties," discussions of the laws of association, contrasting emphases between reason and the will, speculations about evolution's implications for "our instinctive and passional constitution," claims for the importance of the data of the psychological laboratory, and attempts to study in some scientific fashion abnormalities in brains and in states of consciousness (*PP* 3:1482–83).⁷

James was thus working at a transitional point in Western psychology, described by one commentator as a change from "a branch of Philosophy with some scientific trimmings to a genuinely scientific psychology with some philosophical entanglements."⁸ In 1875 he presented the situation to Harvard president Charles William Eliot as one in which psychology professors "whose education has been exclusively literary or philosophical, are too apt to show a real inaptitude for estimating the force & bearing of physiological arguments when used to help define the nature of man." It would thus be wise for the college to appoint a professor—namely himself—"whose scientific training fits him fully to realize the force of all the natural history arguments, whilst his concomitant familiarity with writers of a more introspective kind preserves him from certain crudities of reasoning which are extremely common in men of the laboratory pure & simple." Only in this way, James thought, could Harvard present psychology "as a living science" (*C* 4:527–28; cf. *ML* 3).⁹ In another context, he writes in 1888 that "to know how to handle a chronograph, or a Bunsen cell, and to dissect out a frog's sciatic nerve, even if not a dog's, are beginning to be held as important requisites in a professor of mental science, as that polite learning and power of introspection, which were formerly an all-sufficient equipment for his work" (*EPs* 216).

While James and others believed that psychology was in the process of becoming the "science" of mind, he was convinced that it was not there yet. There had been as yet no major breakthroughs "at the hands of the zoological school," he writes in 1888, and the current enthusiasts seemed animated less by what had been accomplished than by what they thought they were "upon the eve of doing" (*EPs* 216–17). Four years later he notes that "it is indeed strange to hear people talk triumphantly of 'the New Psychology,' and write 'Histories of Psychology,' when into the real elements and forces which the word covers not the first glimpse of clear insights exist" (*PBC* 400–401). To that point, psychology was "hardly more than what physics was before Galileo [Galilei], what chemistry was before [Antoine] Lavoisier." More specifically, he continues, psychology is "a mass of phenomenal description, gossip, and myth, including, however, real material enough to justify one in the hope that with judgment and good-will on the part of those interested, its study may be so organized even now as to become worthy of the name of natural science at no very distant day" (*EPs* 270; cf. *C* 7:53, 89, 353). For the present, however, psychology is "no science, it is only the hope of a science" (*PBC* 401). In this context, we remember that part of James's intention in writing *The Principles* was "by treating Psychology *like* a natural science, to help her become one" (*EPs* 270).[10] A few years later he again writes that, despite the fact that "we have been having something like a 'boom' in psychology in this country" with the appearance of laboratories and chairs and journals, "there *is* no 'new psychology' worthy of the name. There is nothing but the old psychology which began in Locke's time, plus a little physiology of the brain and senses and theory of evolution, and a few refinements of introspective detail" (*TT* 14–15). He continues in this theme in 1901, indicating some sense of his hesitation about where the "new" psychology was going:

> Behind the minute anatomists and the physiologists, with their metallic instruments, there have always stood the out-door naturalists with their eyes and love of concrete nature. The former call the latter superficial, but there is something wrong about your laboratory-biologist who has no sympathy with living animals. In psychology there is a similar distinction. Some psychologists are fascinated by the varieties of mind in living action, others by the dissecting out, whether by logical analysis or by brass instruments, of whatever elementary mental processes may be there. (*EPR* 202)[11]

For his own part, James had continued respect for psychology as a developing science, but he was a thinker who used psychology as a method of inquiry without being limited by any scientific pretensions. While he valued the work of those who wanted to understand human nature without the "soul" talk by adopting a more physiological and comparative stance, he was not inclined to abandon the personal and individualistic issues with which the "soul" talk dealt, however badly. "Physiological psychology is really nothing but a collection of experimental investigations, set apart for convenient study, but quite incapable of leading to any general conclusions without interpretation," he writes in 1887. "And in the interpretation all the problems and difficulties of the 'older' psychology come up afresh, and its 'speculative' methods have to be used again" (*ECR* 398).

Psychology and Philosophy

In a 1911 editorial statement in James Rowland Angell's *Psychological Review*, we read that "at the time of his death, James was generally regarded as a philosopher rather than as a psychologist. And a philosopher he was in the best sense of the word, a devoted and courageous seeker after the deepest truths of life. But he was also a psychologist, easily first among his countrymen." This sort of praise of James as "America's psychologist" has many forms, almost all of them requiring a recognition of the prevalence of psycholophy. In 1940 Otto F. Kraushaar writes that the publication of *The Principles* was "the opening gun in the intellectual war of American philosophical independence." Ralph Barton Perry further notes in 1942 that "the *Principles* lives today, despite the immense advance of psychology during the last sixty years, because it records the reflections and insights of a great mind dealing with the perennial problems of philosophy." Earlier, William McDougall had written of James's central role in bringing "the study of the human mind down from the cloudy heights of academic dispute and mak[ing] it the universally accepted basis of all the humanities, which it is now fast becoming.... James, in short, has humanised psychology." Part of this humanization of psychology was the result of his style. Edwin Bissell Holt points to the way that "James admits the reader to his workshop; where he, the whole man and untrammeled by academic mannerisms, is examining the facts, all the facts and all appearances that present themselves as facts, and trying to find for them some intelligible arrangement." In particular, Holt continues, "inconvenient items are not banished into corners to get them out of sight. And where outstanding contradictions exist, there they are, exposed to view." James's openness to the fullness of experience led Dickinson Sergeant Miller to write that for James, inquirers "must be ready to learn from any quarter whatsoever," to consider what Gardner Murphy calls "the whole wealth of human experience."[12] While James was certainly not the "founder" of American psychology,[13] for many years he was its creative spirit.[14]

As time went on, James drifted away from the professionalizing interests of the American Psychological Association, especially as its members sought to make psychology more like a natural science.[15] It might, perhaps, be more accurate to say that he stayed where he had been, fundamentally interested in what the professionalizing discipline increasingly dismissed as "metaphysical" issues. He never was much of an experimentalist himself; he was, in fact, of two minds about experimentation. On the one hand, as he shows in *The Principles*, he was skeptical of the value of what he calls the "microscopic psychology" that had arisen in Germany. This experimental approach "taxes patience to the utmost, and could hardly have arisen in a country whose natives could be *bored.*" The field of experimental psychology was filling with younger researchers "bent on studying the *elements* of the mental life, dissecting them out from the gross results in which they are embedded, and as far as possible reducing them to quantitative scales" (*PP* 1:191–92). In 1903 James writes more broadly that most American universities had become "Teutomaniac" in this sense, with "ideals of scholarship and of the scholarly character" rooted in the German university and laboratory. "Research into minute points, first-hand contact with some bit of the crude fact, the student pushing into holes and corners some methods of investigation invented by the master—this is the basis of our higher teaching, and this is all that we have absolutely required of our disciples." With some reluctance, James praised the virtues that go with this experimental spirit: "sincerity, veracity, fidelity and patience," and especially its long-term commitment that "if the workers all keep faithful, we trust that the great edifice of truth will in the end be reared." On the other hand, however, he points to the shortcomings of this method: its "lack of urbanity, . . . poor literary form often, redundancy of detail, or oddity of emphasis" (*ECR* 79). Still, it is impossible to overemphasize the importance of the life sciences in his work, especially when he is compared to other philosophers in the pragmatic tradition in his day or later—beginning with Charles Sanders Peirce, C. I. Lewis, and W. V. O. Quine—whose inclinations were more toward logic, mathematics, and physics.[16] In James's day, however, psycholophy was still a powerful prediscipline; when the split became more pronounced philosophers came to neglect psychology in general and *The Principles* in particular.[17]

James had always been interested in religious and ethical and metaphysical themes; he was certainly more interested in them than in developing a "scientific" career.[18] In his early writings, we see James the psycholopher working out two lines of inquiry simultaneously. In part, he is exploring the implications of an emerging voluntaristic, theistic, and pluralistic philosophical perspective. Many of these essays later reappeared in one form or another in *The Will to Believe.* At the same time, he is developing his understanding of the meaning and possibilities of the naturalistic and materialistic "new" psychology that he presents in *The Principles.* Initially, he had hoped that this science could proceed without having to answer any metaphysical questions, but later he realized that it could not be adequate if it failed to consider these questions, and he rejected his provisional dualism.

In *The Principles*, James offers the following definition of metaphysics: "Metaphysics means nothing but an unusually obstinate effort to think clearly" (*PP* 1:148; cf. *PBC* 395; *C* 6:409). He writes later that a more precise definition of metaphysics remains elusive, and he suggests that inquiries focus instead on its content, namely "various obscure, abstract, and universal questions which the sciences and life in general suggest but do not solve." Some of these questions, "relating to the whole of things, or to the ultimate elements thereof," are: "What are 'thoughts' and what are 'things' and how are they connected? ... How comes there to be a world at all? and might it as well not have been? ... Is unity or diversity more fundamental? ... Is everything predestined, or are some things (our wills for example) free?" (*SPP* 21). Metaphysical inquiries, he writes, constitute "a serious branch of learning" (*SPP* 23), and he believes that, as we move into the future, we will need metaphysicians to carry them out. The special sciences may for the most part overlook metaphysical problems, but they should not therefore reject metaphysics. "A geologist's purposes fall short of understanding Time itself," he writes, and "a mechanist need not know how action and reaction are possible at all." Closer to home, James notes that the psychologist need not normally puzzle over "how both he and the mind which he studies are able to take cognizance of the same outer world." Still, he maintains that "problems irrelevant from one standpoint may be essential from another," and, if our intent is "the attainment of the maximum of possible insight into the world as a whole," metaphysics cannot be abandoned (*PBC* 395–96; cf. *EPs* 271; *MEN* 263, 265).

This mind-set explains why James could provisionally present as his goal the establishment of psychology as a "natural science," that is, without metaphysics; it also explains why he did not succeed.[19] As he writes in 1892, while the phrase "psychology as a natural science" means "a sort of psychology that stands at last on solid ground," no such grounded psychology exists. In fact, any "scientific" psychology will be one "into which the waters of metaphysical criticism leak at every joint, a psychology all of whose elementary assumptions and data must be reconsidered in wider connections and translated into other terms" (*PBC* 400; cf. *EP* 87–88). In a preface for the Italian translation of *The Principles* in 1900, James admits that "by frankly putting psychology in the position of a natural science, eliminating certain metaphysical questions from its scope altogether, and confining myself to what could be immediately verified by everyone's own consciousness," he had hoped to present "a central mass of experience" that "everyone might accept as certain, no matter what the differing ulterior philosophic interpretations of it might be." This is why he "assumed uncritically an external world ... the existence of states of consciousness, and ... that the states of consciousness might 'know' both the external world and each other." While this series of assumptions seemed justifiable in 1890, he continues, in the intervening decade "I have realized more and more the difficulty of treating psychology without introducing some positive philosophic doctrine" (*PP* 3:1483–84).[20]

Although throughout his career James explored the various themes of philosophy, he addressed the question of the nature of the philosophical task most clearly in his final two volumes: *A Pluralistic Universe* and *Some Problems of Philosophy*. In the latter, he takes up the definition of philosophy. He begins the initial chapter with a statistical claim, perhaps designed to win over his audience. He writes that while not all people are theory people—that is, questioners who want explanations for the way things are—he is confident that his readers belong to this select group. Every generation, he writes, "produces some individuals exceptionally preoccupied with theory," individuals who "find matter for puzzle and astonishment where no one else does" (*SPP* 9). Philosophy "sees the familiar as if it were strange, and the strange as if it were familiar" (*SPP* 11; cf. *EP* 4), and the individuals who pursue it are humanity's scholars and prophets and sages. "Philosophy, etymologically meaning the love of wisdom, is the work of this class of minds, regarded with an indulgent relish, if not with admiration, even by those who do not understand them or believe much in the truth which they proclaim." He notes that, over the years, the special sciences like chemistry and astronomy have been spun off from philosophy, and "what remains is manageable enough to be taught under the name of philosophy by one man if his interests be broad enough." The philosophical emphasis remains breadth. When James writes that philosophy has come over time to refer to "ideas of universal scope," he is referring to "the principles of explanation that underlie all things without exception, the elements common to gods and men and animals and stones, the first *whence* and the last *whither* of the cosmic procession, the conditions of all knowing, and the most general rules of human action." In this way, philosophy aims at "explanation of the universe at large, not description of its details," and it thus includes "any very sweeping view of the world ... even tho it may be a vague one." Philosophy is, he continues, "a *weltanschauung*, an intellectualized attitude towards life" (*SPP* 9–10).[21]

For his part, James presents us with an understanding of philosophy as "the completest knowledge of the universe" that includes the results of the various sciences so that science, metaphysics (philosophy more narrowly conceived), and religion "may then again form a single body of wisdom, and lend each other mutual support" (*SPP* 19–20). For philosophy to perform its role in liberal education, it should contain certain elements of science, poetry, religion, logic, and so on. He writes that to be introduced to philosophy, "to catch its influence," benefits students of all inclinations. "By its poetry it appeals to literary minds; but its logic stiffens them up and remedies their softness. By its logic it appeals to the scientific; but softens them by its other aspects, and saves them from too dry a technicality" (*SPP* 11). Using a pair of notions—"tender-minded" and "tough-minded"—that we will explore in chapter 4, James notes that "both types of student ought to get from philosophy a liberal spirit, ought to get more air, more mental background." It is in this sense that he concludes that a person without philosophy is "the most inauspicious and unprofitable of all possible social mates" (*SPP* 11). Philosophy, in this broad conception, is what has drawn our fellows since the dawn of questioning. Rather than being taught in a dry or technical way, or being allowed to wander off into mental gymnastics or word games,[22] philosophy should always stimulate the thoughtful encounter of a person with the fullness of experience.

In addition to the theory-people, however, James writes that there are others who do not like philosophy. These self-styled acolytes of common sense and science often find philosophy to be problematic, and he considers three of their lines of criticism. Their first complaint, he writes, is that "whereas the 'sciences' make steady progress, and yield applications of matchless utility, philosophy makes no theoretic progress, and shows no practical applications." His response to this criticism is to reject the dichotomy between science and philosophy, and thus the dichotomy between the progressive and the nonprogressive. Viewed historically, he reminds us, "the sciences are themselves branches of the tree of philosophy ... and what men call 'philosophy' to-day is but the residuum of questions still unanswered" (*SPP* 12; cf. 17–18).[23] As evidence, James points to two sciences that were then in the process of emerging, psychology and biology, and we might point to logic and aesthetics in our day. Even within philosophy, narrowly considered, he maintains that there has been progress, however slow. For example, he notes that much of philosophy used to be blithely a priori, but the "critical" philosophy of Locke, Hume, and Kant brought progress over earlier methods of inquiry (see *SPP* 13–14). Moreover, when philosophy returns to talk about the world informed by this critical stance—for example, when it is conscious of the problems associated with knowing rather than focusing narrowly on the problem of knowledge—there will be more progress.

"To know the actual peculiarities of the world we are born into is surely as important as to know what makes worlds anyhow abstractly possible," James writes. Unfortunately, "this latter knowledge has been treated by many since Kant's time as the only knowledge worthy of being called philosophical." For the average person, he continues, "the question 'what is Nature like?'" is just as meritorious as "the kantian question 'how is Nature possible?'"; philosophy, to remain a vital human undertaking, "must take some notice of the actual constitution of reality." In a similar fashion, philosophy has no peculiar method of its own. The philosopher may be "thinking about generalities rather than about particulars," but the methods remain the same. The philosopher, like the nonphilosopher, "observes, discriminates, generalizes, classifies, looks for causes, traces analogies, and makes hypotheses." As human thinking evolved out of more primitive thinking over the centuries, little has changed in its "manner"—as distinct from its content—except "a greater hesitancy in asserting its convictions, and the habit of seeking verification for them whenever it can" (*SPP* 14). Philosophical work is slow and difficult, and, sounding almost Peircean, James writes that "two thousand years probably measure but one paragraph in that great romance of adventure called the history of the intellect of man" (*SPP* 18; cf. *P* 106–7).[24] Nonetheless, philosophy has made progress.

A second complaint that James notes against philosophy is that it is "dogmatic, and pretends to settle things by pure reason, whereas the only fruitful mode of getting at truth is to appeal to concrete experience." Here again, science seems to be superior because it "collects, classes and analyzes facts, and thereby far outstrips philosophy." He admits that too often philosophers "have aimed at closed systems, established *a priori*, claiming infallibility, and to be accepted or rejected only as totals." He counters, however, that at present, "it is getting more and more difficult for dogmatists claiming finality for their systems, to get a hearing in educated circles," because of the growing incorporation of the hypothetical methods of science, with their possibilities "for indefinite self-correction and increase," into philosophy (*SPP* 18–19).

As a third complaint, James points to the criticism that "philosophy is out of touch with real life, for which it substitutes abstractions." While reality is "various, tangled, painful," he notes that it has been the inclination of philosophers "almost without exception" to treat reality as "noble, simple, and perfect, ignoring the complexity of fact, and indulging in a sort of optimism that exposes their systems to the contempt of common men, and to the satire of such writers as Voltaire and Schopenhauer." In response, James admits that this criticism of philosophy has historical merit. He rejects, however, any suggestion that there is something in the nature of philosophy that makes the discipline abstract. As philosophy advances, he continues, "the thin and noble abstractions may give way to more solid and real constructions, when the materials and methods for making such constructions shall be more and more securely ascertained." Were this to happen, philosophers might be able to "get into as close contact as realistic novelists with the facts of life" (*SPP* 19). He grants that the philosopher is driven by a particular set of interests, especially "that of reducing the manifold in thought to simple form." This passion, which James calls the "aesthetic Principle of Ease," is the "pleasure at finding that a chaos of facts is at bottom the expression of a single underlying fact" (*EP* 35). He recognizes, however, that this kind of simplification may appear to nonphilosophers as simply abstraction, "a most miserable and inadequate substitute for the fulness of the truth. It is a monstrous abridgement of life, which, like all abridgements is got by the absolute loss and casting out of real matter." Because of this felt abstraction, he writes, "so few human beings truly care for philosophy" (*WB* 61; cf. *EP* 55).[25] The purpose of *Some Problems of Philosophy*, on the contrary, was to provide a clear instance of nondogmatic and non-abstract thinking about the "big questions" that did have some practical application to the members of his audience.

A second discussion of the nature of philosophy is to be found in *A Pluralistic Universe*. Here James considers the nature of any philosophical system, which he describes as "a summary sketch, a picture of the world in abridgment, a foreshortened bird's-eye view of the perspective of events" (*PU* 9).[26] We fashion these sketches using "the only material we have at our disposal": "the various portions of that world of which we have already had experience." Philosophers—theists and pantheists, monists and pluralists—formulate their visions "after the analogy of some particular feature of it which has particularly captivated their attention." We each *carve out order* as we find it. In true pluralist fashion, James writes that "different men find their minds more at home in very different fragments of the world." Unfortunately, he continues, even though our personal versions are "accidents more or less of personal vision," each of us is "prone to claim that his conclusions are the only logical ones, that they are necessities of universal reason" (*PU* 9–10).[27]

Philosophy is a field that is inclined toward intellectualization and abstraction. As James writes in 1905, "professors of Philosophy are almost always rationalists," and their students usually find in their lectures a world that is "so abstract, pure, and logical, and perfect" that the students cannot see there "any resemblance of character to the struggling and disjointed sum of muddy facts" that they know as the wider world (*EP* 141; cf. *ML* 378–80). He continues that, for too many, philosophy "doesn't lie flat on its belly in the middle of experience, in the very thick of its sand and gravel." For such people, he continues, philosophy is "essentially the vision of things from above" that is less concerned with feeling "the detail of things" than with comprehending "their intelligible plan." Philosophy seeks "forms and principles . . . categories and rules . . . order and necessity" (*PU* 125). Philosophers seldom take the poetic approach that they are attempting to tell the world's story as best they can from their limited experience. Rather, they prefer to dispute with others who fail to see the world the way that they believe it is.[28] James's poetic approach to our competing philosophical visions calls on us to recognize that we all share "the same essential interests," and to portray a universe in which our "differences are all secondary to this deep agreement." For him, all of these differences are "minor matters" that need to be subordinated to the simple fact that, "whether we be empiricists or rationalists, we are, ourselves, parts of the universe and share the same deep concern in its destinies." Although all of us would like to feel "more truly at home" with the universe, and "to contribute our mite to its amelioration," we find ourselves as philosophers allowing "small aesthetic discords" to keep us divided. The technical writings of professional philosophers, who fortify their presentations with reasons and arguments, are especially guilty here. James recognizes the value of such philosophical presentations, noting that "what distinguishes a philosopher's truth is that it is *reasoned*." While others may come upon their beliefs "they know not how," philosophers live by a higher standard that requires technical language, careful presentation, a survey of the relevant literature, and so on (*PU* 10–11). Still, the value of such protective armor is limited.[29]

Considering the problem of free will, for example, James writes that the average philosopher is less likely to feel in tune with a nonphilosopher who might share his position "by a sort of inborn intuition" than with a fellow philosopher "who should use the same technical apparatus, making the same distinctions, etc., but drawing opposite conclusions" (*PU* 12). When the presentation of philosophy gets infected with this sort of "shop-tradition" and begins to exclude "the open air" of more general thinking, philosophers lose sight of larger issues, and "if by chance anyone writes popularly and about results only, with his mind directly focussed on the subject, it is reckoned *oberflächliches zeug* [superficial stuff] and *ganz unwissenschaftlich* [totally unscientific]." For James, however, "to teach philosophy so that the pupils' interest in technique exceeds that in results is surely a vicious aberration" that reduces the academic enterprise to intellectualized and technical abstractions. Unfortunately, this sort of narrow professionalism seems to have had a great impact in recent scholarship—he writes of the appalling "over-technicality and consequent dreariness of the younger disciples at our american universities"—and in the growth of the understanding of the academic life as a "professorial game" in which the participants "think and write from each other and for each other and at each other exclusively" (*PU* 13–14).[30]

For James, on the contrary, the most important element of philosophy is vision. As he writes, "philosophy is more a matter of passionate vision than of logic ... logic only finding reasons for the vision afterwards" (*PU* 81). Understood in this way, the history of philosophy emerges as a history of visions—systematized metaphysical pictures of how our world is best comprehended. Whether the author of the vision is Plato or Descartes, Spinoza or Royce, each philosopher is attempting to show us how to comprehend our world, and each philosopher's vision is "the great fact about him." These visions are not necessarily argued for, since argumentation—like beauty and human well-being—is itself an element more or less prominent in each vision. "If we take the whole history of philosophy," he writes, "the systems reduce themselves to a few main types" that, despite our imaginative presentations, are "just so many visions, modes of feeling the whole push, and seeing the whole drift of life, forced on one by one's total character and experience, and on the whole *preferred*—there is no other truthful word—as one's best working attitude" (*PU* 14–15). Recognizing the importance of James's "working," we must realize that philosophy's aim should be to present a fulfilling vision of our place in existence so that we can function successfully.[31] Of course, for James the psycholopher, philosophy must also maintain contacts with the growing discipline of psychology.

The Principles of Psychology

The psychology text that James submitted to Henry Holt in May 1890 was the product of twelve years' effort and had grown to nearly 1,400 printed pages.[32] In the course of this study, James demonstrates both a feel for the human animal as a live creature, and a close familiarity with the most recent European thinking in the field. As a psycholopher, he offers a balance of old-fashioned, introspective psychology and "modern" physiological psychology.[33] Still, rather than pretending to offer a complete account of the field in this two-volume study, his presentation is admittedly impressionistic and highly personal,[34] focusing at length on some themes while virtually ignoring others, such as sex.[35] Given the limits of space in the present study, I will follow suit—although even now, readers will benefit in ways expected and unexpected from the careful study of the entire work.[36] The value that many professors found in *The Principles* led to the publication of a one-volume edition, *Psychology: Briefer Course*, designed to be more suitable for classroom use.[37] Later, James produced another volume, *Talks to Teachers on Psychology and to Students on Some of Life's Ideals*, that drew upon his presentations on psychological themes to popular audiences. Since the latter two volumes did not involve new research, but rather rephrasings and reemphases of the earlier material, I will treat them all together, noting only when the later presentations differ from the earlier ones.

In his review of *The Principles*, Josiah Royce indicates that, for him, the value of James's volumes is to be found "rather in their manifold study of facts, in their wide range, in their novelty of suggestion, than in their systematic finish." If to some this comment suggests a lack of organization, James can rest easy, Royce continues, because "psychology is at present an essentially tentative, growing, suggestive, and formless doctrine," and any author who would produce a "finished" book would "contribute fallacious generalizations to his science, instead of empirically well-founded summaries."[38] Charles Sanders Peirce writes in a similar vein, although with a more negative evaluation. While granting that *The Principles* is "the most important contribution that has been made to the subject for many years," he complains that "as a piece of bookmaking" the volumes do not attain "the completeness of a thorough treatise." Rather, they appear to contain "a large assortment of somewhat heterogeneous articles loosely tied up in one bag, with tendencies towards sprawling." All in all, he also notices something "destructive" in this "highly original, or at least novel" work. James, he finds, is too interested in proving "that we do not know what it has been generally supposed that we did know," and "that given premises do not justify the conclusions which all other thinkers hold they do justify." As Peirce summarizes, "the one thing upon which Prof. James seems to pin his faith is the general incomprehensibility of things."[39]

In *The Principles*, James defines psychology as "the Science of Mental Life, both of its phenomena and of their conditions." The phenomena of mental life are "such things as we call feelings, desires, cognitions, reasonings, decisions, and the like" (*PP* 1:15), and the conditions are the bodily factors that he explores in the subsequent chapters. In *Psychology: Briefer Course*, he borrows the definition of psychology of George Trumbull Ladd that had appeared the previous year as "the *description and explanation of states of consciousness as such*."[40] James continues, offering that "by states of consciousness are meant such things as sensations, desires, emotions, cognitions, reasonings, decisions, volitions, and the like. Their 'explanation' must of course include the study of their causes, conditions, and immediate consequences, so far as these can be ascertained" (*PBC* 9). He recognizes that there is a difference between this "provisional body" of propositions about aspects of the mind as part of "Psychology considered as a natural science" and the larger questions that are aspects of "the total body of Philosophy" where "the formulas of Psychology will appear with a very different meaning" from that which appears when they are considered only as part of "an abstract and truncated 'natural science'" (*PBC* 10, 14).

There is a tension between these two foci in James's psychology, and his solution to this provisional dualism is to come. In *The Principles*, however, he adopts "the *psychological* point of view," which he describes as "the relatively uncritical non-idealistic point of view of all natural science, beyond which this book cannot go" (*PP* 263).[41] Psychology, like every other natural science "assumes certain data uncritically, and declines to challenge the elements between which its own 'laws' obtain, and from which its own deductions are carried on." For psychology, he continues, the assumed data are "(1) *thoughts and feelings,* and (2) *a physical world* in time and space with which they coexist and which (3) *they know."* As a natural science, psychology assumes that "thoughts and feelings exist and are vehicles of knowledge," and that there is an "empirical correlation of the various sorts of thought or feeling with definite conditions of the brain." Of course, James is making no ultimate claims here. "Men must keep thinking," he writes, "and the data assumed by psychology, just like those assumed by physics and the other natural sciences, must some time be overhauled." His hypothetical stance, however, is that to attempt to advance the project of physiological psychology, it is necessary temporarily to suspend metaphysical questionings as "outside the province of this book" (*PP* 1:6).

While *The Principles* remains to this day a masterpiece of descriptive psychology that deserves to be studied from cover to cover, on this occasion I will be able to consider only four of its twenty-eight chapters: "The Stream of Thought," "Habit," "The Consciousness of Self," and "Will." "The Stream of Thought," or "The Stream of Consciousness" in *Psychology: Briefer Course,* is not an ontological discussion that considers what sort of "thing" thought or consciousness might be.[42] It is, rather, a descriptive account of the contents of thought or consciousness or, as James phrases it, a "study of the mind from within." He notes that most psychology books "start with sensations, as the simplest mental facts, and proceed synthetically, constructing each higher stage from those below it." The problem with this approach is that "no one ever had a simple sensation by itself." On the contrary, he continues, from birth onward, consciousness is "of a teeming multiplicity of objects and relations, and what we call simple sensations are results of discriminative attention, pushed often to a very high degree" (*PP* 1:219).[43] Unlike the clean and tidy world constructed by Locke and his empiricist and associationist followers, or reconstructed by Kant and his rationalist followers, human consciousness or experience is anything but. Initially, experience is "one great blooming, buzzing confusion" (*PP* 1:462; cf. *PBC* 21),[44] which is then ordered by our efforts as embodied thinkers. We filter and arrange. We describe, and often mis-describe, the flow of experience. "The most persistent outer relations which science believes in," he writes—like "the *elementary* laws of mechanics, physics, and chemistry" and even the "the principle of uniformity in nature"—are not simple "matters of experience." They are the results, rather, of "a process of elimination," of "ignoring conditions which are always present" (*PP* 2:1233). Thus, to advance in our psychological and philosophical discussions, we must always start with the original confusion. It is, James writes, "the re-instatement of the vague to its proper place in our mental life which I am so anxious to press on the attention" (*PP* 1:246).[45]

Experience is, in the words of John J. McDermott, "the most important single concern" in James's philosophy.[46] James frequently emphasizes the need—as we have just seen in his rejection of simplified experience—to encounter experience free of theory. In particular, experience is "the entire process of phenomena, of present data considered in their raw immediacy, before reflective thought has analysed them into subjective and objective aspects or ingredients" (*EP* 95). It is because of his central focus upon experience that James writes that "no philosophy, however wide its sweep or deep its dive, will ever be a substitute for the tiniest experience of life" (*ECR* 489). Elsewhere, he phrases this point more metaphorically: "In the great boarding-house of nature, the cakes and the butter and the syrup seldom come out so even and leave the plate so clean. Indeed, we should view them with scientific suspicion if they did" (*WB* 27). Here, James suggests that we should start with the most general pre-"metaphysical" description that consciousness contains thinking. As he puts it, "the only thing which psychology has a right to postulate at the outset is the fact of thinking itself . . . *thinking of some sort goes on*" (*PP* 1:219).[47]

In his examination of the stream of thinking, James selects five characteristics as worthy of particular discussion. The first of these characteristics is that "every thought tends to be part of a personal consciousness" (*PP* 1:220; cf. *PBC* 140). Moving from his initial claim that "thought goes on," he suggests that all thoughts are connected to personal selves. We have no evidence of loose thoughts or leftover bits of consciousness. All thoughts are, for the psychologist, part of the thought processes of particular individuals.[48] In fact, it is extremely difficult—as we all sadly know—to gain access to the thoughts of others. We all experience the difficulties of communication and of sharing ideas, and the ease and frequency of misunderstanding. He continues:

> Each of these minds keeps its own thoughts to itself. There is no giving or bartering between them. No thought even comes into direct *sight* of a thought in another personal consciousness than its own. Absolute insulation, irreducible pluralism, is the law. It seems as if the elementary psychic fact were not *thought* or *this thought* or *that thought*, but *my thought*, every thought being *owned*. Neither contemporaneity, nor proximity in space, nor similarity of quality and content are able to fuse thoughts together which are sundered by this barrier of belonging to different personal minds. (*PP* 1:221/*PBC* 141)[49]

As an addendum to this discussion, James allows that at times persons may not even have access to all of their own thoughts, and he points to *"secondary personal selves"* that can be uncovered through the use of anesthetics and hypnosis (*PP* 1:222–24).

The second characteristic of thinking that James discusses is that "within each personal consciousness thought is always changing" (*PP* 1:220; cf. *PBC* 140). His point is not that "no one state of mind has any duration" (*PP* 1:224/*PBC* 141), and he rejects the notion of a "knife-edge" present for a "now" with a duration of about twelve seconds.[50] James's point, rather, is anti-Lockean: we cannot reduce the flow of experience to "simple ideas"—cold, red, hard, flat, sweet, and so on—and then use their reappearance to establish knowledge by some sort of retrospective comparison. As he puts it, *"no state once gone can recur and be identical with what it was before."* For James, rather, repeated events do not yield the same mental state or the same experience. "Does not the same piano-key, struck with the same force, make us hear in the same way?" he asks. "Does not the same grass give us the same feeling of green, the same sky the same feeling of blue, and do we not get the same olfactory sensation no matter how many times we put our nose to the same flask of cologne?" His answer to all of these questions, although he admits it may initially seem "a piece of metaphysical sophistry," is negative. He grants that there is repetition in these cases: "We hear the same *note* over and over again; we see the same *quality* of green, or smell the same objective perfume." He rejects, however, the claim that *"the same bodily sensation is ever got by us twice."* For James, our practical interest is in "the sameness of the *things* . . . and any sensations that assure us of that will probably be considered in a rough way to be the same with each other."

Thus, in general, we simply overlook "the different way in which the same things look and sound and smell at different distances and under different circumstances" (*PP* 1:224–26; cf. *PBC* 141–42). If they seem to function in the same way, we treat them the same.

In this discussion, James relies on physiological evidence. The initial experience modifies the brain in some way, the second experience occurs in a modified brain and modifies it further, and subsequent experiences continue the process. Sometimes, the repeated hearing of the sound of a child's toy leads to annoyance; at other times, we manage to ignore it. We occasionally try to recreate a special experience, even though we know that its fullness will elude us. There is thus no way to retaste one's first banana, or relive one's first sexual encounter. "When the identical fact recurs, we *must* think of it in a fresh manner, see it under a somewhat different angle, apprehend it in different relations from those in which it last appeared." The overall effect is that experience is constantly remolding us, and "our mental reaction on every given thing is really a resultant of our experience of the whole world up to that date" (*PP* 1:227–28; cf. *PBC* 143). James suggests that, because languages like English do not modify the names for things, we are perhaps led astray. "What after all is so natural as to assume that one object, called by one name, should be known by one affection of the mind?" (*PP* 1:230). Thus, German's declinable nouns—for example, *der Vater* and *dem Vater*—and combinative words—like the contemporary *Geschwindigkeitsbegrenzung* or *Massenvernichtungswaffen*[51]—might be more helpful, because they change "their shape to suit the context in which they lay" (*PP* 1:230).[52] In his discussion of the changeability of thought, he further notes that the emotional impact of any experience depends on our mood. On a bad day, "what was bright and exciting becomes weary, flat, and unprofitable," he writes. "The bird's song is tedious, the breeze is mournful, the sky is sad" (*PP* 1:226/*PBC* 143).

James's third point is that "within each personal consciousness, thought is sensibly continuous" (*PP* 1:220; cf. *PBC* 140). Because of this continuity, he writes, we need to choose our metaphors for consciousness carefully. Consciousness does not appear to be segmented or "chopped up in bits." Consequently, words like "'chain' or 'train' do not describe it fitly as it presents itself in the first instance." Rather than being "jointed," consciousness "flows," and it would be better described as a 'river' or a 'stream.' "*In talking of it hereafter*," he continues, "*let us call it the stream of thought, of consciousness, or of subjective life*" (*PP* 1:233/*PBC* 145). Using another metaphor, he suggests that consciousness is more like a stalk of bamboo than a chain.[53] "The transition between the *thought* of one object and the thought of another is no more a break in the thought than a joint in a bamboo is a break in the wood," he writes. "It is a part of the *consciousness* as much as the joint is a part of the *bamboo*" (*PP* 1:233–34).

Further evidence for the continuity of experience comes from the fact that changes from moment to moment are never absolutely abrupt. This is why interruptions that force us to redirect our activities are so often experienced as a nuisance. In a similar fashion, this pragmatic criterion can be seen in the inertia of our thought processes. When speaking, multilingual people tend to continue in the same language (see *PP* 1:253; cf. *PBC* 153). Further, James indicates that whole bits of discourse that make no sense can carry themselves forward, "sentences with absolutely no meaning may be uttered in good faith and pass unchallenged." As an example of this, he suggests that we consider one of the more obscure passages in a writer like Hegel. In such cases, he continues, "it is a fair question whether the rationality included in them be anything more than the fact that the words all belong to a common vocabulary, and are strung together on a scheme of predication and relation,—immediacy, self-relation, and what not,—which has habitually recurred." James is not challenging "the subjective feeling of the rationality of these sentences" in Hegel himself, nor the fact that occasional readers may "by straining" (*PP* 1:253–55; cf. *PBC* 153–54) have achieved a similar feeling of rationality as well; he only wants to point out that such texts can proceed by a kind of linguistic inertia in the other cases.

There is some physiological explanation for this continuity, which James compares to the "flights and perchings" of birds. "*Let us call the resting-places the 'substantive parts,' and the places of flight the 'transitive parts,' of the stream of thought.*" He continues that "the main end of our thinking is at all times the attainment of some other substantive part than the one from which we have just been dislodged" (*PP* 1:236; cf. *PBC* 146). In light of the importance of "perchings," there would seem to be a pragmatic justification for our emphasis upon substantives: "*the important thing about a train of thought is its conclusion.*" The other parts of the stream that lead up to these substantive parts are only the means of the attainment of the conclusion, and the "relative unimportance" of these transitive parts is made clear by "the fact that when the conclusion is there, we have always forgotten most of the steps preceding its attainment" (*PP* 1:250–51). Because of their apparent function as means to the substantive parts, we sometimes fail to recognize the importance of the transitive parts, "the feelings of relation . . . psychic overtones, halos, suffusions, or fringes about the terms" (*PP* 1:259–60/*PBC* 154). We need to recognize, however, "there is not a conjunction or a preposition, and hardly an adverbial phrase, syntactic form, or inflection of voice, in human speech, that does not express some shading or other of relation which we at some moment actually feel to exist between the larger objects of our thought." To portray this properly, James suggests that we try to talk about "a feeling of *and*, a feeling of *if*, a feeling of *but*, and a feeling of *by*, quite as readily as we say a feeling of *blue* or a feeling of *cold*," although he realizes that our habit of "recognizing the existence of the substantive parts alone" will require fundamental changes in our understanding of language (*PP* 1:238/*PBC* 148; cf. *EPs* 146).[54]

All of these nonsubstantive parts of experience are themselves experienced, James continues, even though our recognition of them is as "*feelings of tendency*, often so vague that we are unable to name them at all." Here he challenges "the ridiculous theory of Hume and Berkeley that we can have no images but of perfectly definite things." For James, on the contrary, the recognition of the vague is not an indication of failure to think clearly, but rather a recognition of the unclear. His metaphorical example notes that "the traditional psychology talks like one who should say a river consists of nothing but pailsful, spoonsful, quartpotsful, barrelsful, and other moulded forms of water." The important point, however, is that "even were the pails and the pots all actually standing in the stream, still between them the free water would continue to flow." This free water is what psychologists who discuss consciousness too often fail to consider. For James, on the contrary, "every definite image in the mind is steeped and dyed in the free water that flows round it" (*PP* 1:246; cf. *PBC* 150–51). Thus, he continues, the analytical psychology that has been at the foundation of modern philosophy is completely wrong. Relations are a real component of experience, although their role is overlooked by the primacy of clarity and simplicity in the empirical tradition. This tradition can find neither "coarse feelings corresponding to the innumerable relations and forms of connection between the facts of the world," nor "*named* subjective modifications mirroring such relations," and as a result has simply denied that such "feelings of relation exist." From the opposite extreme, he notes, Kantianism, committed to the reality of relations causal and temporal that it cannot find in experience, asserts their extra-experiential origin. These relations are known "by something that lies on an entirely different plane, by an *actus purus* [simple act] of Thought, Intellect, or Reason, all written with capitals and considered to mean something unutterably superior to any fact of sensibility whatever" (*PP* 1:237–38; cf. *PBC* 147–48).[55]

The fourth character of thinking to which James points is that thought "always appears to deal with objects independent of itself" (*PP* 220).[56] As a consequence, although our thoughts are (as we have just seen) personal, many people are able to fix on the same objects, to know the same "thing." We find ourselves doing this all the time in conversation, when we discuss a particular novel or film or storm. Psychologists themselves do the same thing when they discuss patients and experiments and the implications of a recent theory. In fact, "the judgment that *my* thought has the same object as *his* thought is what makes the psychologist call my thought cognitive of an outer reality" (*PP* 1:262).

James's fifth characteristic of thinking is that it is "interested in some parts of these objects to the exclusion of others, and welcomes or rejects—*chooses* from among them, in a word—all the while" (*PP* 1:220; cf. *PBC* 140; *PU* 130). We selectively attend to aspects of experience. We accentuate and emphasize; we neglect and disregard. He asks, "What are our very senses themselves but organs of selection?" James continues: "Out of the infinite chaos of movements, of which physics teaches us that the outer world consists, each sense-organ picks out those which fall with certain limits of velocity. To these it responds, but ignores the rest as completely as if they did not exist. . . . Out of what is in itself an undistinguishable, swarming *continuum*, devoid of distinction or emphasis, our senses make for us, by attending to this motion and ignoring that, a world full of contrasts, of sharp accents, of abrupt changes, of picturesque light and shade" (*PP* 1:273–74; cf. *PBC* 155; *EPs* 46–47).

Elsewhere in *The Principles*, he writes that "each of us literally *chooses*, by his ways of attending to things, what sort of a universe he shall appear to himself to inhabit" (*PP* 1:401; cf. 380–81; *ECR* 300). This means that the content of our experience is largely determined by our habits of attention. Although objects may be presented to us thousands of times, if we fail to notice them, they will not be part of any experience. "We are all seeing flies, moths, and beetles by the thousand, but to whom, save an entomologist, do they say anything distinct?" In a similar fashion, most of us are blind to the finer aspects of counterpoint or carpentry, of gardening or the night sky. "On the other hand," he continues, "a thing met only once in a lifetime may leave an indelible experience in the memory." Here he considers a group of tourists in Europe, one of whom returns with "only picturesque impressions—costumes and colors, parks and views and works of architecture, pictures and statues," while another remembers only "distances and prices, populations and drainage-arrangements, door- and window-fastenings, and other useful statistics." For a third, Europe will mean "theatres, restaurants, and public balls, and naught beside"; for a fourth, the trip will amount to "little more than a few names of places through which he passed." In each of these cases, James notes, the individual tourist "has selected, out of the same mass of presented objects, those which suited his private interest and has made his experience thereby" (*PP* 1:275–76/*PBC* 156–57; cf. *EPs* 49–50).

Because of this selectivity, consciousness is at the core of the pluralism that is such an important part of James's vision, as we shall see in chapter 5. He writes that "the mind is at every stage a theatre of simultaneous possibilities." Consciousness operates among these possibilities, comparing them with others, engaging in "the selection of some, and the suppression of the rest by the reinforcing and inhibiting agency of Attention" (*PP* 1:277; cf. *EPs* 51). He continues that "we do far more than emphasize things, and unite some, and keep others apart." In fact, humans "actually *ignore* most of the things before us" (*PP* 1:273/*PBC* 155). Driving an automobile, for example, would be physically impossible if while driving we actually paid attention to all of the stimuli that are presented to us. Learning to drive is largely learning what we can safely ignore. Elsewhere in our lives, we can learn to interpret what we experience by studying optical illusions. By repetition, we also learn to discern within experience the important parts of a card game, or a subway map, or a complex musical score. Further, selection is essential to the work of an artist, who must choose "tones, colors, [and] shapes," so that they "harmonize with each other and with the main purpose of his work." As we shall see in chapter 6, selecting is also essential to the moral agent, who must choose "which *interest* out of several, equally coercive, shall become supreme." Given an infinite series of possible choices—"Shall I commit this crime? choose that profession? accept that office, or marry this fortune?"— the individual is really deciding "between one of several equally possible future Characters" (*PP* 1:276/*PBC* 157–58). People seek values and through their value choices they establish a system of meaning. In our world of virtually unlimited possibilities, James writes, each of us must choose "what being he shall now resolve to become" (*PP* 1:277; cf. *PBC* 158).⁵⁷ Lest this sound too postmodern to us, we recall that James suggests a great degree of overlap among us with regard to "the rejected portions and the selected portions of the original world-stuff." In the process of living our shared lives, we find that "the human race as a whole largely agrees as to what it shall notice and name, and what not" (*PP* 1:277; cf. *PBC* 158).

James's interest in psychology is, of course, broader than just in consciousness. In his discussions of habit, the issue is the relationship between nature and nurture, between instinct and learning. "All our life, so far as it has definite form, is but a mass of habits—practical, emotional, and intellectual—systematically organized for our weal or woe, and bearing us irresistibly towards our destiny, whatever the latter may be" (*TT* 47). He is greatly concerned with the physiological basis of habits. "*An acquired habit, from the physiological point of view,*" he writes, "*is nothing but a new pathway of discharge formed in the brain, by which certain incoming currents ever after tend to escape*" (*PBC* 125). This development of habits is related to the mutability of organic life that makes the human so adaptive.⁵⁸ He writes that "*the phenomena of habit in living beings are due to the plasticity of the organic materials of which their bodies are composed.*" Plasticity, in general, means "the possession of a structure weak enough to yield to an influence, but strong enough not to yield all at once," and nervous tissue is extraordinarily plastic in this sense (*PP* 1:110/*PBC* 126). The "habitualness" of the habit is caused by modifications of nervous pathways. "The currents, once in, must find a way out," James writes, "in getting out they leave their traces in the paths which they take" (*PP* 1:112/*PBC* 127). New currents must follow the old paths or create new ones, but the tendency is to follow the old,⁵⁹ and habits come to replace our plasticity.

Individuals inevitably become less plastic over the years, a problem that is being powerfully felt in society at present as the population ages and the pace of innovation quickens. "Most of us grow more and more enslaved to the stock conceptions with which we have once become familiar, and less and less capable of assimilating impressions in any but the old ways," he writes. "Old-fogyism, in short, is the inevitable terminus to which life sweeps us on" (*PP* 2:754/*PBC* 286). He continues that outside of the ideas pressed on individuals by the pressures of their working lives, the ideas that they gain "before they are twenty-five are practically the only ideas they shall have in their lives." At some point, he writes, "disinterested curiosity is past, the mental grooves and channels set, the power of assimilation gone." While learning will continue, James believes that it will always carry a "sense of insecurity" when compared "with things learned in the plastic days of instinctive curiosity," about which we will "never lose entirely our sense of being at home" (*PP* 2:1021/*PBC* 350).

With the physiology clarified, James turns to the practical effects of habits. The primary effect to which he points is greater simplification and accuracy in the performance of repetitive tasks like playing the piano and typing, with the resultant decrease in fatigue.[60] "If an act require for its execution a chain, *A, B, C, D, E, F, G*, etc., of successive nervous events," he writes, "then in the first performances of the action the conscious will must choose each of these events from a number of wrong alternatives that tend to present themselves." As time goes on and habit develops, however, "each event calls up its own appropriate successor without any alternative offering itself, and without any reference to the conscious will, until at last the whole chain, *A, B, C, D, E, F, G*, rattles itself off as soon as *A* occurs, just as if *A* and the rest of the chain were fused into a continuous stream." Thus, unlike the person who is learning "to walk, to ride, to swim, skate, fence, write, play, or sing" (*PP* 1:119/*PBC* 129) and is constantly concentrating on the doing of each step of the process, the skilled person simply acts. The second important effect for creatures like us is that habit frees up the mind for reverie or thinking.[61] "A strictly voluntary act has to be guided by idea, perception, and volition, throughout its whole course," he notes, but "in an habitual action, mere sensation is a sufficient guide, and the upper regions of brain and mind are set comparatively free." Oftentimes, the mind even "forgets" some of the unimportant information, like the location of the letters on a keyboard, but the fingers "remember." "Few men can tell off-hand which sock, shoe, or trousers-leg they put on first," James continues. "Which way does my door swing? . . . I cannot *tell* the answer; yet my *hand* never makes a mistake" (*PP* 1:120; cf. *PBC* 130). Our habits ride our bikes for us and drive our cars, and if we think about many of these mechanical activities, our performance is often worse.[62]

Although it is not his central concern, James clearly understands the connection between individual habits and the broader social habits that we call custom or tradition. In some contexts the ability to throw a ball accurately is an important habit to develop; in others, kicking it is more valued. In some situations, a good ear and nimble figures will draw a child into a culture of violin playing; in others, that option is not available. He also considers the ethical or pedagogical importance of individual and social habits. Society can only proceed if there is order, but our instincts offer us little help. Our various needs—for food, clothing, shelter, and so on—will somehow be met, but it is usually the traditional diet, customary dress, and familiar structures of our culture that determine just how.[63] "Habit is thus the enormous fly-wheel of society," he writes, "its most precious conservative agent." It is habit alone that "saves the children of fortune from the envious uprisings of the poor" and "prevents the hardest and most repulsive walks of life from being deserted by those brought up to tread therein." If not for habit, James continues, nothing would keep "the fisherman and the deckhand at sea through the winter," or "the miner in his darkness," or the farmer on "his lonely farm through all the months of snow." There is, no doubt, a certain tragedy to a process that "dooms us all to fight out the battle of life upon the lines of our nurture or our early choice," however disagreeable it becomes, "because there is no other for which we are fitted, and it is too late to begin again." On the other hand, he writes, it is a good thing for society that "in most of us, by the age of thirty, the character has set like plaster, and will never soften again" (*PP* 1:125–26/*PBC* 132–33). Moreover, he continues, these traditions and customs are all habits, contained not just in our nerves, but more broadly in our literature and mythology, in our spelling, our ways of designing roadways and dividing the year. Similarly, our customary moralities are communal habits that, for better or worse, combine religious and legal constraints to guide our basic human drives—for companionship, sex, and child rearing—into narrow preselected possibilities. James further denies the often-heard claims that there is an instinct of acquisitiveness that necessarily leads to capitalism, or an instinct of bellicosity that necessarily leads to warfare. For him, our instincts are more plastic, and there are powerful cultural components in their shaping.[64]

While psychology is not necessarily a moral inquiry, it does examine human behavior and thus, it must intersect at times with morality. Habits are of both good and bad sorts, James notes, although our discussions usually emphasize the latter, our habitual vices. People "talk of the smoking-habit and the swearing-habit and the drinking-habit, but not of the abstention-habit or the moderation-habit or the courage-habit" (*TT* 47). Maintaining that the larger the portion of our daily activities that we can consign to "the effortless custody of automatism, the more our higher powers of mind will be set free for their own proper work," he then offers some suggestions for developing better habits. One is to recognize that there are definite temporal limits on human plasticity, either on the learning of languages or "the formation of intellectual and professional habits" (*PP* 1:126/*PBC* 133–34). If the young would realize that they are quickly becoming "mere walking bundles of habits," they would watch their conduct much more carefully while still in "the plastic state," he writes. Drunkards become drunkards, and saints saints, "by so many separate acts and hours of work" (*PP* 1:130–31/*PBC* 138; cf. *ML* 37). Another suggestion is to learn to cooperate with our bodies, "*to make our nervous system our ally instead of our enemy.*" We can accomplish this by making "*automatic and habitual, as early as possible, as many useful actions as we can,* and guard[ing] against the growing into ways that are likely to be disadvantageous to us, as we should guard against the plague" (*PP* 1:126/*PBC* 133–34). James then offers a series of four tips to help people to develop better habits. The first is to make a strong start. The second, allow no exceptions. Third, keep up the effort until the habit has taken root. Finally, he urges us to never relax our efforts: "*Keep the faculty of effort alive in you by a little gratuitous exercise every day*" (*PP* 1:130/*PBC* 137).

While James is rightly criticized for the individualistic focus of his ethical and political views, as we shall see in chapter 6, his descriptive psychology offers a much richer account of the social aspects of the self, an account that influenced such later social thinkers as Mary Whiton Calkins, Charles Horton Cooley, John Dewey, W. E. B. Du Bois, George Herbert Mead, and Josiah Royce. In the chapter "The Consciousness of Self" (or "The Self" in *Psychology: Briefer Course*), he presents us with an understanding of the self as shaped and largely constituted through interactions with our social groups. In contrast with many earlier attempts to understand the self, James believes that the inherited notion of the substantial soul "explains nothing and guarantees nothing." On the contrary, the process of "successive thoughts" remains the only "intelligible and verifiable" aspect of the conscious self, and simply ascertaining "the correlations of these with brain-processes is as much as psychology can empirically do." He recognizes that often more extensive metaphysical claims are made about the soul. Historically, this soul was the bone of contention between the empirical minimalists like Hume and the Kantian and post-Kantian transcendentalists, and it has been frequently abused by theologians. He finds unobjectionable claims that thoughts have some "vague problematic ground" in brain processes, but he rejects any view of the soul that "professes to give the ground in positive terms of a very dubiously credible sort." For him, no soul is necessary to explain the self as a psychological entity. James the psychologist therefore pledges "to discard the word Soul" from *The Principles*, or to use it only "in the vaguest and most popular way." At the same time, he would allow any "reader who finds any comfort in the idea of the Soul . . . to continue to believe in it; for our reasonings have not established the non-existence of the Soul; they have only proved its superfluity for scientific purposes" (*PP* 1:331–32). For scientific psychology, however, only a minimal self is necessary, and the question of the existence of a soul is better treated as a "metaphysical" issue.

Proceeding with his psychological inquiry, James notes that in our familiar understanding of the self, there is a distinction between what he calls the "I"—the aware, knowing part of the self—and the "me"—the known part of the self.[65] He writes: "Whatever I may be thinking of, I am always at the same time more or less aware of *myself*, of my *personal existence*. At the same time it is *I* who am aware; so that the total self of me, being as it were duplex, partly known and partly knower, partly object and partly subject, must have two aspects discriminated in it, of which for shortness we may call one the *Me* and the other the *I*. I call these 'discriminated aspects,' and not separate things, because the identity of *I* with *me*, even in the very act of their discrimination, is perhaps the most ineradicable dictum of commonsense" (*PBC* 159).[66]

James begins his discussion with the latter emphasis: the empirical self, the self-as-known, the *me*. His first point is that there is no sharp line to be found between the *me* and what I call *mine*. The way that we treat our possessions is much the same as we treat ourselves. "Our fame, our children, the work of our hands, may be as dear to us as our bodies are, and arouse the same feelings and the same acts of reprisal if attacked." With regard to our bodies, he wonders, "are they simply ours, or are they *us*?" Using this recognition of the vagueness of the boundary around the self, James necessarily gives us a very broad understanding of the "me": "*In its widest possible sense . . . a man's Self is the sum total of all that he* CAN *call his*, not only his body and his psychic powers, but his clothes and his house, his wife and children, his ancestors and friends, his reputation and works, his lands and horses, and yacht and bank-account" (*PP* 1:279; cf. *PBC* 159–60; *ERE* 76).[67] Extending the boundaries of the self only slightly further, we can begin to understand the actions of the hero, the martyr, and the suicide bomber.

James then refines his discussion into a series of subtopics. The first of these considers the constituents of the "me," which he lists as the material, social, and spiritual "me." The material "me" is, as we have seen, a material object among others. "We all have a blind impulse," he writes, "to watch over our body, to deck it with clothing of an ornamental sort, to cherish parents, wife and babes, and to find for ourselves a house of our own which we may live in and 'improve.'" We all recognize the power of our possessions, and James indicates how most individuals would feel "personally annihilated if a life-long construction of their hands or brains—say an entomological collection or an extensive work in manuscript—were suddenly swept away" (*PP* 1:280–81/*PBC* 161).

The social "me" is a person among others. In spite of James's strong individualism, he recognizes that we are social creatures.[68] We all have a place within a social group; in fact, we have many places within many social groups. He indicates that *"a man has as many social selves as there are individuals who recognize him* and carry an image of him in their mind" (*PP* 1:281–82/*PBC* 162).[69] As an example of this multiplicity, he considers the case of a boy whose saintly persona, familiar to his parents and teachers, is replaced by another that "swears and swaggers like a pirate among his 'tough' young friends." James continues that "we do not show ourselves to our children as to our club-companions, to our customers as to the laborers we employ, to our own masters and employers as to our intimate friends" (*PP* 1:282/*PBC* 162).[70] He indicates that we have learned much of what it means to be a person from our parents, and we interact with them a particular way.[71] We interact differently with our lovers and former lovers, to whom we now present a far different self. On a broader scale, through our interactions in community, we try on the lives and personalities of others and learn more of the fullness of what it is to be human.[72] Eventually, we pick among these social roles as we construct our selves, and with these choices come responsibilities. Each individual operates to defend "his image in the eyes of his own 'set,'" and this image "exalts or condemns him as he conforms or not to certain requirements that may not be made of one in another walk of life." If we decide to be parents, this image demands that we must be good ones; if we choose to be firefighters, we must be brave. James continues that "a layman may abandon a city infected with cholera; but a priest or a doctor would think such an act incompatible with his honor. A soldier's honor requires him to fight or to die under circumstances where another man can apologize or run away with no stain upon his social self. A judge, a statesman, are in like manner debarred by the honor of their cloth from entering into pecuniary relations perfectly honorable to persons in private life" (*PP* 1:282/*PBC* 162–63; cf. *EPs* 175).[73] James also suggests that social rules have situational aspects such that, while lying is in general prohibited, "you may lie as much as you please if asked about your relations with a lady" (*PP* 1:283/*PBC* 163).

Thirdly, there is the spiritual "me," a somewhat less clear notion that recognizes the self as an individual set of beliefs and values among others. We might consider here, for example, James's philosophy as it is understood—or misunderstood—by others, versus how he understood it. "By the Spiritual Self, so far as it belongs to the Empirical Me," he writes, "I mean a man's inner or subjective being, his psychic faculties or dispositions, taken concretely." The spiritual "me" is what we examine when we view others, or ourselves, as thinkers. In other words, I can focus not on thinking, but on myself as a thinker, with a collection of states of consciousness, faculties, dispositions, and so on, and I can do so without at the same time maintaining that I am a "*mere ens rationis* [thinking thing]." He continues that "these psychic dispositions are the most enduring and intimate part of the self, that which we most verily seem to be." He points, for example, to the satisfaction that we derive from thinking "of our ability to argue and discriminate, of our moral sensibility and conscience, of our indomitable will" (*PP* 1:283, 286, 283; cf. *PBC* 163–64). He admits that there is no general agreement about what this "spiritual self" amounts to, especially in its more controversial role as knower (the "I"). As we have seen, empiricists want a minimalist version of the self, while rationalists and transcendentalists want something more expansive. James maintains, however, that whatever the answer is, the spiritual self is not purely rational, not just thinking. The spiritual self, although spiritual, is connected with the body (see *PP* 1:286–88).

James's second subtopic is the feelings and emotions that these aspects of the self arouse. When, for example, we evaluate ourselves—an action explainable only in terms of a distinction like the "I" and the "me"—what is our conclusion? Sometimes, we find that we are complacent, satisfied, proud, vain, conceited, or even arrogant; at other times, we are more modest, dissatisfied, ashamed, disgusted, or contrite. He maintains that usually there is some justifiable relationship between this self-evaluation and our personal accomplishments, writing that "the normal *provocative* of self-feeling is one's actual success or failure, and the good or bad actual position one holds in the world." This means that, on the one hand, a man who has had a successful life is "not likely to be visited by the morbid diffidences and doubts about himself which he had when he was a boy." On the other hand, the man who "still lies in middle life among the failures at the foot of the hill," is far more likely to live without confidence and to avoid risks. Such generalizations, however, are not the whole story because "the barometer of our self-esteem and confidence rises and falls" independently of our friends' estimations for reasons "that seem to be visceral and organic rather than rational" (*PP* 1:292–93/*PBC* 164–65). As we move through life and respond to new situations, we also modify our ideas and choose new reference groups. He writes that "when, as a protestant, I turn catholic; as a catholic, freethinker; as a 'regular practitioner,' homeopath, or what not, I am always inwardly strengthened in my course and steeled against the loss of my actual social self by the thought of other and better *possible* social judges than those whose verdict goes against me now." For James, there is an "ideal social self" that, however remote or unrealizable in this life, can look forward to the appreciation of "future generations" or of "the highest *possible* judging companion"—whether "God, the Absolute Mind, [or] the 'Great Companion'"—"if such companion there be" (*PP* 1:300–301; cf. *PBC* 172).

James's third subtopic involves the actions that these aspects of the self prompt, especially with regard to self-seeking and self-preservation. The material "me," as an organism, must care about food, safety, and so on, and act accordingly. "Each mind," he writes, "must have a certain minimum of selfishness in the shape of instincts of bodily self-seeking in order to exist" (*PP* 1:308). The social "me" acts so as to attain high regard in the eyes of others. "Our social *self-seeking*," he writes, "is carried on directly through our amativeness and friendliness, our desire to please and attract notice and admiration, our emulation and jealousy, our love of glory, influence, and power, and indirectly through whichever of the material self-seeking impulses prove serviceable as means to social ends." He points out that much of our desire for this recognition is not strictly rational. "We are crazy to get a visiting-list which shall be large, to be able to say when anyone is mentioned, 'Oh! I know him well,'" he continues, and even the places and topics with which he might describe himself as familiar—Venice, Monet, Shakespeare, Chopin—"enlarge my Self in a sort of metaphoric social way." The spiritual "me" acts to achieve the highest inward nature. "Under the head of *spiritual self-seeking*," he writes, "ought to be included every impulse towards psychic progress, whether intellectual, moral, or spiritual in the narrow sense of the term." James suggests, however, that much of our apparent spiritual self-seeking—as in our attempts to stay on the good side of a judging God—constitute, in fact, "only material and social self-seeking beyond the grave." He maintains that only the pursuit of "the redeemed inward nature, the spotlessness from sin, whether here or hereafter" should be counted "as spiritual self-seeking pure and undefiled" (*PP* 1:294–95; cf. *PBC* 166–67).

Lest all of this appear too orderly and rational, James turns his discussion to the rivalry among the various aspects of the "me."[74] Given a vast array of conflicting possibilities of who we might become, we must select among the potential selves. As he puts it, "I am often confronted by the necessity of standing by one of my empirical selves and relinquishing the rest. Not that I would not, if I could, be both handsome and fat and well dressed, and a great athlete, and make a million a year, be a wit, a *bon-vivant*, and a lady-killer, as well as a philosopher; a philanthropist, statesman, warrior, and African explorer, as well as a 'tone poet' and saint. But the thing is simply impossible" (*PP* 1:295/*PBC* 167; cf. *WB* 171).

We are thus constantly evaluating and passing judgment on ourselves. We do this by appealing to standards of beauty, intelligence, athletic ability, and so on. Thus, I judge that I am smarter than she is and stronger than he; at the same time, however, I must admit that she is a better musician, and he a better poet. In a similar fashion, we recognize that we all could further develop our spirituality, strengthen our marriages, and be better parents. He believes that these standards of judgment, although they are often mistakenly seen as simple importations from "outside" the self, are more accurately seen as internalized community values that gain their power because they are in fact constituents of the "me." The standards behind these judgments are in some sense chosen, or at least accepted, by us. I construct a "me" in which intelligence matters somewhat, as does physical strength; I fashion an ideal self in which music and poetry, and spirituality and marital success, play their proper roles—"proper," that is, in the value system that I have selectively internalized from society. James elaborates on the selectivity of the process: "I, who for the time have staked my all on being a psychologist, am mortified if others know much more psychology than I. But I am contented to wallow in the grossest ignorance of Greek." To be deficient in languages is no real problem for a psychologist, and a linguist can remain psychologically naive. He points to "the paradox of a man shamed to death because he is only the second pugilist or the second oarsman in the world." In such cases, to be able "to beat the whole population of the globe minus one is nothing" (*PP* 1:296; cf. *PBC* 168) if his target is to defeat that one.

James then offers us a sort of mathematical formula that presents our level of self-esteem as a function of our successes divided by our hopes, "the ratio of our actualities to our supposed potentialities." He is not taking the mathematics in any scientific sense here; the important part is his recognition that we can improve our sense of self-esteem by either increasing the numerator of actual successes or decreasing the denominator of our expectations. Moreover, since the former is not very easy to raise, the secret to improved self-esteem would seem to be lowering the latter. "To give up pretensions is as blessed a relief as to get them gratified," he writes, "and where disappointment is incessant and the struggle unending, this is what men will always do." For example, he continues that there would be "happier women and men to-day, if they could once for all abandon the notion of keeping up a Musical Self, and without shame let people hear them call a symphony a nuisance." Further, he writes, "how pleasant is the day when we give up striving to be young,—or slender! Thank God! we say, *those* illusions are gone" (*PP* 1:296–97/*PBC* 168).

We can now turn to the "I," or the self as knower. James notes that the "I," which has already slipped repeatedly into our prior discussion whenever notions like evaluation and choosing have appeared, is a much harder aspect of the self to understand or inquire into than the "me." The I "is that which at any given moment *is* conscious, whereas the Me is only one of the things which it is conscious *of*." He is willing to characterize the "I" as "the *Thinker*," but to do so leads immediately to the question of the nature of the thinker. "Is it the passing state of consciousness itself, or is it something deeper and less mutable" like "a permanent Substance or Agent"? For many, "this Agent is the thinker; the 'state' is only its instrument or means" (*PBC* 175). James wonders whether we need such an entity, whether it is described as the "soul" or the "spirit" or the "transcendental Ego."

We can begin with a (relatively) easy aspect of the "I," namely attention. James wonders whether we find in consciousness a jumble of ideas—as the empiricists suggest—or a single idea, full of whatever complexities it contains. Considering such statements as "'Columbus discovered America in 1492'" (*PP* 1:265) or "'The pack of cards is on the table'" (*PP* 1:268/*PBC* 176), he maintains that the object is the entire statement, not a portion of it. "The object of every thought," he writes, "is neither more nor less than all that the thought thinks, exactly as the thought thinks it, however complicated the matter, and however symbolic the manner of the thinking may be" (*PP* 1:266). James has a good bit of fun here exploring the complexities of such experiences as drinking lemonade and hearing discords, and questioning whether twelve individuals, each with a separate word in their minds, could ever formulate a sentence. His point in all of this, however, is the important one that mental states are not fusions: "No possible number of entities (call them as you like, whether forces, material particles, or mental elements) can sum *themselves* together. Each remains, in the sum, what it always was; and the sum itself exists only *for a bystander* who happens to overlook the units and to apprehend the sum as such; or else to exist in the shape of some other effect on an entity external to the sum itself" (*PBC* 177; cf. *PP* 1:272; *EP* 76–78). James thus rejects the empiricist answer that "the mind is constituted by a multiplicity of distinct 'ideas' *associated* into a unity." That is, we have an idea of *a* and an idea of *b*, and we combine the two into "an idea of *a* + *b*, or of *a* and *b* together." For him, the correct answer is to be found in the stream of thought or consciousness, by assuming that the "*things that are known together are known in single pulses of that stream.*" These things themselves may be many, and they may cause "many currents in the brain," but, for James, "the psychic phenomenon correlative to these many currents is one integral 'state,' transitive or substantive . . . to which the many things appear" (*PBC* 178–79).

We can also turn our inquiry into the "I" to a consideration of the self as known and as knower. The self-as-known—the "me"—is ever in the process of changing, although the process is slow: alterations are gradual, and continuity is powerful. "As a concrete Me, I am somewhat different from what I was: then hungry, now full; then walking, now at rest; then poorer, now richer; then younger, now older; etc." Still, in many other aspects—what James calls "the essential ways"—the individual remains the same. "My name and profession and relations to the world are identical, my face, my faculties and store of memories, are practically indistinguishable, now and then." Further, he notes that "the Me of now and the Me of then are *continu-*

ous: the alternations were gradual and never affected the whole of me at once. So far, then, my personal identity is just like the sameness predicated of any other aggregate thing." The self-as-knower, on the other hand, is far more changeable. The "I" he notes "at every moment goes out and knowingly appropriates the *Me* of the past, and discards the non-me as foreign." This process often gives rise, unfortunately, to "a permanent abiding principle of spiritual activity identical with itself wherever found." James admits that this sense of "I" often plays a central role in both philosophy and common sense, but for him, it has serious problems. In particular, it is unnecessary: if passing states of consciousness are seen as realities, then "no such 'substantial' identity in the thinker need be supposed." He thus maintains that there is no "*substantial* identity" between yesterday's and today's states of consciousness, only "a *functional* identity." Yesterday's "I" and today's "I" "know the same objects, and so far as the by-gone me is one of those objects, they react upon it in an identical way, greeting it and calling it *mine*, and opposing it to all the other things they know" (*PBC* 180–81).

We can proceed without a substantive self because successive "I's," although "numerically distinct," are "all aware of the same past in the same way." These states are consequently able to "form an adequate vehicle for all the experience of personal unity and sameness which we actually have." While metaphysics or theology may continue to work to *"prove the Soul to exist . . . for psychology the hypothesis of such a substantial principle of unity is superfluous"* (*PBC* 181). James continues that in each instant the "I" appropriates the same "me," because it has a certain "warmth and intimacy" (*PBC* 181/*PP* 1:316) that other available "me-s" do not have. In other words, our own experiences simply feel different from those that have happened to other people. He continues that "the heavy warm mass of my body is there, and the nucleus of the 'spiritual me,' the sense of intimate activity . . . is there" as well. "We cannot realize our present self without simultaneously feeling one or other of these two things." He continues: "Other men's experiences, no matter how much I may know about them, never bear this vivid, this peculiar brand. This is why Peter, awakening in the same bed with Paul, and recalling what both had in mind before they went to sleep, reidentifies and appropriates the 'warm' ideas as his, and is never tempted to confuse them with those cold and pale-appearing ones which he ascribes to Paul." As each "pulse" of consciousness is replaced by a successive one, the latter "knows its own predecessor, and finding it 'warm,' in the way we have described, greets it, saying: 'Thou are *mine*, and part of the same self with me'" (*PBC* 181–82; cf. *PP* 1:316–22). For James, the resultant sense of self-identity—functional rather than substantive—is not strong. For the most part, however, it is enough.

As a final point in his discussion of the self, James considers the relationship between changes in people—in ourselves and in others—and our general sense of identity. In cases of a marked change, belief in a strong "soul" would seem to preclude our inclusion of the new data except as examples of presumed mental "breakdown," demonic possession, or intended fraud. For him, on the contrary, those cases are instances when the "I" has simply connected up with the wrong "me," or with another "me." These sorts of mutations appear in two ways. Sometimes there are alternations in memory that result in a different "me," as when memory loss shrinks the "me" or when dreamt or imagined fictions insert themselves into memory (see *PP* 1:352–54; *PBC* 183–84). At other times, abnormalities in present personality challenge our self-identity—hypnotic states, insanity or delusion, and the psychical anomalies related to mediumship. Some of these themes will be considered below.

Energy, Activity, and Will

James was equally interested in the question of the will. "The willing department of our nature," he writes in *The Will to Believe*, "dominates both the conceiving department and the feeling department; or, in plainer English, perception and thinking are only there for behavior's sake." This means that the mind is "an essentially teleological mechanism," and that "the conceiving or theorizing faculty ... functions *exclusively for the sake of ends* that do not exist at all in the world of impressions we receive by way of our senses, but are set by our emotional and practical subjectivity altogether." The goal of our thinking life is thus the transformation of the world we perceive into "a totally different world—the world of our conception," a transformation that is effected, when it is effected, "in the interests of our volitional nature." The world that we encounter is alien to our individual interests, unwelcoming and unintelligible. "We have to break that order altogether—and by picking out from it the items which concern us, and connecting them with others far away, which we say 'belong' with them, we are able to make out definite threads of sequence and tendency" (*WB* 92, 94–95). These efforts he considers under the topic of will.

In the chapter on the will in *The Principles*, James considers the question of free will, but instead of offering a metaphysical interpretation, dealing with possibility, chance, and related themes,[75] we get a psychological interpretation. If, on the one hand, the will is "really indeterminate," he writes, "our future acts are ambiguous or unpredestinate: in common parlance, our *wills are free*." If, on the other, "the amount of effort" is not indeterminate, but "related in a fixed manner to the objects themselves, in such wise that whatever object at any time fills our consciousness was from eternity bound to fill it then and there, and compel from us the exact effort, neither more nor less, which we bestow upon it,—then our wills are not free, and all our acts are foreordained." It is in this sense that he can write that *"the question of fact in the free-will controversy is thus extremely simple"*: it is a matter of "the amount of effort of attention or consent which we can at any time put forth" (*PP* 2:1175; cf. *PBC* 390–91).

We thus get from James parallel accounts of the question of free will, a "dualism" of psychology and metaphysics. As before, he believes that no answer is to be found in science: "the question of free-will is insoluble on strictly psychologic grounds" (*PP* 2:1176; cf. *PBC* 391; *WB* 124). Psychology simply assumes that free will does not exist, and then goes about its scientific business of trying to uncover regularities and predict outcomes. If a person is seeking to advance the project of psychology, he writes, that person should adopt "the great scientific postulate that the world must be one unbroken fact, and that prediction of all things without exception must be ideally, even if not actually, possible." If, on the contrary, that person is committed to a moral universe, and "the postulate that *what ought to be can be, and that bad acts cannot be fated, but that good ones must be possible in their place*," then the scientific view must be rejected. For James, this question remains open. As he continues, "when scientific and moral postulates war thus with each other and objective proof is not to be had, the only course is voluntary choice, for scepticism itself, if systematic, is also voluntary choice." Lest free will be undermined in the meantime, he suggests that a belief in indeterminism "should be voluntarily chosen from amongst other possible beliefs" (*PP* 2:1177). He grants, however, that "a psychologist cannot be expected to be thus impartial, having a great motive in favor of determinism." The psychologist "wants to build a *Science;* and a Science is a system of fixed relations." Talk of free will introduces independent variables and brings science to an end. Thus, until human volitions are proven to be independent variables, scientific psychology can treat them as "fixed functions" (*PBC* 392).

Even after leaving this question of free will aside and working within the assumptions of science, the psychological examination of the will still has plenty to do. James begins with a consideration of a trio of interrelated terms: desire, wish, and will. "We desire to feel, to have, to do, all sorts of things which at the moment are not felt, had, or done," he writes. "If with the desire there goes a sense that attainment is not possible, we simply *wish;* but if we believe that the end is in our power, we *will* that the desired feeling, having, or doing shall be real; and real it presently becomes, either immediately upon the willing or after certain preliminaries have been fulfilled." Since willing is related to further action, we also need to consider what sorts of actions there are. So, he embarks on a discussion of the physiology of action, full of specific terms and their definitions. On the one hand, there are movements that are often described as reflexive or automatic or instinctive. James calls these all "primary performances," by which he means that "the nerve-centres are so organized that certain stimuli pull the trigger of certain explosive parts; and a creature going through one of these explosions for the first time undergoes an entirely novel experience." There are also voluntary movements that he describes as *"secondary, not primary functions of our organism,"* because we must know that they are possible before we can will to do them. He writes that "when a particular movement, having once occurred in a random, reflex, or involuntary way, has left an image of itself in the memory, then the movement can be desired again, proposed as an end, and deliberately willed" (*PP* 2:1098–99; cf. *PBC* 358–59). Thus, the child learns what actions are possible by having done them, or by having seen them done by others. Conversely, the child too often learns what is impossible—for example, flying—by pain.

James maintains that voluntary movements always result from ideas. (We can, of course, have the ideas but not act upon them.) These ideas are of two sorts: resident or kinesthetic, and remote. The former he describes as the idea of the movement "as it feels, when taking place, in the moving parts"; the latter, as the idea of the movement "as it feels in some other part of the body which it affects (strokes, presses, scratches, etc.), or as it sounds, or as it looks" (*PBC* 359; cf. *PP* 2:1100). As an example, we might consider an itch idea to be remote, and a scratch idea to be resident. The important part is that the next time that we have an itch, we remember how to deal with it, and eventually the process becomes habitual. In the initial process of learning a particular movement, he suggests that "the resident feelings" are primary. As learning continues and habits develop, however, "the more practised we become in a movement, the more 'remote' do the ideas become which form its mental cue." The skilled carpenter, for example, attends more to the nail than to the hammer; the skilled pianist more to the keys than to the fingers. "What we are *interested* in is what sticks in our consciousness; everything else we get rid of as quickly as we can," he writes. "Our resident feelings of movement have no substantive interest for us at all, as a rule." Our interest is in "the ends which the movement is to attain." He continues: "We walk a beam the better the less we think of the position of our feet upon it. We pitch or catch, we shoot or chop the better the less tactile and muscular (the less resident), and the more exclusively optical (the more remote), our consciousness is. Keep your *eye* on the place aimed at, and your hand will fetch it; think of your hand, and you will very likely miss your aim" (*PP* 2:1127–28/*PBC* 362–63). Voluntary action structured by habits does not require "the thought of the innervation which the movement requires," or even a consideration of the muscular means; it requires only "the anticipation of the movement's sensible effects" (*PP* 2:1130/*PBC* 364).

James poses the question whether the idea alone is enough to cause action, or whether we need more—some additional "*fiat, decision, consent, volitional mandate, or other synonymous phenomenon of consciousness.*" In response, he suggests that, while sometimes "the bare idea" is enough for movement to occur, at other times "an additional conscious element" is required. He begins with the former case, when there is "movement upon the mere thought of it" when the movement follows "*unhesitatingly and immediately* the notion of it." These are instances of what he calls "ideo-motor action" (*PP* 2:1130; cf. *PBC* 364), and they include such actions as an involuntary scratch or brushing dust off a sleeve. Such actions occur when an idea pops into the individual's mind and there is no counter-idea to delay its enactment. Examples of such counter-ideas would include our unwillingness to leave a warm bed in cold room, or a child's hesitancy to leave a chair after being told to sit still. The delay is ended if and when the "antagonistic thoughts" (*PP* 2:1134/*PBC* 367) are forgotten or canceled. For James, we are active creatures, inclined to follow our impulses unless they are inhibited by authority or civilization or alternative impulses. "We are an organized machinery for muscular explosion," he writes, "placed in an environment full of things which pull and clamp the triggers of the machinery in various preappointed ways" (*EPs* 225).[76] He continues, saying that "consciousness is *in its very nature impulsive*," and that it functions quite frequently as "a forerunner of activity" without any added "will-force." Human life is thus active life balanced by various restraints, and our behavior is "at all times the resultant of two opposing neural forces." The brain is the focus of currents that are "playing on his motor nerves," at the same time that other currents are "playing on the first currents, damming or helping them, altering their direction or their speed" (*PP* 2:1134–35/*PBC* 367–68).

In the latter instance, when some restraint impedes action, a fiat is needed. James calls such cases "action after deliberation." These include those cases where there are multiple options, and we ponder our options. Should we stay in our warm bed in a cold room, or get up? Must we remain seated, or may we move around a room? In such cases of *"deliberate action,"* cases "when the mind is the seat of many ideas related to each other in antagonistic or in favorable ways," James tells us that the individual mulls over the idea of the action and any further consideration that would "block the motor discharge" or would "solicit it to take place." In this state of *"indecision,"* we deliberate over these "reinforcing and inhibiting ideas"—now called *"reasons* or *motives"*—and eventually we *"utter our voluntary fiat"* (*PP* 2:1136; cf. *PBC* 368–69). In other words, we decide how we will act.

James then enumerates five types of decisions. The first of these he calls *"reasonable,"* referring to "those cases in which the arguments for and against a given course seem gradually and almost insensibly to settle themselves in the mind and to end by leaving a clear balance in favor of one alternative, which alternative we then adopt without effort or constraint." In these cases we wait until the relevant evidence is available and then make our decision based upon it. Our function here is more as a recorder and judge than as a contributor, and the reasons appear "to flow in from the nature of things, and to owe nothing to our will" (*PP* 2:1138/*PBC* 370). James then discusses two types of decision that occur when "no paramount and authoritative reason for either course will come." Consider, for example, the sort of indecision we often face as we ponder the menu at a good restaurant. All the choices seem fine, and "there is no umpire to decide which good should yield its place to the other." At some point, we simply decide. If the final fiat seems to come from within—and I decide to have "the usual"—he considers it an internal "drift" decision. If the fiat comes from without—and I decide to have "what she is having"—he considers it an external "drift" decision. In both of these cases, James continues, we become increasingly tired of the "hesitation and inconclusiveness," and we realize that "even a bad decision is better than no decision at all" (*PP* 2:1139/*PBC* 371). At the opposite end from these drift decisions are conversion decisions. In such cases, "in consequence of some outer experience or some inexplicable inward change, *we suddenly pass from the easy and careless to the sober and strenuous mood,* or possibly the other way." Finally, James considers the cases when we contribute to the outcome by deliberately tipping the scale of the decision, or, as he writes, "we ourselves by our own wilful act" incline the beam (*PP* 2:1140–41/*PBC* 372).

In the process of making decisions, James believes that the individual's will may be functioning properly or improperly—a question that he had studied from the inside during his long battle with depression and neurasthenia.[77] In the case of a "healthy" will, he writes, "*there is a certain normal ratio in the impulsive power of different sorts of motive . . . which is departed from only at exceptional times or by exceptional individuals.*" In this healthy condition, individuals tend to pay attention to powerful states of mind, such as instinctive objects of passion or emotion, possibilities of pleasure and pain, or ideas of habitual interest. In comparison to these vibrant influences, he continues, "all far-off considerations, all highly abstract conceptions, unaccustomed reasons, and motives foreign to the instinctive history of the race, have little or no impulsive power" (*PP* 2:1143; cf. *PBC* 374). In contrast, what he calls "the moral tragedy of human life" results from the fact that sometimes "the link is ruptured which normally should hold between vision of the truth and action." In such cases, the resultant action fails to pursue the good, or as he quotes Ovid: "'*Video meliora proboque, deteriora sequor*' [I see and try to do the better, but I follow the worse]" (*PP* 2:1153/*PBC* 379). The will can be "unhealthy" in many ways, although in any given case it will always be tough for someone else to identify the problem. Sometimes, the will is "*precipitate*," James writes, and the action follows "the stimulus or idea too rapidly, leaving no time for the arousal of restraining associates." The individual thus fails to deliberate when deliberation would seem necessary.

In other cases, the restraints may develop, but "the ratio which the impulsive and inhibitive forces normally bear to each other may be distorted, and we then have *a will which is perverse*" (*PP* 2:1143/*PBC* 375).[78]

James divides the cases of perversity into two groups. In the first type, which he calls the *"obstructed"* will, "normal actions are impossible," whereas in the second, the case of the *"explosive"* will, "abnormal ones are irrepressible" (*PP* 2:1144/*PBC* 375). In the former case of the obstructed will, what would seem to be normal actions are impossible, because of too little impulsion or too much inhibition. He continues that these cases of obstructed will include many familiar ones: "the hopeless failures, the sentimentalists, the drunkards, the schemers, the 'dead-beats,' whose life is one long contradiction between knowledge and action, and who, with full command of theory, never get to holding their limp characters erect" (*PP* 2:1153/*PBC* 379).[79] In the latter cases of the *"explosive"* will, on the contrary, abnormal actions are irrepressible. Sometimes restraints are inadequate, and "impulses seem to discharge so promptly into movements that inhibitions get no time to arise." Here, James points to "the 'dare-devil' and 'mercurial' temperaments, overflowing with animation, and fizzling with talk, which are so common in the Latin and Celtic races, and with which the cold-blooded and long-headed English character forms so marked a contrast." Pushing these stereotypes further, he continues, "monkeys these people seem to us, whilst we seem to them reptilian." The unhealthiness of the will is manifested here by "the absence of scruples, of consequences, of considerations." As a result, there is "the extraordinary simplification of each moment's mental outlook, that gives to the explosive individual such motor energy and ease; it need not be the greater intensity of any of his passions, motives, or thoughts" (*PP* 2:1144–45; cf. *PBC* 375–76). At other times, he notes, the impulses are exaggerated. Even when "the neural tissues preserve their proper inward tone," and "the inhibitory power is normal or even unusually great," it is still possible that *"the strength of the impulsive idea is preternaturally exalted."* In such cases, an impulse that for most individuals would be merely "the passing suggestion of a possibility" becomes instead "a gnawing, craving urgency to act" (*PP* 2:1148/*PBC* 377). James suggests, however, that there is a possible role for effort to deal with these problems of will. Rejecting any sort of determinism, he suggests that effort can neutralize instinctive or habitual impulses, as well as check explosive tendencies and overcome obstructions. In his analysis of the possibilities of effort, he offers a kind of algebraic formula—"I *per se* < P; I + E > P" (*PP* 2:1155/*PBC* 381)—that maintains that while the initial propensity (P) will overcome the ideal (I), that same ideal plus effort (I + E) can overcome propensity.

Many psychological discussions introduce pleasure and pain at this point as central motivators of action, and James recognizes their importance as well. "Objects and thoughts of objects start our action," he writes, "but the pleasures and pains which action brings modify its course and regulate it; and later the thoughts of the pleasures and the pains acquire themselves impulsive and inhibitive power" (*PP* 2:1156/*PBC* 381–82). We continue to perform those actions that are pleasurable, and refrain from those that are painful. Still, he rejects any unguarded claims that all actions follow what Jeremy Bentham calls these "two sovereign masters."[80] Broadening the notion of action to incorporate more recently studied physiological factors, James points to the effects of instinct and emotion on action. "Who smiles for the pleasure of the smiling, or frowns for the pleasure of the frown?" he wonders. "Who blushes to escape the discomfort of not blushing? Or who in anger, grief, or fear is actuated to the movements which he makes by the pleasures which they yield?" Further, he notes that he does not "breathe for the pleasure of the breathing," nor "write for the pleasure of the writing." In the latter case, he keeps writing "simply because I have once begun, and being in a state of intellectual excitement which keeps venting itself in that way, find that I *am* writing still" (*PP* 2:1156, 1158/*PBC* 382, 383).

Now that James has dismissed this overly simplified answer of pleasure and pain, he is ready to attempt a better answer to the question of how actions are caused or determined. For him, the key is what holds our attention or interest. He writes that "we ought to look for the secret of an idea's impulsiveness, not in any peculiar relations which it may have with paths of motor discharge,—for *all* ideas have relations with some such paths,—but rather in a preliminary phenomenon, the *urgency, namely, with which it is able to compel attention and dominate in consciousness*." Following this hypothesis, it is possible to move away from the notion of will as "a relation between the mind and its 'ideas,'" and turn our attention to "the conditions which make ideas prevail in the mind." Once an idea has prevailed, the issue is no longer one of psychology, and the movement that follows is purely physiological in nature. Here James considers a series of cases. "I will to write, and the act follows," he writes. "I will to sneeze, and it does not." In a similar fashion, "I will that the distant table slide over the floor towards me; it also does not.

My willing representation can no more instigate my sneezing-centre than it can instigate the table to activity." All three of these cases were examples of "true and good willing," but the volition is "a psychic or moral fact pure and simple, and is absolutely completed when the stable state of the idea is there" (*PP* 2:1164–65/*PBC* 384–85; cf. *EPs* 107, 228). Thus, will or volition is a matter of attention; and volitional effort is effort of attention. "*The essential achievement of the will, in short, when it is most 'voluntary,' is to* AT-TEND *to a difficult object and hold it fast before the mind*," he writes. "*Effort of attention is thus the essential phenomenon of will*." At times, this attention is misdirected and individuals find themselves drawn to an action better left undone. In such cases, to succumb to the passion or to resist it are equally physically possible. "It is as easy physically to avoid a fight as to begin one, to pocket one's money as to squander it on one's cupidities, to walk away from as towards a coquette's door." The problem is purely "mental": it is the difficulty of keeping the idea of the wiser action before the mind. Individuals often find, however, that when an unwise passion has gripped them, "the tendency is for no images but such as are congruous with it to come up" (*PP* 2:1166–67; cf. *PBC* 386–87).

It is difficult to keep the proper action before the mind because other possible actions tend to crowd it out. The "strong-willed" person, however, is able to maintain this focus, because such a person "hears the still small voice unflinchingly" and "when the death-bringing consideration comes, looks at its face, consents to its presence, clings to it, affirms it, and holds it fast, in spite of the host of exciting mental images which rise in revolt against it and would expel it from the mind." If the idea of this difficult action is kept alive "by a resolute effort of attention," it will grow in support and eventually change "the disposition of the man's consciousness altogether." Effort must be exerted to continue the idea's "undivided presence," to keep it "from flickering and going out." The whole function of effort is thus "to keep affirming and adopting a thought which, if left to itself, would slip away" (*PP* 2:1168–70; cf. *PBC* 387–89). Whether it functions to restrain an explosive will, or to arouse an obstructed one, such effort is the key to successful conduct.

James offers an ethical coda to the chapter on the will in which he notes that we should strive to emulate strong-willed persons rather than "worthless ones." These latter individuals are unable to face the "dark abysses" of life, and "either escape from its difficulties by averting their attention, or if they cannot do that, collapse into yielding masses of plaintiveness and fear."

Far better would be to draw our inspiration from the heroes who are operating within the community. One such hero is the "prophet" who, although he may have "drunk more deeply than anyone of the cup of bitterness," remains able to speak "such mighty words of cheer that his will becomes our will, and our life is kindled at his own." Thus, James maintains that both our morality and our religion "so far as the latter is deliberate," depend upon the contribution that we are willing to make. "*'Will you or won't you have it so?'*" he writes, "is the most probing question we are ever asked" (*PP* 2:1181–82/ *PBC* 393–94).[81]

The issue of the range of human energies or powers ties in with James's broader interests. We can consider the appearance of this theme in his parallel 1907 essays, "The Energies of Men" and "The Powers of Men." As we saw in chapter 1, he was as a young man laid low by a host of difficulties culminating in his vastation. He spent much of the rest of his life "sickly"—collapsed, unable to work, husbanding his limited energies—and feeling very mortal. Yet he was also capable of extraordinary bursts of energy. As we will see in chapter 7, in *The Varieties* he suggests that bursts of energy like these might have a "supernatural" or at least "extra-natural" origin. In his psychological writings, however, these bursts of energy are treated physiologically, almost as a question of public health. James suggests that we need to make "a topographic survey ... of the limits of human power in every conceivable direction, something like an ophthalmologist's chart of the limits of the human field of vision"; with this in hand, we should develop "a methodical inventory of the paths of access, or keys, differing with the diverse types of individual, to the different kinds of power" (*ERM* 145; cf. 161).[82]

James's overall theme is that few of us ever operate at full capacity. We function, instead, well below "our limits of power" (*ERM* 139), wasting potential levels of energy that go untapped. As he continues, "*men habitually use only a small part of the powers which they actually possess and which they might use under appropriate conditions*" (*ERM* 150). Humans seem capable, however, of much more: "Compared with what we ought to be, we are only half awake ... making use of only a small part of our possible mental and physical resources" (*ERM* 131/150). Human performance seldom reaches full capacity because "powers of various sorts" go unused. As he puts it, the individual "energizes below his maximum, and he behaves below his optimum" (*ERM* 144; cf. 151). In extreme cases, like those of "the formidable neurasthenic and psychasthenic conditions" (*ERM* 131/150) that James had seen in the literature and had himself lived, continued existence seems of little or no value. As significant as this problem is for individual persons, he continues, it is also a major social problem. "In rough terms, we may say that a man who energizes below his normal maximum fails by just so much to profit by his chance at life; and that a nation filled with such men is inferior to a nation run at higher pressure." He then poses two questions for society: "how can men be trained up to their most useful pitch of energy? And how can nations make such training most accessible to all their sons and daughters"? As he sees the issue, the problem of maximizing our powers is "only the general problem of education, formulated in slightly different terms" (ERM 149).

James then offers a number of instances. One has to do with the ability of country people to adjust to the pace of urban existence—"the rapid rate of life, the number of decisions in an hour, the many things to keep account of"—and to live there in relative calm. He believes that what once seemed like "a permanent earthquake" becomes normal after the newcomer has "caught the pulse-beat," and "the new level of energy becomes permanent" (ERM 151–52). Another example draws upon John Stuart Mill's recognition of women's ability for sustained moral effort. "Every case of illness nursed by wife or mother is a proof of this," James writes, "and where can one find greater examples of sustained endurance than in those thousands of poor homes, where the woman successfully holds the family together and keeps it going by taking all the thought and doing all the work" (ERM 152). Cases of the emergence of heroes in crises, such as among trapped miners or the shipwrecked, provide him with other instances. "Despair lames most people," he writes, "but it wakes others fully up" (ERM 153). He also points to "the stores of bottled up energy and endurance" that he had witnessed among the survivors and rescuers of the 1906 San Francisco earthquake (ERM 134; cf. EPs 331–38). Next he considers the power of conversion, and to the "very copious unlocking of energies by ideas, in the persons of those converts to 'New Thought,' 'Christian Science,' 'Metaphysical Healing,' or other forms of spiritual philosophy, who are so numerous among us to-day" (ERM 143; cf. 159).[83] These various sets of "healthy-minded and optimistic" ideas "all tend to the suppression of what Mr. Horace Fletcher has termed 'fearthought.' Fearthought he defines as the 'self-suggestion of inferiority'" (ERM 143; cf. 159).[84]

After listing these various cases, James wonders why science has shown so little interest in the topic of energy. Because "the mind-cure movement" is "essentially a religious movement," he suggests that it is rejected by "academically nurtured minds" and by "medical politicians, and ... the whole trades-union wing of that profession" (*ERM* 160). Psychology, in particular, because of its "scientific" interests in what is universal and replicable, has virtually overlooked this entire question.[85] Without denying any possible connection to a "more,"[86] he turns his attention to the mechanisms of human action and points to the theme of will power that we considered previously. "Either some unusual stimulus fills us with emotional excitement, or some unusual idea of necessity induces us to make an extra effort of will," he writes. "*Excitements, ideas, and efforts*, in a word, are what carry us over the dam" (*ERM* 132; cf. 151). Because emotional excitements tend to act discontinuously, however, and allow the remainder of life "to close in and shut us off" the rest of the time, he notes that "the best practical knowers of the human soul have invented the thing known as methodical ascetic discipline to keep the deeper levels constantly in reach" (*ERM* 136/156). Thus, he considers yoga to be "simply a methodical way of *waking up deeper levels of will-power than are habitually used,* and thereby increasing the individual's vital tone and energy" (*C* 11:220). He also points to the role of certain ideas in concentrating the will. He writes that in addition to the effects of particular ideas on particular individuals, there are more general ideas that tend to affect individuals in general, and awaken their "energies of loyalty, courage, endurance, or devotion." Among the many "energy-releasing abstract ideas," James points to "'Fatherland,' 'the Union,' 'Holy Church,' the 'Monroe Doctrine,' 'Truth,' 'Science,' 'Liberty,' Garibaldi's phrase, 'Rome or Death,' etc." These ideas, and others like them, can take over an individual's life and "transfigure it, unlocking innumerable powers which, but for the idea, would never have come into play" (*ERM* 142; cf. 158).[87] In a similar fashion, he also points to the power of pledges and oaths to help individuals sustain efforts to rebuild their lives.[88]

The Fringes of Psychology

"Psychical research," Ralph Barton Perry writes, "was only one of many examples of James's fondness for excursions to the scientific underworld."[89] While Perry's statement is accurate, its tone betrays science's preference for a simple world. James's preference, on the other hand, was for an account that was more complete, however disorderly it might prove to be. "Round about the accredited and orderly facts of every science," he notes, "there ever floats a sort of dust-cloud of exceptional observations, of occurrences minute and irregular and seldom met with, which it always proves more easy to ignore than to attend to" (*WB* 222; cf. *EPs* 247). Among these presumably ignorable phenomena we find the whole field of "psychic" topics: the various claims of clairvoyance and automatic writing, of telepathy and mediums; the contested explanations of hypnotism and hallucinations; the disputed calls to investigate the mind-altering power of drugs, the alleged potentials of "mind-cure" religion that we have just considered; and so on.[90]

If the goal of science is to present "a closed and completed system of truth," James continues, fringe phenomena, especially those that result from "vague and indirect" reports, function more as "marvels and oddities," and we are able to neglect or deny them "with the best of scientific consciences." While individuals whom we consider "crackpots" might show great interest, only occasional scientists—"Galileos, [Luigi] Galvanis, [Augustin-Jean] Fresnels, [Jan Evangelista] Purkinjes, and Darwins" (*EPs* 247–48)—paid much heed to these exceptional cases. For his part, James admits that the study of the psychical is often "tedious, repellent and undignified," but he maintains that "to reject it for its unromantic character is like rejecting bacteriology because *penicillium glaucum* grows on horse-dung and *bacterium termo* lives in putrefaction" (*EPR* 367). He also suggests that there were even those in the scientific community who believed that "if the facts of telepathy, &c., *were* true, the first duty which every honest man would owe to Science would be to deny them, and prevent them, if possible, from ever becoming known" (*EPR* 112). For James, however, it is only the incorporation of these "irregular phenomena" into more complete explanations, and thus the inclusion of psychological fringe areas, that will enable science to move forward (*WB* 223/*EPs* 248). Such progress will also require abandoning the general sense of the worthlessness of "occultism" that allows the qualified scientists who might be able to identify the frauds within the paranormal to refuse to get involved. As he puts it, it is "high time that a realm of phenomena which have played a prominent part in human history from time immemorial should be rescued from the hands of uncritical enthusiasm and charlatanry, and conquered for science." This will only occur, however, when "educated medical men, who are daily forced up to the very threshold, shake off the discreditable shyness which has hitherto characterized them, and walk boldly in to take possession" (*ECR* 246; cf. *PP* 1:375/*PBC* 190). For the present, the work does not get done, and the haughty prejudice continues unchallenged. As he writes, "there is no source of deception in the investigation of nature which can compare with a fixed belief that certain kinds of phenomen[a] are *impossible*" (*C* 6:105–6).[91]

In 1886 James wrote to a correspondent that "the fulness of truth is not given to any one type of mind." After admitting his own prior doubts about those who worked with matters psychical, he asserts that he had come to believe that "that type of mind takes hold of a range of truths to which the other type is stone blind" (*C* 6:125). In 1909, after years of reading and consultations with various researchers and many hours of "witnessing (or trying to witness) phenomena," he admits that "I am theoretically no 'further' than I was at the beginning" (*EPR* 362).[92] His interest had been strong enough to work together with other like-minded individuals, both in the Society for Psychical Research (founded in London in 1882), of which he was president in 1894–96, and its short-lived cousin, the American Society for Psychical Research (founded in 1884).[93] What was driving him in this research was his recognition of the "more." He did not necessarily agree with any of the standard explanations of these phenomena, but he thought that there was something worthwhile in attempting to understand the puzzling array of fringe experiences. Over the years, he presented a series of overlapping testimonials to the importance of research into these questions, including "What Psychical Research Has Accomplished" (1892) and "The Confidences of a 'Psychical Researcher'" (1909).[94] These reports attempt to summarize his efforts in these fringe areas to see what can be understood about the "paranormal." In all of the work that he did, it is clear that James was seeking to better understand the "more."

These questions are highly complex, both as to the nature of the phenomena and as to their possible causes. James maintains, however, that there seems to be something to these phenomena, if only because they continue to be discussed. In spite of the many times that such matters have been "triumphantly despatched and buried," they continue to reemerge: "How often has 'Science' killed off all spook-philosophy, and laid ghosts and raps and 'telepathy' away underground as so much popular delusion." Still, he writes, they continue to reappear despite all the pronouncements of "scientific orthodoxy." For him, this means that what was being demonstrated was not "a mere chapter in human gullibility," but rather "a genuine realm of natural phenomena" (*EPR* 363). Thus, while James admitted to being "constantly baffled" with regard to various accounts, and wary about all of the potential sources of error, he maintains that "weak sticks make strong faggots; and when the stories fall into consistent sorts that point each in a definite direction, one gets a sense of being in presence of genuinely natural types of phenomena" (*EPR* 371).

James concedes the insignificance of much of what goes on in the psychic realm, for example "the extreme triviality of most of the communications." He continues, "what real spirit, at last able to revisit his wife on this earth, but would find something better to say than that she had changed the place of his photograph?" (*EPR* 83). The baroque procedures of the mediums, "the cabinet, the darkness, the tying, suggest a sort of human rathole life exclusively" (*EPR* 371), and the scientific investigator quite sensibly suspects fraud.[95] He also admits that, unfortunately, there is also much proven fraud and chicanery associated with the psychical. He notes, for example, the mysterious demonstrations of Leonora Evelina Piper and Eusapia Paladino,[96] neither of whom he ever fully trusted.[97] "*Falsus in uno, falsus in omnibus*, once a cheat, always a cheat, such has been the motto of the english psychical researchers in dealing with mediums." This policy he supports—"Tactically, it is far better to believe much too little than a little too much"—and the great value of the *Proceedings* of the Society for Psychical Research "is due to the fixed intention of the editors to proceed very slowly." Still, James wonders how well this high bar functions as "a test of truth." He writes that "in most things human the accusation of deliberate fraud and falsehood is grossly superficial. Man's character is too sophistically mixed for the alternative of 'honest or dishonest' to be a sharp one" (*EPR* 363–64). Thus, while he accepts that "an indefinite majority of instances" represents some sort of swindle, he nevertheless continues to suggest that these swindles bear some relation to reality. Remarkably, he even maintains that "if we look at human imposture as a historic phenomenon, we find is always imitative." That is, even though each swindler "imitates a previous swindler," if we continue back along the line we will discover that "the first swindler of that kind imitated someone who was honest" (*EPR* 371). For James, clearly at his most overly generous,[98] something is happening. Even when we take account of imposture and coincidence, and factor in prior knowledge and skill in piecing together information unwittingly offered by subjects, he writes that "those who have the fullest acquaintance with the phenomena admit that in good medium *there is a residuum of knowledge displayed* that can only be called supernormal" (*EPR* 367).

James's complex hypothesis about these phenomena has several aspects. First, as we have seen, scientific evaluation is now and presumably forever incomplete. Second, it is possible that at least some of what some of these individuals are doing is legitimate. Third, one major aspect of a complete explanation might be that the laws of nature are not as fully settled as science would like us to believe. He thus suggests that, if we read "the theory of evolution radically," we would need to apply it not only to the products of evolution—the animals, plants, and planets—but also to its process: the laws of nature themselves. Granted the initial chaos of existence, he writes, "little by little, out of all the haphazard possibilities of that time, a few connected things and habits arose, and the rudiments of regular performance began." Over time, the general level "of law and order" increased to its present state, but "the aberrant and inconstant variations" might still have preserved themselves, "imperfectly connected with the part of the world that had grown regular, as only to manifest their existence by occasional lawless intrusions, like those which 'psychic' phenomena now make into our scientifically organized world" (*EPR* 369). If this account is accurate, he suggests that these phenomena could be "forever intractable to intellectual methods," since their connections with the more orderly parts of the cosmos would only be enough "to affect its periphery every now and then, as by a momentary whiff or touch or gleam, but not enough [to] ever be followed up and hunted down and bagged." James is willing to live for now with such "stray vestiges of that primordial irrationality, from which all our rationalities have been evolved," but he also believes that, with continued efforts by dedicated psychical researchers, sufficient data will be gathered to make possible "some sort of rational treatment" of these phenomena (*EPR* 369–70).[99] In any case, the many unusual phenomena remain real and in need of scientific explanation, and he maintains that "there is 'something in' these never ending reports of physical phenomena, although I haven't yet the least positive notion of the something." The phenomena remain "a very worthy problem for investigation," even though there is scant scientific interest. He notes that these phenomena are more common than is generally believed and that, "in the midst of all the humbug," is to be found "*really supernormal knowledge . . .* knowledge that cannot be traced to the ordinary sources of information" (*EPR* 371–72).

For James, any overall explanation of these fringe phenomena seems to require some sort of "cosmic consciousness" to tie up all the loose ends. "My own dramatic sense tends instinctively to picture the situation as an interaction between slumbering faculties in the automatist's mind and a cosmic environment of *other consciousness* of some sort which is able to work upon them," he writes. Perhaps the universe contains "a lot of diffuse soul-stuff, unable of itself to get into consistent personal form, or to take permanent possession of an organism, yet always craving to do so," that manages on occasion to enter "weak spots in the armor of human minds, and slipping in and stirring up there the sleeping tendency to personate." His overall conclusion to this theme is that "we with our lives are like islands in the sea, or like trees in the forest." On the surface, the various trees "may whisper to each other with their leaves," and nearby islands may "hear each other's foghorns"; below, however, "the trees also commingle their roots in the darkness underground, and the islands also hang together through the ocean's bottom." Without the metaphors, James writes, "there is a continuum of cosmic consciousness, against which our individuality builds but accidental fences, and into which our several minds plunge as into a mother-sea or reservoir." What he calls our "normal" consciousness is focused on successful existence in our mundane environment, but this individual barrier is "weak in spots, and fitful influences from beyond leak in, showing the otherwise unverifiable common connexion" (*EPR* 373–74; cf. *ECR* 545).

James Rowland Angell wrote shortly after James's death that nothing "so radically divided professional opinion of James as his support of the Psychical Research Movement." In America, "James for years stood almost alone among men of high intellectual repute, and although he was eminently conservative in his estimate of the results of the work of the society, he nevertheless committed himself to belief in certain mediumistic phenomena in a way which seriously offended many of his professional colleagues." As a result, he developed a reputation "at best . . . as a man whose judgment could not be trusted, at worst as an unwitting backer of quackery and fraud." Angell continues, however, that James's approach was "all of a piece with his insistent and never failing protestantism, his passion for fair play, and a just hearing for all sides of every question." He had questions that science was not addressing, and, as we shall see in chapter 3, following his pragmatic principle that called for the pursuit of truth over the avoidance of error, he was willing to risk mistakes to try to answer them. Angell concludes that

James knew that making mistakes was "a regular part of the day's work," and he had "a wholesome contempt ... for the pose of infallibility and essential omniscience assumed by certain distinguished scholars. It seemed to him at once petty and contemptible."[100]

Joseph Jastrow, writing in 1900, had a more negative reaction to the field of psychical research and to James's openness to the fringes of psychology. He grants that "the legitimate problems of Psychical Research are equally and necessarily genuine problems of Psychology," even if they were not "especially important, nor interesting, nor profitable, nor well comprehended." Still, he has fundamental objections to what he saw as the illegitimate work that had been done in the name of psychical research. Overall, he writes, "the debit side of the ledger far outbalances the credit side." He rejects in particular the bifurcation of research that suggests that "while the psychologist may be listened to with respect and authority in one portion of his topic, the layman and the member of the Society for Psychical Research are equally or more competent to pronounce judgments in a closely allied field"; he calls, as does James, for the investigation of "psychical" problems "by the same methods and in the same spirit as are other psychological problems." Jastrow also complains that the growing acceptance of psychical research "has disseminated a totally false estimate on the part of the public at large of the scope and purposes of modern Psychology; and has quite possibly given an unfortunate twist to the trend of recent psychological thought." He continues that when the mysterious and the mystical are emphasized—"when the twilight phenomena of mental life are dwelt upon ... to the neglect of the luminous daylight actualities"—the general public will find it difficult to distinguish "between what is authentically scientific and in accordance with the advancing ideals of psychology, and what is but the embodiment of unfortunate traditions, or the misguided effort of the dilettante, or the perverse fallacy of the prepossessed mystic." For psychology to succeed, he maintains, it is necessary that the public become more critical and logical. "Rationality is doubtless a characteristic tendency of humanity," he admits, "but logicality is an acquired possession, and one by no means firmly established in the race at large." For him, "only as logical thoroughness comes to prevail over superficial plausibility, as beliefs come to be formed and evidence estimated according to their intrinsic value rather than according to their emotional acceptability, will the propagandum of the occult meet with greater resistance and aversion."[101] In line with these general criticisms of work in psychical research, Jastrow notes in his 1911 remembrance of James that he had been "inclined to views that by tolerance of possibility, if not by conviction of plausibility, made a place for telepathy and rare powers of mediums and the significance of premonitions." This tolerance, Jastrow believed, opened up an "interpretation of the universe or any small corner thereof for a personal significance." James's approach to the fringes of psychology was rejected as a "dubious path" by many other psychologists, and it caused them to hold "the authority of his name as unfortunate."[102] Any resolution to this issue—to the extent that it is possible—will be found in chapter 7.

CHAPTER 3

Rationality and Belief

This chapter explores James's attempts to address the topics of rationality and belief by methods that were neither narrowly logical nor cripplingly scientific. First to be considered is his 1897 essay "The Sentiment of Rationality," a reworking of two essays from around 1880. He begins this piece with an exploration of the question of what rationality is experienced as from the standpoint of psychology. After suggesting a number of criteria of rationality that he believes we use in particular cases, he then considers whether religious faith would be rational under these criteria. In "The Dilemma of Determinism" (1884), he discusses the question of free will under similar criteria of rationality and decides that the determinism that science seeks—while it cannot be disproven—can be accepted only at a very high cost. A third central essay in this chapter is "The Will to Believe" (1896). Here James discusses our right to believe in some cases—particularly those of morality, personal relations, and religion—where we cannot prove that our positions are true but we believe them justifiable in terms of their potential results. He further defends the right of individuals to be free from the demands of the more narrowly scientific, those who would require them to withhold their assent until decisive evidence is given.

Rationality as a Sentiment

In *The Principles*, James indicates that we are of two minds about the role of rationality in human life. On the one hand, we value the recognition and pursuit of long-term goals:

> In all ages the man whose determinations are swayed by reference to the most distant ends has been held to possess the highest intelligence. The tramp who lives from hour to hour; the bohemian whose engagements are from day to day; the bachelor who builds but for a single life; the father who acts for another generation; the patriot who thinks of a whole community and many generations; and, finally, the philosopher and saint whose cares are for humanity and for eternity,—these range themselves in an unbroken hierarchy, wherein each successive grade results from an increased manifestation of the special form of action by which the cerebral centres are distinguished from all below them. (*PP* 1:35/*PBC* 97–98)

While we thus value the rational ordering of life, we also recognize that "reason is only one out of a thousand possibilities in the thinking of each of us." Our mental lives are also full of "silly fancies," "grotesque suppositions," and "utterly irrelevant reflections." Our situation is so skewed that we cannot even claim that our "prejudices and irrational beliefs" make up a smaller portion of our mental lives than our "clarified opinions" (*PP* 1:521; cf. *PBC* 224; *ECR* 263). He continues that we routinely "believe as much as we can," and that "we would believe everything if we only could" (*PP* 2:928). Similarly, in a later discussion of war James notes that, with regard to most particular actions, reason is "one of the very feeblest of Nature's forces." While we "rational" creatures often pretend to decide actions in a "rational" fashion, in fact what usually happens is that we act out of "prejudices, partialities, cupidities and excitements." Reason in such situations is "like a small sandbank in the midst of a hungry sea ready to wash it out of existence." He is still able to sustain some hope for the peace movement, as we shall see in chapter 6, because "weak as reason is, it has the unique advantage over its antagonists that its activity never lets up and that it presses always in one direction, while men's prejudices vary, their passions ebb and flow, and their excitements are intermittent" (*ERM* 120–21). More specifics will emerge as we consider the operations of reason and belief.

"The Sentiment of Rationality"[1] is a combination of two related themes. The first is the psychological theme of the nature of rationality. James is thus interested not in philosophical or logical questions related to abstractions and proofs, but in a psychological question related to felt experience: How does rationality *feel*?[2] His second theme is the metaphysical question of the rationality of religious faith. Throughout the essay, his tone is descriptive rather than prescriptive. He begins with the general introductory question of why people philosophize at all, and he suggests that they "desire to attain a conception of the frame of things which shall on the whole be more rational than that somewhat chaotic view which everyone by nature carries about with him under his hat." Even if we set rationality as our goal, however, we would still need to recognize when we have attained it. James believes we do so by noting "certain subjective marks" by which rationality affects us. When a belief or an assumption feels rational to us, then, how does it feel? He initially points to "a strong feeling of ease, peace, rest." Thus, "the transition from a state of puzzle and perplexity to rational comprehension is full of lively relief and pleasure." This criterion seems to be a negative one, suggesting that "the feeling of rationality is constituted merely by the absence of any feeling of irrationality" (*WB* 57; cf. *EP* 32). More positively, rationality is recognized by a sort of comfort, as when we "exchange a hard high stool for an arm-chair or prefer travelling by railroad to riding in a springless cart" (*EP* 33). Further, rationality appears to be a feeling of ease, without worry or anxiety or confusion. It is, in other words, a state of mind that "in its *practical* aspect" allows for "unimpeded mental function" (*WB* 65).

There is a Darwinian advantage in this kind alertness, in being able to clear our minds of all sorts of secondary matters to concentrate on whatever is the task at hand. Open-ended doubt is disadvantageous; it can lead to a kind of mental paralysis, whether the question is "did I turn off the oven?" or "can we trust our neighbors?" To survive and prosper, we need to act, to solve our problems, to face the future. We need confidence in the regularity of our world—in the healthfulness of our meals and the stability of our structures—and the faithfulness of those individuals—our spouses and physicians—who play central roles in our lives. Unfounded doubt in such cases is almost always harmful.

As a prescriptive note, we can mention here an issue that will return shortly: the evident inclination in our nature that allows us to be satisfied with beliefs that are traditional and simplistic, and even superstitious. One factor that needs to be considered here is familiarity: the customary seems proper, it sedates. Novelty, on the other hand, is almost always an irritant. Humans thus have a tendency to live comfortably with illusions and prejudices that seem "rational" unless they are challenged to justify themselves, and the ongoing array of public opinion surveys indicates our myriad failings in this regard. To avoid this problem, we need to show more restraint than we normally do when fixing our beliefs. Chastened by such thinkers as Charles Sanders Peirce, we should strive to be more skeptical and logical.[3] James, for his part, seems more concerned to defend individuals against interference with their beliefs from others who claim to know better.

Returning to James's psychological discussion, we see that he applies this sense of rationality as systemic satisfaction in a descriptive fashion to consider the sorts of beliefs that tend to function successfully in our lives. He offers a series of four general criteria. The first two—simplicity and particularity—exist in a kind of balance. Simplicity is a Darwinian criterion that distills the diverse facts of the world down to an order that we are able to find intelligible. "The passion for parsimony, for economy of means in thought," he writes, "is the philosophic passion *par excellence*" (*WB* 58; cf. *EP* 36). He continues:

> Who does not feel the charm of thinking that the moon and the apple are, as far as their relation to the earth goes, identical; of knowing respiration and combustion to be one; of understanding that the balloon rises by the same law whereby the stone sinks; of feeling that the warmth in one's palm when one rubs one's sleeve is identical with the motion which the friction checks; of recognizing the difference between beast and fish to be only a higher degree of that between human father and son; of believing our strength when we climb the mountain or fell the tree to be no other than the strength of the sun's rays which made the corn grow out of which we got our morning meal?

Our enjoyment at reducing "a chaos of facts" to "a single underlying fact" comes from the greater intelligibility of the result; it is "like the relief of the musician at resolving a confused mass of sound into melodic or harmonic order" (*WB* 58–59). He admits that we cannot demonstrate why the philosophically inclined are more susceptible to the delight "of reducing the manifold in thought to simple form" than we can explain "the passion some persons have for matching colours or for arranging cards in a game of solitaire" (*EP* 35). In any case, the resulting simplification can be managed "with far less mental effort" than the original confusing array, and "a philosophic conception of nature is thus in no metaphorical sense a labor-saving contrivance." For James, then, one mark that a philosophical conception must have is this "universality or extensiveness" (*WB* 58–59). His second criterion is particularity. He writes that in addition to our "passion for simplification" we also have "the passion for distinguishing." Some individuals, in other words, prefer "to be *acquainted* with the parts rather than to comprehend the whole." They are able to tolerate any amount of what would seem to others as "incoherence, abruptness and fragmentariness" in their quest to recognize the "full completeness" of the particulars. They reject what they see as "an abstract way of conceiving things that, while it simplifies them, dissolves away at the same time their concrete fulness" (*WB* 59; cf. *EP* 37–38).

James continues that integrating the criteria of simplicity and particularity offers "a real dilemma" for every thinker, who must find a level of each that is acceptable to his or her individual personality. "A man's philosophic attitude is determined by the balance in him of these two cravings," he writes. "No system of philosophy can hope to be universally accepted among men which grossly violates either need, or entirely subordinates the one to the other" (*WB* 59; cf. *EP* 41). We can consider in this regard the history of past philosophies, a history that he sees as a series of swervings from excessive simplicity, as in the case of Spinoza and the rationalist tradition, to excessive particularity, as in the case of Hume and the empiricist tradition (see *WB* 59–60; *EP* 38).

James's own admitted inclination is toward the latter value of particularity, and he maintains that, despite the fact that speculative reductions are prominent in the history of philosophy, they are of only modest value. "When, for example, we think that we have rationally explained the connection of the facts A and B by classing both under their common attribute x," he writes, "it is obvious that we have really explained only so much of these items as is x." If x is to stand for woman, for example, then other properties that A and B share—he lists them as "l, m, n, and o, p, q," standing perhaps for dog lover, chemist, left-handed, born in Kansas, and so on—do not reduce themselves to x. Each of these other particulars carries its own information. "A single explanation of a fact only explains it from a single point of view." This reminder of the importance of particularity is indicative of his overall view that any philosophical position that simplifies too much is inadequate. As he writes, "the simple classification of things is, on the one hand, the best possible theoretic philosophy, but is, on the other, a most miserable and inadequate substitute for the fulness of the truth." While any abridged version of life, which succeeds "by the absolute loss and casting out of real matter," may possess the advantage of simplicity, "a simple conception is an equivalent for the world only so far as the world is simple." For him, on the contrary, while the world may "harbor" simplicity, it is at the same time "a mightily complex affair." Betraying his own preference for particulars, James maintains that people will refuse to be satisfied with theory: they will want the fullness of life. "The entire man, who feels all needs by turns," he writes, "will take nothing as an equivalent for life but the fulness of living itself." Those who on occasion find themselves "weary of the concrete clash and dust and pettiness" may temporarily refresh themselves "by a bath in the eternal springs, or ... a look at the immutable natures" (*WB* 60–62; cf. *EP* 55–56). They will, however, only want to visit these oases of excessive simplicity. They will not want to live their lives there.

Still, James admits, we do go on with our systematizing, if only because of our need to have—and thus to create—order. Recognizing the level of order to be found in the world, and our urgent desire to raise it, makes theorizing "one of the most invincible of human impulses." As he writes, "the quest of the fewest elements of things is an ideal that some will follow, as long as there are men to think at all." He continues that classification is only a way of handling experience "for some particular purpose," and, as a result, "conceptions, 'kinds,' are teleological instruments." As tools, their function is specific, and no concept "can be a valid substitute for a concrete reality except with reference to a particular interest in the conceiver." Consequently, James believes that no thinking person is ever totally satisfied with such teleological constructs; we have devised them and we will always see through them. "Our mind is so wedded to the process of seeing an *other* beside every item of its experience," he writes, "that when the notion of an absolute datum is presented to it, it goes through its usual procedure and remains pointing at the void beyond, as if in that lay further matter for contemplation" (*WB* 62–63; cf. *EP* 56–58).[4]

Thus, for James rationality as a theoretical or logical matter incorporates two competing values: simplicity or order, and particularity or richness. What happens when two ideas or beliefs or plans seem to satisfy these criteria equally well? He emphasizes the importance of resolution to ongoing practical activity, and he rejects the possibility that long-term deadlock would be an acceptable conclusion. Moving on with his descriptive account, he suggests that in such situations individuals will consider it rational to introduce additional criteria. What other possible criteria might there be to choose between the two alternatives? He notes that "of two conceptions equally fit to satisfy the logical demand, that one which awakens the active impulses, or satisfies other aesthetic demands better than the other, will be accounted the more rational conception, and will deservedly prevail." In a recognition of the broad range of pluralism, he continues, "the supposition that an analysis of the world may yield a number of formulae, all consistent with the facts" is quite probable. Thus, two systems, evaluated as equivalently simple and particular, "equally satisfying to our purely logical needs," would face the further test of "our aesthetic and practical nature" (*WB* 66). Elsewhere and with slightly different emphases, James writes that "of two competing views of the universe which in all other respects are equal, but of which the first denies some vital human need while the second satisfies it, the second will be favored by sane men for the simple reason that it makes the world seem more rational" (*MT* 5).⁵

Considering what these aesthetic and practical criteria might be, James suggests first that an idea or belief or plan will more likely to be adopted if it helps us to project some order into future experience. Emphasizing "the relation of a thing to its future consequences," he proposes "as the first practical requisite which a philosophic conception must satisfy" the criterion that *"it must, in a general way at least, banish uncertainty from the future"* (*WB* 67). We are Darwinian creatures, and, as he notes elsewhere, "above all things common-sense craves for a stable conception of things," even if this means the continued use of demonstrably problematic notions like "substance" or "phlogiston" or "soul." Human beings want to know what we can expect will happen in the near and distant future. Once we have settled "into an attitude towards life both as to its details and as a whole," he writes, we find it undesirable when disturbances "disconcert all our judgments, and render our efforts vain." Fortunately, however, "we do live in a world from which as a rule we know what to expect" (*ECR* 304), and our traditional systems of explanation tend to hold up.

James offers as a second aesthetic and practical criterion his belief that an idea or belief or plan will be more likely to succeed if it contains a place for us and nourishes our hopes. "For a philosophy to succeed on a universal scale," he writes, "it must define the future *congruously with our spontaneous powers.*" He notes that any philosophy that contradicts "our active propensities" by giving them "no object whatever to press against" will similarly fail to achieve widespread acceptance. Here James considers Materialism in particular. He believes that it "will always fail of universal adoption, however well it may fuse things into an atomic unity, however clearly it may prophesy the future eternity," because it "denies reality to the objects of almost all the impulses which we most cherish." By rejecting "our most intimate powers," Materialism makes our desires irrelevant to the purposes of nature. "A nameless *unheimlichkeit* [feeling of being ill-at-ease] comes over us," he continues, "at the thought of there being nothing eternal in our final purposes, in the objects of those loves and aspirations which are our deepest energies" (*WB* 70–71). In contrast, he suggests, "if we survey the field of history and ask what feature all great periods of revival, of expansion of the human mind, display in common, we shall find, I think, simply this: that each and all of them have said to the human being, 'The inmost nature of the reality is congenial to *powers* which you possess.'" He interprets such prophets as John Wesley, Jean-Jacques Rousseau, and Johann Wolfgang von Goethe to be offering such a sense of revival. His interpretation of Ralph Waldo Emerson is similar: "Emerson's creed that everything that ever was or will be is here in the enveloping now; that man has but to obey himself— 'He who will rest in who he *is*, is a part of Destiny'—is in like manner nothing but an exorcism of all scepticism as to the pertinency of one's natural faculties." While James admits that "the universal essence has hardly been more defined by any of these formulas than by the agnostic *x*," he maintains that "the mere assurance that my powers, such as they are, are not irrelevant to it, but pertinent; that it speaks to them and will in some way recognize their reply ... suffices to make it rational to my feelings in the sense given above" (*WB* 73–74). Summing up these two aesthetic and practical criteria, he writes that "no philosophy will permanently be deemed rational by all men"—even if it satisfies the prior "logical demands"—if it does not also serve to "determine expectancy," and "in a still greater degree make a direct appeal to all those powers of our nature which we hold in highest esteem" (*WB* 89).

James's descriptive account of these four criteria of rationality remains very general, but it does help us to understand how differing individual personalities order experience in their own ways. Among the many philosophers whom he knew personally, we need only consider how different the interpretations of rationality were by Peirce, Josiah Royce, and George Santayana, as they sought to do justice to the importance of science, religion, and art respectively. In our broader world, we recognize that our fellow humans find order for their lives through sociology or literature or engineering, through farming or nursing or sports. "Men's active impulses are so differently mixed," James writes, "that a philosophy fit in this respect for [Otto von] Bismarck will almost certainly be unfit for a valetudinarian poet." While we can know in general that "a philosophy which utterly denies all fundamental ground for seriousness, for effort, for hope, which says the nature of things is radically alien to human nature, can never succeed," it is still impossible to predict "what particular dose of hope, or of gnosticism of the nature of things," will successfully appeal to any individual. He concludes that "personal temperament" will be the decisive factor, and that "although all men will insist on being spoken to by the universe in some way, few will insist on being spoken to in just the same way" (WB 75).[6] We will return to this theme in chapter 4 in a consideration of his account of "tender-minded" rationalistic thinkers and "tough-minded" empiricist thinkers (P 13).

James, for his part, is temperamentally drawn to Theism, and he offers in the next few pages of "The Sentiment of Rationality" the beginnings of a defense of the rationality of religious faith, and a rejection of the restrictive intellectual stance of the forces of science. Both of these grow out of his aesthetic and practical criteria. In considering whether faith is rational, he begins with the following definition: "Faith means belief in something concerning which doubt is still theoretically possible; and as the test of belief is willingness to act, one may say that faith is the readiness to act in a cause the prosperous issue of which is not certified to us in advance." This sort of faith, which he sees as a parallel to "courage in practical affairs," finds little traction among philosophers more inclined toward certainty. For the average person, however, "the power to trust, to risk a little beyond the literal evidence, is an essential function," and he believes that any philosophy that appeals to "this generous power," and makes us feel like we are "individually helping to create the actuality of the truth" that we assumed metaphysically, will gain a large following (WB 76).

When James suggests that a philosophy that makes room for faith will have a higher tendency to succeed, he means to include the philosophies of scientifically trained individuals as well. He believes that such individuals live by their own faith: a faith in the laws of nature as a determining order. In fact, he writes, "the only escape from faith is mental nullity" (*WB* 78). The problem to which he points is that their scientific faith leaves them mistakenly opposed to any other sort of faith. "The necessity of faith as an ingredient in our mental attitude is strongly insisted on by the scientific philosophers of the present day," he writes, "but by a singularly arbitrary caprice they say that it is only legitimate when used in the interests of one particular proposition—the proposition, namely, that the course of nature is uniform." In all other cases of possible truth, it seems, "an attitude of faith is not only illogical but shameful" (*WB* 76–77). He thus recognizes and accepts the fact that thinkers like Thomas Henry Huxley and William Kingdon Clifford find power in adopting certain restrictions on believing; his complaint is that they would impose the restrictions that appeal to them on others. "The rules of the scientific game," James writes, "burdens of proof, presumptions, *experimenta crucis* [decisive experiments], complete inductions, and the like, are only binding on those who enter that game." For him, however, there are other games to be played, and the only common feature of them all is that we need faith to play them. He continues that "we cannot live or think at all without some degree of faith." For him, faith is "synonymous with working hypothesis," and the only crucial difference among various hypotheses is that while some "can be refuted in five minutes, others may defy ages." In the meantime, with regard to a whole series of broadly metaphysical questions—"God, immortality, absolute morality, and free-will"—James thinks that it is possible to maintain an hypothetical stance. The "non-papal believer," as he puts it, "can always doubt his creed" (*WB* 78–79).[7]

The Dilemma of Determinism

In our examination of James's psychological consideration of the will in chapter 2, we saw that he was not so much concerned with the metaphysical question of free will as with action, especially voluntary action. It is his position that, when you ask a scientific psychologist about "free" actions, the psychologist will hear a question about voluntary movements. Humans are actional beings. We sometimes act upon ideas (motor cues), and very frequently habits do the work. The will is the power to hold an idea in place until the action occurs, to delay and deliberate when appropriate among possible goods. Some people are precipitate in their actions: they act too quickly when they should still be contemplating. Others are perverse in their actions, unable to act upon what is right or unable to resist what is wrong. In a person with a healthy will, however, there is deliberation when necessary and sufficient energy to focus attention until the action takes place. The strong-willed person can resist temptation and do what must be done.

James begins his essay "The Dilemma of Determinism" with the recognition that the issue of free will versus determinism might seem to be exhausted. "A common opinion prevails that the juice has ages ago been pressed out of the free-will controversy" (*WB* 114). He suggests, however, that, while we might be exhausted by the debate, the issue is in no way settled. In particular, he maintains that the issue of free will cannot be settled by science. With most scientific questions, an impasse like this would lead to delay and additional inquiry. The faith of a scientist is that, if we do not know how to deal with a problem, further study will eventually give us the necessary guidance. He believes that with some questions, however, this approach is inadequate. In these cases, the answer will not come soon enough, and we must adopt tentative responses in advance of definitive data. Consider, for example, the need to act in the HIV-AIDS crisis without knowing exactly what actions will be most effective. In other cases, those that James calls "metaphysical," the answer is not coming at all. These cases may be few, but they are important. The issue of whether we live our lives as if we are free would seem to be important enough to require that we go beyond any logical stalemate and come to some rationally acceptable stance.

James abandons any pretense of proving that the will is free. His intention is the far more modest one of inducing some readers "to follow my own example in assuming it true, and acting as if it were true." He sees this free choice of freedom to be fitting. As he puts it, "our first act of freedom, if we are free, ought in all inward propriety to be to affirm that we are free" (*WB* 115; cf. *ECR* 266).[8] Making use of the four criteria that we have just examined, he finds the acceptance of freedom to be rational. Here, he notes that "when we make theories about the world and discuss them with one another, we do so in order to attain a conception of things which shall give us subjective satisfaction." This conception must feel rational, in the sense we have just considered. He also assumes that "if there be two conceptions, and the one seems to us, on the whole, more rational than the other, we are entitled to suppose that the more rational one is the truer of the two."

So, for example, if some conception of our situation in nature violates our "moral demand," we are justified to doubt or abandon it "as if it disappointed my demand for uniformity of sequence," since, as he continues, the latter demand is just as "subjective and emotional" as the former. James views the postulate of causality, for example, as "an empty name covering simply a demand that the sequence of events shall some day manifest a deeper kind of belonging of one thing with another than the mere arbitrary juxtaposition which now phenomenally appears." For him, however, any such scientific or philosophical ideal is "as much an altar to an unknown god as the one that Saint Paul found in Athens" (*WB* 115–16).

All of this has been prelude to James's discussion of the issue of determinism. He recognizes that freedom, chance, and so on, are multivalent or ambiguous terms, with softer versions of determinism allowing for the use of "freedom" when one is able to do what one wants to do, even though what one wants to do may not be a matter of choice, and harder versions approximating fatalism and necessity. In an attempt to clarify the language of his position, he indicates that determinism professes "that those parts of the universe already laid down absolutely appoint and decree what the other parts shall be." This means that in a determined world "the future has no ambiguous possibilities hidden in its womb: the part we call the present is compatible with only one totality." So, in the case of a volition, he notes, "the determinists swear that nothing could possibly have occurred in its place." Indeterminists, on the contrary, believe that some other volition might have occurred; indeterminism as a view maintains "actualities seem to float in a wider sea of possibilities from out of which they are chosen" (*WB* 117–19). In general, indeterminism means the existence of loose play and real possibilities in the universe. "The quarrel which determinism has with chance," James continues, "is a quarrel altogether metaphysical." While determinism "affirms that nothing future can be ambiguous . . . indeterminate future volitions *do* mean chance" (*WB* 123). As we saw in chapter 2, the question of free will versus determinism would seem to be a simple, true-or-false question: "The truth *must* lie with one side or the other, and its lying with one side makes the other false" (*WB* 118). As we all know, however, no definitive answer seems possible, since we cannot prove that something else might have happened. While we know that what happened was possible, we cannot know that what did not happen was not.

In any case, James suggests, proof seem to have little to do with settling the issue of freedom and determinism. Here as elsewhere, he believes that "belief follows psychological and not logical laws" (*EPR* 73), and even the philosopher is "at bottom an advocate pleading to a brief handed over to his intellect by the peculiarities of his nature and the influences in his history that have moulded his imagination" (*MEN* 4). Thus, he notes that "facts practically have hardly anything to do with making us either determinists or indeterminists." Rhetorically, of course, there is much trooping of evidence—determinists asserting infallible predictions of others' conduct and indeterminists rejecting them—but he urges us to recognize "the wretched insufficiency of this so-called objective testimony on both sides" and to seek for a more adequate explanation. "What divides us into possibility men and anti-possibility men," he writes, "is different faiths or postulates—postulates of rationality." To one person the world only appears rational "with possibilities in it," whereas to another a rational world only comes "with possibilities excluded." Regardless of any evidentiary claims, James continues, "what makes us monists or pluralists, determinists or indeterminists, is at bottom always some sentiment" of this sort (*WB* 119). In other words, those who accept determinism reject a sloppy world of chance, with loose ends and ever-looming chaos. They want order to their world, regularity and law, even at the cost of freedom.[9] As he writes, "many persons talk as if the minutest dose of disconnectedness of one part with another, the smallest modicum of independence, the faintest tremor of ambiguity about the future, for example, would ruin everything, and turn this goodly universe into a sort of insane sand-heap or nulliverse, no universe at all" (*WB* 121; cf. 137–38). On the other hand, those who accept indeterminism find the idea of chance to be positive, not some force of randomness and disorder, but simply the reality of options.

Now James attempts to move toward a resolution. In "The Sentiment of Rationality," he spoke of deciding "logically" indeterminate questions in terms of aesthetic and practical criteria. Here, his attempt at a resolution of the determinism standoff through these latter criteria appears in the form of the traditional rhetorical tool of the dilemma. He suggests that, if we assume that determinism is true, and then examine the consequences of this assumption, we will find them aesthetically and practically unacceptable. As a result, we will find indeterminism to be a more adequate position. James begins with the first horn of the dilemma by noting that there is a great deal of wanton cruelty in the world, cruelty that calls for "judgments of regret" on our part. The world would have been better some other way, but, since it is by assumption determined, it had to be this way. While these cruel actions may represent "a perfect mechanical fit to the rest of the universe," they represent "a bad moral fit." The deterministic philosophy, however, must view all of this cruelty as "necessary from eternity." Moreover, "we stubbornly . . . stick to our judgment of regret": we call this cruelty bad, and maintain that the world would have been better planned without it. "Calling a thing bad means, if it means anything at all, that the thing ought not to be, that something else ought to be in its stead" (WB 124–25). It would seem sensible for us to give up our regret for these horrible actions and events since they are determined, but at the same time, we recognize that in a determined world our regret is itself determined. If we are truly determinists, judgments of regret would seem to be a kind of "blasphemy." Yet, if these judgments of regret are wrong, "other judgments, judgments of approval presumably, ought to be in their place." If the regrets are determined, however, they cannot be replaced, and "the universe is just what it was before—namely, a place in which what ought to be appears impossible." So, for example, he notes that both the existence of murder and treachery, and our regret of their existence, are "foredoomed" under these assumptions; as a result, "something must be fatally unreasonable, absurd, and wrong in the world" (WB 126–27). On this horn, we have pessimism as we confront the painful realities of existence.

On the other horn of the dilemma, we have what James calls "gnosticism," in which the events of the world are less important than their effects on our consciousness. "The world must not be regarded as a machine whose final purpose is the making real of any outward good," he writes, "but rather as a contrivance for deepening the theoretic consciousness of what goodness and evil in their intrinsic natures are." Thus, he continues, "life is one long eating of the fruit of the tree of *knowledge*." He suggests that if the determinist of this sort is to avoid pessimism, it will be necessary to "leave off looking at the goods and ills of life in a simple objective way, and regard them as materials, indifferent in themselves, for the production of consciousness, scientific and ethical, in us" (WB 128–29). James himself rejects this sort of subjectivism as being antinomian or romantic. If we reject the idea that "certain duties are good in themselves, and that we are here to do them, no matter how we feel about them," and replace it with the idea that "our performances and our violations of duty are for a common purpose, the attainment of subjective knowledge and feeling, and that the deepening of these is the chief end of our lives," he wonders when this decline is to stop on its way to "a nerveless sentimentality or a sensualism without bounds" (*WB* 132).

James thus believes that the potential determinist is forced by this dilemma to choose between the undesirable options of a pessimism of accepting preordained evil or a subjectivism in which the presumed evil is something else. Given an open but necessary choice between determinism and freedom, which one helps us to organize a future that is amenable to our powers? For him, it is not determinism, under which either the cruelty of the world is as necessary—while we want it to be otherwise, we know that it cannot be—as is our regret, or the suffering of the world serves only to advance our understanding of its sad reality, and we become more insightful chroniclers of the inner meaning of living as we contemplate it.

Either way, determinism is an unacceptable choice. This does not mean that determinism is false—we cannot know if it is—but only that believing it is very costly. For James, a far better Weltanschauung to adopt would be freedom. Freedom remains equally unproven, of course, and undermined in the minds of some by its open-endedness. He admits again that some people are unhappy with the messiness of this position. "The indeterminism I defend, the free-will theory of popular sense based on the judgment of regret, represents that world as vulnerable, and liable to be injured by certain of its parts if they act wrong," he writes. "It gives us a pluralistic, restless universe" (*WB* 136).[10] This pluralistic world, however messy, is less offensive to James than the alternative of a pessimism that would preclude morality. "I know that chance means pluralism," he continues, and the possibility "that in moral respects the future may be other and better than the past has been" (*WB* 137; cf. *TT* 111–12). The great advantage of freedom in James's mind is thus the aesthetic and practical one of offering us lives that make a difference in the struggle. We want a life rich in emotion and challenges; we want not just good, but good triumphing over evil (see *WB* 129–31, 134). This struggle is another aspect of his pluralism. "What interest, zest, or excitement can there be in achieving the right way," he asks, "unless we are enabled to feel that the wrong way is also a possible and a natural way—nay, more, a menacing and an imminent way?" (*WB* 135).[11]

The Right to Believe

"The Will to Believe" began as a lecture that James read with some success to a number of undergraduate philosophy clubs. It later provided the culmination to the series of metaphysical essays that he had written over the previous two decades, and it became the title essay of his 1897 collection. He offers the essay as "something like a sermon on justification by faith . . . I mean an essay in justification *of* faith, a defence of our right to adopt a believing attitude in religious matters, in spite of the fact that our merely logical intellect may not have been coerced." He felt that this defense was particularly important in the context of his contemporary higher education situation, because he believed that the average scientifically inclined student saw "voluntarily adopted faith" to be in conflict with "the logical spirit"—despite the fact that these same students were "personally all the time chock-full of some faith or other themselves" (*WB* 13).[12] James presents the whole volume of *The Will to Believe* as being "largely concerned with defending the legitimacy of religious faith." While he admits that humans in general lack "criticism and caution" and are "only too prone to follow faith unreasoningly," and consequently need "no preaching nor encouragement in that direction," he maintains that "academic audiences, fed already on science, have a very different need." They suffer from "paralysis of their native capacity for faith and timorous *abulia* [loss of will power] in the religious field," caused by the belief, "carefully instilled, that there is something called scientific evidence by waiting upon which they shall escape all danger of shipwreck in regard to truth." For him, on the contrary, there is "no scientific or other method by which men can steer safely between the opposite dangers of believing too little or of believing too much" (*WB* 7; cf. *C* 8:143).

James begins "The Will to Believe" with a series of definitions of the terms that he will be using. "Let us give the name of *hypothesis* to anything that may be proposed to our belief," he writes, "and just as the electricians speak of live and dead wires, let us speak of any hypothesis as either *live* or *dead*." The former type would be "one which appeals as a real possibility to him to whom it is proposed"; the latter type would not. He emphasizes that "deadness and liveness in an hypothesis are not intrinsic properties, but relations to the individual thinker. They are measured by his willingness to act." For example, he notes that the typical members of his audience would find belief in the Mahdi to be without "any credibility at all." For a Muslim, he continues, such a belief might be within "the mind's possibilities" and thus be "alive" (*WB* 14).[13] He next introduces the notion of "option," which he defines as "the decision between two hypotheses." He believes that options are of several sorts. "A living option is one in which both hypotheses are live ones." So, for example, "if I say to you: 'Be a theosophist or be a mahomedan,' it is probably a dead option.... But if I say: 'Be an agnostic or be a Christian,' it is otherwise." Second, an option is either forced or avoidable. James writes that "if I say to you: 'Choose between going out with your umbrella or without it,' I do not offer you a genuine option, for it is not forced." You could always stay home. On the other hand, "if I say, 'Either accept this truth or go without it,' I put on you a forced option, for there is no standing place outside of the alternative." Third, he continues, "if I were Dr. [Fridtjof] Nansen and proposed to you to join my North Pole expedition, your option would be momentous; for this would probably be your only similar opportunity, and your choice now would either exclude you from the North Pole sort of immortality altogether or put at least the chance of it into your hands." An option that is forced, living, and momentous he calls "a genuine option" (*WB* 14–15), and a person who finds himself or herself in the midst of a genuine option, traveling on a runaway train, for example, must decide—at great personal risk either way—whether to jump off or to ride it out.

How do we decide what to believe, or how to act, when faced with such a live option? What is the rational course to follow? As he had written earlier in "The Sentiment of Rationality," for James rationality is a sentiment or feeling that is largely negative in nature: it consists of the absence of the discomforting feeling of irrationality. As we have seen, he suggests that there is a series of four factors that contribute to our sense of rationality. The first two are logical or theoretical: the belief or explanation must bring simplicity or order to our understanding of the world without surrendering a sense of its richness or particularity. Two further criteria are aesthetic and practical in nature: they require that the belief or explanation make sense of the future and offer us a participating role within it.[14] James begins "The Will to Believe" in complete accord with this position, noting the importance that our beliefs conform to the facts. We cannot, "by just willing it, believe that Abraham Lincoln's existence is a myth." Nor can we, "by any effort of our will, or by any strength of wish that it were true, believe ourselves well and about when we are roaring with rheumatism in bed." Similarly, we cannot will to believe "that the sum of the two one-dollar bills in our pocket must be a hundred dollars" (*WB* 15).[15] We may, of course, say any of these things, but we cannot believe them. He continues that "the whole fabric of the truths that we do believe in" is constituted by such realities: "matters of fact, immediate or remote, as Hume said, and relations between ideas, which are either there or not there for us if we see them so, and which if not there cannot be put there by any action of our own" (*WB* 16).

James's assertion that we cannot believe just anything simply by will power without some kind of evidence points to what he sees as the silliness of Blaise Pascal's wager about salvation. The nature of this wager is that we have two potential paths for our lives: we can choose to live a sober and religious life, assuming that there is a God, or a riotous and profane life, assuming that there is none. While our choice of life path has no effect, of course, on the existence of God, we can still weigh the potential costs and benefits of each option. In terms of potential rewards, in fact, Pascal suggests that the former approach makes more sense, since any level of eternal pain will far outweigh all possible temporal pleasures. For James, however, believing based on such calculations would be both psychologically impossible and theologically illegitimate. Believing cannot be accomplished by pure volition, and, even if we could do it, no self-respecting God would fall for such a cynical scheme. He notes that "a faith in masses and holy water adopted willfully after such a mechanical calculation would lack the inner soul of faith's reality; and if we were ourselves in the place of the Deity, we should probably take particular pleasure in cutting off believers of this pattern from their infinite reward" (*WB* 16).

Now we can turn to what James considers to be advice from the opposite extreme. Instead of a view that advocates belief based on personal choice, he considers belief based solely upon conviction by public evidence. If we are to follow the "scientific" approach, he suggests that we need to avoid the personal. If we use the scientific method, however, how should we proceed when the evidence is not decisive? Should we believe—and do—nothing? James writes that "the magnificent edifice of the physical sciences" was created by the "patience and postponement" and the "submission to the icy laws of outer fact" of legions of disinterested scientists. In the face of such an ideal, he writes, "how besotted and contemptible seems every little sentimentalist who comes blowing his voluntary smoke-wreaths, and pretending to decide things from out of his private dream!" (WB 17). He adopts Clifford as his representative scientist, and he quotes him as follows:

> Belief is desecrated when given to unproved and unquestioned statements, for the solace and private pleasure of the believer.... Whoso would deserve well of his fellows in this matter will guard the purity of his belief with a very fanaticism of jealous care, lest at any time it should rest on an unworthy object, and catch a stain which can never be wiped away.... If [a] belief has been accepted on insufficient evidence [even though the belief be true, as Clifford on the same page explains], the pleasure is a stolen one.... It is sinful, because it is stolen in defiance of our duty to mankind. That duty is to guard ourselves from such beliefs as from a pestilence which may shortly master our own body and then spread to the rest of the town.... It is wrong always, everywhere, and for anyone, to believe anything upon insufficient evidence. (WB 17–18; cf. ECR 358–59)

Clifford, like Peirce, was a champion of the expansion of scientific method, and his larger theme was the danger of indoctrination by established religions. James's great fear was different from Clifford's (and Peirce's): the crushing of faith by scientific indoctrination.[16]

Clifford's primary focus is on the social consequences of mistaken or, more precisely, unjustified beliefs. His central example is that of a shipowner who irresponsibly assumes that his ship is safe without adequate evidence, and who is subsequently responsible for the deaths of many when it sinks. Although the owner had had some doubts whether the ship was seaworthy, Clifford notes, he overcame "these melancholy reflections" because the ship had survived multiple voyages and storms in the past. Thus, he continues, the shipowner "acquired a sincere and comfortable conviction that his vessel was thoroughly safe and seaworthy." For Clifford, of course, "the sincerity of his conviction" is irrelevant "because *he had no right to believe on such evidence as was before him.*" His belief, however compelling to him, was not the honest result of patient investigation, but rather of stifled doubts. What is more, he continues, our beliefs are not "a private matter" that concerns ourselves alone: "forasmuch as no belief held by one man, however seemingly trivial the belief, and however obscure the believer, is ever actually insignificant or without its effect on the fate of mankind, we have no choice but to extend our judgment to all cases of belief whatever." We thus have a "universal duty of questioning all that we believe." To believe "on insufficient evidence" is to "deceive ourselves by giving us a sense of power which we do not really possess," and to fail our fellow humans because our pleasure is "stolen in defiance of our duty to mankind . . . to guard ourselves from such beliefs as from a pestilence, which may shortly master our own body and then spread to the rest of the town." To summarize Clifford's view, we can repeat the passage that James had just quoted: "it is wrong always, everywhere, and for anyone, to believe anything upon insufficient evidence."[17]

To believe nothing without sufficient evidence might seem in the abstract like good advice, but James wonders if this standard is impossibly high. In response to Clifford, he notes that we do in fact believe a great deal without this sort of proof. "Here in this room," he writes, "we all of us believe in molecules and the conservation of energy, in democracy and necessary progress, in Protestant Christianity and the duty of fighting for 'the doctrine of the immortal Monroe,' all for no reasons worthy of the name." James's point here is almost purely descriptive. We are believers for whom not "insight," but rather "the *prestige* of the opinions, is what makes the spark shoot from them and light up our sleeping magazines of faith." As a result, we are quite satisfied, "in nine hundred and ninety-nine cases out of every thousand of us," if our reason can present "a few arguments that will do to recite in case our credulity is criticized by someone else." He continues that most of the time "our faith is faith in some one else's faith." As an example, he wonders about "our belief in truth itself . . . that there is a truth, and that our minds and it are made for each other—what is it but a passionate affirmation of desire, in which our social system backs us up?" For the most part, then, "our non-intellectual nature does influence our convictions" (*WB* 18–19; cf. *ERM* 106).

James maintains that even in philosophy there is a "characteristic sort of happiness" found in "the conviction felt by each successive school or system that by it bottom-certitude had been attained." Philosophers are all too often wont to assert that "'other philosophies are collections of opinions, mostly false; *my* philosophy gives standing-ground forever.'" Such is the spirit of any philosophical system that "to be a system at all, must come as a *closed* system, reversible in this or that detail, perchance, but in its essential features never!" More broadly, he continues, we are all inclined toward this rigidity when we are not careful: "Of some things we feel that we are certain: we know, and we know that we do know." He writes that metaphorically, "there is something that gives a click inside of us, a bell that strikes twelve, when the hands of our mental clock have swept the dial and meet over the meridian hour." Even those who claim to live solely by evidence are "only empiricists on reflection," but when they are "left to their instincts, they dogmatize like infallible popes" (*WB* 21). James thus rejects the notion, frequent among those whom he calls "working philosophers," that "any philosophy can be, or ever has been, constructed without the help of personal preference, belief, or divination." He maintains, on the contrary, that "every philosopher, or man of science either, whose initiative counts for anything in the evolution of thought, has taken his stand on a sort of dumb conviction that the truth must lie in one direction rather than another, and a sort of preliminary assurance that his notion can be made to work; and has borne his best fruit in trying to make it work." These diverse mental inclinations in different individuals are the results of "spontaneous variations" within the population (*WB* 77–78; cf. *VRE* 66–67).

James continues that "when the Cliffords tell us how sinful it is to be Christians on such 'insufficient evidence,' insufficiency is really the last thing they have in mind." He believes, on the contrary, that Clifford and the others find the evidence to be "absolutely sufficient"—just in favor of science. For them, "Christianity is a dead hypothesis from the start" (*WB* 21–22).[18] For him, however, such a stance is absolutistic, and the partisans of science cannot in any real sense prove their position. As he writes, "this very law which the logicians would impose upon us . . . is based on nothing but their own natural wish to exclude all elements for which they, in their professional quality of logicians, can find no use" (*WB* 19). Following their own inclinations, the scientists have sought the "ideal logical and mathematical harmonies" that "lie hidden between all the chinks and interstices of the crude natural world." Virtually all scientific laws, and even facts, are the products of individuals' efforts "often with sweat and blood, to gratify an inner need." James does not dispute the scientists' reality. His only complaint is about their blindness to the fact that "the inner need of believing that this world of nature is a sign of something more spiritual and eternal than itself is just as strong and authoritative in those who feel it, as the inner need of uniform laws of causation ever can be in a professionally scientific head" (*WB* 51; cf.

ECR 115–17). For him, both scientists and religious thinkers "live on some inclined plane of credulity" that "tips one way in one man, another way in another; and may he whose plane tips in no way be the first to cast a stone!" (*WB* 236).

James's own thesis is a defense of our "will" to believe, which he later modified to a "right" to believe[19]: "*Our passional nature not only lawfully may, but must, decide an option between propositions, whenever it is a genuine option that cannot by its nature be decided on intellectual grounds; for to say, under such circumstances, 'Do not decide, but leave the question open,' is itself a passional decision—just like deciding yes or no—and is attended with the same risk of losing the truth*" (*WB* 20).[20] To move from this descriptive account to a more prescriptive one—where "we have the right to believe at our own risk any hypothesis that is live enough to tempt our will" (*WB* 32; cf. 52)[21]—we must read James's thesis through his approach to moral philosophy, which will be considered in chapter 6. Doing so will enable us to grasp the centrality of his emphasis on individualism and noninterference with the pluralistic array of beliefs present in society. He reminds us that, among the opinions for which have been claimed "objective evidence and absolute certitude" are to be found contradictory views like the following: "The world is rational through and through—its existence is an ultimate brute fact; there is a personal God—a personal God is inconceivable." He continues that there is probably no position that "someone has not thought absolutely true, whilst his neighbor deemed it absolutely false," and none of those holding the contradictory positions seems to have realized that "the trouble may all the time be essential, and that the intellect, even with truth directly in its grasp, may have no infallible signal for knowing whether it be truth or no" (*WB* 23).

James is less concerned with the need for self-restraint on our part—the main interest of the Cliffords and other would-be "scientists"—than he is with preventing us from imposing restraints on others and with preventing them from imposing restraints on us.[22] We must, he tells us, resist our natural inclination toward absolutism. Empiricism can work only within the context of fallibilism, within which we adopt a tolerant stance toward the beliefs of others. Since whatever warrants we get come from experience, there is no justification for certainty (see *WB* 22–24). "When the true prophet arises the right will be sifted from the wrong in Clifford's doctrines, and in those of all of us," James writes. "Till then we should all be left free to mix our mental porridge as we please" (*ECR* 360).[23] In particular, in the process of living our lives, he wants us to be able to decide whether we want to be directed by Clifford's ideal of "the avoidance of error" or his own ideal of "the chase for truth" (WB 24; cf. SPP 112).²⁴ Clifford tells us, James continues, to "believe nothing . . . keep your mind in suspense forever, rather than by closing it on insufficient evidence incur the awful risk of believing lies." For James, on the contrary, "the risk of being in error is a very small matter when compared with the blessings of real knowledge," and he admits himself "ready to be duped many times" in his life "rather than postpone indefinitely the chance of guessing true." As he puts it, "worse things than being duped may happen to a man in this world" (WB 24–25; cf. ECR 293–94).²⁵

We can consider some possible applications of these theoretical positions. Sometimes, it would be quite sensible to follow Clifford and take as our maxim the avoidance of error. Most obviously, in those cases where we merely report on the events of the world—mathematical and chemical formulae, dates, account balances, court decisions, sports scores, election results, and so on—it would be a mistake to report too soon. In such cases, we might on occasion guess correctly in advance of the factual results, but most of the time we will not. It thus makes more sense to wait and "save ourselves from any chance of *believing falsehood*, by not making up our minds at all till objective evidence has come." James continues that "in our dealings with objective nature we obviously are recorders, not makers, of the truth; and decisions for the mere sake of deciding promptly and getting on to the next business would be wholly out of place" (WB 25–26; cf. SPP 112). In these sorts of recording cases, we can almost always wait for the results to come in.

There are, however, other cases—contribution cases—where we cannot wait for the results to come in, because our actions influence the results, and without our actions the outcome would be different. In effect, deciding to wait in these cases is choosing a different outcome. He writes that "there is a certain class of truths of whose reality belief is a factor as well as a confessor; and that as regards this class of truths faith is not only licit and pertinent, but essential and indispensable." In these cases, truths do not come into existence "till our faith has made them so" (WB 80; cf. EP 21). Unlike the sports reporter who is recording the results of the game, a player in the game cannot lie back until the final score is determined. Athletes, in fact, should seek to create the truth that their team is better than their opponents' team. In games, and in all sorts of similar contribution cases—Will I be able to quit drugs? Will my parents end up in the poorhouse? Will some particular institution (like a community garden) remain a viable entity?[26]—our contributions will influence the outcome. As William Ernest Hocking writes, "the surgeon, not knowing whether an operation will save a life, will never find out by 'suspending judgment': he must adopt a working hypothesis, and act on it."[27]

Some commentators have a clear recognition of the central Jamesian distinction between recording and contribution cases. Marcus Singer, for example, writes of James's "sharp distinction between two kinds of truths or facts: (a) truths or facts that are what they are independently of what we do and of what we believe; and (b) truths about those things that are dependent on our actions for their existence."[28] Other commentators fail to grasp this distinction, and write as if James saw all cases as contribution cases. Dickinson Sergeant Miller, for example, writes that James "took the worst weakness of the human mind, the bribery of the intelligence, and set it up as a kind of ideal." This destructive approach, he believes, produces both individual and social ills. "The intervention of 'our passional nature,' of which James approves, is that which chiefly interferes, in all human beings, with good and trustworthy judgment," and this interference "is the magnetism in the human mind that keeps tampering with the compass by which alone we can safely steer." Miller concludes the "'the will to believe' is the will to deceive oneself; it is the will to regard something as true which is doubtful."[29]

Perhaps the least charitable reading of James in this regard comes from G. E. Moore, who approaches James's position in the following way:

> I may have the belief that it will rain to-morrow.... And this belief may be true. It will be true, if it does rain to-morrow. But ... would anyone think of saying that, in case it is true, I had *made* it true? Would anyone say that I had had any hand *at all* in making it true? Plainly no one would. We should say that I had a hand in making it true, if and only if I had a hand in *making the rain fall.* In every case in which we believe in the existence of anything, past or future, we should say that we had helped to make the belief true, if and only if we had helped to cause the existence of the fact which, in that belief, we believed did exist or would exist.

Moore then offers a similar interpretation of whether the sun will rise to-morrow. He next allows for the distinction between recording and contribution cases—and uses it against James. "That some of our truths are man-made—indeed, a great many—I fully admit. We certainly do make some of our beliefs true," he writes. "Men certainly have the power to alter the world to a certain extent; and, so far as they do this, they certainly 'make true' any beliefs, which are beliefs in the occurrence of these alterations." Moore maintains, however, that there is "no reason for supposing that they 'make true' *nearly* all those of their beliefs which are true."[30] Why Moore believes that this is James's position is not clear. He cites as James's position Schiller's view (that James had repeated) that "to an unascertainable extent our truths are man-made products"—a claim that James characterizes as "Mr. Schiller's butt-end-foremost statement of the humanist position" (*P* 117).

James had made this distinction between recording and contribution cases previously in "The Sentiment of Rationality." In his understanding of the world, where people must live by faith because they often do not have adequate knowledge, "belief (as measured by action) not only does [but] must continually outstrip scientific evidence." We can consider here the many cases of belief to whose as-yet-indeterminate outcome we contribute. In these cases, "faith is not only licit and pertinent, but essential and indispensable," he writes. "The truths cannot become true till our faith has made them so." As an example, he asks us to consider the case of a person climbing in the Alps who, after some misjudgment, is forced to make a risky leap to escape from danger. James indicates the likely doubts in the mind of the climber, but he suggests that the climber also has the option of adopting "hope and confidence" that the leap will succeed. If, on the contrary, the climber adopts the attitude of "fear and mistrust"—if, "having just read [Clifford's] 'Ethics of Belief,'" it seems "sinful to act upon an assumption unverified by previous experience"—the climber will likely hesitate, lose all confidence, fail in the jump, and "roll into the abyss." He continues: "In this case (and it is one of an immense class) the part of wisdom clearly is to believe what one desires; for the belief is one of the indispensable preliminary conditions of the realization of its object. *There are then cases where faith creates its own verification.* Believe, and you shall be right, for you shall save yourself; doubt, and you shall again be right, for you shall perish. The only difference is that to believe is greatly to your advantage" (*WB* 80; cf. 53; *EPs* 54).[31] If we set aside his casual assurance that confidence would guarantee success, and admit only his considered view (as we shall see shortly) that confidence is more likely to contribute to success, as fear is more likely to contribute to failure, we will still recognize the side on which the advantage lies.[32]

James's point is that these contribution cases are unlike the recording cases—such as the paths of celestial bodies or the events of past history, about which we can only report—and that they are of extreme importance in human life. In fact, the really important issues in individuals' lives are almost always contribution cases. "The future movements of the stars or the facts of past history are determined now once for all, whether I like them or not. They are given irrespective of my wishes" (WB 80; cf. MT 56). With regard to these sorts of truths, he continues, "subjective preference should have no part; it can only obscure the judgment." The situation is completely different, however, in those cases when "personal contribution" plays a role, because in these cases, where "subjective energy" must be expended, "the future fact is conditioned by my present faith in it" and "the course of destiny may be altered by individuals" (WB 81–82). As a further example, he notes that individuals must decide for themselves whether living is worthwhile. If a person sees the world as a vale of wickedness and misery, and as a result commits suicide, this individual "adds to the mass M of mundane phenomena, independent of his subjectivity, the subjective complement x, which makes of the whole an utterly black picture illumined by no gleam of good." This new state, to which he has contributed, "$M + x$ expresses a state of things totally bad." Still, he continues, $M + y$ was also possible: "suppose that instead of giving way to the evil he braves it, and finds a sterner, more wonderful joy than any passive pleasure can yield in triumphing over pain and defying fear; suppose he does this successfully, and however thickly evils crowd upon him proves his dauntless subjectivity to be more than their match." This more optimistic response to the admittedly evil situations "can come about only by help of a moral energy born of the faith that in some way or other we shall succeed in getting it if we try pertinaciously enough. The world *is* good, we must say, since it is what we make it—and we shall make it good." There can be no guarantees, of course. For James, the moral universe rests "on a series of *shoulds* all the way down" (WB 83–85). As we have seen, we must commit to its morality in advance, with our "answer" likely to come only much later. In fact, he continues, any verification of a moral universe will not occur "in the life of a single philosopher." Instead, "the experience of the entire human race must make the verification," and the decision will require the contribution of the last person. In the meantime, all of our contributions matter. The facts of the situation as they stand are "inadequate to justify a conclusion either way in advance of my action." But, if we assume that the world is like a moral lock, and "if we try the moral key *and it fits*, it is a moral lock" (WB 87–88; cf. 56), and the universe a moral one.

James discusses the contribution cases, which cannot "wait for sensible proof," under three subheadings. The first group is what he calls moral cases, cases that deal not with "what sensibly exists," but with "what is good, or would be good if it did exist." Science, he writes, can help us with what does exist, but not with what should exist. "The question of having moral beliefs at all or not having them is decided by our will," he continues. "Are our moral preferences true or false, or are they only odd biological phenomena, making things good or bad for *us*, but in themselves indifferent?" (WB 27–28). Further, do we live in a world in which morality even matters? Should I allow moral considerations to influence my evaluations of possible courses of action? Is a promise made to be carried out? Should I pursue the greatest good for the greatest number?

James's second subheading of contribution cases concerns "personal relations, states of mind between one man and another." Here the answer to the question *"Do you like me or not?"* will depend "in countless instances, on whether I meet you half-way, am willing to assume that you must like me, and show you trust and expectation" (WB 28). Whether persons will be liked by others is largely dependent on what they themselves do to foster that liking;[33] whether social organizations will thrive is related to their members' actions. The results are not simple facts to be recorded, but depend on the contributions of the various participants. Thus, in many cases of personal relations—choosing spouses, careers, and political affiliations—we cannot wait for the facts, since the facts will depend on our prior actions. On the larger scale, he notes that "a social organism of any sort whatever"—and he lists as examples "a government, an army, a commercial system, a ship, a college, an athletic team"—succeeds "because each member proceeds to his own duty with a trust that the other members will simultaneously do theirs." Without this faith, however, the result will be different. He writes, for example, that "a whole train of passengers (individually brave enough) will be looted by a few highwaymen, simply because the latter can count on one another, while each passenger fears that if he makes a movement of resistance, he will be shot before anyone else backs him up." If, on the contrary, the individual passengers believed that their fellows would help them to resist the bandits, he concludes that "train-robbing would never even be attempted." For James, then, there are "cases where a fact cannot come at all unless a preliminary faith exists in its coming." In this set of cases, however limited, *"where faith in an fact can help create the fact,"* he maintains that it would be "an insane logic which should say that faith running ahead of scientific evidence is the "lowest kind of immorality" into which a thinking being can fall." Still, he continues, this logic is the one being recommended by "our scientific absolutists" (*WB* 29).[34]

The third subheading of these contribution cases, and the actual focus of James's essay, is the group of religious cases for which the discussions of morality and personal relations were functioning as analogies.[35] The predominant interpretations of religion in the West with which James was familiar—the various forms of Christianity and Judaism—suggest that religion is a recording case. The various doctrines of creation, sin, and redemption are all presented as factual claims. Our job is to recognize these facts ("revelations"), adopt the proper religious lifestyle ("conversion"), and live in conformity with the appropriate requirements ("commandments"). Atheists often see religion this way as well, though for them its claims are false—that is, based on inaccurate reports. For James, contrary to both of these views, religion is not a simple recording case. What he calls *"the religious hypothesis"* is a complex cluster that contains at least some contribution: "First, she [religion] says that the best things are the more eternal things, the overlapping things, the things in the universe that throw the last stone, so to speak, and say the final word.... The second affirmation of religion is that we are better off even now if we believe her first affirmation to be true" (*WB* 29–30). The contribution aspect, especially prominent in the second affirmation, admits that this religious hypothesis is indeterminate, but it suggests that we should act as if it were true and see if our lives turn out better after our contribution.[36]

The question of leading a religious life would seem to be, as were the other contribution cases, a potentially live option. If it has any traction in a person's life, religion is a live hypothesis; since it could lead to vital goods, it is a momentous hypothesis; and because it must be believed or not, it is a forced hypothesis. If an individual finds the message of religion to be a live option, and finds the logical criteria to be indecisive, James suggests that such an individual is justified in moving on to the aesthetic and practical criteria. If these criteria suggest value for living, then that individual is justified in accepting religion. In such a case, he writes, to follow the scientists' rule and wait would be a mistake: *"a rule of thinking which would absolutely prevent me from acknowledging certain kinds of truth if those kinds of truth were really there, would be an irrational rule"* (WB 31–32). Thus, he writes elsewhere, while "it is *usually* poor policy to believe what isn't verified ... sometimes the belief produces verification" (C 11:404). Consequently, any Clifford-like requirement that we wait, "acting of course meanwhile more or less as if religion were *not* true—till doomsday, or till such time as our intellect and senses working together may have raked in evidence enough," seems to James to be "the queerest idol ever manufactured in the philosophic cave." For him, choosing to believe or not should be our decision, since either way we are "taking our life in our hands." As a corollary, he believes that we should leave others alone. "No one of us ought to issue vetoes to the other, nor should we bandy words of abuse," he writes. "We ought, on the contrary, delicately and profoundly to respect one another's mental freedom—then only shall we bring about the intellectual republic" (WB 32–33). Once again, we see that he is less concerned with self-restraint than he is with external stifling of potential believers by the apparitors of science.[37]

James returns to the theme of faith at the end of the posthumously published volume *Some Problems of Philosophy*, when in an appendix, "Faith and the Right to Believe," he again considers the difference between recording and contribution cases. This time the discussion is in terms of the evils of "Intellectualism" that he describes as "the belief that our mind comes upon a world complete in itself, and has the duty of ascertaining its contents; but has no power of re-determining its character, for that is already given." He distinguishes between rationalizing intellectualists, like Hegel and Royce, who "lay stress on deductive and 'dialectic' arguments, making large use of abstract concepts and pure logic," and empiricist intellectualists like Clifford and Karl Pearson, who "are more 'scientific,' and think that the character of the world must be sought in our sensible experiences, and found in hypotheses based exclusively thereon" (SPP 111). Whether of the idealist or the realist stripe, however, these intellectualists all agree that the personal or idiosyncratic should be eliminated from philosophy. Only public evidence, from reason or science, should guide our thinking; personal factors, like preference and inclination and faith, have no place. For these intellectualists, James continues, believing wrongly—that is, believing without evidence or "proof," not believing the wrong answer—is worse than believing nothing.[38] He readily admits here, as he had done in "The Will to Believe," that sometimes—when the truth exists already, or when it will come without our contribution, or when there is no pressing need to decide—such restraints are valuable. At other times, however, as when "the character of the world's results may in part depend upon our acts," such restraints are disastrous. He notes that oftentimes we cannot wait: we "must act, somehow; so we act on the most *probable* hypothesis, trusting that the event may prove us wise." Further, he emphasizes that refusing "to act on one belief, is often equivalent to acting as if the opposite belief were true," and in such cases "inaction would not always be as 'passive' as the intellectualists assume" (SPP 112; cf. ECR 325–26).

Whether the intellectualists admit it or not, James continues, their stance demonstrates its own kind of faith.[39] While Intellectualism maintains that his doctrine of the will to believe is "a pure disturber of truth," he maintains that Intellectualism is an act of "arbitrary" faith that stands "in the way of a pluralistic universe's success, such success requiring the good-will and active faith, theoretical as well as practical, of all concerned, to make it 'come true.'" Thus, he notes that it is an adequate objection to Intellectualism to recognize that it would veto in advance any possible contribution on our part to "a 'pluralistically' organized, or 'co-operative' universe," to any "'melioristic' universe" that, although it might turn out to be true, was not antecedently proven. Because we need faith to live, James is much more comfortable with what he calls the "faith-ladder." This ladder is a series of steps that describe a natural progression of beliefs. "Such faith-tendencies are extremely active psychological forces, constantly outstripping evidence" (SPP 112–13), and he thinks it is possible to list the possible levels of belief, in what he conceives as their ascending order:

1. There is nothing absurd in a certain view of the world being true, nothing self-contradictory;
2. It *might* have been true under certain conditions;
3. It *may* be true, even now;
4. It is *fit* to be true;
5. It *ought* to be true;
6. it *must* be true;
7. It *shall* be true, at any rate true for *me*.[40]

For James, this descriptive account of psychological progression is not intended as any sort of logical proof: "this is no intellectual chain of inferences, like the *Sorites* of the logic-books." It is rather the account of "a slope of good-will on which in the larger questions of life men habitually live" (*SPP* 112–13; cf. *ERM* 125; *PU* 148). This process demonstrates "life exceeding logic" (*PU* 148), and it recognizes that we live our lives forward, without proof. In some matters that occur regularly, like mortality rates and frequency of house fires, it is possible to extract probabilities and to develop schemes of insurance. In such cases, Pascal's calculating approach to rationality might be appropriate. Many other questions, however, do not allow for such mathematical analyses, or what James calls "fractional solutions." For example, he wonders: "If the probability that a friend is waiting for you in Boston is 1–2, how should you act on that probability? By going as far as the bridge?" As a second example, he suggests that "if the probability is 1–2 that your partner is a villain," the worst possible response would be "treating him as a villain one day, and confiding your money and your secrets to him the next." Even though the probability in each of these cases is assumed to be 50 percent, it is not sensible to perform halfway actions, like traveling halfway from Cambridge to Boston or alternately trusting and fearing a partner. "In all such cases we must act wholly for one *or* the other horn of the dilemma," he writes. "We must go in for the more probable alternative as if the other one did not exist, and suffer the full penalty if the event belie our faith." This is especially true related to the big questions of metaphysics and religion: questions "of the *character* of the world, of life being moral in its essential meaning, of our playing a vital part therein, etc." With regard to such questions, James writes, we have to take some attitude, and "no insurance-company is there to cover us." Moreover, should we choose wrongly, "our error, even though it be not as great as the old hell-fire theology pretended, may yet be momentous" (*SPP* 114–15; cf. *ML* 416–17).

Do we live, for example, in a melioristic universe? For James, this question is not a simple and settled factual one, the answer to which we can wait to record. It is, rather, a question about a contribution case. A universe that is to grow better will require widespread contributions, and we are likely to contribute only if we have some level of faith in a positive outcome. "The melioristic universe," he writes, requires "a pluralism of independent powers," and it will succeed or fail depending on their contributions. "If none work, it will fail. If each does his best, it will not fail." Of course, this is not exactly true: we might all contribute and still fail. He continues more carefully that, "as individual members of a pluralistic universe, we must recognize that even though we do *our* best, the other factors also will have a voice in the result. If they refuse to conspire, our good-will and labor may be thrown away. No insurance-company can here cover us or save us from the risks we run in being part of such a world." Just what the "other factors" are, he does not say here, but it is clear that this is not a simple recording case, and there are no guarantees. Thus, James admits that "*if* we do *our* best, *and* the other powers do *their* best," there is still only a possibility that "the world will be perfected." The destiny of this potential melioristic universe, he maintains, "thus hangs on an *if*, or on a lot of *ifs*." Because it is not yet finished, "its total character can be expressed only by *hypothetical* and not by *categorical* propositions." Still, he maintains, the future possibility of a moral universe remains overall a contribution case: "we can *create* the conclusion.... We can and we may, as it were, jump with both feet off the ground into or towards a world of which we trust the other parts to meet our jump—and *only so* can the *making* of a perfected world of the pluralistic pattern ever take place." Again, there are no guarantees here; our efforts may not pay off: "There is no inconsistency anywhere in this, and no 'vicious circle' unless a circle of poles holding themselves upright by leaning on one another, or a circle of dancers revolving by holding each other's hands, be 'vicious.' The faith circle is so congruous with human nature that the only explanation of the veto that intellectualists pass upon it must be sought in the offensive character *to them* of the faiths of certain concrete persons" (*SPP* 115–17).[41] Elsewhere, as we shall see in chapter 7, James notes that his class—the "educated" and "scientific" and "cosmopolitan" class—has been trained to reject this option.

CHAPTER 4

Pragmatism

This chapter considers Pragmatism, a philosophy that had deep roots in American culture, and that was prominent in the thought of such figures as Benjamin Franklin and Ralph Waldo Emerson. The latter, as we saw in chapter 1, played an especially important role in James's thought. The major pragmatic influence on James was Charles Sanders Peirce. In James's central pragmatic works, "Philosophical Conceptions and Practical Results," *Pragmatism*, and *The Meaning of Truth*, he set out to modify Peirce's Pragmatism to make it more useful to his own philosophical purposes. The results of these modifications were, on the one hand, to alienate Peirce from his project but, on the other, to make Pragmatism available to a wider circle of thinkers as a tool for making our lives richer and more satisfying. After exploring James's position and examining how it was received and criticized, I attempt a tentative resolution that presents his pragmatic legacy as a means to open us up to a perspectival world through a reconsideration of the way that meaning and truth operate in our lives, and to offer us a way to move forward in our attempts to attain our goals.

Historical Background

As a philosophic approach, Pragmatism itself has had legions of defenders and critics. Among the former, we find such supporters as Henry Steele Commager, who notes:

> Practical, democratic, individualistic, opportunistic, spontaneous, hopeful, pragmatism was wonderfully adapted to the tem-

perament of the average American. It cleared away the jungle of
theology and metaphysics and deterministic science and allowed
the warm sun of common sense to quicken the American spirit
as the pioneer cleared the forests and the underbrush and allowed the sun to quicken the soil of the American West.... No
wonder that despite the broadsides of more formidable philosophers, pragmatism caught on until it came to be almost the official philosophy of America.

Commager continues that James's Pragmatism presented an understanding of "reason that was organic and evolutionary, that adjusted itself to the whole range of human experience, [and] that regarded the intellect not as a thing apart but as an agent in the creation of truth."[1]

Among the critics of Pragmatism we can count Paul Carus, who maintains in 1908 that "Pragmatism does indeed come from America; but, thank God, the movement has not yet conquered the entire land." He continues that it is "an illness that has resulted from the search to create something completely new and original." From his point of view, however, "what is true in Pragmatism is not new; and what is new, is false."[2] A few years later, Carus notes that Pragmatism "appeared cometlike on our intellectual horizon," and that the "nucleus" of this comet is the "brilliant but erratic" William James. Carus continues on that he considers Pragmatism's widespread American success to be "a symptom of the immaturity and naivete that obtains sometimes even in the professional circles of our universities. With all due respect for Professor James, for whose extraordinary and fine personality I cherish an unbounded admiration, I must confess that I would deem it a misfortune if his philosophy would ever exercise a determinating and permanent influence upon the national life of our country."[3] Another critic, Lewis Mumford, notes of James's philosophy that "one cannot doubt that it worked. What one doubts is whether the results of this work were valuable." A third critic, May Brodbeck, writes: "It is a fact of life that men tend to believe what they like to believe. Pragmatism is the only philosophy that makes a virtue of this human weakness."[4] I hope to convince readers that these critical comments are misguided.

Regardless of evaluation, however, there is no doubt that Pragmatism is the central stream of American philosophy, although not in any statistical sense is it the dominant stream.⁵ It represents the attempted integration of culture and philosophy that some philosophers reject but others require. Pragmatism in this sense contains at least four themes. The first is a recognition of our place within the larger system of nature. The second is a focus on the importance of experience as providing us criteria for belief and action. Third, Pragmatism stresses the melioristic role that openness and possibility play in human living. Finally, there is a concern with the life of the community and the role that it plays in human well-being. My intent here is to explore Pragmatism in this broad sense and to note its connections with the larger American culture. Pragmatism means a kind of intellectuality, long central to the American way of thinking, that emphasizes the importance of action, of getting the task done, of the practical rather than the ceremonial. As Benjamin Franklin wrote in 1782, Americans are more concerned with what a person can do than with that person's pedigree: in America, "People do not enquire concerning a Stranger, *What* is *he?* but *What can he* DO?"⁶ Pragmatism as a philosophy represented the introduction of this perspective on knowledge into the hallowed halls of academia.⁷

We can consider a pair of general themes, beginning with the term itself. "Pragmatism" was in the air at the turn of the twentieth century, although it conveyed no univocal meaning, then or now. As Addison Webster Moore notes in 1910, "a few years ago 'pragmatism' was a technical term known to a small circle of metaphysicians and makers of philosophical dictionaries. Now, it is a sweet morsel in the mouth of the undergraduate, a favorite theme of 'culture' clubs and 'advanced' pulpits, and a 'feature' of the Sunday paper and the popular magazine." Even within academia, Ralph Barton Perry continues in 1912, "it is characteristic of pragmatism that it does not readily lend itself to summary definition. It can neither be identified with a fixed habit of mind, as naturalism can be identified with the scientific habit of mind, nor can it be reduced to a single cardinal principle, as can idealism." He further notes, however, that at least in one regard Pragmatism can be identified. It "means, in the broadest sense, *the acceptance of the categories of life as fundamental. It is the bio-centric philosophy.*"⁸ The three Americans who were most closely connected with Pragmatism—Peirce, James, and John Dewey—continued to work out what the philosophy meant.⁹

A second theme to consider is the origin of the term "pragmatism." James tells us that it is "derived from the same Greek word πράγμα, meaning action, from which our words 'practice' and 'practical' come" (P 28). Peirce himself is more expansive:

> for one who had learned philosophy out of Kant, as the writer, along with nineteen out of every twenty experimentalists who have turned to philosophy, had done, and who still thought in Kantian terms most readily, *praktisch* and *pragmatisch* were as far apart as the two poles, the former belonging in a region of thought where no mind of the experimentalist type can ever make sure of solid ground under his feet, the latter expressing relation to some definite human purpose. Now quite the most striking feature of the new theory was its recognition of an inseparable connection between rational cognition and rational purpose; and that consideration it was which determined the preference for the name *pragmatism*.[10]

In his discussion of the roots of Pragmatism, James points to such proto-Pragmatists as Socrates, Aristotle, Locke, Berkeley, and Hume (see P 30, 268–69; SPP 65–66). Peirce, for his part, singles out Socrates, Aristotle, Spinoza, Kant, and Auguste Comte.[11] In contrast to this concern with origins, Dewey is in general more interested in Pragmatism's flowerings within American culture, regardless of its roots. "Instrumentalism," he writes, "assigns a positive function to thought, that of *reconstituting* the present stage of things instead of merely knowing it."[12]

The initial chapter of James's public connection with Pragmatism was his 1898 address at the Philosophical Union at Berkeley entitled "Philosophical Conceptions and Practical Results." While this talk is often presented as the beginning of the Pragmatic movement, the movement had gained a public place with a series of six essays by Peirce in *Popular Science Monthly* in 1877–78,[13] and in earlier essays by James himself.[14] By the turn of the twentieth century, the audience was becoming ready. After the Berkeley address, and a number of further efforts,[15] James published *Pragmatism: A New Name for Some Old Ways of Thinking* in 1907, dedicated to the memory of John Stuart Mill "from whom I first learned the pragmatic openness of mind and whom my fancy likes to picture as our leader were he alive today" (P 3). This volume was, and remains, one of the most famous—if not influential—philosophy books ever published.¹⁶ *Pragmatism* was based on a series of public lectures that he offered in Boston and then in New York City in 1906–7. James began to prepare the final manuscript in January 1907, and the finished text appeared in May of that year. The volume attained its fame in part because it was fresh and engaging, and in part because of the firestorm of criticisms that it unleashed.¹⁷

In the preface to *Pragmatism,* James writes that his intention in the volume was "to unify" the current philosophical picture "as it presents itself to my eyes, dealing in broad strokes, and avoiding minute controversy" (*P* 5).¹⁸ Attempting to clarify the many diverse themes that were present in the pragmatic movement was something that James had been thinking about doing for a number of years. Pragmatism is "not a single hypothesis or theorem," he writes, "and it dwells on no new facts." The pragmatic approach was "rather a slow shifting in the philosophic perspective, making things appear as from a new centre of interest or point of sight" (*MT* 70). Moreover, because Pragmatism was not an exclusively academic project, he saw it as a philosophy for everyman. It was not to be "a practical substitute for philosophy, good for engineers, doctors, sewage-experts, and vigorous untaught minds in general to feed upon," but rather an approach to the task of philosophizing that has proven "so over-subtle that even academic critics have failed to catch its question, to say nothing of their misunderstandings of its answer" (*MEN* 227–28; cf. C 3:344).¹⁹

The background themes in his Berkeley talk, which took place in the afterglow of the victorious Spanish-American War, deal with California, the future of the Pacific Ocean, the American relationship with the British empire, and "the English spirit in philosophy," which he writes is "intellectually, as well as practically and morally, on the saner, sounder, and truer path" than the work of Kant and his followers. James continues:

> Kant's mind is the rarest and most intricate of all possible antique bric-a-brac museums, and connoisseurs and dilettanti will always wish to visit it and see the wondrous and racy contents. The temper of the dear old man about his work is perfectly delectable. And yet he is really . . . at bottom a mere curio, a "specimen." I mean by this a perfectly definite thing: I believe that Kant bequeathes to us not one single conception which is both indispensable to philosophy and which philosophy either did

not possess before him, or was not destined inevitably to acquire after him through the growth of men's reflection upon the hypotheses by which science interprets nature.

For James as a result, the real course of "philosophic progress" was to be found "not so much *through* Kant as *round* him to the point where now we stand," by outflanking him and returning to "the older English lines" (*P* 269; cf. *EP* 138–39; *C* 9:460).[20]

James begins his lecture with the rhetorical sweetener that he is not going to bore his audience with the usual sort of academic talk. Rather than discussing "philosophy" or "words," or some other arcane material, he intends to talk about matters of practical importance to life.[21] James introduces his discussion of these matters through the ideas of the then little-known Peirce, "with whose very existence as a philosopher I dare say many of you are unacquainted." Peirce, he continues, "is one of the most original of contemporary thinkers; and the principle of practicalism—or pragmatism, as he called it, when I first heard him enunciate it at Cambridge in the early '70's—is the clue or compass by following which I find myself more and more confirmed in believing we may keep our feet upon the proper trail" (*P* 258). James's story here thus takes us back to Cambridge, Massachusetts, in the early 1870s to look at the "Metaphysical Club,"[22] an informal group of well-educated young men who were by training and career lawyers, Nicholas St. John Green and Oliver Wendell Holmes Jr.; a physician, James; a mathematician, Chauncey Wright; and a chemist, Peirce. These individuals were not ministers or classical scholars or "romantics"—like the Concord Transcendentalists and the Illinois Platonists—who were interested in exploring notions like "soul" or "nature." Nor were they educators or social leaders or judges—like the St. Louis Hegelians—who were interested in developing proposals for directly advancing community life. The members of the Cambridge Metaphysical Club came together to discuss the meaning and possibilities of science. Especially through the ideas of Peirce and James, the members had a major impact on academic philosophy in America beginning in the late 1890s.

The brightest star in this group was Peirce, whom all consider the founder of Pragmatism, and many consider the greatest American philosopher. Peirce and James lived much of their lives in close relation to each other: from their work together in the Metaphysical Club, through James's ongoing attempts to bring the ideas of Peirce into wider appreciation in the intellectual community, and finally through his economic subvention to slow the decline of the ever-spiky Peirce into penury. "Peirce's principle," James notes in the talk, was that "the soul and meaning of thought ... can never be made to direct itself towards anything but the production of belief, belief being the demicadence which closes a musical phrase in the symphony of our intellectual life." When our thinking has come to a secure belief, "then our action on the subject can firmly and safely begin. Beliefs, in short, are really rules for action; and the whole function of thinking is but one step in the production of habits of action" (P 258–59). He continues that *the true opposites of belief, psychologically considered, are doubt and inquiry, not disbelief*" (PP 2:914). As Peirce himself had written, "the action of thought is excited by the irritation of doubt, and ceases when belief is attained; so that the production of belief is the sole function of thought."[23] Peirce had not yet introduced any consideration of the quality of these beliefs, and, as we shall shortly see, addressing this question leads to important differences between him and James about the need for restraining our inclinations to believe.

What does a term or an idea mean? Writing in a Peircean spirit, James notes that "to attain perfect clearness in our thoughts of an object, then, we need only consider what effects of a conceivably practical kind the object may involve—what sensations we are to expect from it, and what reactions we must prepare" (P 259). In Baldwin's *Dictionary* shortly afterward, James continues that Pragmatism is "the doctrine that the whole 'meaning' of a conception expresses itself in practical consequences, consequences either in the shape of conduct to be recommended, or in that of experiences to be expected, if the conception be true." Should the conception be untrue, then the consequences would be different from those anticipated. In a related point, James notes that for Peirce "if a second conception should not appear to have other consequences, then it must really be only the first conception under a different name" (EP 94). Peirce suggests, for example, that a simple term like "hard" means that the object to which it is applied "will not be scratched by many other substances." For him, the "whole conception" of hard, and of such terms as "weight," "force," "path," and "reality," is to be found "in its conceived effects."[24]

James set out to adapt Peirce's Pragmatism to his own philosophical purposes. He takes this principle and modifies it—for good or ill—expanding upon, perhaps undermining, perhaps saving, Peirce.[25] The results of these modifications were, on the one hand, to divorce their two projects but, on the other, to enable a wider circle of thinkers to use Pragmatism in their attempts to make their lives more rich and satisfying.[26] The legacy of James's Pragmatism was to open us up to a perspectival world through a reconsideration of the way that meaning and truth operate in our lives, and to offer us a means to move forward in our attempts to attain our goals. Instead of using Pragmatism only to determine the meaning of concepts or ideas, James wanted to take on bigger game. He writes that the principle "should be expressed more broadly than Mr. Peirce expresses it." For James, "the effective meaning of any philosophic proposition can always be brought down to some particular consequence, in our future practical experience, whether active or passive; the point lying rather in the fact that the experience must be particular, than the fact that it must be active" (P 259). He has thus made three revisions to Peirce's pragmatic principle. First, he wants to apply it to philosophical positions and beliefs rather than just terms. Second, he wants to apply it to particular situations rather than to classes or groups of situations. As James writes, "the whole function of philosophy ought to be to find out what definite difference it will make to you and me, at definite instants of our life, if this world-formula or that world-formula be the one which is true" (P 260). Third, he shifts the emphasis of the discussion of Pragmatism from meaning to truth.[27]

So far, we have been exploring the pragmatic method as James outlined it in his Berkeley address. We now turn to his evaluation of it. He chooses as his first test of Pragmatism the case of religion, and he suggests that we consider the world from the competing perspectives of Materialism and Theism. If we are just looking retrospectively, he notes, either account would seem to be adequate. As we saw in chapter 3, his logical criteria require that our explanations cover the facts, offering generality but also particularity. Materialism is thought by many to satisfy these criteria, as is Theism; supporters of evolutionary accounts of the origin of human existence find them adequate, as do those of the various creation stories. Partisans for each side may not accept the others' position, but neutral thinkers will have to admit that either viewpoint is minimally adequate to explain whatever has already happened. There are, in other words, no counter-examples to the materialistic evolutionary perspective that would prove a theistic creation (or vice versa), and each perspective carries much secondary baggage, either because of the impossibility of replication or the reliance on an unproven deity. In each case, what we have actually experienced would be covered by Materialism or Theism. Retrospectively, therefore, the two perspectives are functionally equivalent, pragmatically the same. James then wonders about a world that is continuing on into the future. In such a world, there would seem to be a clear difference between Materialism and Theism as they are evaluated by the aesthetic and practical criteria. When considered "prospectively," he notes, Materialism and Theism point "to wholly different practical consequences, to opposite outlooks of experience" (*P* 263; cf. 53).

A second possible test for the Pragmatic approach would be to attempt to uncover the practical meaning of contemporary Idealism. James maintains that the inherited interpretation of religion—"the old monarchical notion of the Deity as a sort of Louis the Fourteenth of the Heavens"—is slipping, and that idealistic interpretations are growing in strength. But what do these idealistic interpretations mean? He suggests that, "in the philosophy of the Absolute, so called, that post-Kantian form of idealism which is carrying so many of our higher minds before it," we find the rebirth of what had been called "the pantheistic heresy—I mean the conception of God, not as the extraneous creator, but as the indwelling spirit and substance of the world" (*P* 266). He wonders, however, whether there can still be freedom for us in such a world. As a third test, James considers what difference it would make in our experience if we believe that the world is one or many. He writes that if we were to subject Monism and Pluralism to pragmatic testing, rather than approaching the topic "in an absolute and mystical way," this seemingly insoluble quarrel "might be completely smoothed out to the satisfaction of all claimants." He maintains that current forms of Monism and Pluralism are too abstract. It is a mistake, he continues, to suggest that "the world must be either pure disconnectedness, no universe at all, or absolute unity," and to insist that "there is no stopping-place half way." He rejects in particular the view that there can be any connection only "if there be still more connection, until at last we are driven to admit the absolutely total connection required" (*P* 268). For him, it was the British philosophers—Locke, Berkeley, Hume, and those who followed—who were the real "critical" philosophers because they, not Kant with his "circuitous and ponderous artificialities," demanded experiential equivalencies for all philosophical ideas. The British philosophers needed only to become more radical empiricists and "to track the practical results completely enough to see how far they extend" (*P* 269).²⁸ To have done so would have indicated to them that, among other things, relations are experienced too, as we shall see in chapter 5.

Pragmatism

James's early attempt to flesh out his approach to Pragmatism at Berkeley was followed by a greatly expanded presentation in *Pragmatism*. He begins with a discussion of what he calls "The Present Dilemma in Philosophy." By this, he is referring to the choice that was confronting the members of his audience in their philosophizing. For him, as we saw in chapter 2, the real aim of philosophy is not "professional"—not constructing concise logical formulae or elegant categorial schemes to fill learned tomes—but rather helping to make people's lives richer. In this regard, he cites a passage from Gilbert Keith Chesterton, who maintains that "'the most practical and important thing about a man is still his view of the universe.'" While a landlady is justified in her concern about a lodger's income, it remains more important for her "'to know his philosophy'" (*P* 9; cf. *PU* 14). To update this passage a bit, James's view is that philosophy helps us to recognize that what should matter in life is not looks or money or stuff, but hopes and dreams, values and culture. After a few chapters, he returns to this theme, noting that "the really vital question for us all is, What is this world going to be? What is life eventually to make of itself?" Moreover, to answer this question, he believes that "the centre of gravity of philosophy" has to shift from its concerns with "the glories of the upper ether" to a concern with "the earth of things" (*P* 62).

A second introductory theme in *Pragmatism* is the importance of the personal or temperamental in our intellectual work. James emphasizes that philosophers are normally uncomfortable admitting such inclinations, at least as regards philosophy. Even today, while we are quite willing to accept unjustified personal likings in music and poetry, or in sports and religion, we feel that philosophy should be a different matter. He writes, however, that "the history of philosophy is to a great extent that of a certain clash of human temperaments." Recognizing that this stance will strike many philosophers as "undignified," he still maintains that it explains "a good many of the divergencies of philosophers" (*P* 11). What each system presents as "a picture of the great universe of God" is in fact "the revelation of how intensely odd the personal flavor of some fellow creature is" (P 24). Even though temperament is not a "conventionally recognized reason," he continues, it—more than "any of his more strictly objective premises"—inclines the philosopher's thinking. "It loads the evidence for him one way or the other, making for a more sentimental or a more hard-hearted view of the universe, just as this fact or that principle would." Moreover, since the philosopher cannot claim any sort of authority "on the bare ground of his temperament," our philosophic discussions are all at least in part insincere because "the potentest of all our premises is never mentioned" (P 11; cf. WB 40). As we saw in chapter 1, James believes that some are inclined toward a world that is finished and settled, while others, more pluralistic like himself, can live in a world that is a bit frayed around the edges. He presents his own view: "The world we live in exists diffused and distributed, in the form of an indefinitely numerous lot of *eaches,* coherent in all sorts of ways and degrees." While individuals like him can tolerate this "insecurity," others want to reinforce this world with "'another and a better' world in which the eaches form an All and the All a One that logically presupposes, co-implicates, and secures *each* without exception" (P 126–27).

James believes that most of us are temperamentally complex and that our actions reflect this fact. Our temperaments are "a mixture of opposite ingredients, each one present very moderately." As budding philosophers, he writes, we combine aspects of Empiricism and Rationalism, "'empiricist' meaning your lover of facts in all their crude variety, 'rationalist' meaning your devotee to abstract and eternal principles." He describes those who incline toward Rationalism as "THE TENDER-MINDED": "Rationalistic (going by 'principles'), Intellectualistic, Idealistic, Optimistic, Religious, Free-willist, Monistic, Dogmatical." Those who incline toward Empiricism he calls "THE TOUGH-MINDED": "Empiricist (going by 'facts'), Sensationalistic, Materialistic, Pessimistic, Irreligious, Fatalistic, Pluralistic, Sceptical" (P 11–13).[29] The empiricists think of the rationalists as "sentimentalists and soft-heads," while the tender-minded regard the tough-minded as "unrefined, callous, or brutal" (P 14).[30] Unfortunately, however, because this difference "breeds antipathies of the most pungent character between those who lay the emphasis differently," we find it quite useful "to express a certain contrast in men's ways of taking their universe, by talking of the 'empiricist' and of the 'rationalist' temper," thus making this contrast "simple and massive" (P 12).

In our everyday lives, we want to have both: we cannot "live an hour without both facts and principles" (*P* 12). As a rule, we "have a hankering for the good things on both sides of the line," James writes. We want the facts of Empiricism and the principles of Rationalism. As an example of how Pragmatism might help, he presents the following: "The world is indubitably one if you look at it in one way," he writes, "but as indubitably is it many, if you look at it in another." Because our experience is of both the one and the many, he suggests facetiously that we might advocate "a sort of pluralistic monism." Continuing on in this light tone, he speculates that a "free-will determinism" or a pessimistic optimism would not alarm the "ordinary philosophic layman," who has "never straightening out his system" and lives "vaguely in one plausible compartment of it or another to suit the temptations of successive hours." In our lives as philosophers, however, James recognizes that we crave, instead of this casual mixture of beliefs, a higher level of intellectual order. We who aspire to philosophy, he notes, are "vexed by too much inconsistency and vacillation in our creed." To preserve "a good intellectual conscience," we cannot mix "incompatibles from opposite sides of the line," even if the result is that we find ourselves adopting either "an empirical philosophy that is not religious enough" or "a religious philosophy that is not empirical enough" (*P* 14–15; cf. 141).

In consequence, people who begin to pursue philosophy are drawn, or pushed, one way or the other by the need for consistency, intellectually or conceptually denying the fullness of their experience. As developing philosophers, they take their cues from "the experts and professionals ... already in the field" (*P* 15). Thus we find, on the one hand, the tough-minded students of Clifford and his followers, who allow themselves to be made still tougher in their pursuit of science and facts, and their refinement of the skeptical stance of no belief without proof. From James's perspective, this was the perspective that unfortunately seemed to have the upper hand in 1907. "Never were as many men of a decidedly empiricist proclivity in existence as there are at the present day," he writes. "Our children, one may say, are almost born scientific" (*P* 14).[31] On the other hand, we find the tender-minded followers of religious philosophies then being eclipsed. These religious philosophies were not philosophies of facts or particulars, but philosophies of the whole that would explain experience by something beyond. James expresses a certain admiration for religious philosophies, especially how they can refashion "the world of concrete personal experiences"—"multitudinous beyond imagination, tangled, muddy, painful and perplexed"—into something "simple, clean and noble," a "marble temple shining on a hill" (*P* 17–18). He complains, however, that this approach offers "far less an account of this actual world than a clear addition built upon it, a classic sanctuary in which the rationalist fancy may take refuge from the intolerably confused and gothic character which mere facts present." Thus, instead of presenting an "*explanation* of our concrete universe," religious philosophies give us "a substitute for it, a remedy, a way of escape" (*P* 18), "a pallid outline for the real world's richness" (*P* 40), particularly with regard to evil and suffering. James continues that one clear failing of these tender-minded philosophies is that they tend to be overly optimistic. He notes that "while Professors Royce and Bradley and a whole host of guileless thoroughfed thinkers are unveiling Reality and the Absolute and explaining away evil and pain, this is the condition of the only beings known to us anywhere in the universe with a developed consciousness of what the universe is. What these people experience *is* Reality." The idealistic philosophers, on the other hand, are "dealing in shades, while those who live and feel know truth" (*P* 21–22; cf. *EP* 140–41).

Thus, for James, the latter approach of religious philosophy offers a system that is vague on particulars; the former approach of scientific philosophy offers these specifics but no overall picture. He continues that people want a philosophy that is richer than either of these one-sided approaches; they want both facts and principles, science and human values. Instead of an Empiricism committed to "inhumanism and irreligion," or a Rationalism that "may call itself religious, but that keeps out of all definite touch with concrete facts and joys and sorrows," people want a philosophy that can combine both "the scientific loyalty to facts and willingness to take account of them, the spirit of adaptation and accommodation, in short, but also the old confidence in human values and the resultant spontaneity, whether of the religious or of the romantic type" (*P* 17).[32] Because of its emphasis on experience rather than on doctrine, and because of its focus on consequences, James believes that Pragmatism offers just this sort of philosophy.

While intellectual and social pressures in academia are pushing individuals to purer but more costly extremes, James offers Pragmatism as a bridge to connect the values on both sides. Pragmatism is "a philosophy that can satisfy both kinds of demand," he writes. "It can remain religious like the rationalisms, but at the same time, like the empiricisms, it can preserve the richest intimacy with facts" (*P* 23). He continues that Pragmatism is "a mediator and reconciler," with "no prejudices whatever, no obstructive dogmas, no rigid canons of what shall count as proof." This neutrality gives Pragmatism its great advantage over "positivistic empiricism, with its antitheological bias," and "religious rationalism, with its exclusive interest in the remote, the noble, the simple, and the abstract in the way of conception." He suggests, for example, that in our search for God, unlike Rationalism that "sticks to logic and the empyrean" and Empiricism that "sticks to the external senses," Pragmatism is more versatile and thus more likely to be successful. He writes: "Pragmatism is willing to take anything, to follow either logic or the senses, and to count the humblest and most personal experiences. She will count mystical experiences if they have practical consequences. She will take a God who lives in the very dirt of private fact—if that should seem a likely place to find him. Her only test of probable truth is what works best in the way of leading us, what fits every part of life best and combines with the collectivity of experience's demands, nothing being omitted" (*P* 43–44). James believes that Pragmatism might be successful in combining the goods from the empiricist and the rationalist sides because it forces the disputants to come back from their intellectual and conceptual battle stations to the realm of normal experience.

James begins the second chapter of *Pragmatism*, "What Pragmatism Means," in just this way, with the story of the most famous rodent in philosophy. Besides being a clever little tale, the importance of this interlude is that it enables him to remind us of the seemingly endless and futile disputes that plague philosophy and prevent competing perspectives from reconciling. A squirrel, he tells us, became the focus of "a ferocious metaphysical dispute" among his friends about the relative positions of a man and the squirrel as that squirrel is clinging to the opposite side of a tree trunk while the man is circling the tree. He writes: "The resultant metaphysical problem now is this: *Does the man go round the squirrel or not?* He goes round the tree, sure enough, and the squirrel is on the tree; but does he go round the squirrel?" James's resolution to this dispute was squarely pragmatic. It begins by asking what we mean by "going round" the squirrel. "'If you mean passing from the north of him to the east, then to the south, then to the west, and then to the north of him again, obviously the man does go round him, for he occupies these successive positions.'" If, however, we mean "'being first in front of him, then on the right of him, them behind him, then on his left, and finally in front again, it is quite as obvious that the man fails to go round him, for by the compensating movements the squirrel makes, he keeps his belly turned towards the man all the time, and his back turned away'" (P 27–28). James's pragmatic resolution to this insignificant dispute is based on the methodical use of experience.

When James continues that "the pragmatic method is primarily a method of settling metaphysical disputes that otherwise might be interminable" (P 28), he means more by the term "metaphysical" than that the disputes seem likely to go on forever, as we saw in chapter 2. In particular, he means that the disputes as formulated seem to allow for no possible resolution. "Is the world one or many?—fated or free?—material or spiritual?—here are notions either of which may or may not hold good of the world; and disputes over such notions are unending" (P 28). He believes that Pragmatism offers a way to reformulate and settle these disputes. He notes that "in every genuine metaphysical debate some practical issue, however conjectural and remote, is involved" (P 52; cf. 262), and he hopes that by using the pragmatic method in these cases, by interpreting "each notion by tracing its respective practical consequences," we can reach a resolution. If any dispute is a serious one, if any metaphysical problem is genuine, it should be possible "to show some practical difference that must follow from one side or the other's being right." But if no practical difference of any sort can be found, "then the alternatives mean practically the same thing, and all dispute is idle" (P 28; cf. WB 99). James believes that many philosophical disputes, like the dispute about the squirrel, "collapse into insignificance the moment you subject them to this simple test of tracing a concrete consequence." He thus rejects the possibility that there could be a "difference in abstract truth that doesn't express itself in a difference in concrete fact and in conduct consequent upon the fact, imposed on somebody, somehow, somewhere, and somewhen," and he suggests that "the whole function of philosophy ought to be to find out what definite difference it will make to you and me, at definite instants of our life, if this world-formula or that world-formula be the true one" (P 30; cf. 260).[33]

At this point, James reintroduces Peirce, although he has drifted a good bit from the latter's position. He notes that Peirce maintained that "our beliefs are really rules for action," and that to uncover the meaning of a thought, "we need only determine what conduct it is fitted to produce: that conduct is for us its sole significance." James continues that for Peirce: "To attain perfect clearness in our thoughts of an object, then, we need only consider what conceivable effects of a practical kind the object may involve—what sensations we are to expect from it, and what reactions we must prepare. Our conception of these effects, whether immediate or remote, is then for us the whole of our conception of the object, so far as that conception has positive significance at all" (P 28–29; cf. 259; VRE 351).³⁴ In the previous section, we considered how James modified Peirce's position by shifting the emphasis from terms to philosophical positions, by abandoning the long-term test for a test within the compass of a single person's experience, and by concerning himself with truth more than meaning. Peirce, for his part, rejected these intended improvements and renamed his view "Pragmaticism."³⁵

James emphasizes that Pragmatism is a way of doing philosophy more than a philosophy itself. It is a method without any preferred outcome. Pragmatism "does not stand for any special results. It is a method only." He continues that it "has no dogmas, and no doctrines save its method." Drawing upon the suggestion of a young Italian colleague, Giovanni Papini, James notes that Pragmatism "lies in the midst of our theories, like a corridor in a hotel" (P 31–32). Pragmatism, he continues elsewhere, is fundamentally pluralistic: "It is like a corridor in a hotel, from which a hundred doors open into a hundred chambers. In one you may see a man on his knees praying to regain his faith; in another a desk at which sits some one eager to destroy all metaphysics; in a third a laboratory with an investigator looking for new footholds by which to advance upon the future. But the corridor belongs to all, and all must pass there. Pragmatism, in short, is a great *corridor-theory*" (EP 146).³⁶

The key to using this pluralistic corridor-like method is to carry on philosophical discussions not in individual rooms each dedicated to cultivating private beliefs, but in the public corridor at the level of shared experience. We need to return from the theoretical level to explain what practical differences might result from each and every intellectual distinction. James sees this pragmatic approach as grounded in the empirical tradition of British philosophy—without, as we shall see in chapter 5, the fragmentariness that plagues much of that tradition's unradical empiricism. He notes that "it is the English-speaking philosophers who first introduced the custom of interpreting the meaning of conceptions by asking what difference they make for life." Their approach to finding the meaning of a conception "is to ask yourself right off, 'What is it *known as*? In what facts does it result? What is its *cash-value*, in terms of particular experience? and what special difference would come into the world according as it were true or false?'" Following in this tradition, he notes that Peirce "has only expressed in the form of an explicit maxim what their sense of reality led them all instinctively to do" (P 268; cf. VRE 350).³⁷ The pragmatic attitude thus rejects "resolutely and once for all ... a lot of inveterate habits dear to professional philosophers." James consequently advocates turning "away from abstraction and insufficiency, from verbal solutions, from bad *a priori* reasons, from fixed principles, closed systems, and pretended absolutes and origins," and turning instead "towards concreteness and adequacy, towards facts, towards action and towards power." This empiricist, antirationalist stance demonstrates, he continues, "the open air and possibilities of nature, as against dogma, artificiality, and the pretence of finality in truth" (P 31).

James realizes the power within Rationalism of verbal solutions. The universe, he writes, "has always appeared to the natural mind as a kind of enigma, of which the key must be sought in the shape of some illuminating or power-bringing word or name." When we have that name, we have "the universe's *principle* ... the universe itself." Although he admits that there has never been any general agreement about what that word is—he notes that some suggestions have been "'God,' 'Matter,' 'Reason,' 'the Absolute,' and 'Energy'"—he recognizes the power attributed to the many "solving names." When the metaphysician has found the proper one, the "metaphysical quest" is over. For James, on the contrary, "if you follow the pragmatic method, you cannot look on any such word as closing your quest." Rather, it is necessary to find the "practical cash-value" of each word and "set it at work within the stream of your experience." It thus appears "less as a solution ... than as a program for more work, and more particularly as an indication of the ways in which existing realities may be *changed*" (P 31–32; cf. SPP 37–38). The pragmatic method thus brings along an attitude: "*The attitude of looking away from first things, principles, 'categories,' supposed necessities; and of looking towards last things, fruits, consequences, facts*" (P 32).³⁸ As a result, he continues, Pragmatism "unstiffens all our theories, limbers them up and sets each one at work." For James, theories are tools. "*Theories thus become instruments, not answers to enigmas, in which we can rest*," he writes. "We don't lie back upon them, we move forward, and, on occasion, make nature over again by their aid" (P 32; cf. 94).

In chapters 3 and 4 of *Pragmatism*, James considers a series of five metaphysical problems by means of the pragmatic method to see if they are genuine. His aim here is, in part, to show us how to use the method, but it is also by using it to show us how these problems are insoluble if formulated independently of experiential consequences. The first of these problems—and to James's mind the "driest"—is that of substance. Using the familiar distinction between a substance and its attributes, he distinguishes between a piece of chalk and its "whiteness, friability, cylindrical shape, insolubility in water, etc., etc." He further distinguishes between wood and a desk, wool and a coat, and even chalk, wood and wool and the "still more primal substance, *matter.*" The problem with this way of thinking, he continues, is that we know only the properties, the attributes, but never the substance. "A group of attributes is what each substance here is known-as, they form its sole cash-value for our actual experience," he writes. "The substance is in every case revealed through *them*" (*P* 45–46; cf. *SPP* 38). If this is true, however, what function does substance serve? Realists tell us that we need it to make sense of the world; nominalists tell us that we do not. Pragmatically, James urges us to consider whether there are any actual experiential differences between a realistic position on substance and a nominalistic one.[39]

The second metaphysical dispute that James considers is whether, as the materialists say, we can explain all "higher phenomena by lower ones," or, as the theists maintain, higher phenomena require something more. According to the former position, "the laws of physical nature are what run things," and all of the intellectual achievements of humanity "might be ciphered by one who had complete acquaintance with the facts." The latter position—Theism or Spiritualism—tells us "that mind not only witnesses and records things, but also runs and operates them: the world being thus guided, not by its lower, but by its higher element" (*P* 49). James begins by interjecting an almost Emersonian passage aimed at undermining any antimaterialistic residuum: "To anyone who has ever looked on the face of a dead child or parent the mere fact that matter *could* have taken for a time that precious form, ought to make matter sacred after all." He then returns to his prior point that, while materialistic or theistic analyses of the past might be equally adequate, when we turn to consider the future, the meaning of each is very different. He writes:

> It makes not a single jot of difference so far as the *past* of the world goes, whether we deem it to have been the work of mat-

ter or whether we think a divine spirit was its author. Imagine, in fact, the entire contents of the world to be once for all irrevocably given. Imagine it to end this very moment, and to have no future; and then let a theist and a materialist apply their rival explanations to its history. The theist shows how a God made it; the materialist shows, and we will suppose with equal success, how it resulted from blind physical forces. (P 50)

If we place ourselves in a world with a future, however, in a world that is "uncompleted whilst we speak," he believes that we will quickly recognize that in this "unfinished world" the choice between Materialism and Theism becomes an "intensely practical" question (P 52).

James grants that a materialistic universe, ruled by "the theory of mechanical evolution," would still contain all the past goods that it does, but it would be directed by laws that are "fatally certain to undo their work again, and to redissolve everything that they have once evolved." A theistic universe, on the contrary, "however inferior it may be in clearness to those mathematical notions so current in the mechanical philosophy, has at least this practical superiority over them, that it guarantees an ideal order that shall be permanently preserved." Even if the world were to "burn up or freeze," the theistic universe would still have a God "mindful of the old ideals and sure to bring them elsewhere to fruition; so that, where he is, tragedy is only provisional and partial, and shipwreck and dissolution not the absolutely final things." For James, this need for "an eternal moral order"—"not in hair-splitting abstractions about matter's inner essence, or about the metaphysical attributes of God"—remains one of the fundamental requirements of human fulfillment. As he continues, Theism "means the affirmation of an eternal moral order and the letting loose of hope," Materialism means "simply the denial that the moral order is eternal, and the cutting off of ultimate hopes" (P 53–55; cf. 263–64).[40] Thus, the dispute between Materialism and Theism makes a great deal of difference as we contemplate the meaning of the future experience.[41]

James's third metaphysical problem is that of design. "It is strange," he notes, "considering how unanimously our ancestors felt the force of this argument, to see how little it counts for since the triumph of the darwinian theory." He believes that we have learned from Darwin to see "the power of chance-happenings to bring forth 'fit' results if only they have time to add themselves together," and "the enormous waste of nature in producing results that get destroyed because of their unfitness." We have learned, in other words, that design is unnecessary and that there need not have been a prior plan to arrive where we are. He further points to the number of adaptations that, if actually designed, would indicate an evil rather than a good designer. For example, "to the grub under the bark the exquisite fitness of the woodpecker's organism to extract him would certainly argue a diabolical designer." Viewed from the evolutionary perspective, the design argument will explain whatever our current situation happens to be as the result of design; or, as he puts it, "the abstract word 'design' is a blank cartridge" (P 57–58; cf. 39). Pragmatically, the notion of design gets us little, he maintains, unless we combine it with Theism:

> "Design," worthless tho it be as a mere rationalistic principle set above or behind things for our admiration, becomes, if our faith concretes it into something theistic, a term of *promise*. Returning with it into experience, we gain a more confident outlook on the future. If not a blind force but a seeing force runs things, we may reasonably expect better issues. This vague confidence in the future is the sole pragmatic meaning at present discernible in the terms design and designer. But if cosmic confidence is right not wrong, better not worse, that is a most important meaning. That much at last of possible "truth" the terms will then have in them. (P 59)

The question of design is thus a serious metaphysical question because, at least in its theistic version, it offers us the possibility of hope.

In introducing his next topic, the free-will problem, aspects of which we have already considered in chapters 2 and 3, James notes that "most persons who believe in what is called their free-will do so after the rationalistic fashion," by which he means that free will "is a principle, a positive faculty or virtue added to man, by which his dignity is enigmatically augmented." Determinists thus "diminish man" in their eyes by saying that "individual men originate nothing, but merely transmit to the future the whole push of the past cosmos of which they are so small an expression." He believes that the majority of his audience has an "instinctive belief in free-will, and the admiration of it as a principle of dignity has much to do with your fidelity" (P 59). He suggests, further, that the discussion of free will usually gets sidetracked by considerations of blame and accountability: if we are totally free, there is no responsibility but rather chaos; if, on the other hand, we are completely determined, there is no responsibility but rather fatalism. Pragmatically considered, however, the issue of free will really means the existence of *"novelties in the world,* the right to expect that in its deepest elements as well as in its surface phenomena, the future may not identically repeat and imitate the past." James grants, of course, that there is imitation, and a high level of uniformity in nature, and "persons in whom knowledge of the world's past has bred pessimism (or doubts as to the world's good character, which become certainties if that character be supposed eternally fixed) may naturally welcome free-will as a *melioristic* doctrine." Still, he believes that because free will leaves room for improvements, while determinism "assures us that our whole notion of possibility is born of human ignorance, and that necessity and impossibility between them rule the destinies of the world" (P 60–61), our choice on this metaphysical topic—"What is this world going to be? What is life eventually to make of itself?" (P 62)— will have serious experiential consequences.

James's final metaphysical problem—the one that he takes to be the most important—is the ancient philosophical puzzle of Monism and Pluralism. It is, he writes, "the most central of all philosophic problems, central because so pregnant." He continues that knowing "whether a man is a decided monist or a decided pluralist" will tell us more about the remainder of his beliefs "than if you give him any other name ending in *ist*" (P 64; cf. 141; SPP 61–62). Using the pragmatic method, and focusing on experience, he notes that we all find some sort of unity to the world, but what sort of unity is it? Do we mean by unity that we can recognize continuities and causality, or that we can recognize uniform purposes and perhaps a unified Knower (see P 66–72). For him, there are "many systems, kinds, purposes, and dramas" that bring unity to the world. He is even willing to entertain the hypothesis that there may be "one sovereign purpose, system, kind, and story" as long as this does not also mean that there has to be *"one Knower"* behind it all. Rationalism believes in a "focus of information ... from which the entire content of the universe is visible at once." In contrast, Empiricism is "satisfied with that type of noetic unity that is humanly familiar." By this, James means that, while in a pluralistic account, "everything gets known by *some* knower ... the knowers may in the end be irreducibly many, and the greatest knower of them all may yet not know the whole of everything, or even know what he does know at one single stroke:—he may be liable to forget." Either way, there would still be a noetic universe, either "absolutely unified" or, in his favored understanding, "strung along and overlapped" (P 71–72), and our choice between Monism and Pluralism makes a difference.

Although his inclinations are fairly apparent, James has made no claims thus far about answering any of these metaphysical questions. He has simply been trying to clarify, by means of the pragmatic method, what the different possible answers would mean in terms of experience, thus showing that they are genuine metaphysical problems. As we saw in chapter 3, "sometimes alternative theoretic formulas are equally compatible with all the truths we know, and then we choose between them for subjective reasons." In such cases, decisions are not matters of pure logic; aesthetic and practical reasons play a role. We find ourselves supporting a theory that satisfies one inclination, whether for "'elegance' or 'economy,'" more than another. Moreover, "consistency both with previous truth and with novel fact is always the most imperious claimant" (P 104).[42]

In the fifth chapter, "Pragmatism and Common Sense," James lays out his account of the developing stages of consciousness. He writes that there are multiple levels of thinking, prominent among which are common sense, critical science, and critical philosophy. He also discusses a prior level that was present at the childhood of the race, before the development of common sense. In this primary phase of thinking—the level that we still find at work in young children—there are neither things, nor laws of nature, nor fixed systems of time or space. Instead, there is a realm that comfortably incorporates magic and superstition, witchcraft and dreams. As he writes, animals and young children "know no more of time or space as world-receptacles, or of permanent subjects and changing predicates, or of causes, or kinds, or thoughts, or things, than our common people know of continental cyclones." So, for example, when a rattle is dropped, "the baby looks not for it," he writes. "It has 'gone out' for him, as a candle-flame goes out; and it comes back, when you replace it in his hand, as the flame comes back when relit." At this pre–common sense level of thinking, the enduring presence of an object remains an undeveloped notion. Any idea of the objective being of an enduring thing, with a "permanent existence . . . between its successive apparitions," has not yet occurred to the developing mind. Operating at this level of thinking, he continues, people living "in primitive times . . . mixed their dreams with their realities inextricably." Even the process of recognizing thoughts and things as distinct is a process that he believes "originated historically and only gradually spread." Such notions as "one Time" and "one Space" that give each event and thing a single location are abstractions of great value to us at present, but they do not function in "the loose unordered time-and-space experiences of natural men!" For such individuals, "cosmic space and cosmic time, so far from being the intuitions that Kant said they were, are constructions as patently artificial as any that science can show." James continues that, even in his day, "the great majority of the human race never use these notions, but live in plural times and spaces, interpenetrant and *durcheinander* [all mixed up]." When we think of permanent things, and kinds of things, of causality and possibility, we are making use of human achievements. Moreover, he reminds us that "everything that happens to us brings its own duration and extension, and both are vaguely surrounded by a marginal 'more' that runs into the duration and extension of the next thing that comes" (*P* 85–87).

For James, the shadowy and mysterious world of early humans contained little that could be considered philosophy. He notes, for example, that "in the earliest stages of human intelligence . . . thought proper must have had an exclusively practical use" (*SPP* 38), and residents of this world were too close to the harsh realities of nature for much intellectualizing about "reality." "The thought of very primitive men has hardly any tincture of philosophy," he writes. "Nature can have little unity for savages" (*PU* 15).[43] Nature as experienced was "a walpurgis-nacht procession, a checkered play of light and shadow, a medley of impish and elfish friendly and inimical powers. 'Close to nature' tho they live, they are anything but wordsworthians." The mysteries of natural existence, and the meager human powers of response, may have given rise to some curiosity, and certainly to fear, but seldom to anything we would call philosophical. "Tempests and conflagrations, pestilences and earthquakes," he writes, "reveal supramundane power, and instigate religious terror rather than philosophy" (*PU* 15). Eventually, however, the mind emerged, and brought with it common sense, science, and philosophy.

If we leave aside this prior stage of remembrance and fantasy, we can focus on James's "three well-characterized levels, stages or types of thought" about our place in the world. We thus come to realize that "the notions of one stage have one kind of merit, those of another stage another kind."

These stages of common sense, critical science, and critical philosophy offer us different answers to the fundamental questions of living, and he maintains that it is impossible "to say that any stage as yet in sight is absolutely more *true* than any other." He begins with common sense, which is "the more *consolidated* stage, because it got its innings first, and made all language into its ally." In spite of its head start, however, common sense cannot be seen as the final answer: "If common sense were true, why should science have had to brand the secondary qualities, to which our world owes all its living interest, as false, and to invent an invisible world of points and curves, and mathematical equations instead?" (P 92; cf. 94).

The great advantage of common sense is its vast improvement on the prior childlike perspective. It "satisfies in an extraordinarily successful way the purposes for which we think." For the most part, it keeps us alive. "'Things' do exist, even when we do not see them. Their 'kinds' also exist. Their 'qualities' are what they act by, and are what we act on; and these also exist." Common sense took the initial confusion of pure experience and ordered it in ways that the prior perspective could not, and, because it was a very useful tool, it caught on. The individuals who were inclined to think this way survived and reproduced, and at this commonsense level, "all non-European men without exception have remained" (P 89).[44] Our experiences are not initially "ticketed and labelled"; we must take the encountered appearances and perceptions and create some sort of unity "by our wits." Our usual process is "to frame some system of concepts mentally classified, serialized, or connected in some intellectual way." James has in mind here such concepts as "'Thing; The same or different; Kinds; Minds; Bodies; One Time; One Space; Subjects and attributes; Causal influences; The fancied; The real." We use this system "as a tally by which we 'keep tab' on the impressions that present themselves." Each aspect of experience is thus given its place in the organizational system and is "thereby 'understood'" (P 84–85).

Further, James notes, these "very ancient modes of thought" that constitute common sense have managed to survive more or less intact in human thought. Comparing our socially inherited ways of understanding to various inherited body parts—"our five fingers, our ear-bones, our rudimentary caudal appendage, or our other 'vestigial' peculiarities"—he suggests that both groups "may remain as indelible tokens of events in our race-history." Those who have gone before us came upon certain useful ways of thinking that they might not have come upon, but "once they did so, and after the fact, the inheritance continues." Thus, many of our fundamental interpretations of experience are *"discoveries of exceedingly remote ancestors, which have been able to preserve themselves throughout the experience of all subsequent time,"* he writes. "They form one great stage of equilibrium in the human mind's development, the stage of *common sense*" (P 83; cf. 89).

Over time, we—or at least some of us—have come to recognize the limitations of common sense, and we have begun to think in more critical ways that we now call philosophical and scientific. While for "utilitarian practical purposes" commonsense notions "amply suffice," for other purposes they do not. For example, "we assume for certain purposes one 'objective' Time that *aequabiliter fluit* [flows evenly], but we don't livingly believe in or realize any such equally-flowing time." Also, how does common sense differentiate things? "Is a constellation properly a thing? or an army? or is an *ens rationis* [mental entity] such as space or justice a thing? Is a knife whose handle and blade are changed the 'same'? Is the 'changeling,' whom Locke so seriously discusses, of the human 'kind'? Is 'telepathy' a 'fancy' or a 'fact'?" James maintains that as soon as we move beyond "the practical use" of common sense categories to a "curious or speculative way of thinking," we are unable to apply these categories as usefully (P 89–90).[45]

James points to various individuals who have abandoned this common sense approach for what he calls "the 'critical' level of thought." He notes, in fact, that only "highly sophisticated" thinkers "have ever even suspected common sense of not being absolutely true." Among their number he includes both those of a philosophical bent—"your Humes and Berkeleys and Hegels"—and also the more scientifically inclined "practical observers of facts"—"your Galileos, [John] Daltons, [and Michael] Faradays"—none of whom were able "to treat the *naïfs* sense-termini of common sense as ultimately real" (P 89–90). Science and philosophy are thus able to "burst the bounds of common sense." With the former "'secondary' qualities become unreal; primary ones alone remain," while with the latter "havoc is made of everything." Naive realism and its commonsense approach to thinking are no longer seen as representing "anything in the way of *being.*" They represent, rather, the "sublime tricks of human thought, our ways of escaping bewilderment in the midst of sensation's irremediable flow." Science as a method gives us great power, greatly exceeding "the scope of the old control grounded on common sense." At the same time, however, James admits that on occasion the power of science to remake the world may exceed our wisdom, and we may drown "like a child in a bath-tub, who has turned on the water and who cannot turn it off." Moreover, the novelties that this critical science creates, for example "the corpuscular and etheric world," while "definitely conceived, should not be held for literally real." While it may seem that they exist, "in reality they are like co-ordinates or logarithms, only artificial short-cuts for taking us from one part to another of experience's flux." For its part, critical philosophy may offer us intellectual satisfaction, but it can give us "no new range of practical power" (*P* 91–92; cf. *MT* 74/*ERE* 101). Overall, as we deal with the various problems that we encounter in living, we operate at different levels using the tools that we find more adequate.

The practical impact of this discussion is that, if James's position has general value, we need to reconsider how we look at the term "truth" itself. It arose within the level of common sense, and has been carried over—not without serious problems—to the other levels. He notes that, when comparing these different types of thinking, there is no way to determine which is "the more absolutely true." The tool that we should choose depends on the particular problem that we are facing: "Common sense is *better* for one sphere of life, science for another, philosophic criticism for a third; but whether either be *truer* absolutely, Heaven only knows." James urges us to consider the concept of "truth" itself. He writes: "The whole notion of truth, which naturally and without reflexion we assume to mean the simple duplication by the mind of a ready-made and given reality, proves hard to understand clearly. There is no simple test available for adjudicating offhand between the divers types of thought that claim to possess it. Common sense, common science or corpuscular philosophy, ultra-critical science, or energetics, and critical or idealistic philosophy, all seem insufficiently true in some regard and leave some dissatisfaction." The result of "the conflict of these so widely differing systems" indicates to James the need "to overhaul the very idea of truth"—a process that he is about to undertake—because "at present we have no definite notion of what the word may mean" (*P* 93–94). As we move from one perspective to another, however, the issue of truth becomes problematic because our traditional understanding of truth is itself embedded in the common sense perspective.

Until the middle of the nineteenth century, James writes, the general belief was that the sciences "expressed truths that were exact copies of a definite code of non-human realities." Since that time, however, "the enormously rapid multiplication of theories . . . has well-nigh upset the notion of any one of them being a more literally objective kind of thing than another." His world contained multiple geometries and logics, conflicting hypotheses and classifications, each of which was "good for so much and yet not good for everything." As a result, he suggests that perhaps "even the truest formula" is in fact "a human device and not a literal transcript." It is in this sense, he continues, that scientific laws are "now treated as so much 'conceptual shorthand,' true so far as they are useful but no farther." The mind has come to accept "symbol instead of reproduction . . . approximation instead of exactness . . . plasticity instead of rigor" (*MT* 40).[46] In such a world, James believed, people were ready for a new understanding of "truth."

James's Emphases within "Truth"

As we have seen, Peirce was mainly interested in meaning and did not have a great deal to say about truth. Moreover, when the issue came up, he was more interested in improving the general methods of inquiring than in solving specific problems. Truth as he saw it is related to eventual agreement among careful researchers. "The opinion which is fated to be ultimately agreed to by all who investigate," he writes, "is what we mean by the truth." As a correlate, he further notes that "the method of science . . . must be such that the ultimate conclusion of every man shall be the same."[47] Thus, an important Peircean issue might be attempting to answer questions like these as they arise within the HIV-AIDS epidemic: What is the origin of the virus? How is it so successful in overcoming our immune system? By what measures can its spread be controlled and new cases ultimately prevented? As a result of Peirce's focus, the issue of answering the particular questions that interested James—like the prognosis of any particular patient—remained a side issue.

James begins chapter 6, "Pragmatism's Conception of Truth," with a light introduction that discusses the career of an idea. He writes that he fully expects to see the pragmatic theory of truth advance through what he calls "the classic stages of a theory's career." After a new theory is initially condemned as "absurd," and later reevaluated as "true, but obvious and insignificant," the final stage that he expects for Pragmatism is that its contemporary opponents will "claim that they themselves discovered it" (*P* 95). James, as the pragmatist who most strongly emphasizes the topic of truth, draws the strongest criticisms regarding it. While discussing the shift in the focus of the discussion from meaning to truth, he indicates—in the passive voice—that "the word pragmatism has come to be used in a still wider sense, as meaning also a certain *theory of truth*" (P 32–33). Elsewhere, he writes that "the pivotal part of my book named *Pragmatism* is its account of the relation called 'truth' which may obtain between an idea (opinion, belief, statement, or what not) and its object" (*MT* 3; cf. *P* 96; *MEN* 227).[48]

In his discussion of truth, as in many other places, James lights on one theme after another, without emphasizing any particular sequence. His lack of systematic presentation has cost him dearly here, because critics have often hooked onto one isolated point or another without attempting to grasp his overall position. For that matter, they have also neglected the connections between his Pragmatism and the rest of his thought, like his prior distinction between recording and contribution cases that we saw in chapter 3, and his frequent shifts between description and prescription. When considering his complex position on truth, we can approach it in terms of five separable themes, none of which is independent of the others, but each of which will benefit from temporary isolation. In no particular order, these themes are truth as agreement with reality, absolute truth, truth and learning, dynamic truth, and truth as a good thing. There is something important in each of his interrelated emphases—we might even say in a Jamesian fashion that there is "some truth" in each—although the novelty of his approach and the phrasing of his formulations have proven problematic.[49]

We can begin with a consideration of the relationship between "truth" and "reality." "Truth, as any dictionary will tell you, is a property of certain of our ideas," James writes. "It means their 'agreement,' as falsity means their disagreement, with 'reality.'" He continues that both pragmatists and their opponents accept this definition, quarreling "only after the question is raised as to what may precisely be meant by the term 'agreement,' and what by the term 'reality,' when reality is taken as something for our ideas to agree with" (P 96; cf. 117; MT 59–60). When considering what we mean by these terms, he suggests that there are three distinguishable aspects of reality to consider. He begins with simple cases of matters of fact like the address of a friend's house or the access code to a bank account: if we have the correct information, then we arrive at the party or can withdraw our money. These are examples of recording cases, and in such cases, agreement simply means an accurate one-for-one copying of the world by our idea. James then presents the more demanding example of a mechanical clock. After noting that "a true idea must copy its reality," he suggests that with regard to even a minimally complex machine like a clock we may not need to copy it in great detail. While amateurs may conjure up "a true picture or copy of its dial" (P 96), only a clock-maker needs to have any adequate idea of the clock's gears and other parts. Given such cases of indefinite copying, his emphasis is not that we know so little, but that "agreement" is a complex notion, and that our interest is more with the functioning of the clock than with its structure. "Verif*iability* of wheels and weights and pendulum" is, for most of us, enough. James also allows for generalized agreement, such that "when we have once directly verified our ideas about one specimen of a kind, we consider ourselves free to apply them to other specimens without verification" (P 99–100).

James then turns to the second area of agreement: the relations of ideas. "*Relations among purely mental ideas* form another sphere where true and false beliefs obtain," he writes, "and here the beliefs are absolute, or unconditional." By this he means that "it is either a principle or a definition that 1 and 1 make 2, that 2 and 1 make 3, and so on; that white differs less from gray than it does from black; that when the cause begins to act the effect also commences. Such propositions hold of all possible 'ones,' of all conceivable 'whites and 'grays' and 'causes.'" Unlike matters of fact, "the objects here are mental objects" and thus "no sense-verification is necessary." Further, in these cases, "once true, always true, of those same mental objects. Truth here has an 'eternal' character." We can manipulate these mental relations, integrating "one abstract idea with another, framing in the end great systems of logical and mathematical truth," systems that sometimes "hold good of realities also." Moreover, he continues, if we have done our calculations properly, our conclusions will be "already true in advance of special verification" (P 100–101).[50] James writes: "We can no more play fast and lose with these abstract relations than we can do so with our sense-experiences. They coerce us; we must treat them consistently, whether or not we like the results. The rules of addition apply to our debts as rigorously as to our assets. The hundredth decimal of π, the ratio of the circumference to its diameter, is predetermined ideally now, tho no one may have computed it" (P 101; cf. MT 108–12).[51] These cases of relations of ideas are, like the prior cases of matters of fact, recording cases. "Between the coercions of the sensible order and those of the ideal order," he writes, "our mind is thus wedged tightly." The aim of our ideas is to agree with these realities, "be such realities concrete or abstract, be they facts or be they principles, under penalty of endless inconsistency and frustration" (*P* 101; cf. 117–18).

James's third area of agreement is that our new ideas must also agree with our prior set of working hypotheses and beliefs. In addition to the "concrete facts" and "abstract kinds of things and relations perceived intuitively between them," he writes that our new ideas must take account of "the whole body of other truths already in our possession" (*P* 102; cf. 118). Here he is not pointing to a different kind of truth beyond matters of fact and relations of ideas; he is only indicating that in habitual creatures like us there is discomfort with the novel. Most of the time, loyalty to "the older truths"—whether matters of fact or relations of ideas—remains our "first principle." New opinions will thus be accepted as true just to the extent that they satisfy "the individual's desire to assimilate the novel in his experience to his beliefs in stock" (*P* 35–36). Similarly, when we introduce a new theory into our web of "funded truths" (*P* 111), it "must mediate between all previous truths and certain new experiences. It must derange common sense and previous belief as little as possible, and it must lead to some sensible terminus or other that can be verified exactly. To 'work' means both these things; and the squeeze is so tight that there is little loose play for any hypothesis. Our theories are wedged and controlled as nothing else is" (*P* 104). Within this large system of agreement, James suggests, for example, that "the truth of 'God' has to run the gauntlet of all our other truths. It is on trial by them and they on trial by it." As a result, our final position on the God question cannot be determined until "all the truths have straightened themselves out together" (*P* 56; cf. 43).

A second emphasis in James's discussion of truth is his assurance that we do not live in a fantasy world: there is some sort of real world of objective truth to which we must conform.[52] "To admit," he writes, "as we pragmatists do, that we are liable to correction (even tho we may not expect it) *involves* the use on our part of an ideal standard" (*MT* 142; cf. 117; *WB* 146). Elsewhere he warns: "Woe to him whose beliefs play fast and loose with the order which realities follow in his experience: they will lead him nowhere or else make false connexions" (*P* 99). In a poetic vein, James renders his appreciation of the interconnectedness of this pervasive reality as follows: "Can we realize for an instant what a cross-section of all existence at a definite point of time would be? While I talk and the flies buzz, a sea-gull catches a fish at the mouth of the Amazon, a tree falls in the Adirondack wilderness, a man sneezes in Germany, a horse dies in Tartary, and twins are born in France." James rejects the notion that there is "a rational bond" among these many events, while insisting that "such a collateral contemporaneity, and nothing else, is a real order of the world" (WB 95–96). His account of objective truth is thus compatible with Peirce's call for a commitment from inquirers to explore as long as is necessary to find answers, a commitment on Peirce's part that moves easily from "sufficient inquiry" to "fifty generations of arduous experimentation" to "endless investigation." Peirce can follow this continuum because he believes that there are answers to be found. Facts are, for him, "hard things which do not consist in my thinking so and so, but stand unmoved by whatever you or I or any man or generations of men may opine about them."[53] Combining this realistic account of the independence of facts with limitless inquiry leads Peirce to believe that, with proper method, there will be continued growth of agreement among all inquirers.

James continues in this vein that "the 'absolutely' true, meaning what no farther experience will ever alter, is that ideal vanishing-point towards which we imagine that all our temporary truths will some day converge" (P 106–7).[54] In daily living, however, he emphasizes that "we have to live to-day by what truth we can get to-day, and be ready to-morrow to call it falsehood" (P 107). Peirce offers similar comments about what he calls "matters of real practical concern,"[55] suggesting that he and James differ less over the nature of truth than over which truths are more important. For Peirce, these are the generic truths, the laws of various sorts and the unchanging. For James, the focus remains instead on individuals living their lives, searching for particular meaning or value. From this perspective, individuals do not lead lives of indefinite inquiry: we choose spouses and careers, we accept or reject religious doctrines, and we buy and sell houses. With his shift in emphasis from "absolute" truths to finite and grounded human living, he calls for a shift to a sense of success rooted within the range of the present experience of particular individuals who are attempting to settle, perhaps only tentatively and hypothetically, some piece of the objective world with which they are deeply involved. In such a particular moment, "the immediate experience in its passing is always 'truth,' practical truth, *something to act on*, at its own movement" (ERE 13).[56]

A third emphasis in James's consideration of truth is that in the course of living we learn or discover truths. He believes that the general process by which individuals settle into new opinions is "always the same" (P 34).[57] The individual, who has "a stock of old opinions," encounters a novel experience that challenges this current stock. For example, someone contradicts one or more of these beliefs, "or in a reflective moment he discovers that they contradict each other; or he hears of facts with which they are incompatible; or desires arise in him which they cease to satisfy." As a consequence of this novel experience, the individual winds up in "an inward trouble to which his mind till then had been a stranger, and from which he seeks to escape by modifying his previous mass of opinions." Because with regard to beliefs we tend to be very conservative, however, we will attempt to retain as much of our old belief systems as possible. The idea that will now be adopted as true, he continues in a descriptive vein, will be the one that "preserves the older stock of truths with a minimum of modification, stretching them just enough to make them admit the novelty, but conceiving that in ways as familiar as the case leaves possible." Our habitual natures tend to reject explanations that violate too many of our preconceptions. "We should scratch round industriously till we found something less excentric," he continues, and even "the most violent revolutions in an individual's beliefs leave most of his old order standing." For example, James reminds us how the discovery of radium "seemed for a moment to contradict our ideas of the whole order of nature," because it challenged the inherited understanding of the conservation of energy. As he puts it, "the mere sight of radium paying heat away indefinitely out of its own pocket seemed to violate that conservation." The eventual solution to this problem was far less radical, and required only a recognition of the "unsuspected 'potential' energy, pre-existent inside of the atoms" (*P* 34–36; cf. *MT* 54; *TT* 96).

"A new opinion counts as 'true' just in proportion as it gratifies the individual's desire to assimilate the novel in his experience to his beliefs in stock," James continues in a descriptive fashion. "It must both lean on old truth and grasp new fact; and its success . . . in doing this, is a matter for the individual's appreciation" (*P* 36). Our beliefs are largely a matter of habit, and we incorporate new beliefs only with some reluctance. He notes that "our knowledge grows *in spots*. The spots may be large or small, but the knowledge never grows all over: some old knowledge always remains what it was. . . . Our minds thus grow in spots; and like grease-spots, the spots spread. But we let them spread as little as possible: we keep unaltered as much of our old knowledge, as many of our old prejudices and beliefs, as we can. We patch and tinker more than we renew. The novelty soaks in; it stains the ancient mass; but it is also tinged by what absorbs it." It seldom happens, he continues, "that the new fact is added *raw*." Rather, the more common occurrence is that our beliefs are thus "resultants of new experiences and of old truths combined and mutually modifying one another" (*P* 82–83).⁵⁸

A fourth emphasis in James's pragmatic approach is that any understanding of truth must recognize the dynamic aspects of living. He writes that "the fundamental fact about our experience is that it is a process of change" (*MT* 54), and contrary to the standard account that emphasizes recording prior truths, he emphasizes the role of humans in recognizing and creating new truths. There can be no static encyclopedia of facts or finished catalogue of truths because our world is neither static nor finished. "The essential contrast is that *for rationalism reality is ready-made and complete from all eternity, while for pragmatism it is still in the making, and awaits part of its complexion from the future*," James writes. "On the one side the universe is absolutely secure, on the other it is still pursuing its adventures" (*P* 123). Elsewhere, he continues that in *Pragmatism* he was "primarily concerned . . . with contrasting the belief that the world is still in process of making with the belief that there is an 'eternal' edition of it ready-made and complete" (*MT* 123).⁵⁹ We can consider here his paraphrasing of the position of the rationalist. "'Truth is not made,'" the rationalist will say:

> "it absolutely obtains, being a unique relation that does not wait upon any process, but shoots straight over the head of experience, and hits its reality every time. Our belief that yon thing on the wall is a clock is true already, altho no one in the whole history of the world should verify it. The bare quality of standing in that transcendental relation is what makes any thought true that possesses it. . . . The quality itself is timeless, like all essences and natures. Thoughts partake of it directly, as they partake of falsity or of irrelevancy." (*P* 105; cf. *ERE* 130–31)

James continues that, whereas Rationalism will allow that our experience and our understanding of truths are in process, it will never allow that "either reality itself or truth itself is mutable." On the contrary, he continues, for the rationalist, "Reality stands complete and ready-made from all eternity," and as a result "truth has nothing to do with our experiences" (*P* 108).⁶⁰

In James's pluralistic view, however, "the truth of an idea is not a stagnant property inherent in it." On the contrary, he writes that "truth *happens* to an idea. It *becomes* true, is *made* true by events" (*P* 97/*MT* 3; cf. *ERE* 29). While this is especially clear in contribution cases—as when a person marries or completes a poem—it is also apparent in recording cases—as when a volcano explodes or a hawk strikes, each independently of human action. While James suggests that "with 'truth' most people go over the border entirely, and treat the rationalistic account as self-evident" (*P* 106), he does not go over the other border and maintain that all truths are in process. He acknowledges, as we have repeatedly seen, that many of our encounters with the world represent recording cases. As he writes, "an enormous quantity of truth must be written down as having pre-existed to its perception by us humans. In countless instances we find it most satisfactory to believe that, tho we were always ignorant of the fact, it always *was* a fact that S was SP" (*ERE* 130). Still, he asserts, it is necessary to separate these cases from cases in which our contributions matter.

James's central point is the importance of these contribution cases, of human creativity, in understanding our place in the world.[61] "Reality," he writes of the standard view, "stands ready-made and complete, and our intellects supervene with the one simple duty of describing it as it is already." For him, on the contrary, "we *add*, both to the subject and to the predicate part of reality." The world is not finished; it "stands really malleable, waiting to receive its final touches at our hands." By our various actions, for example, we make the world a better or worse home for humanity. We create at least some of the facts of our environment. What the world is depends in part on what we do. "Man *engenders* truths upon it" (*P* 123; cf. *MEN* 228–29). Given the sharp distinction between the rationalists and the pragmatists on the role of human contribution, James admits that "it is impossible not to see a temperamental difference at work in the choice of sides." For the rationalists who are temperamentally "of a doctrinaire and authoritative complexion," he writes, "the phrase '*must be*'" is ever present. "The belly-band of its universe must be tight." The pragmatist, on the contrary, is temperamentally "a happy-go-lucky anarchistic sort of creature." James also realizes that rationalists will find the pragmatists' reality "a tramp and vagrant world, adrift in space, with neither elephant nor tortoise to plant the sole of its foot upon." Outside of philosophy, however, people have become used to "living in a state of relative insecurity." In the political and religious realms, we have learned to accept this openness. Still, such liberality has not yet reached our "philosophic class-rooms," where talk of human contributions and created truths smacks of opportunism and disorder. "Such a world would not be *respectable* philosophically," he notes. "It is a trunk without a tag, a dog without a collar, in the eyes of most professors of philosophy" (P 124–25).

Instead of Idealism's buttoned-up package of reality—"the block-universe eternal and without a history" (PU 140; cf. 147–48)—James emphasizes the open-ended, creative aspects of human living. Our world is plastic, with human contribution throughout: "The trail of the human serpent is thus over everything." While he admits that created truths are encountered in the context of "truth independent; truth that we *find* merely; truth no longer malleable to human need; truth incorrigible," and even that these static truths—the focus of "rationalistically minded thinkers"—represent the vast majority of truths, his point is that such truths represent "only the dead heart of the living tree" (P 37). As we live our lives we contribute throughout reality. We determine, at least in part, what exists. We grow gardens and design sailboats, all with the cooperation of nature. In this regard, James even wonders again what an object, or a unit, or a thing is. The answer, he suggests, is "quite arbitrary, for we carve out everything, just as we carve out constellations, to suit our human purposes." He then turns to his auditors in the lecture hall:

> For me, this whole "audience" is one thing, which grows now restless, now attentive. I have no use at present for its individual units, so I don't consider them.... But in your own eyes, ladies and gentlemen, to call you "audience" is an accidental way of taking you. The permanently real things for you are your individual persons. To an anatomist, again, those persons are but organisms, and the real things are the organs. Not the organs, so much as their constituent cells, say the histologists; not the cells, but their molecules, say in turn the chemists.

We develop units where we find them useful for our various purposes. Thus, we cannot "weed out the human contribution," either in our practice or our philosophy. "The great question is: does it, with our additions, *rise or fall in value*? Are the additions *worthy* or *unworthy*?" (P 122–23; cf. MT 56). We humans live in a world that has room for human creativity; it will demonstrate that creativity, however, only if our thinking and practice recognize its possibility.

Again, James is especially interested in exploring the contribution cases that living presents: advancing relationships and building careers, developing medicines and creating works of art, mastering dance routines and repairing decayed teeth. For writers, these contribution cases largely involve editing and rewriting to make the eventual product more closely approximate—be "truer" to—what they had intended to say, or even in some cases to help them refine that intention. Truth is in large part individually and socially created. For him, "the knower is not simply a mirror floating with no foot-hold anywhere, and passively reflecting an order that he comes upon and finds simply existing." On the contrary, "the knower is an actor, and co-efficient of the truth on one side, whilst on the other he registers the truth which he helps to create." As a result, "mental interests, hypotheses, postulates" function as "bases for human action—action which to a great extent transforms the world" and thus "help to *make* the truth which they declare." James stresses that "there belongs to mind, from its birth upward, a spontaneity, a vote." In his dynamic understanding of truth, the active person is "in the game, and not a mere looker-on" (*EP* 21).

Fifth, James emphasizes that having true beliefs is a good thing. Such beliefs enable us to solve our problems and to live happier, more fulfilling lives. As he writes, "the possession of true thoughts means everywhere the possession of invaluable instruments of action" (*P* 97). Through discoveries of previously unknown facts about the workings of our natural situation we develop more effective surgeries, erect safer buildings, and achieve better harvests. "We live in a world of realities that can be infinitely useful or infinitely harmful," he continues. "Ideas that tell us which of them to expect count as true ideas in all this primary sphere of verification, and the pursuit of such ideas is a primary human duty." Truths are useful for dealing with reality because they take us out of problems and toward favorable results. For example, he writes of a starving traveler lost in the woods who comes upon and follows a cow path in the hope that it will bring him to a dwelling. If this belief turns out to be true, it "is useful here because the house which is its object is useful." Thus, for James, Pragmatism's "general notion of truth" is "something essentially bound up with the way in which one moment in our experience may lead us towards other moments which it will be worth while to have been lead to," or to put it another way, "the truth of a state of mind means this function of *a leading that is worth while*" (*P* 98).⁶² Ideas that help us to deal with our problems, that help us to avoid frustration and adapt "our life to the reality's whole setting" (*P* 102), will give us better lives. For the pragmatist, then, truth becomes broadly "a class-name of all sorts of definite working-values in experience" (*P* 38). James continues that agreement is thus:

> essentially an affair of leading—leading that is useful because it is into quarters that contain objects that are important. True ideas lead us into useful verbal and conceptual quarters as well as directly up to useful sensible termini. They lead to consistency, stability and flowing human intercourse. They lead away from excentricity and isolation, from foiled and barren thinking... in the end and eventually, all true processes must lead to the face of directly verifying sensible experiences *somewhere*, which somebody's ideas have copied. (*P* 103)

Switching to a slightly different metaphor, he continues that "any idea upon which we can ride ... any idea that will carry us prosperously from any one part of our experience to any other part, linking things satisfactorily, working securely, simplifying, saving labor; is true for just so much, true in so far forth, true *instrumentally*" (*P* 34; cf. 36; *MT* 5; *C* 12:18). We recognize how useful these truths are, and we stockpile them for use in future problems. As James writes, "since almost any object may some day become temporarily important, the advantage of having a general stock of *extra* truths, of ideas that shall be true of merely possible situations, is obvious" (*P* 98).⁶³

In the context of his emphasis on the usefulness of truths, James rejects the criticism that pragmatists believe that "by saying whatever you find it pleasant to say and calling it truth you fulfill every pragmatistic requirement" (*P* 111).⁶⁴ There are clearly conditions imposed on the notion of "working" by all the pragmatists. As James writes, for example, "the true is what works well, even though the qualification 'on the whole' may always have to be added.... What immediately feels most 'good' is not always most 'true,' when measured by the verdict of the rest of experience" (*VRE* 361, 22).⁶⁵ Thus, when he speaks of working or useful or expedient, he means "in the long run and on the whole" because what meets the requirements of present experience "won't necessarily meet all farther experiences equally satisfactorily. Experience, as we know, has ways of *boiling over*, and making us correct our present formulas" (*P* 106; cf. 42).[66]

Some Criticisms and a Tentative Resolution

Given these five separable emphases in James's understanding of truth, it was perhaps to be expected that critics would fail to deal with them as an interrelated set. Further, given the novelty of some of his formulations, it was also to be expected that critics would bristle. In this regard, Martin Gardner writes that "James never seemed to comprehend that the storm aroused by his 1907 book was the result of using 'truth' in a way that violated ordinary language." He continues that James believed that "if the meaning of truth could be put more in harmony with scientific method—instead of saying a hypothesis works because it is true in some absolute sense, we turn the words around and say it is probably true because it works—this new way of talking about truth would inject enormous clarity into philosophical speculation and eliminate all sorts of metaphysical muddles."[67] James was admittedly attempting to reconstruct our understanding of "truth," and, if we start from this recognition, some initially problematic aspects of James's position seem to dissolve. For example, as we have seen, he frequently talks about "truths" rather than "ideas" or "beliefs" that were, or were thought to be, true. His position would allow us to maintain, for example, that Ptolemy's astronomy was true—or at least a "truth"—in his day, even though we no longer recognize it to be so.[68] Based on our familiarity with James's use of both descriptive and prescriptive accounts, we can maintain a clearer distinction between what we may believe to be true and what is true.[69] Although we can easily understand what James means when he says informally that "new truths thus are resultants of new experiences and of old truths combined and mutually modifying one another" (*P* 83), we realize that what he refers to as "old truths"—or, for that matter, even "new truths"—are not necessarily true. In another formulation, he notes that "ptolemaic astronomy, euclidean space, aristotelian logic, scholastic metaphysics, were expedient for centuries," and thus were accepted as true. Recent advances in thinking, however, have caused us to consider them "only relatively true, or true within those borders of experience. 'Absolutely,' they are false." That is, within these conceptual systems certain beliefs functioned quite well, but now that we have abandoned these systems, we have abandoned these beliefs as well. At the same time, he notes that "when new experiences lead to retrospective judgments, using the past tense, what these judgments utter *was* true, even tho no past thinker had been led there" (*P* 107).⁷⁰

James also maintains that, although there is a reality that is largely beyond our experience, the facts of this reality when part of our experience should not be called true. "The 'facts' themselves ... are not *true*. They simply *are*." For James, "truth is the function of the beliefs that start and terminate among them" (*P* 108; cf. *MT* 76/*ERE* 103). In the course of living, for example, each day brings new weather, new births and new deaths, but these new facts are not true. "The new contents themselves are not true, they simply *come* and *are*. Truth is *what we say about* them, and when we say that they have come, truth is satisfied by the plain additive formula" (*P* 36). This means that "realities are not *true*, they *are*; and beliefs are true *of* them" (*MT* 106). Moreover, if these realities never enter consciousness as beliefs, they cannot be called "true." There are thus facts, and beliefs about these facts. Some of the beliefs are true, others false. James does not want to complicate the discussion with talk of propositions. In particular, propositions that critics like Bertrand Russell and G. E. Moore "make the exclusive vehicles of truth are mongrel curs that have no real place between realities on the one hand and beliefs on the other" (*C* 11:526).⁷¹

A third issue with James's unfamiliar position on truth is his use of comparative and superlative versions of "true."⁷² While the sequence of good–better–best works quite well in English, for the most part the sequence of true–truer–truest does not. (Nor does right–righter–rightest.) The problem is not that we cannot understand in general what he means when he uses such terms as "more true" (*P* 121; cf. 92) or "less true" (*MT* 88), or when he discusses a "truer idea" (*MT* 89) or a "truer belief" (*MT* 105), or when he suggests that an idea can be "truest" (*P* 36).⁷³ The problem is rather that, as a common sense notion, "true" is already a sort of absolute, and the comparative "truer" and the superlative "truest" are either unnecessary or nonsensical. In some related uses of "true," as with bicycles, we are able to make a wheel "truer" by making it more closely approximate a circle, but the mechanical process of "truing" a wheel cannot produce an absolutely "true" wheel that would rival the perfection of a geometric circle. Our inherited sense of the truth of a belief, however, contains this strain of perfection. Related to this problem of the uses of comparative and superlative levels of "true" is the equally novel idea of perspectival truth as in *"true in so far forth"* (*P* 41), "my truth, as I now see it" (*EPR* 371), or "true for *me*" (*SPP* 113).[74] We can understand his perspectival account of reality as "'*whatever excites and stimulates our interest.*'" He continues that when something "so appeals to us that we turn to it, accept it, fill our mind with it, or practically take account of it, so far it is real for us, and we believe it." At the same time, when something does not appeal to us, "we ignore it, fail to consider it or act upon it, despise it, reject it, forget it, so far it is unreal for us and disbelieved." Our sense of reality is thus subjective. To the extent that we are unemotional logical thinkers, "we give reality to whatever objects we think of, for they are really phenomena, or objects of our passing thought, if nothing more." When we are emotionally engaged, however, "*we give what seems to us a still higher degree of reality to whatever things we select and emphasize and turn to* WITH A WILL. These are our *living* realities." Given our subjective presence, we feel "our own present reality with absolutely coercive force," and we "ascribe an all but equal degree of reality, first to whatever things we lay hold on with a sense of personal need, and second, to whatever farther things continuously belong to these" (*PP* 2:924–26; cf. 936–37). This subjective sense of reality yields a perspectival sense of truth.

A more serious pair of problems with James's understanding of truth—problems that point to fundamental difficulties in his position—begins with his discussion of the relation between the "true" and the "useful." Developing his earlier emphasis that truth is a human value, he maintains that the two terms mean the same thing: truth means usefulness. He writes, for example, that when an introduced belief functions successfully, we can say "either that 'it is useful because it is true' or that 'it is true because it is useful.' Both these phrases mean exactly the same thing, namely that here is an idea that gets fulfilled and can be verified" (*P* 98).[75] While it seems quite sensible to say, as James does, that "true ideas would never have been singled out as such, would never have acquired a class-name, least of all a name suggesting value, unless they had been useful from the outset in this way" (*P* 98), this does not mean that we should treat the two terms as meaning the same thing. Even in contribution cases when we are acting to bring about a good, the truth of a belief remains distinguishable from its usefulness.[76]

Using a more traditional understanding of the terms in question, we can consider the following set of possibilities. There are, first of all, beliefs that are both true and useful. Examples of such working beliefs would be: correct social security numbers, telephone numbers, lock combinations, airport gate numbers, and so on. These bits of true information enable us to do what we want to do, whereas false ones would not. Second, there are beliefs that are true but for the most part useless because under normal circumstances they can do no work. Here we might consider beliefs about James's favorite barber, whiskey, composer, and so on. Such beliefs, if true, might have some use in a trivia contest, but seldom in any other context.[77] Third, there are false beliefs that are useless, and often harmful. Beliefs that I need not pay my taxes, or am impervious to bullets or immune to HIV-AIDS, can lead to great personal suffering. Finally, and of great importance to the lives of individuals and their societies, are the false beliefs that are useful. What I have in mind here are, for example, various approximations and generalizations that, although ultimately not true, work well enough under most circumstances.[78] Also in this class, however, are the sinister examples of undying prejudices of all sorts, from the most pedestrian to the most horrible, that function quite powerfully despite being false.[79] Considering these cases makes it clear that there is still value in distinguishing between truth and usefulness.

In a somewhat humorous vein, Josiah Royce wonders whether a pragmatist who was testifying in court might be allowed to replace the familiar oath with what he sees as its pragmatic equivalent: "'I promise to tell whatever is expedient and nothing but what is expedient, so help me future experience.'" For Royce, the answer is negative, rejecting the notion that "this witness has expressed, with adequacy, that view of the nature of truth that you really wish a witness to have in mind." While he grants that "a typical pragmatist ... would indeed be delighted to hear his testimony on the witness-stand or anywhere else,"[80] he believes that no one else would. Bertrand Russell also has a great deal of fun with what he takes to be James's position. We can consider a number of instances. "With James's definition, it might happen that 'A exists' is true although in fact A does not exist," Russell writes. "I have always found that the hypothesis of Santa Claus 'works satisfactorily in the widest sense of the word': therefore 'Santa Claus exists' is true, although Santa Claus does not exist." This sort of analysis of James's position—if it is even accurate to call it that—simply ignores James's emphasis upon logical as well as aesthetic and practical criteria, and his distinction between contribution and recording cases. The basis of Russell's criticism of James's work seems to be its presumed democratic spirit that contrasts "with the usual dictatorial tone of philosophic writings." In James's "humanized" approach, truth functions "like the police force in a democracy, the servant of the people," rather than as Russell believes it should function: as "their master." For Russell, "there is a non-human truth, which one man may know, while another does not," and, as a result, there is also "a standard outside the disputants, to which ... the dispute ought to be submitted." This neutrality means that "a pacific and judicial settlement of disputes is at least theoretically possible." In his reading of James, however, Russell maintains that "there is no longer any principle except force by which the issue can be decided."[81]

Russell is attempting to impose his prescriptive frame on James's largely descriptive account. If we contrast these logical and psychological approaches, and if we note that Russell's James "was primarily a psychologist," we can get a clearer sense of his criticism of James. Russell allows that the pragmatists believe that "their theory alone is based upon a true psychological account of how belief arises," but he rejects the relevance of this descriptive account to what he takes to be the more important logical question: "What is meant by 'truth' and 'falsehood'?" As an example of this assumed primacy, Russell considers "the belief that other people exist." The pragmatists tell us, he continues, that "to say 'it is true that other people exist' *means* 'it is useful to believe that other people exist.'" If this is so, he continues, "then these two phrases are merely different words for the same proposition; therefore when I believe the one I believe the other." Whether this is so, and why the logical should trump the psychological, Russell does not consider. For him it is enough to note that, from his logical perspective, "the word 'true' represents for us a different idea from that represented by the phrase 'useful to believe,'" and that as a consequence "the pragmatic definition of truth ignores, without destroying, the meaning commonly given to the word "true," which meaning, in my opinion, is of fundamental importance."[82]

James himself responds to the first of Russell's points by asserting that the claim that something exists may be true, even when it does not exist, is "the usual slander, repeated to satiety by our critics" (*MT* 147) that overlooks all that he says about the criteria of belief that we saw in chapter 3.[83] In response to Russell's second point about the primacy of logic over psychology, James writes: "The social proposition 'other men exist' and the pragmatist proposition 'it is expedient to believe that other men exist' come from different universes of discourse." As such, each can be believed independently of the other. "The first expresses the object of a belief," he writes, "the second tells of one condition of the belief's power to maintain itself," but it is a mistake "to treat them as mutually substitutable" (*MT* 150).[84] James continues, stating that Russell is distinguishing between a "more abstract" account as found in logic and a "more concrete account" as found in psychology, and then accusing "those who favor the latter of 'confounding psychology with logic.'" For Russell, James notes, when pragmatists are asked "what truth *means*," they respond to this logical question psychologically "by telling only how it is *arrived-at*." Further, "since a meaning is a logical relation, static, independent of time, how can it possibly be identified, they say, with any concrete man's experience, perishing as this does at the instant of its production?" In response, James opposes the attempt to abstract logic from psychology. He writes: "I defy anyone to show any difference between logic and psychology here. The logical relation stands to the psychological relation between idea and object only as saltatory abstractness stands to ambulatory concreteness. Both relations need a psychological vehicle; and the 'logical' one is simply the 'psychological' one disemboweled of its fulness, and reduced to a bare abstractional scheme" (*MT* 85–86).[85]

A second serious problem with James's position on truth is his presentation of the role of verification. Developing upon his earlier emphases that truth is dynamic and related to learning, he maintains that the "verity" of an idea "*is* in fact an event, a process: the process namely of its verifying itself, its veri-*fication*. Its validity is the process of its valid-*ation*" (*P* 97/*MT* 4). Continuing on in this processive vein, he continues, "truth for us is simply a collective name for verification-processes, just as health, wealth, strength, etc., are names for other processes connected with life, and also pursued because it pays to pursue them." In our world, truth "is *made*, just as health, wealth and strength are made, in the course of experience" (*P* 104). The difficulty with these unqualified formulations is a lack of sensitivity to the fact, to which he repeatedly pointed elsewhere, that some of these truths were made long ago and may have since been recorded, whereas others are still in the making and still require our contributions. An example of the former can be found in simple recording cases like the unknown number of coins in a jar. While the answer may not yet be known by anyone, that answer was determined once and for all by the filling of the jar. This is clearly a case where the eventual counting of the items is just the process of verification. The answer remains true but unknown until verification; it is not made true by the verification. The jar case differs from the related contribution case of a lottery in which the process of selecting the winning numbers both determines and reveals the winner. James fails to distinguish these two types of cases here, and H. S. Thayer writes that he "confuses *truth* and *verification*." Emphasizing recording cases, Thayer notes that "the verification of some Belief-assertion, or corroborating our belief in it, is distinct from the truth of that Belief-assertion . . . the truth value is logically prior to and distinct from the verification."[86] Some unverified beliefs are true, others false; at least with regard to recording cases, the eventual process of testing them cannot change their status.

We often find accounts of truth that separate it from the learning process, sometimes even from knowing itself. It is possible, for example, to focus on cases like the number of corn stalks in Nebraska at any given moment or the number of dead in Tiananmen Square in 1989. These cases are examples of facts ("truths") that exist antecedently although they are unknown and unknowable, except perhaps to an omniscient deity or a battery of National Security Agency computers. There are many philosophers who are fascinated with these unknown, and even unknowable, facts.[87] These "rationalists," James writes, are primarily concerned with logic and epistemology, and they have little interest in psychology or human experience. For them, even though no being, human or divine, "should ever ascertain" any particular truth, "the word would still have to be defined as that which *ought* to be ascertained and recognized" (P 109).

As we have seen, James is quite comfortable admitting the existence of truths that are independent of learning and verification. His point is simply that they exist outside of present human experience, and consequently they play no significant role in it. He writes, for example, that at least sometimes "truth exists *per se* and absolutely, by God's grace and decree, no matter who of us knows it or is ignorant, and it would continue to exist unaltered, even though we finite knowers were all annihilated" (PU 18). He is thus able to point to the existence of "innumerable events in the history of our planet of which nobody ever has been or ever will be able to give an account, yet of which it can already be said abstractly that only one sort of possible account can ever be true" (MT 155). Should any of these events—the cause of the death of the last dinosaur, the name of George Washington's least favorite horse, the coldest day in the year 500 CE in the place that later became Innsbruck—ever become known, "the nature of the knowledge is already to some degree predetermined" (*MT* 157). On this point, James is in complete agreement with those who say that "truth is what we *ought* to believe ... even tho no man ever did or shall believe it, and even tho we have no way of getting at it save by the usual empirical processes of testing our opinions by one another and by facts" (*MT* 143). He is even willing to discuss "the truth which precedes actual knowledge of a fact" as long as we mean by this "only what any possible knower of the fact will eventually find himself necessitated to believe about it." For the present, however, "it is knowledge anticipated, knowledge in the form of possibility merely" (*MT* 157–58).

This realm of unknown truths is not a problem for James's analysis; more significantly, it is not a problem for him in daily living. He recognizes that we live fallibly in a realm of unknowns.[88] As we live our lives, in fact, we live without guarantees:

> The overwhelming majority of our true ideas admit of no direct or face-to-face verification—those of past history, for example, as of Cain and Abel. The stream of time can be remounted only verbally, or verified indirectly by the present prolongations or effects of what the past harbored. Yet if they agree with these verbalities and effects, we can know that our ideas of the past are true. *As true as past time itself was,* so true was Julius Caesar, so true were antediluvian monsters, all in their proper dates and settings. That past time itself was, is guaranteed by its coherence with everything that's present. True as the present *is,* the past *was* also. (*P* 103; cf. *MT* 54, 120–22)

Some of these unknowns are settled recording cases; others, to-be-determined contribution cases. For example, a student's grade in a particular course is in no way predetermined, unlike the number of coins in the jar is, by some prior process. The grade is the result of what the student is able to learn and demonstrate. Further, some of these unknowns will eventually be revealed in the process of testing beliefs; others will not. For our part, "we live on speculative investments, or on our prospects only," he writes. "But living on things *in posse* [potentially] is as good as living in the actual, so long as our credit remains good" (*ERE* 43). James continues descriptively that "we live on credits everywhere." This means that "we continually curtail verification-processes, letting our belief that they are possible suffice" (*MT*

91; cf. 76).⁸⁹ Instead of "direct verification" we often settle for verification of an indirect sort: "if everything runs on harmoniously, we are so sure that verification is possible that we omit it." Although James is surely correct that we are "usually justified by all that happens" (*P* 100; cf. 105), we run the risk of believing too easily. In our more prescriptive moments, we realize that we should show more restraint.

This chapter has been largely an attempt to lay out James's position on truth in the hope of understanding it better. Much more remains to be done as we move toward an evaluation of James's view, especially with regard to integrating his more extreme statements with our inherited notions of truth. A partial and tentative resolution to the questions circling around his view seems more likely if we remind ourselves of the themes that stand behind his position. First of all, it is necessary to keep in mind the complex issues of Idealism and what he saw as its "block universe" of settled truth against which he was struggling. Next, it is necessary to recognize both James's inadequate presentation of his views, and the inadequate efforts that his critics made to understand him. He admits, as we have seen, that *Pragmatism* was intended as a sketch to be improved later, and he confesses to "certain offhand habits of speech" in which he had "assumed too great a generosity" on the part of his audience (*MT* 111).⁹⁰ As a result, he continues, some of his critics seem "to labor under an inability almost pathetic, to understand the thesis which they seek to refute" (*MT* 10). He also admits it was a mistake to speak "elliptically," thereby giving Pragmatism's critics the opportunity to boggle "at every word they could boggle at" and to concentrate upon "the letter of our discourse" rather than "the spirit." He allows that "the fantastic character of the current misconceptions" may indicate the unfamiliarity of what Pragmatism is attempting to advance, but pragmatists themselves "understand each other at a hint, and can converse without anxiously attending to their P's and Q's" (*MT* 99). Third, it is necessary to come to his analysis of truth though his larger perspective as displayed in *The Principles of Psychology* and *The Will to Believe*, especially as they remind us of James's dual emphases of description and prescription, and his distinction between cases where we merely record what has happened and those where we contribute to the outcome.

The most problematic issue with James's position on truth is related, as I have been suggesting, to his view on verification. He begins descriptively with a consideration of familiar aspects of our lives, noting that truth lives on "credit," that our beliefs rely on the beliefs of others. He continues that the process of individual verification is generally only partial. He recognizes, of course, the importance of distinguishing between "knowing as verified and completed" and "knowing as in transit and on its way." As he writes, until we have verified the actual results of our ideas in experience, we are not "actual knowers" but only *virtual* knowers." The issue, however, is a question of balance. For James, "the immensely greater part of all our knowing never gets beyond this virtual stage." The process of verification is seldom if ever "completed or nailed down." We quite rightly take on credit and do not verify our ideas "of imperceptibles like ether-waves or dissociated 'ions,' or of 'ejects' like the contents of our neighbors' minds." At the same time, we often do not bother to test the ideas "which we might verify if we would take the trouble, but which we hold for true altho unterminated perceptually, because nothing says 'no' to us, and there is no contradicting truth in sight." When our beliefs are functioning well to deal with our problems, we tend to accept them as true. "*To continue thinking unchallenged is,*" he writes, "*ninety-nine times out of a hundred, our practical substitute for knowing in the completed sense.*" As long as the stream of our experience flows smoothly, so that "we nowhere feel a collision with what we elsewhere count as truth or fact," we find ourselves willing to commit "to the current as if the port were sure" (*MT* 67–68/*ERE* 34; cf. *MT* 91).[91]

What is fundamentally problematic in James's understanding of verification is that he would allow us, using Peirce's term, to "fix" our beliefs too soon,[92] to use a private and, what Clifford would consider to be, a lax standard of truth. Phrased differently, of course, one of James's greatest philosophical achievements is his championing of an open and personal approach to believing that uses beliefs to open up the future. As we have seen, he believes that an individual will consider a new opinion "true" to the extent that it satisfies that "individual's desire to assimilate the novel in his experience to his beliefs in stock," and that the success of this assimilation will be "a matter of an individual's appreciation" (*P* 36). He similarly writes that when we maintain that one theory solves a problem "on the whole more satisfactorily" than another, we mean "more satisfactorily to ourselves, and individuals will emphasize their points of satisfaction differently. To a certain degree, therefore, everything here is plastic" (*P* 35).[93] James follows this descriptive account of why we believe what we believe with a consideration of the extent of our tendency to believe what others believe. "Orthodoxy is almost as much a matter of authority in science as it is in the Church," he notes. "We believe in all sorts of laws of nature which we cannot ourselves understand, merely because men whom we admire and trust vouch for them." He continues that so strong is this largely wholesome tendency on our part that, if a set of highly regarded scientists like Hermann Ludwig Helmholtz and Louis Pasteur "were simultaneously to announce themselves as converts to clairvoyance, thought-transference, and ghosts," we would have to anticipate "a prompt popular stampede in that direction." Our inclinations are such, he writes descriptively, that "we should hasten to invoke mystical explanations without winking, and fear to be identified with a by-gone *regime* if we held back" (*EPR* 99–100). Even if James is largely accurate here—and he may be—we should offer some sort of resistance. The problem, as we saw in chapter 3, is that this individual standard is simply too low. He admits that for much of our history "truth was what had not yet been contradicted" (*VRE* 390), but we need more restraint. We need to worry about the positive results, however occasional, from false beliefs. We need to search for trouble, and to challenge what feels comfortable. We need not cripple ourselves in the way that James believes Clifford would, by believing nothing that we cannot prove, but we do need to be more skeptical than James would seem to require. In the aesthetic realm "interesting" is not "good," we need further testing; in the moral realm "acceptable" is similarly not "right"; and in the intellectual realm "believable" is not "true."[94]

I am not offering an overall complaint about James's pragmatic theory of truth, a theory that offers us a number of values. Primary among these is the way that it relocates questions about truth into the larger processes of living. To prevent confusion, we may still want to follow Dewey and avoid the term "truth" itself, because it is a commonsense notion that does not translate well into our new scientific context. Rather, we may want to move toward Dewey's preferred term "warranted assertibility" to replace ambiguities in terms like "truth," "belief," and "knowledge," and to emphasize the central role of inquiry.[95] My complaint is rather about James's position on inquiry. In his desire to save the particular individual, the unpopular viewpoint, and the minority perspective, he has simply gone too far. While it is admittedly important to protect the religious student from the intellectual bullying of aggressively "scientific" professors and classmates, and the patients of nontraditional healers from the rigidities of orthodox medicine—both of which James attempted to do—it is also important to call upon such individuals, and others, to engage in the long-term social inquiry that could lead to increased social warrant for their beliefs. As James himself writes on at least one occasion, *"introspection is difficult and fallible; and . . . the difficulty is simply that of all observation of whatever kind."* Even though we do the best we can to experience and report, "we may go astray, and give a description more applicable to some other sort of thing." We thus need to balance out our fallible positions with the criticisms and corroborations of others. "The only safeguard is in the final *consensus* of our farther knowledge about the thing in question, later views correcting earlier ones, until at last the harmony of a consistent system is reached" (*PP* 1:191).

CHAPTER 5

Radical Empiricism and Pluralism

In this introductory examination of James's radical empiricism and pluralism, I begin with a consideration of his understanding of the tradition of British Empiricism. Although he believed that this empirical philosophy is firmly grounded in particulars, he also believed that it is more successful at keeping out the non-experiential than at recognizing all that experience contains. Particularly in its denial of experienced relations, traditional Empiricism substitutes a fragmented mosaic for our flowing experience. One consequence of this failure is the opening given to Rationalism to propose some sort of unexperienced power (eventually an Absolute) to bring the necessary order to our lives. James's understanding of Hegel, and of his own contemporaries like F. H. Bradley and Josiah Royce, indicates that the eventual result of Rationalism is what he calls a "block-universe" that is as dangerous to our understanding of a meaningful individual existence as reductive science ever was. The core of the problem in the work of each of these thinkers is what James calls "vicious intellectualism," the flaw of a philosophical method that arrays its conceptualizations into a pattern that supplants reality. For his part, he sees concepts pragmatically, as constructed meanings that we use in our attempts to understand what we are about. A fundamental pluralism follows necessarily from this pragmatic approach.

Inadequate Empiricism

In volumes like *The Will to Believe*, *The Varieties of Religious Experience*, and *Pragmatism*, James was able to display his vision, but for reasons that will emerge in this chapter, this vision did not convince the majority of other philosophers. Phrased differently, while he had a feel for his own vision from the inside, he could not formulate it in a way that was generally convincing. Over the years, he came increasingly to recognize how novel his philosophical approach—encompassing pure experience, pragmatism, radical experience, and pluralism—was. Late in his life, he attempted to clarify his position for a broader audience. One part of this project was to present an integrated volume, with the working title of *The Many and the One*, on the theme of radical empiricism; between late 1904 and mid-1905 he published a set of eight preliminary essays,[1] some of which will be considered in this chapter. All of these pieces are tentative, and they should be approached collectively as a cluster of hypotheses rather than as an extended argument. James never did manage to reformulate these essays into the intended book. Perhaps the task was impossible, or at least beyond his ability,[2] or perhaps he was simply too distracted as he dealt with the continuing fallout from the controversy over *Pragmatism*.[3] Some of the radical empiricist material found its way into *A Pluralistic Universe* and *The Meaning of Truth* in 1909, and into the posthumous *Some Problems of Philosophy*; the eight essays and other related materials were published as a volume in *Essays in Radical Empiricism* in 1912. In the discussion of radical empiricism and pluralism that follows, I will occasionally be integrating materials from beyond these volumes to indicate the range of James's thinking on this topic.[4]

James was, and was writing as, a radical empiricist long before he explicitly formulated the position in 1897. In this initial presentation, he indicates that by "empiricism" he intends to treat his "most assured conclusions concerning matters of fact as hypotheses liable to modification in the course of future experience," and by "radical" he intends to treat "the doctrine of monism itself as an hypothesis." Here he is differing from other, inadequate empiricisms—"positivism or agnosticism or scientific naturalism"—that treat monism as a dogma "with which all experience has got to square." For him it is a mistake to simplify experience to conform to prior beliefs. "*Prima facie* the world is a pluralism," James writes, "as we find it, its unity seems to be that of any collection"; too often, however, "our higher thinking consists chiefly of an effort to redeem it from that first crude form" (*WB* 5–6; cf. *PP* 2:1230–31). Still, while philosophy wants simplicity and unity rather than the initial plurality, no absolute unity should be anticipated. As he puts it, "the negative, the alogical, is never wholly banished." Radical empiricism takes as its hypothesis the assumption that pluralism is "the permanent form of the world" of which "the crudity of experience remains an eternal element." In other words, "absolute unity, in spite of brilliant dashes in its direction, still remains undiscovered.... 'Ever not quite' must be the rationalistic philosopher's last confession concerning it." He continues: "There is no possible point of view from which the world can appear an absolutely single fact. Real possibilities, real indeterminations, real beginnings, real ends, real evil, real crises, catastrophes, and escapes, a real God, and a real moral life, just as common-sense conceives these things, may remain in empiricism as conceptions which that philosophy gives up the attempt either to 'overcome' or to reinterpret in monistic form" (*WB* 6–7; cf. *SPP* 74). While this pluralism may appear less than fully rational to those who are committed to a more ordered version of reality, for James pluralism is necessary to appreciate experience in its fullness.

In 1904 James offered a second formulation of radical empiricism. "To be radical, an empiricism must neither admit into its constructions any element that is not directly experienced, nor exclude from them any element that is directly experienced," he writes. In particular, it is important to recognize that "*the relations that connect experiences must themselves be experienced relations, and any kind of relation experienced must be accounted as 'real' as anything else in the system*" (*ERE* 22). A third, somewhat different, attempt appeared in 1909, emphasizing the "coalescence of next with next in concrete experience" and noting that "all the insulating cuts we make there are artificial products of the conceptualization faculty." In this way, he distinguishes his radical empiricism "from the bugaboo empiricism of the traditional rationalist critics, which (rightly or wrongly) is accused of chopping up experience into atomistic sensations, incapable of union with one another until a purely intellectual principle has swooped down upon them from on high and folded them in its own conjunctive categories" (*PU* 147; cf. 126). Also in 1909 James offered a fourth formulation of radical empiricism, again with slightly different emphases. This time he tells us that radical empiricism incorporates a postulate, a statement of fact, and a generalized conclusion. Beginning with the postulate, he writes that "the only things that shall be debatable among philosophers shall be things definable in terms drawn from experience." He follows this assumption with the factual statement that "the relations between things, conjunctive as well as disjunctive, are just as much matters of direct particular experience, neither more so nor less so, than the things themselves." Finally, as a "generalized conclusion" he notes that "the parts of experience hold together from next to next by relations that are themselves parts of experience." As a result, "the directly apprehended universe needs, in short, no extraneous trans-empirical connective support, but possesses in its own right a concatenated or continuous structure" (*MT* 6–7).[5]

A related discussion of connectedness occurs in "The Knowing of Things Together." Here, James discusses positions with which contemporary readers are likely to have slight familiarity. Still, he is taking up a question that was hotly debated in his day. At issue is how we decide between a number of guests and a party, or between separate musical notes and a chord. At what point does a collection of trees become a forest, or lemon and sugar in water lemonade? "Common sense simply says that the mind 'brings the things together,'" he writes, "and common psychology says the 'ideas' of the various things 'combine,' and at most will admit that the occasions on which ideas combine may be made the subject of inquiry." For him, however, to adopt this view is to beg the question. He emphasizes that the initial phenomenon is "that of *knowing things together*; and it is in those terms that its solution must, in the first instance at least, be sought." Still, how does this "fundamental fact of our experience" (*EP* 72) actually work?[6]

James decides to take apart the phrase "to know things together," and to analyze the pieces one at a time, beginning with what we mean by "things." He offers initially the position of idealistic philosophy that "things have no other nature than thoughts have, and we know of no things that are not given to somebody's experience." Thus, he continues, for Idealism: "When I see the thing white paper before my eyes, the nature of the thing and the nature of the sensations are one.... A thing may be my phenomenon or some one else's; it may be frequently or infrequently experienced; it may be shared by all of us; one of our copies of it may be regarded as the original, and the other copies as representatives of that original; it may appear very differently at different times; but whatever it be, the stuff of which it is made is thought-stuff." Further, when we speak of something as "out of our own mind," we are speaking of something "that was or will be in our own mind on another occasion; or, finally, we mean a thing in the mind of some other possible receiver of experiences like ours" (*EP* 72–73).

James then turns to the question of what we mean by "know," noting that the concept "knowledge" is ambiguous in English. We may say that we know a person, place, or thing, or that we know something about the person, place, or thing. As an initial example, we can consider how different is it to "know" Venice by immediate acquaintance from a gondola or to "know" it only mediately from a description in a book or on a website. "There are two ways of knowing things," he writes, "knowing them immediately or intuitively, and knowing them conceptually or representatively." As an example of the former, he points to a sheet of "white paper before our eyes"; as examples of the latter—and of "most of the things we know"—he suggests "the tigers now in India . . . or the scholastic system of philosophy," either of which we can only known "representatively or symbolically." Our conceptual knowing of the Indian tigers consists in "having them, however absent in body, become in some way present to our thought" or "mentally *pointing* towards them" (*EP* 73).[7] He continues: "The pointing of our thought to the tigers is known simply and solely as a procession of mental associates and motor consequences that follow on the thought, and that would lead harmoniously, if followed out, into some ideal or real context, or even into the immediate presence, of the tigers. It is known as our rejection of a jaguar, if that beast were shown us as a tiger; as our assent to a genuine tiger if so shown." James maintains that such "representative knowledge" is in no way mysterious. "*To know an object is here to lead to it through a context which the world supplies*" (*EP* 74).

James's consideration of these two ways of knowing the world is directly related to his discussion of concepts and percepts. He writes that the relation of concepts to percepts is "like that of sight to touch" (*SPP* 42). When our thinking is fluid, we move comfortably back and forth between them. "Percepts and concepts interpenetrate and melt together, impregnate and fertilize each other," he writes. "Neither, taken alone, knows reality in its completeness" (*SPP* 34). Thus, to live successful lives in our world, we need both of these "mental functions." Perception, for its part, "awakens thought," and thought, for its part, "enriches perception." As a result, he continues, "the more we see, the more we think; while the more we think, the more we see in our immediate experiences, and the greater grows the detail, and the more significant the articulateness of our perception." The long-term consequences of this dual process are that "the world we practically live in is one in which it is impossible (except by theoretic retrospection) to disentangle the contributions of intellect from those of sense." The conceptual and the perceptual, "the universal and the particular parts of the experience are literally immersed in each other, and both are indispensable." Rendering this point more poetically, he notes that "concepts are like evaporations out of the bosom of perception, into which they condense again whenever practical service summons them" (*SPP* 58–59).

Focusing more closely on concepts—the more troublesome half of the partnership—James notes that they have specific values. First, they are of practical use. Conception is "a *teleological instrument*" for him. "It is a partial aspect of a thing which *for our purpose* we regard as its essential aspect.... In comparison with this aspect, whatever other properties and qualities the thing may have, are unimportant accidents which we may without blame ignore" (*EP* 34; cf. *PP* 1:436). Because of this power, concepts are able to "steer us practically every day," he writes, "and provide an immense map of relations among the elements of things, which map, tho not now yet on some possible future occasion, may help to steer us practically" (*SPP* 43). Much of this usefulness results from simplification. For example, when we are able to substitute "a whole conceptual order ... for the immediate perceptual flow," we thereby fashion a much wider "mental panorama." Without concepts, we would have to deal with each moment of experience as it comes, "as the sessile sea-anemone on its rock receives whatever nourishment the wash of the waves may bring." Because we have concepts, however, we can "go in quest of the absent, meet the remote, actively turn this way or that, bend our experience, and make it tell us whither it is bound." Thus, the "primary function of conception" is for "practically adapting us to a larger environment than that of which brutes take account." Because of concepts, we are able to "*harness* perceptual reality ... in order to drive it better to our ends" (*SPP* 39; cf. *P* 34; *PU* 111). Second, concepts can provide a fuller understanding of percepts. Concepts "bring new values into our perceptual life, they reanimate our wills, and make our action turn upon new points of emphasis" (*SPP* 43). When we know better what our percepts are, "we can tell all sorts of farther truths about them, based on the relation of those whats to other whats" (*SPP* 39–40). Also, concepts offer the possibility of a priori sciences like mathematics and logic (see *SPP* 40–42). Third, James writes, "concepts not only guide us over the map of life, but we *revalue* life by their use." The map that we frame by means of concepts is "an object which possesses, when once it has been framed, an independent existence. It suffices all by itself for purposes of study. The 'eternal' truths it contains would have to be acknowledged even were the world of sense annihilated" (*SPP* 42–43).

James notes that percepts are continuous with one another, but concepts remain discrete in their meanings. "Each concept means just what it singly means, and nothing else," whereas perception "*means* nothing, and is but what it immediately is." Thus, each moment of perception is "always a much-at-once, and contains innumerable aspects and characters which conception can pick out and isolate, and thereafter always intend." Each moment contains "duration, intensity, complexity or simplicity, interestingness, excitingness, pleasantness or their opposites" (*SPP* 32; cf. *EP* 76–77). If we could abstract our conscious life "from all conceptual interpretation" and return to the "immediate sensible life," we would "find it to be what someone"—that is, James himself—"has called a big blooming buzzing confusion [see *PP* 1:462; *PBC* 21], as free from contradiction in its 'much-at-onceness' as it is all alive and evidently there." From "this aboriginal sensible muchness" our attention "carves out" the objects that conception "names and identifies forever." This dual process, as we saw in chapter 4, is the origin of the constellations in the sky, and of the many distinctions on earth that separate marshes and swamps, wolves and dogs. In a similar fashion, we extract hours and seasons from within the continuous flow of time. "We say *what* each part of the sensible continuum is, and all these abstracted *whats* are *concepts*" (*SPP* 32–33). Still, while the names by which we label these distinctions "cut them into separate conceptual entities," James reminds us that "no cuts existed in the continuum in which they originally came" (*PU* 129; cf. *EP* 169). Percepts, because they are incessantly changing particulars that "never return exactly as they were before," bring with them "an element of concrete novelty into our experience." Concepts, on the contrary, offer no novelty because they are "abstracted from experiences already seen or given" and can present any novelty only "in ready-made and ancient terms." They are, as he continues, "post-mortem preparations" derived from experiences had that are only more or less applicable to the new (*SPP* 54–55).[8]

While he admits that concepts are as "real" as percepts, since "we cannot live a moment without taking account of them," James maintains that what he calls "the 'eternal' kind of being" that concepts enjoy is "inferior" to the "temporal kind" of being of percepts. This is so because the nature of concepts is "so static and schematic and lacks so many characters which temporal reality possesses." He continues that it is necessary for philosophy to "recognize many realms of reality which mutually interpenetrate." Among these are "the conceptual systems of mathematics, logic, aesthetics, [and] ethics." These and other realms are "each strung upon some peculiar form of relation," but each differs from "perceptual reality" because in none of these realms "is history or happening displayed." James notes, however, that "perceptual reality involves and contains all these ideal systems, and vastly more besides" (*SPP* 56).

With regard to percepts and concepts, James continues, "there has always been a tendency among philosophers to treat conception as the more essential thing in knowledge" (*SPP* 44). While he presumes that all would admit that "complete knowledge of fact" requires the contribution of both sense and intellect, he believes that long ago philosophers developed "the notion that a knowledge of so-called 'universals,' consisting of concepts of abstract forms, qualities, numbers, and relations, was the only knowledge worthy of the truly philosophic mind" (*SPP* 34). Our perceptual senses, understood in this way as "organs of wavering illusion," interfere with knowledge in any ultimate sense. For philosophers, the senses were thus a problem on which they could "safely turn their backs" as they pursued an "intelligible order" that would "supersede the senses rather than interpret them" (*SPP* 44). Unlike the fickle percepts, concepts never vary, and "between such unvarying terms the relations must be constant and express eternal verities." By means of such concepts, we are able to contrast "the knowledge of universals and intelligibles, as godlike, dignified, and honorable to the knower, with that of particulars and sensibles as something relatively base which more allies us with the beasts" (*SPP* 34). Given this view, he notes that our intellectual life *"consists almost wholly in . . . substituting a conceptual order for the perceptual order in which . . . experience originally comes"* (*SPP* 33; cf. *PU* 113).

James then considers "what is gained and what is lost when percepts are translated into concepts." The former are "solely of the here and now," whereas the latter are "of the like and unlike, of the future, of the past, and of the far away" (*SPP* 43). Conceptual systems, since they are "monstrous abridgments" of the fullness of perception (*SPP* 53), offer us a conceptual map that presents "only a surface." By this he means that a conceptual map contains only "abstract signs and symbols of things that in themselves are concrete bits of sensible experience." If we compare conceptual "extent" with perceptual "content," or if we measure conceptual "spread" against perceptual "thickness," we will recognize that "for some purposes the one, for other purposes the other, has the higher value" (*SPP* 43; cf. *PU* 111–12). This recognition, however, undermines philosophy's traditional conceptual bias. As he writes, "conceptual knowledge is forever inadequate to the fulness of the reality to be known." Thus, despite the value of the conceptual approach, we must admit that it "remains superficial through the abstractness, and false through the discreteness of its terms; and the whole operation, so far from making things appear more rational, becomes the sources of quite gratuitous unintelligibilities." Moreover, because "reality consists of existential particulars as well as of essences and universals and class-names," and because we can become aware of these particulars "only in the perceptual flux," we can never abandon that flux. James writes that "we must carry it with us to the bitter end of our cognitive business," keeping perception always in the discussion even when conception "proves illuminating," and returning to perception alone when the discussion breaks down (*SPP* 45; cf. *ECR* 518–19).[9]

To make more specific the difficulty with concepts, James considers two problems. The first is that conception is "a secondary process" built upon perception, "which is self-sufficing, as all lower creatures in whom conscious life goes on by reflex adaptations show." Before we can understand a concept, we must recognize its meaning as "some *this*, or some abstract portion of a *this*, with which we first made acquaintance in the perceptual world, or else some grouping of such abstract portions." Conceptual content is thus second hand: "to know what the concept 'colour' means you must have *seen* red or blue, or green." While it may be possible to fashion novel concepts like the unicorn out of prior elements, he believes that those elements "must have been perceptually given." The second problem with concepts is that, if we are not careful, they can "falsify as well as omit, and make the flux impossible to understand." As we will shortly see with the race of Achilles and the tortoise, filtering "perceptual reality" through concepts can make it appear "paradoxical and incomprehensible." If taken to the extreme, the conceptual approach can lead us "to the opinion that perceptual experience is not reality at all, but an appearance or illusion" (*SPP* 45–46; cf. 51–53). Thus, when concepts are taken as primary, there is trouble.[10]

Concepts are less adequate means for grasping reality than are percepts. Similarly, definitions are not complete and final for James; rather, they are pragmatic graspings, more adequate for some times and situations than for others. He believes that it is far better to treat concepts pragmatically as tools. We should "use concepts when they help, and drop them when they hinder, understanding; and take reality bodily and integrally up into philosophy in exactly the perceptual shape in which it comes" (*SPP* 53). To live successfully, however, we need both percepts and concepts "as we need both our legs to walk with" (*SPP* 34). James asks "who can decide off-hand which is absolutely better, to live or to understand life?" We must continue alternatively to live perceptually and understand conceptually, and a "man can no more limit himself to either than a pair of scissors can cut with a single one of its blades" (*SPP* 43–44; cf. 55; *C* 12:396). To use another analogy, he writes that "without abstract concepts to handle our perceptual particulars by, we are like men hopping on one foot." By using both feet, however, we are able to walk. "We throw our concept forward, get a foothold on the consequence, hitch our line to this, and draw our percept up, traveling thus with a hop, skip and jump over the surface of life at a vastly rapider rate than if we merely waded through the thickness of the particulars as accident rained them down upon our heads" (*MT* 134).

Still, James is greatly concerned to reject the conceptual primacy of much of philosophy. He admits that concepts have a kind of permanence, but precisely because of this, they are unable to adapt to the flux of experience. While concepts offer us "a magnificent sketch-map for showing us our bearings," they cannot replace perception, which remains closer to our existential reality as it is "created temporally day by day" (*SPP* 55; cf. *PP* 1:437). As we saw in chapter 2, philosophy cannot be exclusively perceptual, lying "flat on its belly in the middle of experience" (*PU* 125). Still, we should never forget that percepts must remain primary. Experiencing is more than constructing doctrines about experience; living is only in part the formulation of abstractions.

For James, Empiricism's great value is that it preserves the fullness of the experienced moment. "Rationalistic philosophy has always aspired to a rounded-in view of the whole of things, a closed system of kinds, from which the notion of any essential novelty being possible, is ruled-out in advance" (*SPP* 55). Unlike Rationalism, "with its exclusive interest in the unchanging and the general," and its insufficient appreciation for "the passing pulses of our life," Empiricism points to "our instinctive feeling about immediate experience" that recognizes "the genuineness of each particular moment in which we sensibly feel the squeeze of this world's life, as we actually do work here, or work is done upon us" (*SPP* 59–60).[11] Perceptual reality is not contained by conceptual restraints: "It overflows, exceeds, and alters; and what novelties it may turn into can be known adequately only by following its singularities from moment to moment as our experience grows." The empiricist rejects any antecedent "all-inclusive vision," and proceeds through experience with the help of concepts that are "useful but not sovereign." For the empiricist, "philosophy, like life, must keep the doors and windows open," never pretending that "man's relation to the totality of things as a philosopher is essentially different from his relation to the parts of things as a daily patient or agent in the practical current of events" (SPP 55).

Rationalists prefer concepts as more noble and clean; empiricists want their thinking to be better grounded in particulars. James believes that rationalists view conceptual knowledge as originally arising "independently of all perceptual particulars." As a result, such concepts as "God," "eternity," "truth," and "justice" are unexplainable using only experience. The empiricist James, however, believes that such concepts "do result from practical experience." Still, he is ultimately more interested in the function of concepts than their origin. Rejecting the view that we should leave our concepts "flocking with their abstract and motionless companions," he maintains that *"the significance of concepts consists always in their relation to perceptual particulars."* Concepts are "made of percepts, or distilled from parts of percepts," and their function is "to coalesce with percepts again, bringing the mind back into the perceptual world with a better command of the situation there" (SPP 35–36). The meaning of any concept can be found, "if not in some sensible particular which it directly designates, then in some particular difference in the course of human experience which its being true will make." In any particular case, for example, if two distinct concepts should lead us to expect an identical experience, we would be justified in assuming, as we saw in chapter 4, "that they embody the same meaning under different names" (SPP 37).

After this consideration of percepts and concepts, we can return to James's account of "immediate or intuitive acquaintance with an object," and to the sheet of white paper. He notes that "the thought-stuff and the thing-stuff are here indistinguishably the same in nature . . . and there is no context of intermediaries or associates to stand between and separate the thought and thing." Instead of any "'pointing,'" there is "an allround embracing of the paper by the thought" (EP 74–75). He emphasizes again that our experience is full of examples of immediate acquaintance, and that these instances of direct encounter are fundamental aspects of human existence. He writes: "the paper seen and the seeing of it are only two names for one indivisible fact which, properly named, is *the datum, the phenomenon, or the experience*. The paper is in the mind and the mind is around the paper, because paper and mind are only two names that are given later to the one experience, when, taken in a larger world of which it forms a part, its connections are traced in different directions. *To know immediately, then, or intuitively, is for mental content and object to be identical*" (EP 75–76). For James, the central point of this pragmatic distinction between immediate and representative knowing is to emphasize his belief in the primacy of perceptual knowledge over conceptual knowledge. "*A percept knows whatever reality it directly or indirectly operates on and resembles*," whereas a concept only "*knows a reality, whenever it actually or potentially terminates in a percept that operates on or resembles that reality, or is otherwise connected with it or with its context*" (MT 27–28).[12]

For James, our perceptions yield a sort of community. He writes that "we believe that we all know and think about and talk about the same world, because *we believe our* PERCEPTS *are possessed by us in common*." While there is no proof that my feelings of the world match yours, we assume that they do "as the simplest hypothesis that meets the case" (MT 29–30; cf. PP 1:262).[13] What saves us "from flying asunder into a chaos of mutually repellent solipsisms," he continues, and what allows our individual minds to commune with one another, is "nothing but the mutual resemblance of those of our perceptual feelings which have this power of modifying one another, *which are mere dumb knowledges-of-acquaintance,* and which must also resemble their realities or not know them aright at all." Even though these sensations are condemned by some philosophers, they are "the mother-earth, the anchorage, the stable rock, the first and last limits, the *terminus a quo* [starting point] and the *terminus ad quem* [ending point] of the mind," and attaining these "sensational *termini*" should be the goal of all our intellectual efforts. These perceptual *termini* "end discussion" and "destroy the false conceit of knowledge" to have a higher existence in some conceptual realm. Without percepts, he continues, we would find ourselves "all at sea with each other's meaning." James admits, of course, that concepts are more attractive to ponder. "Beautiful is the flight of conceptual reason through the upper air of truth," he writes. Consequently, it should be no surprise that "philosophers are dazzled by it still, and no wonder they look with some disdain at the low earth of feeling from which the goddess launched herself aloft. But woe to her if she return not home to its acquaintance." Different individuals, in fact, can never be sure whether they are in agreement until they can bring their conceptual discussion to a pragmatic test. "This is why metaphysical discussions are so much like fighting with the air" (*MT* 30–31).[14]

Consciousness

The first of the *Essays in Radical Empiricism*, "Does Consciousness Exist?," is largely duplicated by the eighth, "La Notion de Conscience," and these two should be considered in tandem. The theme being considered is the nature of experience. The topic is not, as it is elsewhere in James's writings, the content of experience, such as its religious aspects or its focus and fringe, although some issues of content remain always nearby. His topic here is knowing or cognition as a fundamental human activity. He had written in *The Principles* that "the *relation of knowing* is the most mysterious thing in the world" (*PP* 1:212). Now he wants to try to make it a bit less mysterious, and to show that "knowing is just a natural process like any other" (*MT* 84). To use the familiar commonsense dualistic framework, he wants to consider what experience tells us about the world. In an attempt to answer this question, we can begin with the understanding of "average persons on the street"—the so-called naive realists—for whom knowledge is not in any way mysterious. Such individuals believe that the world is outside of them, has preceded them, and will continue on after they die. They believe that automobiles have color and make noise and sometimes crash. They believe that there are billions of other people in the world whose experiences—of hunger and exhaustion, of success and love—are similar to their own. They also believe that most of what occurs in the world bears no significant relation to their lives. This position is called "realism" because it posits an ongoing material world as the locus of human activities. Our experiences in this real world are not delusions or empty ideas or some sort of divine theater; our experiences are veridical.[15] This realism is called "naive" because it fails to take any account of numerous, fundamental problems in experiencing with which humans have long been familiar. One such problem is the nonsolidity of matter proposed by the atomic theory, with its implications for our understanding of heat and color. A second problem is the often erratic operations of the human organism. Exhaustion and drugs and illness affect our senses; in addition, we fall victim to all sorts of optical and aural illusions. Any good psychologist—and James was a very good psychologist—

could point to dozens of ways in which the body is a machine that is prone to report falsely on the world. Thus, naive realism is suspect.

James recognizes that there is a certain natural inclination toward dualism, fostered perhaps by this naive realism, and by the psychology of the outside observer who has access to our actions but not to our thoughts. "Common sense and popular philosophy," he writes, "are as dualistic as it is possible to be." We naturally think that thoughts are "made of one kind of substance, and things of another" (*ERE* 69; cf. 3). This dualism is often exacerbated by academic philosophy (see *ERE* 261–62) that assumes this dualism as a given and offers us explanations of it using, for example, the power of platonic ideas, but in the process, sophisticated philosophy gives rise to even worse problems, like those related to skepticism. Some familiar philosophical answers to the problems that result from naive realism are Lockean phenomenalism, which maintains that we have access to our experiences but not to the world; Berkeleyan idealism, which maintains that there is no longer a need for the world; Humean skepticism, a more extreme and consistent version of Lockeanism; Kantian Transcendentalism, which repairs Humean skepticism by attributing the ordering of experience to the workings of our minds; Common Sense Realism, which rejects the initial Lockean phenomenalism; Roycean or Bradleyan Idealism, which modify the Kantian solution; and after James, New Realism and Critical Realism, which paved the way for philosophy as a professional endeavor attempting to solve "the problem of knowledge."[16]

James believes that the traditional philosophical solutions to the problem of the dualism of thought and thing are of no use. Fortunately, however, they are also unnecessary, because the problem to which they offer solutions is one that we have created for ourselves. The problem of dualism, as it is usually presented to us, results from a mis-taking of experience that has been perpetuated by philosophical malpractice. So, when James says that he mistrusts consciousness "as an entity," he is not denying that we are conscious beings; rather, he is rejecting consciousness as some sort of thing. Thus, when he denies that consciousness exists, he means "only to deny that the word stands for an entity," although he insists "most emphatically that it does stand for a function." He writes that there is "no aboriginal stuff or quality of being, contrasted with that of which material objects are made, out of which our thoughts of them are made." There is, however, "a function in experience which thoughts perform, and for the performance of which this quality of being in invoked," and this function is *"knowing"* (ERE 4). James summarizes that "consciousness (as it is commonly represented, either as an entity, or as pure activity, but in any case as being fluid, unextended, diaphanous, devoid of content of its own, but directly self-knowing—spiritual, in short) ... is pure fancy" (ERE 267). On the contrary, what does exist is *"the susceptibility possessed by the parts of experience to be reported or known"* (ERE 271). It might thus be better to eliminate as best we can the noun from this discussion: we are individuals who are conscious of many things, but there is no such thing as consciousness.

To begin to think in this functional rather than substantial way, we must move away from our familiar dualistic understanding that bifurcates experience, and begin with "pure" experience.[17] James writes that "if we start with the supposition that there is only one primal stuff or material in the world, a stuff of which everything is composed, and if we call that stuff 'pure experience,' then knowing can easily be explained as a particular sort of relation towards one another into which portions of pure experience may enter." As later events have proven, his use of "easily" was certainly hasty, and he is closer to the mark when he writes that clarifying this relation in which "one of its 'terms' becomes the subject or bearer of the knowledge, the knower, the other becomes the object known ... will need much explanation before it can be understood" (ERE 4–5).

"Pure experience" is what James calls "the immediate flux of life which furnishes the material to our later reflection with its conceptual categories." He notes further: "Only new-born babes, or men in semi-coma from sleep, drugs, illnesses, or blows, may be assumed to have an experience pure in the literal sense of a *that* which is not yet any definite *what,* tho ready to be all sorts of whats; full both of oneness and of manyness, but in respects that don't appear; changing throughout, yet so confusedly that its phases interpenetrate and no points, either of distinction or of identity, can be caught" (ERE 46).[18] Experience in this pure or raw state is "but another name for feeling or sensation." Perhaps it would be better to discuss its *relatively* pure or raw state because, in the process of living, experience "no sooner comes than it tends to fill itself with emphases, and these salient parts become identified and fixed and abstracted"; as a result "experience now flows as if shot through with adjectives and nouns and prepositions and conjunctions." From that point on, only "the proportional amount of unverbalized sensation which it still embodies" can still be characterized as "pure" experience (*ERE* 46).

Pure experience can become either subjective or objective; we make the stuff of pure experience into either thoughts or things. James writes that "pure experience" or "the instant field of the present" is "only virtually or potentially either object or subject as yet." Until we have converted it into a *what*, pure experience is "plain, unqualified actuality or existence, a simple *that*" (*ERE* 13). Thus, he continues that the distinction between "thing" and "thought" is both *"a practical distinction of the utmost importance"* and *"a distinction which is of a* FUNCTIONAL *order only, and not at all ontological as understood by classical dualism."* Things and thoughts are *"made of one and the same stuff, which as such cannot be defined but only experienced; and which, if one wishes, one can call the stuff of experience in general"* (*ERE* 271). In our direct acquaintance with an object, such as the sheet of white paper mentioned above, "the paper seen and the seeing of it are only two names for one indivisible fact which, properly named, is *the datum, the phenomenon, or the experience.*" At one and the same time, "the paper is in the mind and the mind is around the paper," he continues, and this is so "because paper and mind are only two names that are given later to the one experience, when, taken in a larger world of which it forms a part, its connections are traced in different directions" (*EP* 75; cf. *MT* 36).

Experience is thus unlike paint, which James maintains is dualistic by its very nature. "Paint has a dual constitution," he writes, that involves both "a menstruum (oil, size or what not) and a mass of content in the form of pigment suspended therein." Each part can be separated from the other: "We can get the pure menstruum by letting the pigment settle, and the pure pigment by pouring off the size or oil." He believes that this process of "physical subtraction" should not be likened to a presumed process of "mental subtraction" by means of which we separate aspects of experience into thoughts and things, because the process of separating thoughts and things does not involve "isolating them entirely," but only "distinguishing them enough to know that they are two." He thus rejects this paint analogy and its implication that experience is a duality that can be divided into component parts. When properly understood, the distinction within experience of what we call consciousness and content comes, James writes, *"not by way of subtraction, but by way of addition—*the addition, to a given concrete piece of it, of other sets of experiences, in connection with which severally its use or function may be of two different kinds" (*ERE* 6–7; cf. 268, 270).

Using paint in a better analogy, James suggests that "in a pot in a paint-shop, along with other paints, it serves in its entirety as so much saleable matter. Spread on a canvas, with other paints around it, it represents, on the contrary, a feature in a picture and performs a spiritual function." He then develops this analogy: "Just so ... does a given undivided portion of experience, taken in one context of associates, play the part of a knower, of a state of mind, of 'consciousness'; while in a different context the same undivided bit of experience plays the part of the thing known, of an objective 'content.' ... In one group it figures as a thought, in another group as a thing. And, since it can figure in both groups simultaneously we have every right to speak of it as subjective and objective both at once." He notes that we should be more comfortable with "such double-barrelled terms as 'experience,' 'phenomenon,' 'datum,' '*Vorfindung*,'" in place of "the single-barrelled terms of 'thought' and 'thing,'" because the double-barreled words reinterpret the apparent dualism in such a way that, "instead of being mysterious and elusive, it becomes verifiable and concrete." For him, consciousness is "an affair of relations" falling "outside, not inside, the single experience considered," although it is always open to being "particularized and defined" (*ERE* 7). So, for example, to the degree that our experiences "extend in time, enter into relations of physical influence, reciprocally split, warm, illuminate, etc., each other," we consider them to be "a field apart which we call the physical world." But to the degree that "they are transitory, physically inert, with a succession which does not follow a determined order but seems rather to obey emotive fancies," we consider them to be "another field which we call the psychical world" (*ERE* 270).[19]

James then begins a three-point discussion of perception and conception, beginning with the former. He suggests that perceptions, events of seeing, hearing, and smelling, are better understood as relations, not between two things—for example, not between the candle or flower and my brain, as naive realism would have it—but between two pieces of experience. He grants that the commonsense approach to the experience of a person sitting in a room is that the person is experiencing "a collection of physical things cut out from an environing world of other physical things with which these physical things have actual or potential relations." He notes the familiar dualism here and indicates that philosophers have long puzzled over how "what is evidently one reality should be in two places at once, both in outer space and in a person's mind." For him, however, this approach misrepresents the situation. "The puzzle of how the one identical room can be in two places," he writes, is no more than "the puzzle of how one identical point can be on two lines." Just as a single point can be at the intersection of two lines, a pulse of pure experience can be at the "intersection of two processes" and thus operate in two orders. As such "it could be counted twice over, as belonging to either group, and spoken of loosely as existing in two places, although it would remain all the time a numerically single thing" (*ERE* 7–8; cf. 27–29/*MT* 61–63).

James's emphasis is, of course, on the processes. One of these processes is "the reader's personal biography" and the other is "the history of the house of which the room is part"; he believes that these physical and mental processes are not completely compatible:

> As a room, the experience has occupied that spot and had that environment for thirty years. As your field of consciousness it may never have existed until now. As a room, attention will go on to discover endless new details in it. As your mental state merely, few new ones will emerge under attention's eye. As a room, it will take an earthquake, or a gang of men, and in any case a certain amount of time, to destroy it. As your subjective state, the closing of your eyes, or any instantaneous play of your fancy will suffice. In the real world, fire will consume it. In your mind, you can let fire play over it without effect. As an outer object, you must pay so much a month to inhabit it. As an inner content, you may occupy it for any length of time rent-free. (*ERE* 8–9; cf. 14–15, 269)[20]

Thus, from the side of personal biography, much is true of the room that is not true when the room is considered as part of the history of the house, and vice versa. Still, we cannot say that "the psychical and the physical" processes are "absolutely heterogeneous." They are in fact "so little heterogeneous that if we adopt the common-sense point of view ... this sensible reality and the sensation which we have of it are absolutely identical with the other at the time the sensation occurs." Thus, he continues, far from being "small inner duplicates of things," our sensations are "the things themselves in so far as the things are presented to us." Thus, if we set aside what he calls the "private life of things," and concentrate on their "public life"—that is, on the "present actuality with which things confront us, from which all our theoretical constructions are derived and to which they must all return and be linked under penalty of floating in the air and in the unreal"—we will recognize that this actuality is "homogeneous—nay, more than homogeneous, but numerically one—with a certain part of our inner life" (ERE 263).

A second central consideration in his sketch of epistemology is conception—imagination, memory, and so on—which, while more complex than perception, reveals "the same essential homogeneity." If we consider a case of "pure thought, as it occurs in dreams or reveries, or in remembrance of the past," James writes, we will recognize that "the stuff of experience" performs "a double duty," with the physical and the psychical intermingling and fusing. "If I dream of a golden mountain," he continues, "doubtless it does not exist outside of the dream; but *in* the dream the mountain is of a perfectly physical nature or stuff, it is *as* physical that it appears to me" (ERE 263–64). Similarly, he notes that "if at this moment I think of my hat which a while ago I left in the cloak-room, where is the dualism, the discontinuity between the hat of my thoughts and the real hat?" How different is the real hat that I can hold in my hand and the "idea-hat" that I can go and retrieve? (ERE 264–65; cf. ERE 28/MT 62). He continues: "If we take conceptual manifolds, or memories, or fancies, they also are in their first intention mere bits of pure experience, and, as such, are single *thats* which act in one context as objects, and in another context figure as mental states.... Any single non-perceptual experience tends to get counted twice over, just as a perceptual experience does, figuring in one context as an object or field of objects, in another as a state of mind" (ERE 9–10). In each case, the single experience serves double duty: the seen room is also a field of consciousness, and the conceived or recollected room, a state of mind. "It plays two different roles, being *Gedanke* and *Gedachtes*, the thought-of-an-object, the object-thought-of, both in one." So, for example, the room as an object of thought may have a longer existence than the thought of it. "In the reader's personal history the room occupies a single date—he saw it only once perhaps, a year ago," he continues. "Of the house's history, on the other hand, it forms a permanent ingredient" (ERE 12–13). Of course, it is also possible that the house may live on in a person's memory long after the structure has been destroyed.

A third central epistemological consideration—perhaps the most significant—is the knowing of perceptual by conceptual experience. Here again, James sees "an affair of external relations." By this he means that "one experience would be the knower, the other the reality known," and that the knowing of percepts by concepts could be "perfectly well" defined without any use of "consciousness" if it were seen as "leading-towards . . . and terminating-in percepts, through a series of transitional experiences which the world supplies" (*ERE* 14).[21] As an example he offers an encounter with Harvard's Memorial Hall. How could we know, he wonders, that we were "thinking truly" of this building? "My mind may have before it only the name, or it may have a clear image, or it may have a very dim image of the hall," he writes, "but such an intrinsic difference in the image makes no difference in its cognitive function." He continues: "if you ask me what hall I mean by my image, and I can tell you nothing; or if I fail to point or lead you towards the Harvard Delta; or if, being led by you, I am uncertain whether the Hall I see be what I had in mind or not; you would rightly deny that I had 'meant' that particular hall at all, even tho my mental image might to some degree have resembled it." In contrast, James notes, should he be able to take you to Memorial Hall and describe its history and function, or should he when arrived there feel that his idea, "however imperfect it may have been, to have led hither and to be now *terminated*," then his idea "must be, and by common consent would be, called cognizant of reality" (*ERE* 28–29/*MT* 62–63; cf. *ERE* 100–101/*MT* 73–74).

James begins the essay "A World of Pure Experience" with a further consideration of radical empiricism, especially its difference from traditional Empiricism that he sees as a philosophy of parts in search of wholeness. "Rationalism tends to emphasize universals and to make wholes prior to parts in the order of logic as well as in that of being," he writes. In contrast, Empiricism "lays the explanatory stress upon the part, the element, the individual, and treats the whole as a collection and the universal as an abstraction." For him, the proper description "starts with the parts and makes of the whole a being of the second order." It is thus a sort of "mosaic philosophy, a philosophy of plural facts." He admits that his view resembles the ideas of Hume and his followers "who refer these facts neither to substances in which they inhere nor to an absolute mind that creates them as its objects," but James emphasizes that his empiricism is radical because it also incorporates all that is experienced. He continues that "in spite of the fact that conjunctive and disjunctive relations present themselves as being fully co-ordinate parts of experience," traditional Empiricism has been inclined to downplay the former and emphasize the latter. In response to this assumed fragmentation, Rationalism has introduced a supposed repair "by the addition of trans-experiential agents of unification, substances, intellectual categories and powers, or selves." He maintains, however, that if Empiricism had been thoroughly radical and treated conjunctive and disjunctive relations equally then no "artificial correction" would have had to be imported (*ERE* 22–23; cf. *SPP* 74).

James urges us to consider the full range of conjunctive relations—withness, simultaneity in time, before and after, adjacency in space, near and far, similarity, difference, causality, and so on (see *ERE* 23–27). "*Radical empiricism*," he writes, "*does full justice to conjunctive relations*, without, however, treating them as rationalism always tends to treat them, as being true in some supernal way, as if the unity of things and their variety belonged to different orders of truth and vitality altogether" (*ERE* 23). Although he had just referred to his philosophy of plural facts as a "mosaic" philosophy, he steps back from that metaphor because "in actual mosaics the pieces are held together by their bedding," and Rationalism was only too happy to portray its role as providing the necessary bedding—"substances, transcendental egos, or absolutes"—to turn the pieces into a world. He writes, however, that for radical empiricism "there is no bedding; it is as if the pieces clung together by their edges, the transitions experienced between them forming their cement." As a result, he continues, "experience itself, taken at large, can grow by its edges" with its various moments merging into others. "Life is in the transitions," James writes, "as much as in the terms connected" (*ERE* 42). Consequently, conjunctive relations and disjunctive relations are both central to experience. Neither is primary; both are real and co-equal. Experience seeps and drifts and flows because of these relations.

Pluralism versus Monism

James's 1909 volume, *A Pluralistic Universe*, resulted from a series of lectures that he had given the year before at Manchester College, Oxford.[22] Once again, the lectures were written for a "popular" audience, a setting in which he was very effective. Although he had said that he wanted to write something more systematic, he was drawn back to the podium, perhaps by the honorarium, certainly by the prestige.[23] The subtitle of this volume was

The Present Situation in Philosophy, and it is clear from everything that he says that the central issue for him in contemporary philosophy was advancing the challenge to Idealism. As he writes to his brother Henry, he was "eager for the scalp of the Absolute" (C 3:360). He believed that contemporary philosophers, even at Oxford, were sensing a revolt. "Oxford, long the seed-bed, for the english world, of the idealism inspired by Kant and Hegel, has recently become the nursery of a very different way of thinking," he writes. Pluralism or humanism, rooted in "ancient english empiricism" but long considered less respectable than "nobler sounding germanic formulas" (PU 7), was recovering itself. He admits that Idealism had done good work, especially in its challenging of the excesses of Empiricism that had left a whole generation of philosophers feeling "as if it had fed on the chopped straw of psychology and of associationism long enough," and craving "a little vastness, even tho it went with vagueness." Particularly in the work of Thomas Hill Green, James notes, there was a challenge to "the crudity of the older english thinking, its ultra-simplicity of mind," and a "deepening of philosophic consciousness." This challenge had come to England from Germany, but, as he writes, it flourished in its new home without any "german technicality and shrillness." The thought of Green and his followers was able to remain "in the english fashion, devout." Green rejected "the disconnectedness of the reigning english sensationalism," and saw in Kant a means for overcoming the dominant Empiricism and fashioning a new school of philosophy, James continues, that then "reigned supreme at Oxford and in the scottish universities" (PU 8–9; cf. 16). Idealism, however, had excesses of its own, and he saw Pragmatism as the overall cure.

After setting the stage, James notes that there are, in general, two types of philosophy dominant in the West: Materialism and Spiritualism. He suggests further that these two philosophies have roots in "cynical" and "sympathetic" human temperaments respectively. Materialistic philosophy defines the world "so as to leave man's soul upon it as a sort of outside passenger or alien," while "the spiritual way of thinking" asserts that "the intimate and human must surround and underlie the brutal" (PU 15–16). Since Materialism—including the variants of Spencer and Huxley and Clifford—was not a viable opponent at Oxford, James does not consider it in these lectures. His discussion focuses, rather, on Spiritualism. It too has a number of variants, of which he is interested in two: "the more intimate one of which is monistic and the less intimate dualistic." The latter dualistic species of Spiritualism, which is theistic and prominent in scholastic philosophy, pictures "God and his creation as entities distinct from each other," and thus "leaves the human subject outside of the deepest reality in the universe." Since in this approach God and his creatures "have absolutely *nothing* in common," philosophic theism "makes us outsiders and keeps us foreigners in relation to God." As a result, God is not "heart of our heart and reason of our reason," but plays the role of "magistrate" and "mechanically to obey his commands, however strange they may be, remains our only moral duty" (*PU* 16–17). Because of the impacts of scientific evolutionism and social democratic ideals on our imaginations, however, "the older monarchical theism is obsolete or obsolescent," and he believes that people now seek a "more organic and intimate" interaction with the divine. James admits that, while "an external creator and his institutions may still be verbally confessed at church in formulas that linger by their mere inertia," there is no life for us there. As he writes, we want "a more intimate *weltanschauung*," a pantheism, "the vision of God as the indwellling divine rather than the external creator" that can offer us a sense of belonging to some larger whole. In good Emersonian fashion, he notes that "not to demand intimate relations with the universe, and not to wish them satisfactory, should be accounted signs of something wrong" (*PU* 18–20).[24] Instead of this dualistic Spiritualism, James advocates the former species of pantheistic Spiritualism. Still, he notes that monistic pantheism commonly maintains that the human can become "fully divine only in the form of totality," or what he calls "the *all*-form." He offers instead "the *each*-form," a pluralistic version of Pantheism that maintains that "there may ultimately never be an all-form at all, that the substance of reality may never get totally collected, that some of it may remain outside of the largest combination of it ever made." Thus, "a distributive form of reality" is as logically and empirically sound as a collective form (*PU* 20).

James continues that if we call the former the "philosophy of the absolute," we may call the latter pluralistic version "radical empiricism" (*PU* 20). Whereas the former asserts that "the divine exists authentically only when the world is experienced all at once in its absolute totality," radical empiricism grants that "the absolute sum-total of things may never be actually experienced or realized in that shape at all, and that a disseminated, distributed, or incompletely unified appearance is the only form that reality may yet have achieved" (*PU* 25).[25] Phrased more positively, he writes elsewhere that according to pluralism, "the truth is too great for any one actual mind, even though that mind be dubbed 'the Absolute,' to know the whole of it. The facts and worths of life need many cognizers to take them in" (*TT* 4; cf. *WB* 224).

Pluralism is initially encountered as a negative hypothesis,[26] James notes, contradicting the monistic belief "that there is absolutely *no* disconnection" within reality. As such, "the irreducible *outness* of *any*thing however infinitesimal, from *any*thing else, in *any* respect, would be enough, if it were solidly established, to ruin the monistic doctrine." He continues that, on this one criterion alone, monism surely must be rejected "for we find practical disconnections without number." As examples of such disconnections, he points to the fact that his "pocket is disconnected with Mr. [J. P.] Morgan's bank-account, and King Edward VIIth's mind is disconnected with this book" (*SPP* 62). James writes: "We can easily conceive of things that shall have no connexion whatever with each other. We may assume them to inhabit different times and spaces, as the dreams of different persons do even now. They may be so unlike and incommensurable, and so inert towards one another, as never to jostle or interfere. Even now there may actually be whole universes so disparate from ours that we who know ours have no means of perceiving that they exist." The connections that we find in existence are sometimes major, sometimes minor. "There is thus neither absolute oneness nor absolute manyness from the physical point of view," he continues, "but a mixture of well-definable modes of both." Thus, if our situation is to be accurately presented, we have to admit that "neither the oneness nor the manyness seems the more essential attribute." Rather, both are "co-ordinate features of the natural world" (*SPP* 66–67). There is also a temporal aspect, because Monism sees with an eternal eye. "If a thing were once disconnected," James writes, "it could never be connected again." Thus, he emphasizes the "pragmatic difference" between Pluralism and Monism: "if *a* is once out of sight of *b* or out of touch with it, or, more briefly, 'out' of it at all, then, according to monism, it must always remain so," and *a* and *b* can never connect; "whereas pluralism admits that on another occasion they may work together, or in some way be connected again." From the monistic point of view, however, there are "no such things as 'other occasions' in reality" (*PU* 146; cf. *SPP* 62–63). Pluralism, on the contrary, "triumphs over monism if the least morsel of disconnectedness is once found undeniably to exist. 'Ever not *quite*' is all it says to monism; while monism is obliged to prove that what pluralism asserts can in no amount whatever possibly be true—an infinitely harder task" (*SPP* 74; cf. *WB* 6–7).

James allows that Monism seems to have had a rhetorical or eulogistic advantage, and that there has been a long tradition of attempts to present something—for example, "Substance"—as the fundamental One. As he writes, Oneness offers to many "a *value*, an ineffable illustriousness and dignity upon the world, with which the conception of it as an irreducible 'many' is believed to clash." In addition, he notes that "a through-and-through noetic connexion of everything with absolutely everything else" is held by many to be a precondition of a rational world. "Only then might we believe that all things really do *belong* together, instead of being connected by the bare conjunctions 'with' or 'and.'" While James admits that pluralism may "make the world partly alogical, or non-rational, from a purely intellectual point of view," he is far more comfortable with such a world than with one that is "a consolidated unit, within which each member is determined by the whole to be just *that*, and from which the slightest incipiency of independence anywhere is ruled out" (*SPP* 71).[27]

Before exploring his own position further, James develops his critique of Absolute Idealism. Talking generally about the systematizing inclinations of most philosophy, he suggests that Pluralism has always suffered because it does not share the vision that philosophy should aim at "cleaning up the litter with which the world apparently is filled." In the place of such system, he admits that his pluralistic approach can offer only "a sorry appearance" which he describes as "a turbid, muddled, gothic sort of an affair, without a sweeping outline and with little pictorial nobility" (*PU* 26). The idealistic tradition, from Pythagoras and Plato onward, had always presented its systematizing aspect as its central value. Within the flux and chaos of daily living, Idealism uncovers the true thread of meaning—number or form or essence—concealed in experience.[28] In this process, however, Idealism demotes the remainder of experience to mere appearance. James, as we might suspect, finds a serious problem here, a problem that he names "'vicious intellectualism'" for the process of "*treating of a name as excluding from the fact named what the name's definition fails positively to include*" (*PU* 32).[29] In other words, as James sees the situation, Idealism constructs an intellectual system that is complete and necessary, and then mistakes its own creation for Reality. The negative side to the completeness that Absolutism offers, and to which James was particularly sensitive, is the fact that the role of the individual is not made secure. In its desire to be complete and compelling, Idealism presents the Absolute in the context of what he calls, as we saw in chapter 4, a "block-universe" in which all relations are internal (*PU* 147). He offers as an example the work of Bradley, which demonstrates an extreme "intolerance to pluralism." Bradley's philosophy contains throughout what James calls "the vice of intellectualism, for abstract terms are used by him as positively excluding all that their definition fails to include" (*PU* 36). In a similar fashion, James notes, Royce tells us that in our philosophical thinking "the only alternative we have is to chose the complete disunion of all things or their complete union in the absolute One" (*PU* 33).[30] All must be related in the Absolute, or we have chaos.[31]

If we step back a bit from attempting to understand James's view, we have to admit the inadequacy of his discussion of his idealist opponents. His presentation, of course, includes his prior assumptions that philosophies are personal visions (see *PU* 14–15), and that we require a plurality of approaches to get a fuller picture. He thus seems predisposed to reject in advance any absolute answer. Still, we recognize that his story is still too simple.[32] The post-Kantian idealist tradition is rich and diverse, with numerous thinkers and multiple interpretations of the thought of each of them.[33] In James's defense, it would not seem out of place to note that, in general, creative philosophers have seldom been able to fully understand other creative philosophers. (This recognition, in fact, would seem to be a corollary of James's ideas). His Darwinian approach at least offers us a reason why disagreements are so prominent — unlike others who comfortably assert that their opponents are simply wrong.[34] Despite his weaknesses, however, we can take James to be an accurate witness to his own personal situation, and the way that Absolute Idealism affected him.

Turning from these monistic forms of Spiritualism, or absolutistic forms of Idealism, James wants to develop a pluralistic philosophy that is more faithful to experience, however messy and open-ended that philosophy turns out to be. He makes a number of points. The first is a defense of "the flux of sensible experience" to provide a rationality that has been neglected in the midst of the systematizations of Rationalism. Far better would it be to trust experience than to retreat to "the pseudo-rationality of the supposed absolute point of view." Secondly, there are, from his perspective, levels of rationality: relations can be of all sorts, and the final product need not be all-inclusive. While he grants that "the universe must be rational," he still wonders what "that eulogistic but ambiguous word" means. For the absolutists, "rationality is one and indivisible: if not rational thus indivisibly, the universe must be completely irrational, and no shadings or mixtures or compromises can obtain." For James, on the contrary, there are "degrees in rationality" and "things can be consistent or coherent in very diverse ways" (*PU* 38–39). In a similar fashion, chance need not mean chaos. He writes that "if chance is spoken of as an ingredient of the universe, absolutists interpret it to mean that double sevens are as likely to be thrown out of a dice box as double sixes are." The pluralist rejects the notion that "the only categories inwardly consistent and therefore pertinent to reality are 'all' and 'none,'" and defends "the legitimacy of the notion of *some*: each part of the world is in some ways connected, in some other ways not connected with its other parts." Finally, James maintains that there are external as well as internal relations. He thus rejects the absolutist claim that "all the relations with other things, possible to a being, are pre-included in its intrinsic nature and enter into its essence," and he defends the view that at least some relations are external. As an example, he offers the copy of his lecture on the desk. "The relation of being 'on' doesn't seem to implicate or involve in any way the inner meaning of the manuscript or the inner structure of the desk," he writes, "these objects engage in it only by their outsides, it seems only a temporary accident in their respective histories" (*PU* 40–41; cf. *ERE* 140–41).

The eventual focus of James's critique of Idealism is Hegel, in his eyes the original propounder of the view that there must be an all-encompassing Absolute. Despite numerous criticisms that are present here and there in his works—for example, his rejection of Hegel's "abominable habits of speech" (*PU* 44; cf. *PP* 1:254–55; *SPP* 51) and of his excessive use of "the apodictic words *must be* rather than ... those inferior hypothetic words *may be*" (*PU* 50)—James, who had learned much about the Hegelian approach from heretics like Royce and apostates like Dewey, had a healthy amount of respect for Hegel.[35] James tells us that there are two aspects of Hegel's thought that merit particular consideration, his "vision" and his "technique." Hegel's vision was "of a world in which reason holds all things in solution and accounts for all the irrationality that superficially appears by taking it up as a 'moment' into itself"; his technique was "the so-called dialectic method" (*PU* 43). James believes that the former aspect is valuable and, if we focus on it, we will learn a great deal. If we are not careful, however, the latter aspect will suck us into the inescapable "whirlpool" of Absolute Idealism (*EP* 174; cf. *WB* 204, 216).

On the one hand, James finds in Hegel—as he finds in Darwin—a clear recognition of the provisionality of human existence. "The impression that any naif person gets who plants himself innocently in the flux of things is that things are off their balance" (*PU* 44). Natural disasters, social crises, intellectual puzzles, and religious doubts all challenge our well-being. "Of no special system of good attained does the universe recognize the value as sacred," he writes. "Down it tumbles, over it goes, to feed the ravenous appetite for destruction of the larger system of history in which it stood for a moment as a landing-place and stepping-stone." What he calls "this dogging of everything by its negative . . . this perpetual moving on to something future which shall supersede the present" is Hegel's recognition of "the essential provisionality, and consequent unreality, of everything empirical and finite." So far, James writes, "Hegel is not only harmless, but accurate." Our study of "the whole constitution of concrete life" reveals process. Unfortunately, he continues, "Hegel saw this undeniable characteristic of the world we live in in a non-empirical light," and thus allows the world of "sensible facts" to fall victim to "the conceptual way of treating them" (*PU* 45–46). James continues: "Clinging as he did to the vision of a really living world, and refusing to be content with a chopped-up intellectualist picture of it, it is a pity that he should have adopted the very word that intellectualism had already pre-empted. But he clung fast to the old rationalist contempt for the immediately given world of sense and all its squalid particulars, and never tolerated the notion that the form of philosophy might be empirical only" (*PU* 46). James thus praises Hegel "as a reporter of certain empirical aspects of the actual," but he complains that Hegel set as his goal "being something far greater than an empirical reporter" (*PU* 49–50). Further, James maintains that Hegel's vision, freed from his own restrictive machinery, is clearly pluralistic. The dialectical movement in things "can be described and accounted for in terms of the pluralistic vision of things far more naturally than in the monistic terms to which Hegel finally reduced it." This pluralism emphasizes context and environment, that everything exists in "a surrounding world of other things," where it meets "with friction and opposition from its neighbors" (*PU* 45; cf. *WB* 214–17).

For James, Absolute Idealism sees the world as a place of change and decay, and ultimately chaos, unless it is explained by means of a Oneness that preserves its "rationality." While granting, as we saw in chapter 3, that "men are once for all so made that they prefer a rational world to believe in and to live in" (*PU* 54–55), he rejects the absolutist version of rationality as the only one possible. In fact, he maintains that "the hypothesis of the absolute ... from the intellectual point of view, remains decidedly irrational" (*PU* 60), because it mistakenly commits us to an intellectual resolution of the problem of evil. The assumption of the Absolute "introduces a speculative 'problem of evil,'" he writes, that forces us to wonder "why the perfection of the absolute should require just such particular hideous forms of life as darken the day for our human imaginations." If these evils were forced upon the Absolute from outside, we might be able to accept them, even though we would be unwilling to present the situation "as the most rational one conceivable." Our situation is different, however, and "the absolute is represented as a being without environment, upon which nothing alien can be forced, and which has spontaneously chosen from within to give itself the spectacle of all that evil rather than a spectacle with less evil in it" (*PU* 57). In a pluralistic metaphysic, on the contrary, James continues, "the problems that evil presents are practical, not speculative," and our concern is not "why evil should exist at all, but how we can lessen the actual amount of it" (*PU* 60; cf. *SPP* 72). Or, as he had written in *Pragmatism*, the way to escape from evil is "*not* by getting it 'aufgehoben' [transcended]" or by claiming that "the absolute makes all good things certain, and all bad things impossible" (*P* 142, 135), but by creating a world in which evil plays a lesser role.

In summary, James urges us to recognize "that the absolute is not forced on our belief by logic, that it involves features of irrationality peculiar to itself, and that a thinker to whom it does not come as an 'immediate certainty' ... is in no way bound to treat it as anything but an emotionally rather sublime hypothesis." In the place of this Monism, he defends what he calls "the strung-along unfinished world in time." What he calls "the anti-absolutist hypothesis" is simply the assumption that *"reality* MAY *exist in distributive form, in the shape not of an all but of a set of eaches, just as it seems to."* This distributive version of reality has the clear advantage of appearing in the experience of everyone, he indicates, "whereas the absolute has as yet appeared immediately to only a few mystics, and indeed to them very ambiguously" (*PU* 62). Pluralism thus insists upon "taking perceptual experience at its face-value," and placing "conceptual abstractions" in a secondary place. While we cannot "*explain* conceptually *how* genuine novelties can come," we certainly can experience *that* they come. "We do in fact experience perceptual novelties all the while." For James, the *thats* of perceptual experience are thus more trustworthy than the *whys* of conceptual reason. "So the common-sense view of life, as something really dramatic, with work done, and things decided here and now, is acceptable to pluralism." Moreover, Pluralism, because it accepts the universe "unfinished, with doors and windows open to possibilities uncontrollable in advance, gives us less religious uncertainty than monism, with its absolutely closed-in world" (*SPP* 73).

In James's pluralistic understanding of knowing, "everything in the world might be known by somebody, yet not everything by the same knower, or in one single cognitive act." What he calls this "concatenated knowing" is unlike the "consolidated knowing" that is the trademark of the Absolute, and while it yields "a coherent type of universe," that universe remains one "in which the widest knower that exists may yet remain ignorant of much that is known to others" (*SPP* 68–69). This gives us a world that is "'one' in some respects, and 'many' in others." This is what "oneness" pragmatically means for James, and "a world coherent in any of these ways would be no chaos but a universe of such or such a grade." This, he writes, "is the *cash-value* of the world's unity, empirically realized." It has a "total unity," but that unity is "the sum of all the partial unities." James admits that this pluralistic approach "outrages rationalistic minds, which habitually despise all this practical small-change." Monism insists upon "a deeper, more through-and-through union of all things in the absolute, 'each in all and all in each,' as the *prior condition* of these empirically ascertained connexions." For him, however, these intellectual demands represent "the usual worship of abstractions, like calling 'bad weather' the cause of to-day's rain, etc., or accounting for a man's features by his 'face,' when really the rain *is* the bad weather, is what you *mean* by 'bad weather,' just as the features are what you mean by the face" (*SPP* 70).

Pluralism on Its Own

James rejects the materialistic view that we are alone in the world, as well as the dualistic theistic view that we are isolated or cut off from our source of meaning. Further, he maintains that the Absolute that Hegel and his followers had developed was a mistaken formulation that at best approximated the truth. At this point, he shifts the focus of *A Pluralistic Universe* away from attacking the Absolute, which he believes has "crumbled in our hands" (*PU*

63), toward constructing his pluralistic alternative. In doing so, he introduces material that suggests a way to understand our place in existence that was more novel to his Oxford audience. In the positive half of the volume, James supplements his own thoughts with similar ideas from a German and a French thinker, perhaps to simplify the task for his listeners (and readers). The German thinker is Gustav Fechner—virtually forgotten today—who proposed a panpsychism that offered a fuller elaboration of what James had designated as the "more." The French thinker was Henri Bergson—somewhat better known then and now—whose presentation of experience was in close accord with James's distinction of percepts and concepts.

Chapter 4 examines aspects of the thought of Gustav Theodor Fechner (1801–87), a physician with interests in physics and experimental psychology. James had presented Fechner unfavorably on several occasions in *The Principles*,[36] but later he came to view Fechner as "a philosopher in the 'great' sense of the term" (*ERM* 117) and a fellow seeker after answers to the larger questions of human meaning.[37] James notes that in his late thirties Fechner suffered "a terrific attack of nervous prostration with painful hyperaesthesia of all the functions, from which he suffered three years, cut off entirely from active life." James believed that advances in medicine by his day could have treated Fechner's condition, but half a century earlier, "it was treated as a visitation incomprehensible in its malignity, and when he suddenly began to get well, both Fechner and others treated the recovery as a sort of divine miracle." In any case, James continues, this bout of illness brought Fechner "face to face with inner desperation" and "made a great crisis in his life." James then quotes Fechner: "'Had I not then clung to the faith . . . that clinging to faith would somehow or other work its reward, *so hätte ich jene zeit nicht ausgehalten*' [I would not have made it through]" (*PU* 69).[38] Fechner believed that his faith had saved him, and that he was directed to communicate its power to the world.

Fechner worked at the amorphous intersection of philosophy, psychology, and panpsychism. At the core of his thought is the belief that the entirety of being is alive and in some sense conscious. James emphasizes, as he did with Hegel, that Fechner's vision is more important than his technique. "Few professorial philosophers have any vision," he writes; Fechner did, however, and "that is why one can read him over and over again, and each time bring away a fresh sense of reality" (*PU* 77). James continues that

Fechner's philosophy is "thick" rather than "thin" (see *PU* 64–65), and that it presents "'the daylight-view'" rather than "the night-view." This "daylight-view" is "the anti-materialistic view,—the view that the entire material universe, instead of being dead, is inwardly alive and consciously animated" (*ERM* 117).[39] James notes that Fechner's means for presenting this daylight view is analogy. There is "not a rationalistic argument is to be found in all his many pages—only reasonings like those which men continually use in practical life." For example, if a house requires a builder, then so does the world; if a body moves under some direction of feelings and the will, then so must "the sun, moon, sea, and wind." James greatly appreciates his power to perceive analogies, and he points as well to Fechner's ability to recognize disanalogies. "Most of us," James writes, "reasoning justly that since all the minds we know are connected with bodies, therefore God's mind should be connected with a body, proceed to suppose that the body must be an animal body over again, and so paint an altogether human picture of God." All that is required, however, is some sort of body, and "if God have a physical body at all, it must be utterly different from ours in structure" (*PU* 71).

"Throughout his writings Fechner makes difference and analogy walk abreast," James continues, "and by his extraordinary power of noticing both, he converts what would ordinarily pass for objections to his conclusions into factors of their support." One particular point that he wants to draw out of his brief survey of Fechner's thought is the analogy that the relation of our senses to our consciousness is like the relation of human lives to a higher life. Another point is that our body is related to our soul as the world is related to God. James writes:

> The vaster orders of mind go with the vaster orders of body. The entire earth on which we live must have, according to Fechner, its own collective consciousness. So must each sun, moon, and planet; so must the whole solar system have its own wider consciousness, in which the consciousness of our earth plays one part. So has the entire starry system as such its consciousness; and if that starry system be not the sum of all that *is*, materially considered, then that whole system, along with whatever else may be, is the body of that absolutely totalized consciousness of the universe to which men give the name of God.

James continues that in Fechner's theological universe there is room "for every grade of spiritual being between man and the final all-inclusive God." Further, Fechner believes in an "earth-soul" and "he treats the earth as our special human guardian angel" to which we can pray "as men pray to their saints." Fechner's Supreme Being is "left thin and abstract in his majesty," James notes, "men preferring to carry on their personal transactions with the many less remote and abstract messengers and mediators whom the divine order provides" (PU 71–72).[40] Continuing on in this spirit, James notes that "visual consciousness goes with our eyes, tactile consciousness with our skin." Even though "neither skin nor eye knows aught of the sensations of the other," still these sensations combine themselves "in the more inclusive consciousness which each of us names his *self*." In a similar fashion, Fechner supposes that "my consciousness of myself and yours of yourself, altho in their immediacy they keep separate and know nothing of each other, are yet known and used together in a higher consciousness, that of the human race, say, into which they enter as constituent parts" (PU 72). Individual persons thus function as "so many sense-organs of the earth's soul." When an individual dies, "all *perceptive* contributions from that particular quarter cease," but "the memories and conceptual relations" that have resulted from that individual's contributions continue on "in the larger earth-life" just as "our own distinct objects of thought, once stored in memory, form new relations and develop throughout our whole finite life" (PU 79; cf. EPR 358). It would seem unnecessary at this point to note that, while the suggestive power of analogy is strong, its evidentiary value is minimal. Of course, Fechner's position might be true. James notes that it is certainly "not without direct empirical verification" (PU 139), although this is a standard that would hardly satisfy Clifford or Peirce. Nor, I believe, should it satisfy us.[41]

Chapter 6 of *A Pluralistic Universe* explores aspects of the thought of Henri Bergson (1859–1941). Bergson, a mathematically trained professor of philosophy, was a correspondent and friend of James, and James praises him for his originality and clarity. (As in the case of Fechner, James would seem to be praising Bergson for qualities that he himself also demonstrates.)[42] Like James, Bergson strongly emphasized a distinction between intellect and intuition, between the conceptual or symbolic and the immediate. Bergson writes:

philosophers, in spite of their apparent divergencies, agree in distinguishing two profoundly different ways of knowing a thing. The first implies that we move round the object; the second that we enter into it. The first depends on the point of view at which we are placed and on the symbols by which we express ourselves. The second neither depends on a point of view nor relies on any symbol. The first kind of knowledge may be said to stop at the *relative*; the second, in those cases where it is possible, to attain the *absolute*.[43]

Bergson's "relative knowledge" corresponds to what James calls "knowledge about"; his "absolute knowledge," to James's "knowledge by acquaintance."

One way to enter into Bergson's thought is through his analysis of Zeno's paradox and the problem of time. In a race between Achilles and a tortoise, Zeno maintains that Achilles can never catch the tortoise. The reason, James notes, is simple: "if space and time are infinitely divisible . . . by the time Achilles reaches the tortoise's starting-point, the tortoise has already got ahead of *that* starting-point, and so on *ad infinitum*" (PU 102–3; cf. SPP 81–82). Thus, although in Zeno's conceptual world Achilles might be forever getting closer, he will never catch up. As we all know, however, things work differently in the perceptual world of experience and action, where mail gets delivered and assassins sometimes succeed, where tomatoes ripen and children come home after school. In our world, the tortoise stands no chance of winning. The reason is that the "minimal pulses of experience"—unlike concepts—"run into one another continuously and seem to interpenetrate," James writes. These pulses of experience are "pent in by no such definite limits as our conceptual substitutes for them are confined by" (PU 127–28; cf. ERE 46–47; EP 76–77).

The paradox here is rooted in how we understand time. James writes that, for Bergson, time can be approached either scientifically or experientially. James suggests that we consider the elapsing of a period of twenty seconds scientifically:

> If time be infinitely divisible, and it must be so on intellectualist principles, they [the twenty seconds] simply cannot elapse, their end cannot be reached; for no matter how much of them

has already elapsed, before the remainder, however minute, can have wholly elapsed, the earlier half of it must first have elapsed. And this ever-rearising need of making the earlier half elapse *first* leaves time with always something to do *before* the last thing is done, so that the last thing never gets done. Expressed in bare numbers, it is like the convergent series ½ plus ¼ plus ⅛ . . . , of which the limit is one. But this limit, simply because it is a limit, stands outside the series, the value of which approaches it indefinitely but never touches it.

If we leave this intellectualism behind and return to the experiential world, however, James reminds us that "nature doesn't make eggs by making first half an egg, then a quarter, then an eighth, etc., and adding them together." On the contrary, nature "either makes a whole egg at once or none at all, and so of all her other units." To offer another example, he notes that "if a bottle had to be emptied by an infinite number of successive decrements, it is mathematically impossible that the emptying should ever positively terminate." In fact, he continues, "bottles and coffee-pots empty themselves by a finite number of decrements, each of definite amount. Either a whole drop emerges or nothing emerges from the spout." For James, then, all of our immediate experience comes to us "in drops." Moreover, "time itself comes in drops" (*PU* 103–4).[44]

Thus, for Bergson and James, scientific time and experiential time are not the same, and the experienced world of perception cannot be understood fully using an abstract conceptual or mathematical model. James recognizes that successful human living requires some—maybe a great deal of—conceptualization. "We of course need a stable scheme of concepts, stably related with one another," he writes, "to lay hold of our experiences and to co-ordinate them withal." Moreover, on the occasion when an experience strikes us "with sufficient saliency to stand out," we preserve the idea of it for future situations: we "store it in our conceptual system." Our conceptual system thus becomes more complete and the new realities that we encounter are then "named after and conceptually strung upon this or that element of the scheme which we have already established." James notes that one of the great practical values of such an "abstract scheme" is that "the same identical terms and relations in it can always be recovered and referred to—change itself is just such an unalterable concept." These conceptual moments remain, however, abstractions from the flow of experience. He continues that, "as flowers gathered, they are only moments dipped out from the stream of time, snap-shots taken, as by a kinetoscopic camera, at a life that in its original coming is continuous." But we will be unable, by means of these snapshots, to explain "what makes any single phenomenon be or go ... for you cannot make continuous being out of discontinuities, and your concepts are discontinuous." It is the nature of change that it "inhabits what your definition fails to gather up, and thus eludes conceptual explanation altogether" (*PU* 105–6; cf. *VRE* 395).[45]

James believes that philosophers, as we have seen, have a tendency to forget that these concepts are our pragmatic constructs, and to treat them as Reality. "The ruling tradition in philosophy," he writes, "has always been the platonic and aristotelian belief that fixity is a nobler and worthier thing than change." Reality thus is "one and unalterable." Only concepts, themselves "fixities," can match "the fixed nature of truth," and "for any knowledge of ours to be quite true it must be knowledge by universal concepts rather than by particular experiences, for these notoriously are mutable and corruptible" (*PU* 106). Philosophers are so used to what he calls "the conceptual decomposition of life" that James fears that challenging it will be seen as "putting muddiest confusion in place of clearest thought, and relapsing into a molluscoid state of mind." Still, he does challenge the presumed superiority of any intellectual approach if it predicts "impossibility in tasks which sense-experience so easily performs." While the flow of life is fragmented by "retrospective conception," this flow is primary. It is important to recognize that the smallest portion of experience has "its quality, its duration, its extension, its intensity, its urgency, its clearness, and many aspects besides." Further, none of these aspects can manage to exist "in the isolation in which our verbalized logic keeps it." They are able to exist, he writes, "only *durcheinander* [in confusion]" (*PU* 114). He continues:

> Terms like A and C appear to be connected by intermediaries, by B for example. Intellectualism calls this absurd, for "B-connected-with-A" is, "as such," a different term from "B-connected-with-C." But real life laughs at logic's veto. Imagine a heavy log which takes two men to carry it. First A and B take it. Then C takes hold and A drops off; the D takes hold and B drops off, so that C and D now bear it; and so on. The log meanwhile never drops,

> and keeps its sameness throughout the journey. Even so it is with all our experiences. Their changes are not complete annihilations followed by complete creations of something absolutely novel. There is partial decay and partial growth, and all the while a nucleus of relative constancy from which what decays drop off, and which takes into itself whatever is grafted on, until at length something wholly different has taken its place. (*PU* 115)

It is in this sense that James can describe the Absolute as an unnecessary solution to an unreal problem. As he puts it, they have "invoked the absolute" as "the peculiar inner form" that can "overcome the contradictions with which intellectualism has found the finite many as such to be infected" (*PU* 133).

For James, as we saw in chapter 4, the conceptual or intellectualist approach feeds into the unresolvable split between traditional Rationalism and traditional Empiricism. Each side treats "intellectualist logic" as "authoritative": "the absolutists smashing the world of sense by its means, the empiricists smashing the absolute—for the absolute, they say, is the quintessence of all logical contradictions." He notes that Bergson, however, challenges this intellectualist approach, denying that "mere conceptual logic can tell us what is impossible or possible in the world of being or fact" (*PU* 108–9). He maintains that this view is not an instance of irrationalism;[46] both he and Bergson defend the primacy of logic in its proper sphere. "In the first place, logic, giving primarily the relations between concepts as such, and the relations between natural facts only secondarily or so far as the facts have been already identified with concepts and defined by them, must of course stand or fall with the conceptual method." Still, this does not constitute the whole of our access to the world. James continues that "to understand life by concepts is to arrest its movement, cutting it up into bits as if with scissors, and immobilizing these in our logical herbarium where, comparing them as dried specimens, we can ascertain which of them statistically includes or excludes which other" (*PU* 109).[47] Too often, he continues, concepts "fail to connect us with the inner life of the flux, or with the causes that govern its direction." Rather than functioning as "interpreters of reality," these concepts "negate the inwardness of reality altogether." For the pragmatist James, however, our intellectual life should serve our practical life. He writes that Bergson also insists that "the function of the intellect is practical rather than theoretical." Our world of novelties and problems is too complex to be managed one particular at a time. If we use just our perceptions, "to get from one point in it to another we have to plough or wade through the whole intolerable interval." But with "our faculty of abstracting and fixing concepts," we can move instantaneously, "skipping the intermediaries as by a divine winged power, and getting at the exact point we require without entanglement with any context" (*PU* 110–11).

Still, there is a cost to be paid for this wondrous power. As James writes, "theoretic knowledge, which is knowledge *about* things, as distinguished from living contemplation or sympathetic acquaintance with them, touches only the outer surface of reality." This outer surface can be as expansive as the mind can manage—"it may dot the whole diameter of space and time with its conceptual creations"—but it travels only on the surface and "does not penetrate a millimeter into the solid dimension." The "inner dimension of reality" is available only through direct experience. "Thought deals thus solely with surfaces," he continues. "It can name the thickness of reality, but it cannot fathom it, and its insufficiency here is essential and permanent, not temporary." Thus, for Bergson as for James, intellectual knowledge is ultimately the inferior sort. "Instead of being the only adequate knowledge, it is grossly inadequate, and its only superiority is the practical one of enabling us to make short cuts through experience and thereby to save time" (*PU* 111–12). James continues: "Dive back into the flux itself, then, Bergson tells us, if you wish to *know* reality, that flux which platonism, in its strange belief that only the immutable is excellent, has always spurned; turn your face towards sensation, that flesh-bound thing which rationalism has always loaded with abuse" (*PU* 113). Sounding as much like Emerson as anyone else—although he continues to call upon Bergson—James continues that we must experience life fully and directly and perceptually. "The only way in which to apprehend reality's thickness is either to experience it directly by being a part of reality one's self, or to evoke it in imagination by sympathetically divining some one else's inner life" (*PU* 112).

Human life requires the use of both concepts and percepts. On the one hand, "what we thus immediately experience or concretely divine is very limited in duration"; on the other, by conceptual abstraction, "we are able to conceive eternities." James continues that "direct acquaintance and conceptual knowledge are thus complementary of each other; each remedies the other's defects." Our focus at any given moment will be determined by the task that we have before us. "If what we care most about be the synoptic treatment of phenomena, the vision of the far and the gathering of the scattered like, we must follow the conceptual method." If, on the other hand, we are metaphysicians, "we are more curious about the inner nature of reality or about what really *makes it go*, we must turn our backs upon our winged concepts altogether, and bury ourselves in the thickness of those passing moments over the surface of which they fly, and on particular points of which they occasionally rest and perch" (*PU* 112). Our conceptual schemes are "discontinuous and fixed," and they present life only to the extent that it too is discontinuous and fixed. Using another metaphor, he notes that "you can no more dip up the substance of reality" with concepts "than you can dip up water with a net, however finely meshed." We speak, for example, of past, present, and future as distinct concepts; in terms of experience, however, "the literally present moment is a purely verbal supposition, not a position; the only present ever realized concretely being the 'passing moment' in which the dying rearward of time and its dawning future forever mix their lights" (*PU* 113).

Once we have broken up reality "into concepts" we cannot "reconstruct it in its wholeness," James writes. "Out of no amount of discreteness can you manufacture the concrete." The conceptual approach represents "a retrospective patchwork, a post-mortem dissection," that "can follow any order we find most expedient." Moreover, James maintains that unless we live full perceptual lives, we cannot even understand conceptualized philosophies. He writes that, if we can place ourselves "at the centre of a man's philosophic vision," we will be able to understand the fullness of this position. On the one hand, if we approach this view from the "outside," using our "post-mortem method," trying "to build the philosophy up out of the single phrases, taking first one and then another and seeking to make them fit 'logically,'" we will surely fail. From the "outside," we will "crawl over the thing like a myopic ant over a building, tumbling into every microscopic crack or fissure, finding nothing but inconsistencies, and never suspecting that a centre exists" (*PU* 116–17).

The process by means of which individuals conceptualize their flowing experience guarantees that the history of philosophy will never come to an end: each philosophical vision is a personal simplification.[48] We recognize from the complexity of human experiences, James writes, "that the world can be handled according to many systems of ideas, and is so handled by different men, and will each time give some characteristic kind of profit, for which he cares, to the handler, while at the same time some other kind of profit has to be omitted or postponed" (*VRE* 104–5). Regardless of whatever we manage to incorporate into any philosophical system, there is always something left out, some remainder, a "more," and, however broadly we treat what we have included, there remain other ways to treat it. He wants an account of the world that recognizes this radical plurality. While monism "insists that when you come down to reality as such, to the reality of realities, everything is present to *everything* else in one vast instantaneous co-implicated completeness," pluralism requires "only that the sundry parts of reality *may be externally related.*" Relations are multifarious. "Things are 'with' one another in many ways, but nothing includes everything, or dominates over everything," James writes. "The word 'and' trails along after every sentence." Regardless of how careful we are in our formulations, something will manage to escape, and our attempts to attain "all-inclusiveness" will continue to fall short. As pluralists, however, our accounts of reality cannot go beyond "what we ourselves find empirically realized in every minimum of finite life," and must recognize that "nothing real is absolutely simple ... every smallest bit of experience is a *multum in parvo* [much in little] plurally related" (*PU* 145). Pluralism can thus accept a reality as it presents itself in experience. James describes this pluralism as "the each-form" or distributive form, in contrast with "the all-form or collective-unit form" of monism, and since the each-form is "the eternal form of reality" as well as the form of "temporal appearance," our world remains coherent, despite the criticisms of absolutists (*PU* 146).[49] "Our 'multiverse' still makes a 'universe,'" he writes, "for every part, tho it may not be in actual or immediate connexion, is nevertheless in some possible or mediated connexion, with every other part however remote, through the fact that each part hangs together with its very next neighbors in inextricable interfusion." The sort of union that James is recognizing is neither "the monistic type of *alleinheit* [all-inclusiveness]," nor "a universal co-implication, or integration of all things *durcheinander.*" His pluralistic sort of union is "the strung-along type, the type of continuity, contiguity, or concatenation" (*PU* 146–47) that has numerous implications, including those for his ethical and social thought.

CHAPTER 6

Ethics and Social Thought

This chapter considers the nature and importance of James's moral thinking. It begins with his 1891 essay, "The Moral Philosopher and the Moral Life," in which he addresses fundamental aspects of moral living. A background theme in this essay, which becomes more prominent in two 1899 essays, "On a Certain Blindness in Human Beings" and "What Makes a Life Significant," is his dual emphasis on advancing personal fulfillment and on respecting the life plans of others. His goal in all three essays is to attempt to forge a community of tolerance based on recognizing and overcoming our animal partiality. Next, a few instances of his approach to specific moral problems will be considered. Finally, in the last of his central ethical essays, "The Moral Equivalent of War" of 1910, we see him exploring the issues of violence and warfare from a social-psychological, rather than from a political, standpoint. James admits that the roots of our militarism are to be found in the inherited tendencies of human nature, but he offers a possibility for discharging these violent impulses through socially valuable struggles to modify our natural environment. A consideration of these themes makes clear the value of his ethical writings for helping us to understand more about ourselves, about our attempts at bettering human existence, and about the complex nature of morality itself.

Philosophy and the Moral Life

James begins the essay, "The Moral Philosopher and the Moral Life," with an explicit statement of its aims. "The main purpose of this paper," he writes, "is to show that there is no such thing possible as an ethical philosophy dogmatically made up in advance." On the contrary, he continues, by means of our ongoing contributions to "the race's moral life" each of us helps "to determine the content of ethical philosophy." As a result, we should anticipate no final truths in ethics "any more than in physics, until the last man has had his experience and said his say" (*WB* 141). James then separates his larger topic into a series of three questions. The first, or psychological, question explores the origins of our opinions about right and wrong. The second, or metaphysical, question—what is now called the meta-ethical question—examines the meanings of ethical terms. Finally, the casuistic question considers how we evaluate particular actions as either right or wrong.

We can begin with the metaphysical question, and consider the meaning of ethical terms. The answer that James offers is naturalistic: morality is not a supernatural matter to be discussed in terms of such notions as "God's will" or "sin" or "damnation." Morality is, rather, a matter of human wellbeing. He rejects as "absurd" the notion that events can be right or wrong in themselves. "Can murders and treacheries," he wonders, "considered as mere outward happenings, or motions of matter, be bad without anyone to feel their badness?" For that matter, he continues, "could paradise properly be good in the absence of a sentient principle by which the goodness was perceived?" (*WB* 129). In an insentient world, he continues, there could be no "*status*" for good or for evil because no "physical fact, considered simply as a physical fact" can be better than any other (*WB* 145). In a world of conscious beings, however, in a world of pleasure and pain, right and wrong do play a central role.[1]

James begins by considering a world with one conscious being. When such a person enters the universe, "there is a chance for goods and evils really to exist." In that individual's consciousness, morality has a place. In so far as this individual "feels anything to be good, he *makes* it good. It *is* good, for him, and being good for him, is absolutely good, for he is the sole creator of values in that universe, and outside of his opinion things have no moral character at all." There is thus no "good or right except so far as some consciousness feels it to be good or thinks it to be right," and, in a world of only one sentient being experiencing pleasure and pain, that individual's role is that of "a sort of divinity, subject to no higher judge" (*WB* 145–47; cf. *ML* 184–85). When we consider a world with multiple sentient beings, however, the moral situation is far more complex. In such a world, one like ours, where there is a flood of various claims that exist independently of—and often in conflict with—each other, decisions about right and wrong are much harder. James notes that philosophers are often troubled by this apparent moral chaos, and in response they attempt to develop some system to order the various claims. By examining the different ideals, philosophers hope to uncover "some which have the more truth or authority; and to these the others *ought* to yield, so that system and subordination may reign" (WB 147).

The principle that James advocates is the democratic principle of inclusiveness. He offers this principle in a pair of interrelated assertions: *"without a claim actually made by some concrete person there can be no obligation,"* and *"there is some obligation wherever there is a claim"* (WB 148). Thus, all claims of sentient beings are to be taken seriously, and no other claim counts. "Whether a God exist, or whether no God exist, in yon blue heaven above us bent, we form at any rate an ethical republic here below" (WB 150). We can now offer James's answer to the metaphysical question: "right" and "wrong" refer to the satisfaction or nonsatisfaction of the demands of earthly sentient beings, especially humans.[2]

Next we can consider what James calls the casuistic question. He means here not "casuistry," the meticulous and often self-serving thinking that seeks to bend general moral principles around particular actions. His focus is the application of moral ideas to particular situations that we now call normative ethics. For example, under what circumstances might killing be moral, or what obligations might the rich have to the poor. As we have seen, philosophers want some sort of moral order to organize thinking about the varieties of human action into a respectable whole, and over the course of the centuries, they have proposed many possible moral systems. James lists just a few of them: "to be a mean between two extremes; to be recognized by a special intuitive faculty; to make the agent happy for the moment; to make others as well as him happy in the long run; to add to his perfection or dignity; to harm no one; to follow from reason or flow from universal law; to be in accordance with the will of God; to promote the survival of the human species on the planet." Collectively, all of these systems, and others, constitute "so many tests, each of which has been maintained by somebody to constitute the essence of all good things or actions so far as they are good" (WB 152).

For his part, James interprets all of these systems as more or less adequate attempts to articulate what he has already suggested under his principle of inclusion, "the *most* universal principle—that *the essence of good is simply to satisfy demand*" (*WB* 153). Assuming that "everything which is demanded is by that fact a good," it would follow that "the guiding principle for ethical philosophy (since all demands conjointly cannot be satisfied in this poor world)" must be "simply to satisfy at all times *as many demands as we can.*" If this is so, then the act is best that "makes for the *best whole,* in the sense of awakening the least sum of dissatisfactions." Further, he notes that "those ideals must be written highest which *prevail at the least cost,* or by whose realization the least possible number of other ideals are destroyed" (*WB* 155). There is, of course, the problem that, while all demands might be satisfied in an ideal world, in our world many goods are denied. "The actually possible in this world is vastly narrower than all that is demanded," he writes, "and there is always a *pinch* between the ideal and the actual which can only be got through by leaving part of the ideal behind" (*WB* 153; cf. *ML* 185).

James believes that we are ourselves largely responsible for many of the unsatisfied demands of others because we are all habituated into particular systems of moral ideas that skew our thinking away from the inclusive ideal that he is proposing. Each of us, he writes, grows up in a society of economic and ethnic and religious practices "whose ideals are largely ordered already." As we are enculturated and as we enculturate, our tendency is to follow "the ideal which is conventionally highest," and to trample the others. As he puts it, "our environment encourages us not to be philosophers but partisans" (*WB* 154). As products of our inherited moral environment, we come to believe that this religion is good and that one bad, that the economy has only one proper arrangement, and that various types of entertainment are proper and others unacceptable. There is, sadly, cultural pressure against even thinking about such matters, or listening to any contradictory demands. Further, instead of fostering tolerance, we attempt to indoctrinate others by creating a wider world that reflects our values—whether they be pet-friendly or bicycle-friendly or gun-friendly—so that our goods will live on.

Because we are partisans of our own moral visions, James continues, no one should be appointed moral dictator over the lives of others. He notes that even our moral saints "must not only be insensible, but be ludicrously and peculiarly insensible, to many goods." As philosophers, fighting to prevent values that they recognize from being "submerged and lost from out of life," these individuals perform a vital function, but, "as schoolmasters deciding what all must think," and attempting "to substitute the content of their clean-shaven systems" for broader visions, or "as pontiffs" able to assert their "temporal powers," these purifying moralists too often attempt to determine "which good shall be butchered and which shall be suffered to survive." From his point of view, he thinks that it would be better to live in the midst of moral chaos rather than in "an order based on any closet-philosopher's rule, even though he were the most enlightened possible member of his tribe" (*WB* 154–55).

What saves James from the pessimism of anticipated moral stagnation here is his belief that there is a progressive development to our shared moral lives. He believes that over time we have the possibility of becoming less partisan, and of learning better how to listen to others.[3] "The course of history," he writes, "is nothing but the story of men's struggles from generation to generation to find the more and more inclusive order." In our search for greater ideals that would incorporate lesser ones, he continues, "society has shaken itself into one sort of relative equilibrium after another by a series of social discoveries quite analogous to those of science." As examples of these moral discoveries, he points to society's rejections of polygamy and slavery, of private warfare and judicial torture, as inherited evils that have "slowly succumbed to actually aroused complaints." He admits that progress here is slow and painful, and that every institution—whether it be private property or monogamous marriage or uniform spelling—crushes the goods of some in its quest for a larger social good. Although "someone's ideals are unquestionably the worse off for each improvement," James maintains that "a vastly greater total number" of these individuals' ideals "find shelter in our civilized society than in the older savage ways" (*WB* 155–56).

Further, James anticipates that each new stasis will be upset by future complaints. He writes that, "as our present laws and customs have fought and conquered other past ones, so they will in their turn be overthrown by any newly discovered order which will hush up the complaints that they still give rise to, without producing others louder still" (*WB* 156). Thus, what he calls "the *highest* ethical life" is lived by those who are able to transcend the inherited moral rules "which have grown too narrow for the actual case." Throughout this process, he continues, there is only "one unconditional commandment," and that is that "we should seek incessantly, with fear and trembling, so to vote and to act as to bring about the very largest total universe of good which we can see" (*WB* 158). Our societies will then decide "through actual experiment by what sort of conduct the maximum amount of good can be gained and kept in this world." These moral experiments themselves are to be evaluated, "not *a priori,* but by actually finding, after the fact of their making, how much more outcry or how much appeasement comes about" (*WB* 157). It is for this reason that "no philosophy of ethics is possible in the old-fashioned absolute sense of the term. Everywhere the ethical philosopher must wait on facts. The thinkers who create the ideals come he knows not whence, their sensibilities are evolved he knows not how; and the question as to which of two conflicting ideals will give the best universe then and there, can be answered by him only through the aid of the experience of other men" (*WB* 158).

James thus views "ethical science" in the same way that he views physical science: "instead of being deducible all at once from abstract principles," ethics must "bide its time, and be ready to revise its conclusions from day to day." Most of the time, however, we can rely upon "the vulgarly accepted opinions" in both cases. He notes that "it would be folly quite as great, in most of us, to strike out independently and to aim at originality in ethics as in physics." He writes that myopic philosophers, with their premade systems of value, cannot lead the process of moral reform. A far better plan, he believes, would be to "follow the windings of the spectacle, confident that the line of least resistance will always be towards the richer and the more inclusive arrangement, and that by one tack after another some approach to the kingdom of heaven is incessantly made" (*WB* 157).[4] James does admit, however, that occasionally society meets with a moral prophet, someone who is "born with the right to be original, and his revolutionary thought or action may bear prosperous fruit." Such a person may, like the person who revises our thinking in physics, "by breaking old moral rules in a certain place, bring in a total condition of things more ideal than would have followed had the rules been kept" (*WB* 157–58). We can now offer James's answer to the normative question: in our moral lives, we should attempt to satisfy as many demands as possible.

Finally, we can consider the psychological question of the origin of moral ideas, a question that because of its descriptive nature has not always been considered "philosophical." This question brings us to the issue of nurture vs. nature, which, as we saw in chapter 4, James considers in the context of the "front door" of the senses and the "back door" of the structure of the mind. He begins here in good empiricist fashion by noting that "association with many remote pleasures will unquestionably make a thing significant of goodness in our minds." At the same time, he continues, it is impossible to account for "all our sentiments and preferences in this simple way." Empiricism's "associations of coexistence and succession" cannot fully explain how our "secondary affections" arrange our impulses and the environmental influences to produce the directions of our lives. He urges us to consider a vast array of human behaviors. "Take the love of drunkenness; take bashfulness, the terror of high places, the tendency to sea-sickness, to faint at the sight of blood, the susceptibility to musical sounds; take the emotion of the comical, the passion for poetry, for mathematics, or for metaphysics." Attributing these diverse behaviors to "incidental complications to our cerebral structure," James notes both the fact that "a vast number of our moral perceptions also are certainly of this secondary and brain-born kind" (*WB* 143),[5] and the importance of this recognition for a fuller appreciation of the centrality of individualism. Because these moral perceptions depend upon individually "felt fitnesses between things," they often oppose values that are more habitual and utilitarian. For example, he writes that "the sense for abstract justice which some persons have is as excentric a variation, from the natural-history point of view, as is the passion for music or for the higher philosophical consistencies which consumes the soul of others." To put the matter quite informally, "the nobler thing *tastes* better, and that is all that we can say" (*WB* 143–44).[6] At the same time, he realizes that there is a large overlap among the people of any society with regard to these valuations, as when he asks: "If a man has shot his wife's paramour, by reason of what subtle repugnancy in things is it that we are so disgusted when we hear that the wife and the husband have made it up and are living comfortably together again?" (*WB* 144). Thus, for James, the answer to the psychological question is that moral evaluations are individual in origin and are then shaped by society.

Blindness to Significance

James notes that the two essays "On a Certain Blindness in Human Beings" and "What Makes a Life Significant," because of their common origin, style, and content, "belong together" (*TT* 4). Both of them arose as public talks to college students, consist largely of long compilations of undigested quotations (presumably read *ad libitum*), and emphasize individuality and tolerance. He begins the former essay with a descriptive psychological paragraph that emphasizes the importance of emotion. "Our judgments concerning the worth of things, big or little, depend on the *feelings* the things arouse in us," he writes. "Where we judge a thing to be precious in consequence of the *idea* we frame of it, this is only because the idea is itself associated already with a feeling." If, on the contrary, we lived by ideas alone, if we were "radically feelingless," we would lose "all our likes and dislikes at a stroke," and find no experience superior to another (*TT* 132). James then develops a prescriptive principle out of this psychological theme, illustrates this principle with a number of examples, and finally offers a conclusion about how we ought to act based upon it. All of this functions as an extension of "The Moral Philosopher and the Moral Life" that we have just considered.

The psychological principle that James develops in these two essays is that we are generally blind and unfeeling to the values "of creatures and people different from ourselves." As "practical beings," we are all "bound to feel intensely" the importance of our own duties and of the situations that require our actions. Still, he continues, "this feeling is in each of us a vital secret," and we look in vain to others who are too absorbed living out their lives to take much interest in ours. The two primary results of our blindness are "the stupidity and injustice of our opinions, so far as they deal with the significance of alien lives," and "the falsity of our judgments, so far as they presume to decide in an absolute way on the value of other persons' conditions or ideals" (*TT* 132; cf. *ERM* 98, 101).[7] Additionally, this blindness leads us to fear those who have abandoned the familiar and common for values of their private devising.

As we have just seen, our partiality results from the fact that we are actors rather than spectators, partisans rather than philosophers. Significance, where we find it, is direct and personal. "Wherever a process of life communicates an eagerness to him who lives it, there the life becomes genuinely significant," James writes. Wherever such receptivity is found, "there is the zest, the tingle, the excitement, of reality; and there *is* 'importance' in the only real and positive sense in which importance ever anywhere can be" (*TT* 134–35). Our beliefs are not catalogues of "orthodoxies and heresies"; they are tools for us "to live by" (*WB* 52). The corollary to this personal significance is that we cannot fully appreciate the lives of others. "Our deadness toward all but one particular kind of joy would thus be the price we inevitably have to pay for being practical creatures." Only in the case of the dreamer or lover—the "philosopher, poet, or romancer" (*TT* 138)—is this fundamental practicality mitigated. He maintains that intellectuals, because of their lives of disengagement from the sharp edges of reality, are weakened in "responsive sensibilities." He writes that the members "of the highly educated classes (so called)" have drifted away from nature. Admitting that he is as guilty as his brethren, he continues in an Emersonian fashion that: "We are trained to seek the choice, the rare, the exquisite, exclusively, and to overlook the common. We are stuffed with abstract conceptions, and glib with verbalities and verbosities; and in the culture of these higher functions the peculiar sources of joy connected with our simpler functions often dry up, and we grow stone-blind and insensible to life's more elementary and general goods and joys." As a remedy for their, and his, situation, James suggests a descent to "a more profound and primitive level": the experience of imprisonment or shipwreck or military life would, he believes, "permanently show the good of life to many an over-educated pessimist." By reconnecting with the lives of "savages and children of nature, to whom we deem ourselves so much superior," we might be able to reanimate our lives because they are often "alive where we are often dead" (*TT* 146).

The second part of the "Blindness" essay is a series of illustrations of this psychological principle. One is a comparison of the values that drive a dog's life versus that of a human. Although the two are connected "by a tie more intimate than most ties in this world," James writes, each is insensible to the values of the other: "we to the rapture of bones under hedges, or smells of trees and lamp-posts, they to the delights of literature and art." In spite of the fox-terrier's general regard for its owner, for example, much of the latter's conduct remains incomprehensible to the faithful pooch, who will never be able to understand the hours spent every day reading, "paralyzed of motion and vacant of all conscious life" (*TT* 132–33).[8] A second illustration involves "african savages," who watch in amazement as an American traveler reads a newspaper, assuming unknown medicinal powers as "the only reason they could conceive of for the protracted bath which he had given his eyes upon its surface." His third illustration is the result of a trip to North Carolina, where he found, in the midst of the "unmitigated squalor" that had been carved out of a place of pristine natural beauty, a local resident who was quite proud of his misguided modifications. James eventually realized that he had missed "the whole inward significance of the situation." When the residents "looked on the hideous stumps, what they thought of was personal victory. The chips, the girdled trees, and the vile split rails spoke of honest sweat, persistent toil and final reward. The cabin was a warrant of safety for self and wife and babes. In short, the clearing, which to me was a mere ugly picture on the retina, was to them a symbol redolent with moral memories and sang a very paean of duty, struggle, and success." Turning the tables as best he can, he admits that he had been "as blind to the peculiar ideality of their conditions as they certainly would also have been to the ideality of mine, had they had a peep at my strange indoor academic ways of life at Cambridge" (*TT* 132–34).[9]

James then turns to discuss a series of literary figures, culminating with Walt Whitman, who he notes is "accounted by many of us a contemporary prophet." He writes that Whitman undermines many familiar distinctions and "brings all conventionalisms into solution." Further, because he celebrates the vibrant simplicities of life, "he becomes a sort of ideal tramp, a rider on omnibus-tops and ferry-boats, and, [is] considered either practically or academically, a worthless unproductive being." James continues that, for many, even Whitman's poems do not work hard enough: "His verses are but ejaculations—things mostly without subject or verb, a succession of interjections on an immense scale" (*TT* 141). Thus, he writes, Whitman's lifestyle seems to represent "a futile way of passing the time," a way of living that is "not altogether creditable to a grown-up man." Still, he remarks, "from the deepest point of view, who knows the more of truth, and who knows the less—Whitman on his omnibus-top, full of the inner joy with which the spectacle inspires him, or you, full of the disdain which the futility of his occupation excites?" (*TT* 144). Particularly with regard to this presentation of Whitman, we recognize the power of James's descriptive account of human feelings and interests. We natural creatures live as practical problem-solvers amidst the uncertainties of our fluid experience. By nature and nurture, we are partisans to certain ways of acting, and he is urging us to recognize our (statistically) normal blindness to the ways of individuals like Whitman, whose modes of living we do not understand.[10]

James's pluralistic conclusion about how we ought to act based upon this principle has two parts. Negatively, he writes, "it absolutely forbids us to be forward in pronouncing on the meaninglessness of forms of existence other than our own." While each individual "gains a partial superiority of insight from the peculiar position in which he stands," we must remember that "neither the whole of truth, nor the whole of good, is revealed to any single observer." Positively, his principle "commands us to tolerate, respect, and indulge those whom we see harmlessly interested and happy in their own ways, however unintelligible these may be to us." Each of us, James continues, "should be faithful to his own opportunities and make the most of his blessings, without presuming to regulate the rest of the vast field" (*TT* 149).[11]

The second essay, "What Makes a Life Significant," continues James's line of thinking. As an example of how we do not understand what makes others "tick," he urges us to consider our inability to grasp why one person falls in love with another. "Every Jack sees in his own particular Jill," he writes, "charms and perfections to the enchantment of which we stolid onlookers are stone-cold." Still, he wonders, who understands the situation better: the smitten Jack or the rest of us who are "victims of a pathological anaesthesia as regards Jill's magical importance?" The advantage that Jack has is that he "realizes Jill concretely, and we do not." Jack's struggle is "towards a union with her inner life, divining her feelings, anticipating her desires, understanding her limits as manfully as he can, and yet inadequately, too; for he is also afflicted with some blindness, even here." As we saw in chapter 5, we may recognize this attraction intellectually or conceptually—we may know about it—but "dead clods that we are," we cannot really know it from within (*TT* 150–51).[12] Thus, if we cannot fully understand others' lives, we should be less hasty to judge them. Our uninformed inclination to disregard the values of others is "the root of most human injustices and cruelties, and the trait in human character most likely to make the angels weep." Neither should we judge others' conduct, nor interfere with how they lead their lives. "The first thing to learn in intercourse with others," James writes, "is non-interference with their own peculiar ways of being happy, provided those ways do not assume to interfere by violence with ours." Others will fail to grasp our "inner secrets," and we theirs, because "beings as essentially practical as we are are necessarily short of sight" (*TT* 150–51; cf. 4; *WB* 154–55). Our response to our blindness should be tolerance.[13]

The new material in this essay is the search for "some principle to make our tolerance less chaotic." James begins with the story of his trip to the institute in the town of Chautauqua, New York, where he spent a week relaxing amidst the soothing music, uplifting lectures and wholesome food. During his stay, he writes, he was "held spell-bound by the charm and ease of everything, by the middle-class paradise, without a sin, without a victim, without a blot, without a tear." After he had moved on, however, he notes a feeling of relief in his return to the real world of sin and tears: "Now for something primordial and savage, even though it were as bad as an Armenian massacre, to set the balance straight again" (*TT* 151–52).[14] Although Chautauqua represented "the realization—on a small, sample scale of course—of all the ideals for which our civilization has been striving: security, intelligence, humanity, and order," he recognizes the paradox of his "instinctive hostile reaction ... of a so-called cultivated man upon such a Utopia" (*TT* 153).

What James thought was missing from life in this "Sabbatical city" was the natural human need for some sense of danger or struggle. For him, a fulfilling life is not a life of creature comforts, but a life of overcoming evil. It was this struggle "that gives to the wicked outer world all its moral style, expressiveness and picturesqueness—the element of precipitousness, so to call it, of strength and strenuousness, intensity and danger." Life there was isolated from our ongoing struggles with the powers of darkness, and from heroism and its occasional victories snatched "from the jaws of death." On the contrary, "in this unspeakable Chautauqua there was no potentiality of death in sight anywhere, and no point of the compass visible from which danger might possibly appear." It was a place where victory was so complete that there was no indication that a battle had previously taken place. Although "what our human emotions seem to require is the sight of the struggle going on," here was an entire town "just resting on its oars." For James, such a mediocre bourgeois world does not offer "human nature *in extremis* [under severe pressure]," and, from his point of view, the world overall was becoming more of a "Chautauquan enclosure" (*TT* 153–54). The world is becoming more "civilized"—more safe, more homogenized, more bland, and worse—he ruminated, and our lives are losing their potential significance.

During his return trip to Cambridge, however, James began to realize that whatever the comforts of his own middle-class existence, and those of his fellow Chautauquans, there remained many others struggling daily to secure their existence. Blind to many instances of "heroism and the spectacle of human nature on the rack," he confesses that he had failed to see the difficulty of his fellows' lives. As he continues, "wherever a scythe, an axe, a pick, or a shovel is wielded," there are struggling people, "sweating and aching and with [their] powers of patient endurance racked to the utmost under the length of hours of the strain" (*TT* 154–55; cf. *ERM* 169). Workers digging subways—even if they are trapped in their jobs by habit—can be just as heroic as generals (and people like James). Then he introduces the message of Leo Tolstoy who, late in his life, gave up his aristocratic lifestyle to live as a peasant. Upon further consideration, however, James suggests that perhaps Tolstoy had gone too far and overcorrected our normal prejudice "when he makes his love of the peasant so exclusive, and hardens his heart towards the educated man as absolutely as he does." Even the Chautauquans, James notes, despite their lack of "moral effort" and their "little sweat or muscular strain," still possessed "some vital virtue not found wanting when required" (*TT* 159).

Thus, for James, the lives of the middle class are not necessarily bad, nor are those of the laborers necessarily good. Each contains a part of what makes a life significant. The problem with the lives of the poor is neither that the dirt nor the poverty makes their lives "hard, barren, hopeless," he suggests; the problem is that these lives are lived without an inner purpose. To have significant lives, it would be necessary that these struggling individuals "worked and endured in obedience to some inner *ideal*." Too often, he remarks, their lives seem to be missing any ideal—although he grants that the ideals of others are "among those secrets that we can almost never penetrate." He continues that "the barrenness and ignobleness of the more usual laborer's life consists in the fact that it is moved by no such ideal inner springs." It is thus not adequate that the workers are willing to endure "the backache, the long hours, [and] the danger" if their goal is simply "to gain a quid of tobacco, a glass of beer, a cup of coffee, a meal, and a bed, and to begin again the next day and shirk as much as one can." It is because of their lack of purpose, he suggests, that there are no monuments to those who dig our subways. We build monuments to our soldiers because they "have followed an ideal," but not to our laborers who "have followed none" (*TT* 161–63).

If we wonder what James means by an ideal, he tells us that it "must be something intellectually conceived, something of which we are not unconscious" that brings with itself "that sort of outlook, uplift, and brightness that go with all intellectual facts." An ideal must also be appropriate for that individual. "Sodden routine is incompatible with ideality," he writes, although he grants that "what is sodden routine for one person may be ideal novelty for another." Further, he maintains that a significant life must both have such an ideal and must also struggle to enact it. He notes that "mere ideals are the cheapest things in life." We all have them to a certain extent. He points to "the most worthless sentimentalists and dreamers, drunkards, shirks and verse-makers," who are full of ideals, even though they "never show a grain of effort, courage, or endurance" to bring them into existence. If simply knowing ideals were enough, he continues, the average college professor, "with a starched shirt and spectacles," would be "the most absolutely and deeply significant of men" (*TT* 163; cf. *PP* 1:129; *PBC* 136–37). A significant life requires both ideals and the "dirt or scars contracted in the attempt to get them realized." Ideals are insufficient if not combined "with pluck and will," James writes, but pluck and will, "dogged endurance and insensibility to danger," are similarly insufficient without ideals. In a truly significant life, he maintains there must be a "fusion" of the two (*TT* 164–65).

Some Problems of Society

In many places in his thought, James emphasized the importance of individuals. This is especially true, as we have just seen in his discussions of the role of prophets in the process of social change. He recognizes the contradictory Spencerian view that social changes are "irrespective of persons, and independent of individual control … due to the environment, to the circumstances, the physical geography, the ancestral conditions, the increasing experience of outer relations." Still, James maintains that social changes over generations are the result of "the accumulated influences of individuals, of their examples, their initiatives, and their decisions" (*WB* 164). He continues that "the relation of the visible environment to the great man is in the main exactly what it is to the 'variation' in the darwinian philosophy." As he sees it, the environment "adopts or rejects, preserves or destroys" individuals, but it does not make them what they are. When the environment adopts the great man and preserves his influence, it is in turn "modified by his influence in an entirely original and peculiar way." Such an individual is the factor of change—"whether he be an importation from without like [Robert] Clive in India or [Louis] Agassiz here, or whether he spring from the soil like Mahomet or Franklin"—who modifies to a greater or lesser extent, the future of the society. He continues: "The mutations of societies, then, from generation to generation, are in the main due directly or indirectly to the acts or the example of individuals whose genius was so adapted to the receptivities of the moment, or whose accidental position of authority was so critical that they became ferments, initiators of movements, setters of precedent or fashion, centres of corruption, or destroyers of other persons, whose gifts, had they had free play, would have led society in another direction" (*WB* 170). In any instance of social change, James reminds us of the importance of both factors. On the one side, there is the individual who derives "his peculiar gifts from the play of physiological and infrasocial forces, but bearing all the power of initiative and origination in his hands." On the other side, there is "the social environment, with its power of adopting or rejecting both him and his gifts." Without the cooperation of both factors change will not occur. "The community stagnates without the impulse of the individual. The impulse dies away without the sympathy of the community" (*WB* 174; cf. 227/*EPR* 92).[15]

James continues that when individuals respond to particular problems it is their uniqueness that makes the difference. "Individuals of genius show the way, and set the patterns, which common people then adopt and follow" (*ECR* 109). The solution to any problem will appear in "one brain, and no other, because the instability of that brain is such as to tip and upset itself in just that particular direction." Here he is pointing to "the personal tone of each mind, which makes it more alive to certain classes of experience than others, more attentive to certain impressions, more open to certain reasons" (*WB* 186), and he emphasizes that this personal uniqueness is the result of the unknown forces within the nervous system that make the brain function one way rather than the other.[16] This unique contribution and others all enter into the process of social selection. "The products of the mind with the determined aesthetic bent," for example, "please or displease the community." If we decide to follow William Wordsworth, we will "grow unsentimental and serene." If, on the contrary, we follow Arthur Schopenhauer, we will learn "the true luxury of woe." In the long run, moreover, whatever attitude is adopted "becomes a ferment in the community, and alters its tone" (*WB* 187).

As a partisan of his own social class, James further notes that it is the individual members of the educated class, not the working class, to whom we should look for whatever progressive social change is to be anticipated. America's college-bred represent, in their capacity as "the only permanent presence that corresponds to the aristocracy in older countries" (*ECR* 110), a force to recognize and rally support for great men who would act as great leaders. "The best claim we can make for the higher education," he writes, is that "it should enable us to *know a good man when we see him.*" Thus, the job of the college is to offer its graduates "a general sense of what, under various disguises, *superiority* has always signified and may still signify." He describes this sense in a number of ways: "the feeling for a good human job anywhere, the admiration of the really admirable, the disesteem of what is cheap and trashy and impermanent ... the critical sense, the sense of ideal values ... the better part of what men know as wisdom" (*ECR* 108). James further notes the importance of intellectuals, out of whose contributions "the essential lines of the future will be drawn" (*C* 11:270; cf. *C* 9:362; *ML* 100–114).

Institutions, for their part, are habitual social responses that tend to promote or stymie individuals' ability to effect social change, and at the same time to foster or prevent the flourishing of individuals. James's evaluation of institutions was mostly negative. He writes, for example, that, when human wants are formalized as institutions, the institutions themselves tend to hamper "the natural gratification" of the wants. Whether the institution is legal or religious, educational or medical, he believes that too often "such institutions frustrate the spiritual purpose to which they were appointed to minister" (*ERM* 77). Rather than advancing justice or holiness, learning or health, such institutions tend rather to advance institutional values like stability and conformity. "*Every* great institution is perforce a means of corruption—whatever good it may also do," he writes to one correspondent. "Only in the free personal relation is full ideality to be found" (*C* 9:41). To another he writes "the bigger the unit you deal with, the hollower, the more brutal, the more mendacious is the life displayed." For his own part, he favors "eternal forces of truth which always work in the individual and immediately unsuccessful way, under-dogs always, till history comes after they are long dead, and puts them on the top" (*C* 8:546).[17] He was a strong individualist who remained ever suspicious of social organizations, cooperation, and interaction.

In James's writings, we find little discussion of social issues that appear central at present. In particular, questions of race and class engaged him only seldom, and questions of gender even less frequently.[18] His focus was elsewhere, on issues of personal fulfillment. As we have just seen, the greatest evil that he saw was the crushing of individuals by social institutions. Those of us who are quick to point out his failure to recognize "obvious" problems in his day must be prepared to be tried ourselves for values we now fail to recognize and evils against which we fail to take action. In any case, we can still learn a great deal from his discussions of the specific social issues that engaged him. Minimally, we can learn something about his understanding of the process of social advance.

James was, as we saw in chapter 2, a leading figure in the dissemination of the early results of experimental physiology and psychology. This work involved research on animals, including vivisection. The very similarities that made comparative studies worthwhile, however, also made them matters of ethical concern. Earlier in this chapter, we encountered his discussions of the importance of sentience to our thinking about moral questions. There was no doubt that the animals that were popular research subjects, like dogs and rabbits, felt pain, and there were many antivivisectionists who complained about the wanton cruelty of the laboratories. He felt himself to be in the middle.

In 1875 James writes that the entire science of physiology is "based, immediately or remotely, upon vivisectional evidence." While he admits that vivisection had so far offered only "minute" therapeutic advances, he believed that its potential for scientific progress required that it be allowed to continue. He writes that "the vivisectional results of to-day, which are liable to be corrected to-morrow, will be corrected by the vivisections of to-morrow and by nothing else." As a result, he continues, "to taboo vivisection is then the same thing as to give up seeking after a knowledge of physiology." To continue with vivisection is thus "a painful duty." At the same time, however, he wants all to admit "without higgling about more or less, that, in principle, vivisection admits of cruelty." He urges us to consider, for example, a canine test-subject "strapped on a board and howling at his executioners, or, still worse, poisoned by curara, which leaves him paralyzed but sentient." This unfortunate dog finds himself "literally in a sort of hell" that he can neither understand nor change. James continues: the dog "sees no redeeming ray in the whole business. Nevertheless, in a world beyond the ken of his poor, benighted brain, his sufferings are having their effect—truth, and perhaps future human ease, are being bought by them. He is performing a function infinitely superior to any which prosperous canine life admits of, and, if his dark mind could be enlightened, and if he were a heroic dog, he would religiously acquiesce in his own sacrifice" (*ECR* 11–12; cf. *WB* 53).

To consider a second scenario, James admits that a rabbit's pain differs completely from that of humans "in that the moral element, the element of subjective *horror*, is absent." Still, this does not eliminate the question of cruelty. The question we need to ask is: "Do we give them all the pain that they are susceptible of suffering, be that much or little? If so, we are cruel; and there is no doubt that vivisectors are often obliged to go to this extreme"

(*ECR* 10–11). Based upon his earlier ethical principle that inflicting pain is wrong, expanded here to maintain that "nothing is more calculated to deaden the moral sensibility of students than familiarity with blood shed for trifling ends," he proposes that it is our duty "to restrict the amount of *useless* vivisection." As far as making the determination of usefulness, however, he would leave that question "solely with the investigator himself." Further, he believes that any broad prohibition would simply fail to be adopted in a society that is so dead to animal pain that it "boils millions of lobsters alive every year to add a charm to its suppers." Throughout the essay, James's commitment is to advancing medical research, and therefore to continuing vivisection. "It is better for many quadrupeds to perish unjustly," he writes, "than for a whole scientific body to be degraded" (*ECR* 12–13; cf. 18–19; *WB* 47–48).

More than three decades later, in 1909, James returns to the subject of vivisection, but by this time his view has shifted. He still recognizes the claims of "the various medical and scientific defenders of vivisection," who protest that "it is *no one's business* what happens to an animal, so long as the individual who is handling it can plead that to increase science is his aim." Now he maintains, however, that this position "flatly contradict[s] the best conscience of our time," and he asserts that "the rights of the helpless, even though they be brutes, must be protected by those who have superior power." James contends that, in the intervening years, the physiologists have neither adopted any "corporate responsibility" or "code of vivisectional ethics for laboratories to post up and enforce" nor proposed any legislation themselves. As a result, it is necessary for outsiders to step in and protect the animals. While he regrets that the agitation of the antivivisection movement—"with all its expensiveness, idiocy, bad temper, untruth, and vexatiousness"—had been necessary to drive home "to the careless or callous individual experimenter the fact that the sufferings of his animals *are* somebody else's business as well as his own" (*ECR* 191–92),[19] the lesson had been learned and changes were necessary.

In the 1890s James made a series of statements on another issue indicating his opposition to contemporary attempts to regularize the practice of medicine through legislation. Suggesting that it is a mistake to see medical practice as a science rather than an art, he writes to a Boston newspaper in 1894 that it is impossible to "secure faultless therapeutics by law." He continues:

> The healing art is not like the apothecary's or plumber's trade, a definite thing where an examination can secure infallibility. A doctor has not first to find a name for his patient's complaint, and then a remedy to fit that name, as if he were a locksmith fitting a lock with a key. Were his duties as plain as that, an examination might insure his adequacy. But in every delicate case it is no mere name that comes before him, but a human being so uniquely compounded that he has never seen the exact mate of him before. The doctor must guess, divine, experiment and make mistakes. (*ECR* 146)[20]

The individual physician is always treating an individual patient, and whatever the overall benefits of scientific generalizations, particular therapeutic interactions remain unique. Further, it is the right of the individual patient "to treat one's own body as one chooses," to select a therapist, and then to "bear the consequences" (*ECR* 145). Only in such a way can we anticipate "the progress of therapeutic knowledge as a whole" (*ECR* 147; cf. 149–50).

Four years later James testified in opposition to a bill designed to limit the practice of medicine in Massachusetts to orthodox physicians. On this occasion, he notes that the members of the medical profession who were advancing this bill saw themselves as defending "true science" against "ignorance and quackery." He saw the situation quite differently. In spite of his presumed identification with the proponents of the bill, due to his medical degree and his long years as a scientist on the Harvard faculty, he maintains that the proponents of the bill were in fact protecting ignorance. The reason was a simple one: the practice of medicine remains in process. "Were medicine at present a finished science," he contends, "with all practitioners in agreement about methods of treatment, such a bill as this, to make it penal to treat a patient without having passed an examination, would be unobjectionable." We recognize, however, that "the whole face of medicine changes unexpectedly from one generation to another" in accord with changes in medical knowledge. As a result, we must anticipate that just as medical practitioners "look back, with a mixture of amusement and horror, at the practice of our grandfathers," much of what we take for scientifically justified practice "will awaken similar feelings in our posterity." Given the state of medical "ignorance and narrowness," the last thing that we need is to enact laws that would "consecrate and perpetuate" these failings (*ECR* 56–58).[21]

James maintains that the Commonwealth of Massachusetts "is not a medical body, has no right to a medical opinion, and should not dare to take sides in medical controversies." Rather, it should remain neutral. Physicians, for their part, because of their commitment to "the growth of medical truth" should support the efforts of those "willing to push out their experiences in the mental-healing direction, and provide a mass of material out of which the conditions and limits of such therapeutic methods may at last become clear." Especially with regard to the problems of mental health, he feared the power of the proposed law to preclude a great deal of potential medical experience. From his point of view, it was necessary that the many possible approaches to "mental therapeutics" be "studied, and its laws ascertained." Granting that both sides want to benefit the patients, James also wants to defend patients' expanded treatment options. He suggests that the legislators not paternalistically impose their personal choices about mind-curers on others, but recognize that "a large number of our citizens, persons as intelligent and well-educated as yourself or I, persons whose number seems daily to increase," believe that the mind-curers are achieving successes, and "that a valuable new department of medical experience is by them opening up" (ECR 58–59; cf. 61). Our job as a society is to allow these experiments and see what happens.

Related to this consideration of medical practice were James's attempts to advance public opinion with regard to the treatment of mental illness. His early studies, as well as his own personal experience, had familiarized him with the seriousness of the problem. Later in his life, he was one of the strong supporters of Clifford Whittingham Beers, the author of an autobiographical study of mental illness that James called "an important human document" (C 12:133).[22] Later still, he served on the executive committee of the "National Committee for Mental Hygiene." His primary duty there seems to have been seeking financial support from John D. Rockefeller. "During my life as a 'psychologist,'" James wrote to Rockefeller in 1909, "I have had much to do with our Asylums, and I have had so painfully borne in upon me the massiveness of human evil which the term 'insanity' covers, and the inadequacy of our arrangements for coping with it." He continues that it is critically necessary to raise the level of care for "insane people" in the United States: "Not only are our asylums gorged with inmates. Not only do their directorships not attract strong men from the profession, not only are ignorance and sodden routine too often found there, but public opinion needs educating in this matter as much as tuberculosis." James emphasizes that American society has no adequate system "of prevention or of aftercare," and, as a result, "what should be regarded as a common functional disease is handled as a social stigma" and treated by imprisonment in asylums. His expressed intention was to enlist Rockefeller's support in what he hoped will be "a tremendous campaign waged for prevention and cure" (C 12:253–54; cf. 416–17), but little seems to have come of James's efforts.

Turning to the labor question, we see that James did not have a favorable understanding of unions. This can be drawn from his 1898 statement about the response of the members of the medical profession to the activities of heterodox healers: "they adopt the fiercely partisan attitude of a powerful trades union, demanding legislation against the competition of the 'scabs'" (ECR 58). In an earlier letter to his brother Henry, then in England, James advises that he not be "alarmed about the labor troubles here. I am quite sure they are a most healthy phase of evolution, a little costly, but normal and sure to do lots of good to all hands in the end." He continues that he is not referring to "the senseless 'anarchist' riot in Chicago"—the Chicago Haymarket Riot of 4 May 1886—which he sees as neither healthy nor normal but "the work of a lot of pathological germans & poles." As James read the newspaper reports on that event, "all the irish names are among the killed and wounded policemen. Almost every anarchist name is continental" (C 2:40). A year later, he indicated to his brother-in-law, William Salter, his belief that society should let the anarchists "suffer all the consequences" of their actions (C 6:285).

James's comments in these cases are an indication of his own sharing in the blindness that resulted from the bifurcation of society into owners and workers. To get some sense of his own class position, we need only examine how he set up the issue in "What Makes a Life Significant." He writes, for example, that the term "labor-question" covers "all sorts of anarchistic discontents and socialistic projects, and the conservative resistances which they provoke." His own social myopia prevents him from seeing any causal factors and provocations the other way around. He continues in a marginally better fashion that the two "'halves'" do not understand each other: "one-half of our fellow-countrymen remain entirely blind to the internal significance of the lives of the other half." Without accepting the percentages implied by the term "half," we can see that, for James, each portion of society fails to grasp the "joys and sorrows" of the other; each misses the "moral virtue" and "intellectual ideals" of the other. He continues:

> Often all that the poor man can think of in the rich man is a cowardly greediness for safety, luxury, and effeminacy, and a boundless affectation. What he is, is not a human being, but a pocket-book, a bank-account. And a similar greediness, turned by disappointment into envy, is all that many rich men can see in the state of mind of the dissatisfied poor.... Each, in short, ignores the fact that happiness and unhappiness and significance are a vital mystery; each pins them absolutely on some ridiculous feature of the external situation; and everybody remains outside of everybody else's sight.

It is clear that James does attempt to overcome his blindness and to recognize the claims of the poor, but he still emphasizes the importance of an ideal and its function in living. He did not believe that the workers' unhappy lives were the result of the selfish attitudes of the capitalists or the unfortunate play of economic conditions, nor did he believe that even radical changes in these attitudes or conditions would give the workers' lives adequate meaning. He does admit that society has to "pass towards some newer and better equilibrium, and the distribution of wealth has doubtless slowly got to change," because such changes are part of the evolution of social life, but he still maintains that, should anyone believe that these changes will bring "any *genuine vital difference*, on a large scale, to the lives of our descendants," they had missed his point. "The solid meaning of life" always involves the combination of human struggle with an ideal (*TT* 165–66; cf. *VRE* 266). Surely James would have said in a clearer moment, however, that many of these workers—and their families—were living in accordance with an ideal that he, as a partisan of his own values, failed to understand.[23]

Race was an issue about which James wrote little.[24] Slavery was a powerful, if increasingly embattled, American institution when he was born in 1842, but the Civil War, which raged between his nineteenth and twenty-fourth birthdays, was widely viewed to be more about preserving the Union than about emancipation, about sectionalism rather than abolition. In any case, as we saw in chapter 1, he took no part in this great struggle, although two of his younger brothers did participate at great personal cost. More than thirty years after Appomattox, on Decoration Day, 31 May 1897, he offered a fine public oration at the ceremony dedicating the Robert Gould Shaw Monument on the Boston Common.[25] In this oration, he notes that "our great western republic had from its very origin" been both a "land of freedom, boastfully so called," and one "with human slavery enthroned at the heart of it." The Founders' reluctance to challenge slavery had left us with a country that was "a thing of falsehood and horrible self-contradiction." He continues that slavery was such a pervasive force that it eventually was "dictating terms of unconditional surrender to every other organ of its life," and that "the only alternative for the nation was to fight or die" (*ERM* 66). One of the black units engaged in this fight was the 54th Regiment of Massachusetts Voluntary Infantry, led by Col. Shaw, who was killed at the battle for Fort Wagner, South Carolina, on 18 July 1863.[26] Describing the actions of this unit as memorialized on the monument, James points first to the troops: "There on foot go the dark outcasts.... There they march, warm-blooded champions of a better day for man." Then he points to Shaw, "on horseback, among them ... sits the blue-eyed child of fortune upon whose happy youth every divinity had smiled." Officers and men, "onward they moved together" (*ERM* 65). He notes that while they failed bravely at Fort Wagner, they were vindicated by the eventual Union victory in the war. As far as the meaning for these events for the present and the future, he reminds his audience that, while "no future problem can be like that problem," and that "no task laid on our children can compare in difficulty with the task with which their fathers had to deal," victory in the Civil War had not solved all of America's problems. As we move forward, "tasks enough await us" and our "democracy is still upon its trial" (*ERM* 73–74).[27]

One of America's future tasks was dealing with continuing racism. James offered a pair of statements in 1903 on the rash of lynchings that had occurred over the last decade and gave little indication of abating. In these pieces, he is especially interested in conveying his sense of the seriousness of the problem. He writes that "negro lynching" is not "a transient contagion destined soon to exhaust its virulence." On the contrary, it is "a profound social disease, spreading now like forest fire, and certain to become permanently endemic in every corner of our country, North and South, unless heroic remedies are swiftly adopted to check it" (*ECR* 170). What he characterizes as this "social retrogression" is being made worse by a "yellow journalism" that panders to "the morbid appetite dormant in our natures" (ECR 174). Writing as a psychologist in the face of this "epidemic of lynching," he maintains that "the average church-going Civilizee realizes . . . absolutely nothing of the deeper currents of human nature, or of the aboriginal capacity for murderous excitement which lies sleeping even in his own bosom." Although the pressure of centuries of religious and legal education has brought a high level of civilization, our "homicidal potentialities" seem to remain free in this one case. In fact, he continues, "Negro lynching claims more and more the character of a public right. It appeals to the punitive instinct, to race antipathy and to the white man's pride, as well as to the homicidal frenzy." Here, he is referring especially to "the young white American of the lower classes," who is learning from recent events that "any negro accused of crime is public spoil, to be played with as long as the fun will last." To men of this mind-set, he wonders, how can other forms of diversion—"dog fights, prize fights, bull fights"—compare to "a man hunt and a negro burning?" (ECR 171–72). Although he is attempting to understand what is behind these harmful actions, James has no tolerance for the actions themselves, and, as a response to this epidemic, he calls for harsh legislation that would guarantee to "every sheriff or every deputy absolute immunity from vengeance or retaliation in cases where it becomes necessary for him to use force to guard his prisoner and maintain the dignity of the law." Simply put, "when the mob threatens, the sheriff should fire instantly and effectively." If these efforts of the sheriff proved inadequate and the prisoner was lynched anyway, "I would have the members of the mob indicted and hanged" (ECR 175). He sees no other alternative for stopping the violence, since under current circumstances there is no chance that local juries will "indict or condemn" the lynchers and execute these "'leading citizens.'" If such harsh new steps are not taken, he warns that there will be "attempts at general massacres of negroes," "collective reprisals by negroes," and perhaps "negro burning in a very few years on Cambridge common and the Boston public garden" (ECR 171–73; cf. C 10:282–83).

With regard to the lesser but related issue of racial discrimination, James seems to have been, however sensitive as a person, comfortable with all sorts of racial and ethnic slurs. We can consider, for example, the numerous unremarked-upon instances of the term "savage" that have peppered this chapter and others.[28] We have just seen him using the term "darkey" to describe Washington and others, and at one point he characterizes W. E. B.

Du Bois as "a mulatto ex-student of mine" (C 3:242). Yet James writes that Washington and Du Bois are "citizens of whom our country may be equally proud; and I should esteem it a national calamity if either of them gave up the cause for which he fights" (ECR 193). He seems comfortable with the notions of "'lower' races" and "inferior populations," and with separating nations into "yellow" and "white."[29] Consider as well his analysis of Italians and Germans. "An untutored Italian," he writes, is "a man of the world" because he has "instinctive perceptions, tendencies to behavior, reactions, in a word, upon his environment, which the untutored German wholly lacks." The German, while in a naive state, is "apt to be a thoroughly loutish person," but, James continues, "the mere absence in his brain of definite innate tendencies enables him to advance by the development, through education, of his purely reasoned thinking, into complex regions of consciousness that the Italian may probably never approach" (PP 2:991; cf. 1144). Similarly, his opinions of the Jews and the Irish are frequently benighted.[30] At the same time, most of James's racial and ethnic criticisms seem balanced in the fashion of the following passage: "Negro-suffrage shows indeed a sorry history, but so, for the matter of that, does white suffrage" (ECR 193).[31]

After a consideration of all of this mixed evidence, we can wonder to what extent we might understand James to be a social reformer. While some commentators believe that we should,[32] I think that we need to use such a characterization very carefully.[33] This is not to deny his powerful social criticisms, like his condemnation of "the moral flabbiness born of the exclusive worship of the bitch-Goddess SUCCESS" as a kind of "national disease" (C 11:267). Rather, it is to see James's overall commitment as inadequate. Merle Eugene Curti presents James as "in temperament and outlook an aristocrat," and Cornell West writes that he exhibited an undeniable "distrust of the masses." For Paul Conkin, James "reflected the standards of a middle-class Victorian gentleman."[34] John J. McDermott complains that James was, despite his heightened awareness of individuality and possibilities, at times blind to the difficulties in the lives of others. "James was genial but self-centered and abysmally ignorant of massive social inequalities," he writes, noting such flaws as "his cavalier approach to the Civil War, the Irish question, suffragettes, or his romanticization of the San Francisco earthquake." Similarly, James seemed to have little recognition of "the enormous importance of the abolition movement and of the end of slavery in the United States."[35] To be sure, James frequently displayed concern and sensitivity regarding those who suffered from the cruelties of life or society, and who were subjected to callous abuse or debilitating harm. Yet his concern seems episodic and inconstant, a function often of dismay that, as he saw it, his fellow citizens were vacillating in their devotion to ideals.

James's felt need to protect individuals from external forces was thus not translatable—as it later was in John Dewey—into a need to unite them in group self-protection to oppose economic and other forces that were too strong for isolated individuals to resist.[36] Both point to the importance of recognizing meaning in all experience, but Dewey's emphasis is on helping to solve social problems through institutional reconstruction. The primary ethical difference between the two is not that they held contradictory positions on particular issues or even on theoretical principles. It is rather that Dewey, along with the other pragmatic social thinkers, emphasizes the social aspect to the downplaying of the individual, whereas James's emphasis is just the reverse. Both Dewey and James would espouse the view that meaning is the result of human, rather than supernatural, contributions, but James wants more meaning, or at least meaning of a different sort, than Dewey can offer. As we shall see in chapter 7, for James there is ultimately an emptiness in human existence that requires some sort of superhuman power able to guarantee "an ideal order that shall be permanently preserved" (*P* 55). Such a guarantee Dewey neither would seek nor could accept. James further believes that our moral responsibility ends when we have performed our duty, and "the burden of the rest we may lay on higher powers" (*WB* 134), the existence of which Dewey rejects. Part of this confidence in "higher powers" is the result of James's belief that as a meliorist it is occasionally acceptable to lie back in the lap of nature. "The universe is a system of which the individual members may relax their anxieties occasionally, in which the don't-care mood is also right for men, and moral holidays in order" (*P* 41) as "provisional breathing-spells, intended to refresh us for the morrow's fight" (*MT* 124; cf. 5; *P* 56).[37]

As we saw in chapter 1, James was defending spiritual or religious values that he believed were endangered by science and materialism. In doing so, he was answering, I would suggest, old questions in a world that was increasingly encountering new problems that gave rise to questions of a different sort. Dewey no longer anguished over the existence of a God, freedom and determinism, the reality of morality, or the question of immortality. Those questions were—in James's terms—not "live" for Dewey. Although Dewey's naturalism offers none of the grandeur that James seeks, it also has to salve none of the anguish that precipitated James's search. Dewey's problems are of a different sort: What future should we try to build for ourselves and for our children? How should the bounty of the earth be managed? How can the members of our society and the peoples of the rest of the world get along with each other? These are the questions of Dewey's good life. They are social questions that require an ethics of reform. Further, James's means for achieving the good life led him away from the position that Dewey was affirming. The answers to these new social questions must be developed through group interaction and collective choice, through a method of social criticism. Addressing these questions seems to require that we turn away from James and his noncritical openness toward Dewey and cooperative inquiry.

James proposes an individually significant life in accord with a vital ideal. A central part of his view is that individuals' values that respect ours are sacred. As a result, his approach does not search for values to undergird contemporary social reform movements, even though our central problem is a lack of sufficient resources for all of us to live according to our separate values. Criticism is an essential part of modern social life, and an essential part of such criticism is the rejection of some individuals' values. It is thus necessary to relegate certain goods to lesser roles, and to close our eyes to their lesser beauty. At the same time, in seeking the most efficient ways to perform the tasks that have to be done, we cannot simply adopt the option that enables us to perform the greatest variety of tasks. Because of his recognition of the social aspect, Dewey calls for attempts at the critical reconstruction of our social and natural environment to facilitate the development of fuller lives for individuals. James's position, with its individualistic tone and its method of inclusion, undermines this type of reconstruction. In his defense of personal values, he opposes institutions as obstacles rather than uses them as means to the fulfillment of individuality. He is unwilling, or unable, to emphasize the need for the reconstruction of our institutions as a means to fuller lives because the institutions themselves, reconstructed or not, are deadening.[38]

The problem is not just that James grew up serenely in the eye of the storm of industrialization.[39] The problem was the nature of his individualism.[40] There is little to suggest that James was cold towards the suffering of others. He recognized the severe social and economic problems of his society. He writes:

> There is nothing to make one indignant in the mere fact that life is hard, that men should toil and suffer pain. The planetary conditions once for all are such, and we can stand it. But that so many men, by mere accidents of birth and opportunity, should have a life of *nothing else* but toil and pain and hardness and inferiority imposed upon them, should have *no* vacation, while others natively no more deserving get no taste of this campaigning life at all—*this* is capable of arousing indignation in reflective minds. (*ERM* 171; cf. *PP* 1:129; *PBC* 136–37).

Still, the question remains of the value of his individualistic approach and his pluralistic method of inclusion for advancing his stated goal of maximizing satisfactions. While James believed that the maldistribution of wealth was decreasing in favor of a more socialistic equilibrium, he did not expect that these eventual changes would make "any *genuine vital difference*, on a large scale" (*TT* 166; cf. *ERM* 170). The thoroughness of his rejection of revolutionary alternatives is perhaps most clearly indicated by his casual remarks, like his statement that it is only habit that "saves the children of fortune from the envious uprisings of the poor" (*PP* 1:125/*PBC* 133). For him, the ethics of fulfillment, at least in his formulation, is in a fundamental way opposed to the ethics of reform. Further, there is no recognition in James that individualism itself could lead to social problems. For him, human atavisms arise in groups, as his discussions of lynching and imperialism indicate. When individuals become part of something external to themselves—lynch mobs as we have just seen, or warring nations as we shall see shortly—their ideality is abandoned. When individuals choose their values in an intelligent and responsible fashion, however, and shape their lives around these vibrant values, social good results.

Turning now to James's possible ethics of reform, we must focus upon the vital process of choosing values for the group. Ethics demonstrates a social aspect that requires that the world be made a better place so that individuals might live decently and happily. But his position—being open to the possibilities of experience and permitting other individuals the freedom to choose their own values—would seem to offer us little. This aspect of his ethical theory, however, is surely there, as we have just seen in his discussions of various social problems. He realizes that to solve these problems, we must transform reality. We must decide and act, further, without the level of confidence that we would like because these contribution cases cannot wait for more evidence. Still, the question that we must ask James at this point is how the group is to identify the evils to be thrown overboard and the goods to be saved. In a world of many people, in a moral pluriverse, the philosopher and ethical reformer normally try to bring order by determining the *desideranda,* the things that should be desired, to which mere *desiderata,* the things that are desired, should yield. The method that he offers, however, is not a method that would exclude some *desiderata* as being in themselves less valuable than others are. His method for choosing social values is rather a method of inclusion. For him, *desideranda* are those *desiderata* that eliminate the fewest competing goods. Thus, the relative unimportance of the ethics of reform for James.

The ethics of fulfillment is an ethics that places little emphasis upon criticism and evaluation, and much emphasis upon openness to the ways in which others understand experience. While the ethics of reform, the ethics of change and of social reconstruction, would seem to be primary at present, it is not the whole of ethics. We lament the past sufferings of humankind as unfortunate; we condemn the present injustices of living as intolerable; and we cry out for and work toward a future when equality will prevail. All the while, we know that human suffering will never end, nor justice and equality triumph. We fear that, even with our contributions, experience will hardly surpass even our most limited expectations. As a result, basing our ethics on attempts at bettering the world resembles the task of Sisyphus.[41] Others view this approach as futile and fully expect the rock to stay up there, at least one of these days, at least for a short while. Such individuals advance an ethics of fulfillment. In this regard, James notes Emerson's early position on the question of slavery: "God must govern his own world, and knows his way out of this pit without my desertion of my post, which has none to guard it but me. I have quite other slaves to face than those negroes, to wit, imprisoned thoughts far back in the brain of man, and which have no watchman or lover or defender but me" (*ERM* 110).[42] Moral thinkers like Emerson and James emphasize the ethics of fulfillment: value is everywhere, life is for rejoicing, let each person find worth wherever possible, judge no one and impose no values on others, allow occasional moral holidays. Moreover, the value of this position, however limited, cannot be denied. The ethics of reform is not itself enough either for a society to be moral, or for its citizens to be fulfilled.[43] Both the ethics of fulfillment and the ethics of reform are necessary for an adequate moral philosophy.

Imperialism and War

While James's moral thought largely undercuts the likelihood of social engagement, his discussion of imperialism and war as social problems is happily another story. His thinking had developed in the context of the Spanish-American War of 1898 and the prior surge of imperialism that had contributed to it. About this public mood, he writes to a correspondent in January 1896 of "the most extraordinary exhibition of a whole nation going fighting-mad in 24 hours." He calls this episode "the most discouraging relapse into barbarism that I have ever seen," and he notes that it demonstrates "how near the surface the fighting instinct remains in Mankind, and how little stimulus is required to touch-off the fighting nerve" (C 8:117; cf. 114). In early 1898 he writes that "we eat, drink and sleep War." While he suspects that the war-madness is attributable "for the most part to deliberate newspaper criminality," he recognizes at the same time that the people are "really crazy" for war "for its own sake." He continues that he is witnessing "collective attacks of genuine madness sweeping over peoples and stampeding them" (C 3:25–26; cf. C 8:540). As the country moved toward war, it seems that James himself was initially caught up in the spirit of the war. He notes, for example, that "with all the certain bad that is in it, there will probably be a lot of good mixed in." Among the positive outcomes, he points to the fact that "our isolation from Europe, absurd abstraction that it was, is pretty well broken into" (C 8:360). In addition, the war will help Americans to finally realize that "we *are not* the quaker nation we once fancied we might be." By forcing us to take up a place in "the general life of the world," and to satisfy "new and diversified responsibilities of a tremendous sort," he continues, "the war is undoubtedly the very best thing that could have befallen us" (C 8:355). In his Berkeley address of August 1898, which we explored in chapter 4, he also indicates some of his own budding imperialism. He remarks, for example, on "the great Anglo-American alliance against the world," an alliance to which he wishes "a God-speed." He also indicates some perceived connection between "the principle of practicalism" that is the heart of Pragmatism, "the whole English tradition in philosophy," and "this wonderful Pacific Coast, of which our race is taking possession" (*P* 269–70).

Quickly, however, James realized problems. In early 1899 he writes that, although pluralism demands "democratic respect for the sacredness of individuality," he believes that the "passionate inner meaning" of such notions had been destroyed by "the pretension of our nation to inflict its own inner ideals and institutions *vi et armis* [with force and arms] upon Orientals" (*TT* 4). Earlier, he had noted that, because of our use of violence, our claim to being "a better nation morally than the rest, safe at home, and without the old savage ambitions, destined to exert great international influence by throwing in our 'moral weight' etc." had been exposed as delusional. "Human Nature is everywhere the same," he continues, "and at the least temptation all the old military passions rise, and sweep everything before them" (*C* 8:373; cf. *ECR* 82). Despite its pretensions, America had been willing to "puke up its own historic soul in five minutes" (*C* 9:4; cf. *C* 11:375; *ECR* 85), and any process of recovery would be lengthy. In the course of the war, the Americans had especially demonstrated a blindness to Filipino values. "We are now openly engaged in crushing out the sacredest thing in this great human world," James writes, "the attempt of a people long enslaved to attain to the possession of itself, to organize its laws and government, to be free to follow its internal destinies according to its own ideals," and in the process, "we are cold-bloodedly, wantonly and abominably destroying the soul of a people who never did us an atom of harm in their lives" (*ECR* 156–57; cf. 160, 179–80). Thus, "the stars and stripes which did truly stand for something ideal, & on the whole mean it, in spite of imperfect ways of fulfillment," has now been exposed as "a lying rag, pure and simple" (*C* 8:523). Although our country had claimed to live by "the faith that a man requires no master to take care of him, and that common people can work out their salvation well enough together if left free to try" (*ERM* 66), it was clear that that faith did not include other peoples.[44]

In his 1910 essay "The Moral Equivalent of War," James demonstrates a recognition that the modern military situation is not amenable to individual control. Too much military power has accumulated in the hands of those who benefit from its use, and a reconstruction of the whole military complex and its role in our society would be necessary before we could hope to move toward a more viable pacifism. His war essay offers a summary statement of a position that he had been developing since at least the 1890s. In this essay, he discusses war primarily as a social-psychological, rather than as a political, phenomenon. As he had noted a few years earlier, the pacifist movement finds its "permanent enemy" in "the noted bellicosity of human nature." The human being is "simply the most formidable of all beasts of prey, and, indeed, the only one that preys systematically on its own species." Because of what evolution has made us, he continues, "a millennium of peace would not breed the fighting disposition out of our bone and marrow, and a function so ingrained and vital will never consent to die without resistance, and will always find impassioned apologists and idealizers." He continues that "the plain truth is that people *want* war ... for itself; and apart from each and every possible consequence." War functions as "the final bouquet of life's fireworks" (*ERM* 121–22). Because of this disposition, it is inadequate simply to blame the militarists and munitions makers. They are able to succeed so well only because their actions integrate with the visceral responses of the general public. We have been molded into societies by "the gory nurse" of combat. "Dead men tell no tales, and if there were tribes of other type than this, they have left no survivors," he writes. We have inherited pugnacity as a central trait, and "thousands of years of peace won't breed it out of us" (*ERM* 164; cf. *C* 8:120).[45] As James had noted in his Shaw address, "war was the gory cradle of mankind, the grim-featured nurse that alone could train our savage progenitors into some semblance of social virtue, teach them to be faithful one to another, and force them to sink their selfishness in wider tribal ends." Whatever our general disregard for government, "the war-tax is still the only tax that men ungrudgingly will pay," he continues. This fact should be no surprise when we realize that we are "the survivors of one successful massacre after another" (*ERM* 72).

James notes that America is a society profoundly ambivalent about warfare, and we must assume the same of all of our presumed enemies. We recognize, on the one hand, that war is the source of unlimited destruction and suffering; on the other hand, we experience in warfare the highest acts of honor and courage.[46] He discusses, as an example, the powerful meaning of the American Civil War, North and South. Few, he believes, would prefer in 1910 to have that war eliminated from our history, since "those ancestors, those efforts, those memories and legends, are the most ideal part of what we now own together, a sacred spiritual possession worth more than all the blood poured out." At the same time, he continues, "not one man or woman would vote" to take up such a war. "In modern eyes, precious tho' wars may be, they must not be waged solely for the sake of the ideal harvest" (*ERM* 162).

James indicates, however, that in practice our ambivalence about war is often overcome by the rhetoric of unscrupulous individuals who wield powerful ideas like "duty" and "destiny" (see *ECR* 81, 157, 164) as tools in the service of militarism. Oftentimes, he admits, these ideas can be forgotten in practical cases. "'Causes,' as anti-slavery, democracy, etc., dwindle when realized in their sordid particulars," he writes, but the ideas still have great potential power, as we saw in chapter 2. "Abstractions will touch us when we are callous to the concrete instances in which they lie embodied." Further, an array of loyal acts gives way to "abstract Loyalty as something of a superior order to be infinitely loyal to." In a similar fashion, philosophers are wont to change facts into "Truth." "So strongly do objects that come as universal and eternal arouse our sensibilities, so greatly do life's values deepen when we translate percepts into ideas! The translation appears as far more than the original's equivalent" (*SPP* 42–43).[47]

One particularly strong idea is "defense," an elevated substitute for the more direct "war." We reject as much as possible, he writes, "the bestial side of military service," and "pure loot and mastery seem no longer morally avowable motives" (*ERM* 164). We can only fight legitimately in self-defense, although at times we can be quite imaginative in our malinterpretations of this concept. "Only when forced upon one," he writes, "only when an enemy's injustice leaves us no alternative, is a war now thought permissible" (*ERM* 162). Fortunately for militarists, we have had no shortage of "unjust" enemies—nor, for their part, do our enemies. Another powerful notion is "patriotism," a value that functions most powerfully when blind and unquestioning.[48] "Patriotism no one thinks discreditable," James writes, and "war is the romance of history." Wrapped in the ambition of victory and unfazed by the possibility of death, "the militarily patriotic and romantic-minded, and especially the professional military class, refuse to admit for a moment that war may be a transitory phenomenon in social evolution" (*ERM* 165). A third powerful notion is "hardihood," a value with which James is more in agreement.[49] He at least partly concurs, as we shall see, that "militarism is the great preserver of our ideals of hardihood, and human life without hardihood would be contemptible," and that we have a duty to keep "military characters in stock" and thus to prevent the "weaklings and mollycoddles" (*ERM* 166), whom Theodore Roosevelt condemns,[50] from taking over society. James continues to characterize the views of his opponents when he notes that war, whatever its negative consequences, is the only way to prevent the triumph "of a world of clerks and teachers, of co-education and zoophily, of 'consumers leagues' and 'associated charities,' of industrialism unlimited, and feminism unabashed. Not scorn, no hardness, no valor any more! Fie upon such a cattleyard of a planet!" (ERM 166).

Operating in the midst of this rhetoric, and with an inheritance of "all the innate pugnacity and all the love of glory" of our ancestors, we have given warfare a religious role in society as "a sort of sacrament" of purification (ERM 163, 165). Although he admits that humans live "by habits," he maintains that what they live "*for* its thrills and excitements," and "from time immemorial wars have been, especially for non-combatants, the supremely thrilling excitement" (ERM 122). In this situation James rightly notes that recognizing the destructiveness, the moral evil, of war will not be enough. Our societal practice needs to be significantly reconstructed. "The military feelings are too deeply grounded to abdicate their place among our ideals until better substitutes are offered than the glory and shame that come to nations as well as to individuals from the ups and downs of politics and the vicissitudes of trade," he writes (ERM 162). As a result, would-be pacifists need "to enter more deeply into the esthetical and ethical point of view of their opponents" (ERM 168) to try to understand the values they have associated with the military life. No society can be expected to abandon war until it feels that it has another way to instill the values that militarism now brings. James thus maintains that we must rescue such notions as "defense," "patriotism" and "hardihood" from the militarists—a task that he does not believe will be easy. As he puts it, "the war against war is going to be no holiday excursion or camping party" (ERM 162).

Because of the problematic make-up of human nature, James fears that our attempts to tame our war selves will allow only "for preventive medicine, not for radical cure" (ERM 122). He had recommended the following steps in 1904: "organize in every conceivable way the practical machinery for making each successive chance of war abortive. Put peace-men in power; educate the editors and statesmen to responsibility.... Seize every pretext, however small, for arbitration methods, and multiply the precedents; foster rival excitements and invent new outlets for heroic energy; and from one generation to another, the chances are that irritations will grow less acute and states of strain less dangerous among the nations" (ERM 123).

His prescription for advancing "the ultimate reign of peace" and "the gradual advent of some sort of socialistic equilibrium" about which he had earlier expressed reservations involves, first, the rejection of "the fatalistic view of the war-function." He writes that war *can* be stopped because "war-making is due to definite motives and subject to prudential checks and reasonable criticisms, just like any other form of enterprise." Further, he notes, war *must* be stopped: "when whole nations are the armies, and the science of destruction vies in intellectual refinement with the sciences of production, I see that war becomes absurd and impossible from its own monstrosity." Eventually, he believes, nations will come to understand this and make "common cause" against war. As he writes, "I look forward to a future when acts of war shall be formally outlawed among civilized peoples" (*ERM* 170). Our only "safeguard" is to keep "the passion of military conquest" forever chained and "never to let it get its start" (*ECR* 154).

Whatever James's antimilitarist beliefs, however, he does not believe that "peace either ought to be or will be permanent on this globe, unless the states pacifically organized preserve some of the old elements of army-discipline." Rejecting any equation of a "peace-economy" with a "pleasure-economy," he continues that in the future "we must still subject ourselves collectively to those severities that answer to our real position upon this only partly hospitable globe." He finds in the military virtues "the enduring cement" of society: "intrepidity, contempt of softness, surrender of private interest, obedience to command." James writes further that "the martial virtues, altho' originally gained by the race through war, are absolute and permanent human goods." Those who turn their backs on hardihood open themselves to "dangerous reactions against commonwealths fit only for contempt," and are "liable to invite attack whenever a centre of crystallization for military-minded enterprise is formed anywhere in their neighborhood" (*ERM* 170).[51]

At this point, a secondary issue emerges in James's essay—a nascent concern with social justice—and an indication that the solutions to the problems of justice and war are intertwined. His concern with a lack of hardihood seems to be focused on well-to-do male college students, who exist comfortably outside of the work economy.[52] We all know, however, that their lives are not the complete story. As we have seen, James recognizes that life is hard for most people. He notes that it is unfair that accidental factors deal out to some people a life of comfort and ease, while others—equally deserving—face only endless days of struggle. While we cannot eliminate toil and pain, however, we can spread it around more equitably. If there is any value to a life of strenuous effort, then developing hardihood more evenly would benefit more individuals, and society at large.

As a moral equivalent of war,[53] James proposes that we replace our partial military conscription with "a conscription of the whole youthful [male] population to form for a certain number of years a part of the army enlisted against *nature*"—*for* nature, we would now phrase this point—that would work to minimize the injustice of selective suffering and result in other benefits to society. Among these would be the following: "The military ideals of hardihood and discipline would be wrought into the growing fibre of the people; no one would remain blind, as the luxurious classes now are blind, to man's relations to the globe he lives on, and to the permanently solid and hard foundations of his higher life." To bring about these goods, he suggests the following program:

> To coal and iron mines, to freight trains, to fishing fleets in December, to dish-washing, clothes-washing, and window-washing, to road-building and tunnel-making, to foundries and stoke-holes, and to the frames of skyscrapers, would our gilded youths be drafted off, according to their choice, to get the childishness knocked out of them, and to come back into society with healthier sympathies and soberer ideas. They would have paid their blood-tax, done their own part in the immemorial human warfare against nature, they would tread the earth more proudly, the women would value them more highly, they would be better fathers and teachers of the following generation. (ERM 171–72)[54]

This kind of conscription, he believed, would be able to preserve, "in the midst of a pacific civilization," the virtues of hardihood that defenders of militarism feared would disappear in peacetime. "We should get toughness without callousness, authority with as little criminal cruelty as possible, and painful work done cheerily because the duty is temporary, and threatens not, as now, to degrade the whole remainder of one's life." By developing a recognition of social place among our youth and a better form of patriotism, and by developing in them a version of the "strenuous honour and disinterestedness" that is found in clergy and physicians, James believes that "the martial type of character can be bred without war" (*ERM* 172; cf. *C* 12:8), and that war thus has a moral equivalent.

Although James's approach has not been the subject of a great deal of commentary recently, it was widely discussed earlier, both for his analysis of human pugnacity and his proposals for redirecting it. We can consider a series of evaluations of his position beginning with Jane Addams's 1906 volume, *Newer Ideals of Peace*, in which she displays a much more positive tone than James. She tells us that our social need is not to redirect our hostile instincts, but to build human solidarity. In a similar fashion, she writes that to talk of channeling our hostilities toward fighting nature is still too negative. Rather than giving a central role to pugnacity (as does James's gendered account), she writes that "the new social morality, which we so sadly need, will of necessity have its origin in the social affections." While Addams admits that war "in the past has done much to bring men together"—for example by "stirring appeal to action for a common purpose" and opening "the channels of sympathy through which we partake of the life about us"—she is adamant that other possible ways of opening those channels exist. The kind of new patriotism that she proposes would come not through conquest and militarism, but through industrial development. "Militarism undertakes to set in order, to suppress and to govern, if necessary to destroy, while industrialism undertakes to liberate latent forces, to reconcile them to new conditions, to demonstrate that their aroused activities can no longer follow caprice, but must fit into a larger order of life."[55] Thus, focusing on expanding the positive aspects of human nature like our social affections rather than on overcoming our pugnacity, Addams's approach would attempt to build peace rather than to minimize war.

Writing in early 1917 Granville Stanley Hall sounds much less hopeful than James, whose suggestions he calls "pallid and academic" in the light of World War I. Hall continues that "it is more or less normal for man at times to plunge back and down the evolutionary ladder, and to immerse himself in rank, primitive emotions and to break away from the complex conventions and routine of civilized life and revert to that of the troglodytes in the trenches, and to face the chance of instant death when the struggle for survival is at its maximum in the bayonet charge."[56] Hall's approach would seem to reject any lasting possibility of redirecting human pugnacity into more socially beneficial practices.

Later in 1917, after the Americans had entered World War I, Mary

Whiton Calkins writes both of "the desire for the end of the Great War" and "the passionate longing for an end of all war." Sounding very much like James, she rejects "the psychological dogma that man is inevitably a fighter and the ethical dogma that through war, and through war alone, he can rise to the supreme height of self-sacrifice." With regard to the former, she notes that "war is not the inevitable result of unmodifiable instinct." While she admits the futility of trying to modify an instinct "in a purely negative way" by simply denying or deflecting it, she maintains that even a harmful instinct can be "directed toward new objects or ... subordinated to another instinct." Thus, she hopes that what are now seen as belligerent instincts can be put to the use of "a strenuous and militant peace." Advocating what she calls "militant pacifism," Calkins hopes "to preserve and even to strengthen the fighting instinct, with all these martial virtues which it inspires, but to direct it to radically new ends": fighting a "New War" against "human ignorance, human injustice ... against Nature and against human greed and sloth and cruelty." Her faith in this possibility also enables her to reject the second dogma of militarism, the belief that "war must be cherished as an awful but necessary human experience which purges men's souls of cowardice and selfishness and fans to a flame the fires of courage and devotion."[57]

Writing in the early 1920s John Dewey similarly advocates the redirection of our violent inclinations, although he is less comfortable with the rigid concept of "instinct" than what he sees as the more flexible concept of "impulse." He writes that "the suggestion of an *equivalent* for war calls attention to the medley of impulses which are casually bunched together under the caption of belligerent impulse; and ... to the fact that the elements of this medley may be woven together into many differing types of activity, some of which may function the native impulses in much better ways than war has ever done." While, on the one hand, the raw materials come from human nature, he continues, "custom furnishes the machinery and the designs." Thus, while wars would not take place "without anger, pugnacity, rivalry, self-display, and such like native tendencies," these impulses could be redirected, and to believe that "they must eventuate in war is as if a savage were to believe that because he uses fibres having fixed natural properties in order to weave baskets, therefore his immemorial tribal patterns are also natural necessities and immutable forms."[58]

A second line of inquiry accepts James's general position on pugnacity but questions whether his proposal for a moral equivalent of war would be an adequate response. Could a social regimen of dish-washing and road-building—to use some of James's examples—or international athletic competitions and educational exchange programs—to use other suggested possibilities—overcome our belligerent tendencies? Writing in 1929 George Herbert Mead registers his doubts. He suggests that to characterize our emotional patriotism-hostility cult as an "instinct" or "impulse" fails to recognize the powerful constitutive role that it plays in our sense of self (what he calls the "me"). "To join ourselves with others in the common assault upon the common foe we have become more than allies," he continues, "we have joined a clan, have different souls, and have the exuberant feeling of being at one with this community." As a result, he doubts the possibility of any easy redirection. Although James suggests that we can "substitute some other cult for the cult of warfare" with an equivalent "emotional result," Mead maintains that "cults are not deliberately created in this fashion," nor "manufactured to order." Thus, while he does not oppose attempts to substitute "a harmless cult for one that is extremely hazardous," the fundamental problem that he sees in James's approach is the continued emotional attachment to a cult of whatever sort. What is necessary to combat war, Mead believes, is an explicitly intellectual response: "We must *think* ourselves in terms of the great community to which we belong," we must create a kind of "international-mindedness." Any moral equivalent of war that will work, he believes, will only be "found in the intelligence and the will both to discover these common interests between contending nations and to make them the basis for the solution of the existing differences and for the common life which they will make possible."[59]

Let me offer just one more perspective. One realist critic, writing anonymously in 1910, disagreed with James because, as he puts it, "so long as evil and injustice remain to be combated wars will be unavoidable in some form or other." War, however unfortunate a means, is sometimes a necessary one to resist the evil of others. "We should believe in the abolition of war only if we believed that some day no criminals will be left and that all the prisons will be closed, and that some day sincere differences of opinion on matters of principle will be impossible." According to this critic, the extremist James fails to recognize the possibility of a good war. "War is not always a giving of the rein to bestial jealousy or avarice," he continues. "It may be waged to preserve the right. Let us never forget that the possession of armed strength in an imperfect world means the *power* to insist on the right."[60] How else, for example, but through the horror of the American Civil War could we have ended the worse horror of human slavery? In response, we can consider James's true, but perhaps irrelevant, comment from 1897: "The lesson that our [civil] war ought most of all to teach us is the lesson that evils must be checked in time, before they grow so great" (*ERM* 73).

James's discussions of the problem of war demonstrate as nowhere else in his thought the importance of the social realm to ethical questions. He indicates here that an important prerequisite of living a good life is antecedently making the world a better place. A world without war would be a place where the positive values of the martial spirit were turned by the people against the true enemies of humankind and not against each other. It still seems, however, that he misses the extent to which an individual country existing within a system of rival nation states cannot simply commit itself to pacifism in isolation from the activities of its neighbors. Thus, it is that the individualistic tone of his moral thought ultimately works against him here also. Perhaps, in 1910 the oceans seemed wide enough for isolated pacifism. The war that began in 1914 proved they were not, and James's notion of a moral equivalent of war was abandoned for the headier moral potions of Woodrow Wilson and others. James was right that a person cannot be an effective pacifist in a country mad with militarism, but he overlooked the fact that neither can a country be pacifist unless the world itself is at peace. Perhaps this strong criticism focusing on James's proposed moral equivalent of war is misplaced, however, and our emphasis should be placed where his was: on the social psychology of war. While we cannot expect him to solve the war problem in single essay, we can better appreciate his clear presentation of the fundamental nature of the problem.

CHAPTER 7

Religion

This chapter explores James's ideas on religion. His personal world was a highly religious one—not in terms of theological doctrine or worship—but in terms of the kind of meaning for human life that he sought to uncover and defend. Further, his sense of human possibilities was always tinged with religious overtones. Part of this chapter discusses his 1902 volume, *The Varieties of Religious Experience: A Study in Human Nature* as exactly that: a psychological study of those highly charged areas of human experience that considers what these mysterious occasions might mean for the rest of us and in the remainder of our lives. A second consideration of this chapter is his willingness to seek meaning in the "more" at the fringes of experience. It was in this penumbra around our more clarified and ordered reality that he sought healing power to fortify his life. Also to be considered is the question of religious truth. Drawing on his later volume *Pragmatism*, this chapter explores our possibility for attaining knowledge about religious matters, and whether we may be justified to act in the absence of such knowledge.

Experiential Religion

James lived in a religious society and practiced the quasi-religious profession of philosophy teaching—a profession that was only then being separated from the duties of the college president, who had almost always been an ordained minister.[1] His father was a religious mystic. He himself, as we saw in chapter 1, suffered a vastation as a young man, and in his later life had at least one more mystical experience.[2] Moreover, one of the themes of his life was the desire for a more vibrant religious life. He wrote to one correspondent in 1900 that the life of religion "as a whole is mankind's most important function" (C 9:186),[3] and to another in 1904 that, while he had "no living sense of commerce with a God," he envied those who did because he believed that "the addition of such a sense would help me immensely." He continues that, in his "*active* life," the "Divine" is strictly a matter of "abstract concepts" that has little power over him "in comparison with what a feeling of God might effect, if I had one." Although James admitted to being without "*Gottesbewus[s]tsein* [a consciousness of God] in the director and stronger sense," he still maintains that "there is *something in me* which *makes response* when I hear utterances made from that lead by others," and that something indicated to him that "'*thither lies truth.*'"[4] In a similar fashion, he notes that he is uncertain how helpful his discussion of mystical states in *The Varieties* will be to readers "for my own constitution shuts me out from their enjoyment almost entirely, and I speak of them only at second hand" (VRE 301). He continues to assert the importance of trying to appreciate others' reports on their mystical and other religious experiences. James further warns "the cleric-academic-scientific" audiences to which he was speaking and for which he was writing, made up of "the officially and conventionally 'correct' type, 'the deadly respectable' type" of individuals, not to ignore the reports of the others since "nothing can be more stupid than to bar out phenomena from our notice, merely because we are incapable of taking any part in them ourselves" (VRE 95).[5]

James did not want conceptual or historical knowledge of religion: he wanted the experience of belief. We can recall this through a quick glance at his other writings that we have considered previously. As we saw in chapter 3, in *The Will to Believe* he writes that "we cannot live or think at all without some degree of faith." For him, faith is essential to living in accordance with the various working hypotheses that direct our advance into the future. Some of these hypotheses "can be refuted in five minutes, others may defy ages." As we live forward, this faith will have the opportunity to verify itself. "Believe, and you shall be right, for you shall save yourself; doubt, and you shall again be right, for you shall perish," he writes. "The only difference is that to believe is greatly to your advantage" (WB 79–80). In those instances where the matter is live, forced and momentous, he continues, "we have the right to believe at our own risk any hypothesis that is live enough to tempt our will" (WB 32). Among the sorts of cases that he considers are ethical matters, personal relations and religion, and within the final class he notes the assumption that "the best things are the more eternal things" (*WB* 29; cf. 48). Moreover, because he views all of these as contribution cases, we cannot wait and see. Then, as we saw in chapter 4, in "Philosophical Conceptions and Practical Results" James discusses the importance of direct religious experience and rejects theology as abstract, conceptual chatter that seldom returns to inform our temporal existence. In that same essay, he notes that Theism is superior to Materialism if for no other reason than it offers "an ideal order that shall be permanently preserved." As he sees it, Materialism denies "that the moral order is eternal," and cuts us off from "ultimate hopes," whereas Theism offers us "the affirmation of an eternal order" and the possibility of hope. He notes further that the desire for such an eternal moral order is "one of the deepest needs of our breast" (*P* 264/55).

Psychological Method

James's Gifford Lectures in Natural Religion that became *The Varieties* were delivered in Edinburgh, Scotland, in two series between May 1901 and June 1902. In accordance with the wishes of the Lectures' founder, and devotee of the works of Emerson,[6] Adam Gifford, the lecturers "may be of any religion or way of thinking, or as is sometimes said, they may be of no religion, or they may be so-called sceptics or agnostics or freethinkers, provided only that the 'patrons' will use diligence to secure that they be able, reverent men, true thinkers, sincere lovers of and earnest inquirers after truth." In particular, Gifford wanted the lecturers "to treat their subject as a strictly natural science,"[7] a clause that meant to James the need to emphasize the importance of religion to human life.[8] His original plan was to divide the twenty lectures in half, discussing in the first series "'Man's Religious Appetites,'" a psychological or descriptive account of our religious propensities, and then in the second series offering a metaphysical consideration of the philosophical significance of these propensities via "'Their Satisfaction through Philosophy'" (*VRE* 5; cf. 13). As he worked to prepare the lectures, however, the amount of psychological material continued to grow and the "metaphysical" material became much less prominent.[9] Still, as I suggested in chapter 2, it is wise to approach James's work in general as a predisciplinary amalgam of psychology and philosophy, as psycholophy.

As he began his lectures in Edinburgh, James admitted that he was "neither a theologian, nor a scholar learned in the history of religions, nor an anthropologist." He was, rather, a skilled psychologist, and as he notes, for the psychologist "the religious propensities of man must be at least as interesting as any other of the facts pertaining to his mental constitution" (*VRE* 12). Thus, he believes that the accounts of nervous instability and psychical visitations, of trances and voices and visions, of melancholy and obsessions and fixed ideas that he details in *The Varieties*, should be just as interesting to the psychologist as are other mental phenomena.[10] Considering the phenomenon of "instantaneous conversion," for example, he notes that, "were we writing the story of the mind from the purely natural-history point of view, with no religious interest whatever, we should still have to write down man's liability to sudden and complete conversion as one of his most curious peculiarities." Regardless of our eventual interpretation of such a conversion—as either "a miracle in which God is present as he is present in no change of heart less strikingly abrupt," or as "a strictly natural process ... neither more nor less divine in its mere causation and mechanism than any other process, high or low, of man's interior life" (*VRE* 188)—the conversion experience itself is an event to which the psychologist should attend. In his careful, almost clinical, introduction to the lectures, James the psychologist proceeds with an inquiry that attempts to provide "a true record of the inner experiences of great-souled persons wrestling with the crises of their fate" (*VRE* 14). For him, experiential religion is of immense importance to a full understanding of human nature, not to be neglected by psychology.

It is further necessary to avoid the prejudices of "medical materialism" (*VRE* 20) that these experiences represent symptomatic evidence of mental illness. One of James's emphases was to reject the view that natural, or even pathological, roots can undermine "the worth of a thing" (*VRE* 193). Using this standard, no religious experience could be eliminated from consideration by indicating its bodily origin. "To the medical mind," he admits, "these ecstasies signify nothing but suggested and imitated hypnoid states, on an intellectual basis of superstition, and a corporeal one of degeneration and hysteria." Still, he maintains that, even knowing "these pathological conditions have existed in many and possibly in all the cases," this knowledge tells us nothing about "the value for knowledge of the consciousness which they induce." Any judgment that we might pass upon those religious states must be based not upon "superficial medical talk," but upon inquiries "into their fruits for life" (*VRE* 327). James admits that those who lead deeply religious lives—saints, martyrs, and others—may be statistically unusual, but he maintains that they are not significantly more unusual than those who devote their lives to opera or gardening, to sports or philosophy.

James assumes the stance of physiological psychology that maintains that "the dependence of mental states upon bodily conditions must be thorough-going and complete" (*VRE* 20). He continues that, while the methods of psychology are far different from those traditionally associated with inquiries into matters spiritual, this mode of inquiry should not be seen as a rejection, or even a disparagement, of religion. While handling the phenomena of religious experience "biologically and psychologically as if they were mere curious facts of individual history" might suggest to some individuals "a degradation of so sublime a subject," or even worse an attempt "to discredit the religious side of life" (*VRE* 14), he sees no necessary connection between his use of the methods of psychological science and any efforts to undermine the potential human value of religion. As he writes, "how can such an existential account of facts of mental history decide in one way or another upon their spiritual significance?" Psychology explores human self-understanding in a manner that applies equally well to "the dicta of the sturdy atheist" and to "those of the Methodist under conviction anxious about his soul" (*VRE* 20). James the psychologist maintains that religious behavior is ultimately human behavior. Thus, the various phenomena of the religious life—melancholy, trances, conversions, and so on—are each "special cases of kinds of human experience of much wider scope" (*VRE* 28). If we hope to understand these religious phenomena as continuous with the rest of human behavior, he continues, "we cannot possibly ignore these pathological aspects of the subject. We must describe and name them just as if they occurred in non-religious men" (*VRE* 17).

As we have just seen, James's introduction of the concept of "pathology" should not be understood as implying that he views religious experiences as episodes of mental disorder. The term should suggest, rather, an amplification or magnification of a sort that he believes is particularly helpful to scientific inquiries.[11] We know that in general he filled these lectures with particular examples and maintained, as we might expect, that "a large acquaintance with particulars often makes us wiser than the possession of abstract formulas, however deep." We know further that James chose many of these examples from among what he calls "the extremer expressions of the religious temperament." While he recognized that his focus on these "convulsions of piety" (*VRE* 5) might make some in his audience uncomfortable, his intention was to portray religion in "its more completely evolved and perfect forms" (*VRE* 12).

While James does not immediately explicate this opaque phrase, we recognize what he has in mind through a series of analogies elsewhere in *The Varieties*. He notes, for example, that "we learn most about a thing when we view it under a microscope, as it were, or in its most exaggerated form" (*VRE* 40; cf. 26, 303). To understand arthritis or diabetes fully, for example, we should not attempt to study the impact of these diseases on patients who are only slightly or moderately afflicted. Similarly, to understand religion fully, we should not focus upon its modest impact on the "ordinary religious believer, who follows the conventional observances of his country, whether it be Buddhist, Christian, or Mohammedan" (*VRE* 15). Physiologists like extreme cases and religious experience is full of psychologically extreme cases. In a second analogy, he suggests that just as "it is a good rule in physiology, when we are studying the meaning of an organ, to ask after its most peculiar and characteristic sort of performance, and to seek its office in that one of its functions which no other organ can possibly exert," a similar rule applies in the case of religion. "The essence of religious experiences, the thing by which we finally must judge them, must be that element or quality in them which we can meet nowhere else," he writes, and we will be able to notice this aspect "in those religious experiences which are most one-sided, exaggerated, and intense" (*VRE* 44). In a third analogy, James treats the more extreme figures as uniquely valuable witnesses. "To learn the secrets of any science, we go to expert specialists, even though they may be excentric persons," he notes, "and not to commonplace pupils" (*VRE* 383). While the latter sort are more frequent and familiar, they are able to offer us none of the special insights of the former who can provide us with the exotic fruits of their extreme experiences. As he writes, "a religious life, exclusively pursued, does tend to make the person exceptional and excentric" (*VRE* 15), and the prophet will often appear as "a mere lonely madman" (*VRE* 270).[12]

For James, it is thus important not to examine individuals for whom religion is "a dull habit"; we should examine those for whom it is "an acute fever." The typical member of the former group he sees as only being religious at "second-hand": "His religion has been made for him by others, communicated to him by tradition, determined to fixed forms by imitation, and retained by habit." Little is to be gained by our study of such believers. Much, however, is to be gained by studying the members of the latter group, made up of individuals who burn with religious fervor. These individuals, whom James characterizes as the "'geniuses'" of religion, have demonstrated in their lives all sorts of "peculiarities" that the average believer has not, but while admitting that these experiences are "ordinarily classed as pathological" (*VRE* 15), he advocates their careful examination.[13] We should stay away from the vague border areas and focus upon the most central and flamboyant instances of religious experience. He writes that "at their extreme of development, there can never be any question as to what experiences are religious. The divinity of the object and the solemnity of the reaction are too well marked for doubt." When there is doubt or hesitation, it is because the religious state of mind is weak, and thus "hardly worthy of our study at all." For him, it is important to concentrate on those "exaggerated" cases "where the religious spirit is unmistakable and extreme" (*VRE* 40).

From his initial focus on "the acute religion of the few against the chronic religion of the many" (*VRE* 98), James develops *The Varieties* in separate directions, which he calls "two orders of inquiry." In the first, he continues the psychological inquiry into the nature of our "religious propensities"; in the second, he offers a philosophical inquiry into their "significance" (*VRE* 13). While the exploration of the religious propensities of his many witnesses makes up the bulk of the volume,[14] this should not suggest that the latter inquiry into the significance of these experiences was of only secondary interest. The experiential data admittedly fascinated him, and he was drawn to explore it more deeply than he had originally intended. At the same time, however, he undertook this project as a would-be believer seeking answers to his own personal questions about religious experience. There is thus a strong tension in *The Varieties*: while the objective psychological method for examining these religious experiences should lead to no conclusions about their overall meaning, he was strongly drawn personally to examine the data of these experiences by his prior beliefs—or at least hopes—about what they might mean.[15] In fact, while James begins the lectures attempting to balance out the contributions of the psychological scientist and the religious believer, during the course of the lectures the believer wins.

As James had anticipated, his psychological approach did not meet with complete acceptance from religious quarters. George B. Stevens, for example, calls *The Varieties* "the most unconventional and the raciest treatment of the philosophy of religion which has yet appeared" because James exhibits "especially the abnormal and bizarre manifestations of religious sentiment." George Albert Coe similarly notes that "no effort is made to separate the typical from the aberrational.... The average religious man is even said to be an imitator of the extremist, who is the 'pattern-setter.'" For Frank Sewall, James's survey of the field through instances of "religious emotional pathology," rather than through "religion as a perfectly normal, healthy, and happy factor in human life," means that he "has treated here of every variety of religious experience, save that of genuine religion itself." Sewell maintains, however, that "to study religion by these examples is to the average religious mind like walking through a medical museum, as compared with watching a body of healthy youth on a spring morning in the athletic field." In like fashion, Adolf Augustus Berle complains that James's "whole method is the method of the pathologist, which is fundamentally false as applied to the spiritual life." Thus, Berle seems especially concerned with the way that James's examples present religion. As he writes, "we do not want, and the Christian people as a whole will not permit, the experiences of the church to be grounded even superficially in these transitory and least impressive elements, which, while furnishing the materials for thought and suggestion, are never to be confounded with the real power which is over and behind them." John Grier Hibben perhaps summarizes the mood of these criticisms of James's psychological method when he writes: "As in philosophy the appeal is so often made to the common sense of the plain man, so also in religion the superior court of appeal resides in the common experiences, the commonplace experiences if you will, of simple conviction and quiet devotion."[16]

Focusing the Inquiry

Turning to the second chapter of *The Varieties*, we find James circumscribing the topic of religion. A familiar starting point would be a definition of what is to be included and excluded by the term,[17] but he maintains that no precise definition of "religion" is possible in advance. The diversity of meanings for the term suggests to him that "the word 'religion' cannot stand for any single principle or essence, but is rather a collective name." It is necessary for us, therefore, to avoid "over-simplification" and the resultant "absolutism and one-sided dogmatism" that plague much writing on the topic by rejecting up front the search for some "one essence" of religion, and to explore rather the "many characters which may alternately be equally important in religion" (*VRE* 30). If we are to come to know religion from within, we must do so experientially, rather than conceptually.[18] Similarly, just as we cannot define "religion," we cannot indicate the "religious" emotion, or point to the "religious" object. Further, he writes that among those who have tried to capture the "religious sentiment," "one man allies it to the feeling of dependence; one makes it a derivative from fear; others connect it with the sexual life; others still identify it with the feeling of the infinite; and so on." These differences should make us skeptical that there is one religious sentiment to be uncovered in psychology. He continues: "religious love is only man's natural emotion of love directed to a religious object; religious fear is only the ordinary fear of commerce, so to speak, the common quaking of the human breast, in so far as the notion of divine retribution may arouse it; religious awe is the same organic thrill which we feel in a forest at twilight, or in a mountain gorge; only this time it comes over us at the thought of our supernatural relations; and similarly of all the various sentiments which may be called into play in the lives of religious persons." While James is willing to grant that religious emotions are "psychic entities distinguishable from other concrete emotions," he still maintains that "there is no ground for assuming a simple abstract 'religious emotion' to exist as a distinct elementary mental affection by itself, present in every religious experience without exception." Rather, he suggests that there is "no one elementary religious emotion, but only a common storehouse of emotions upon which religious objects may draw ... no one specific and essential kind of religious object, and no one specific and essential kind of religious act" (*VRE* 31).

James recognizes, however, that unless he wants to have his inquiry swamped by everything that has been in any way connected with religion, or to be forced to abandon his inquiry as impossible, he needs to narrow and specify his topic somehow. He consequently selects those aspects of religion that will be primary in *The Varieties*. After pointing to the "great partition which divides the religious field" between the "institutional" and the "personal"—between "worship and sacrifice, procedures for working on the dispositions of the deity, theology and ceremony and ecclesiastical organization" on the one hand, and "the inner dispositions of man himself which form the centre of interest, his conscience, his deserts, his helplessness, his incompleteness" on the other (*VRE* 32)—he tells us that his focus will be upon the latter aspects.[19] These personal aspects represent to him the more important part of the religious question, and should others feel that he has jettisoned the vital core of religion, he tentatively allows their worries as long as they are open to considering first the aspects of religion that he will be examining. "I am willing to accept almost any name for the personal religion of which I propose to treat," he writes. "Call it conscience or morality, if you yourselves prefer, and not religion." His sole concern is that his topic be recognized as "equally worthy of our study" (*VRE* 33).

For James, the personal aspects of religion are the core, and all of the rest—the non-experiential—is second-hand. "In seeing freshly, and not in hearing of what others saw, shall a man find what truth is" (*ERM* 111), he writes at his most Emersonian.[20] James notes that personal religion is "the primordial thing," and that it "will prove itself more fundamental than either theology or ecclesiasticism." Churches and other religious institutions, once established by founders as diverse as Christ, the Buddha, Mahomet, and the originators of the various Christian sects, "live at second-hand upon tradition; but the *founders* of every church owed their power originally to the fact of their direct personal communion with the divine" (*VRE* 33; cf. *C* 9:501). We are better off if we concentrate on "the original experiences which were the pattern-setters to all this mass of suggested feeling and imitated conduct" (*VRE* 15; cf. 341, 358–59), and confine our examination to "direct religious experience" instead of "hearsay religion" (*P* 266).

James's personal, even private, approach to his topic runs counter to the social understanding of the religious life that many favor. Hibben, for example, maintains that "the significance of the individual case of personal religious experience can be adequately appreciated only in its general religious setting and historical antecedents." Thus, the meaning of even "the extreme case of religious experience" must be evaluated through a consideration of "its effect upon the community, the tribe, the nation, or the age in which it occurs." Further, Hibben notes that while even "great religious movements" are rooted in "the personal religious experience of a conspicuous leader of thought," at the same time that leader must be "accounted for in a large measure by the religious atmosphere of the age in which he lives." So, while it is true "that Luther founded Protestantism; it is also true that Protestantism produced Luther." In a similar fashion, in his 1918 volume, *The Problem of Christianity*, Josiah Royce notes that, while James limited himself to "the religious experience of individuals," he himself was more interested in "social religious experience," or, in his Pauline context, "the experience of the Church." James had assumed that "the religious experience of a church must needs be 'conventional,' and consequently must be lacking in depth and in sincerity." For Royce, however, James's assumption was "a profound and a momentous error in the whole religious philosophy of our greatest American master in the study of the psychology of religious experience." While Royce grants that all experience has to be individual experience, he maintains that unless religious experience is "*also* social experience, and unless the whole religious community which is in question unites to share it, this experience is but as sounding brass, and as a tinkling cymbal." For him, it is only by understanding what he takes to be "the true and ideal" Christian Church that we can hope to understand the nature of religion.[21]

James, for his part, develops a more precise working definition of "religion as an individual personal function" that "lives itself out within the private breast" (*VRE* 268–69). Religion, he continues, "shall mean for us *the feelings, acts, and experiences of individual men in their solitude, so far as they apprehend themselves to stand in relation to whatever they may consider the divine.*" Out of this understanding of religion as an experiential core, he notes, "theologies, philosophies, and ecclesiastical organizations may secondarily grow" (*VRE* 34), reflecting various potential aspects of this relation. James recognizes that "worship and sacrifice, procedures for working on the dispositions of the deity, theology and ceremony and ecclesiastical organization, are the essentials of religion in the institutional branch" (*VRE* 32). Still, his primary interest remains in the vagaries of individual religious experience, and he demonstrates little or no concern for institutional or doctrinal questions, other than occasional negative comments like the following: "The spirit of politics and the lust of dogmatic rule are . . . apt to enter and to contaminate the original innocent thing" when religion is understood as "an institutional, corporate, or tribal product" (*VRE* 268). Thus, it is for James that, while "religion is man's most important function," most of its "particular manifestation are patently absurd" (*C* 9:422).[22]

James on occasion uses the term "divine," instead of "God," when he wants to emphasize that some important religious approaches are without a god figure. "There are systems of thought which the world usually calls religious," he writes, "which do not positively assume a God." Buddhism is one example. Another is transcendental idealism of the Emersonian sort that "seems to let God evaporate into abstract Ideality." What James calls "the transcendentalist cult" is not interested in "a deity *in concreto*" or in "a superhuman person"; its interest is in "the immanent divinity in things, the essentially spiritual structure of the universe" (*VRE* 34). He continues that "it would be too absurd to say that the inner experiences that underlie such expressions of faith as these and impel the writer to their utterance are quite unworthy to be called religious experiences." On the contrary, the functioning of "Emersonian optimism" and of "Buddhistic pessimism" in human life are "in fact indistinguishable from, and in many respects identical with, the best Christian appeal and response." Thus, he continues, we must "from the experiential point of view, call these godless or quasi-godless creeds 'religions.'" Therefore, when James speaks of "the individual's relation to 'what he considers the divine,'" his intention is to interpret the term "divine" broadly enough to denote "any object that is god*like*, whether it be a concrete deity or not." It is his desire that we recognize and treat as "godlike" whatever is seen as the "most primal and enveloping and deeply true," so that an individual's religion "might thus be identified with his attitude, whatever it might be, towards what he felt to be the primal truth" (*VRE* 36).

While in *The Varieties* James largely follows along with his witnesses' conceptions of an infinite God, in *A Pluralistic Universe* a few years later he asserts his own contrary position that God must be finite. Here he is attempting to distinguish Idealism's abstract notion of the Absolute from "the 'God' of common people in their religion, and the creator-God of orthodox christian theology." He believes that this God is part of a pluralistic, rather than a monistic or pantheistic, system. "He and we stand outside of each other, just as the devil, the saints and the angels stand outside of both of us," James writes. "I can hardly conceive of anything more different from the absolute than the God, say, of David or of Isaiah." That God, James continues, "is an essentially finite being *in* the cosmos, not with the cosmos in him, and indeed he has a very local habitation there, and very one-sided local and personal attachments." As a result, even should it turn out that there is no Absolute, "it will not follow in the slightest degree that a God like that of David, Isaiah, or Jesus may not exist," James continues. "I hold to the finite God" (*PU* 54; cf. *WB* 97–98, 106). This God, who functions in the lives of ordinary religious people, is "the name of the ideal tendency in things, believed in as a superhuman person who calls us to co-operate in his purposes, and who furthers ours if they are worthy." Further, James maintains that "the only God worthy of the name *must* be finite" (*PU* 60).

In part, James is indicating here his sense of the frustration with the conception of an infinite God. He writes that "all the irrationalities and puzzles which the absolute gives rise to, and from which the finite God remains free, are due to the fact that absolute has nothing, absolutely nothing, outside of itself." A finite God, on the contrary, has at least "the minutest fraction of the universe" outside of himself, and is thus "a relative being," rather than an absolute one and thus avoids "all the irrationalities incidental to absolutism" (*PU* 61). He thus suggests that the most sensible choice in both theology and philosophy is "to accept, along with the superhuman consciousness, the notion that it is not all-embracing—the notion, in other words, that there *is* a God, but that he is finite, either in power or knowledge, or in both at once" (*PU* 141).[23] Further, he believes that "common men"—not theologians or philosophers—have usually carried on "their active commerce with God" in just this fashion, and the various "monistic perfections that make the notion of him so paradoxical practically and morally are the colder additions of remote professorial minds" who are working abstractly with only "conceptual substitutes" for God (*PU* 141; cf. *ERM* 60). James even suggests that "the faithfulness of individuals here below to their own poor over-beliefs" may thereby "help God in turn to be more effectively faithful to his own greater tasks" by enabling him to "draw vital strength and increase of very being from our fidelity" (*VRE* 408; *WB* 55; cf. *P* 139–44). We, in cooperation with God, attempt to overcome the actual instances of evil.

In another attempted definition, James writes that "religion, whatever it is, is a man's total reaction upon life, so why not say that any total reaction upon life is a religion?" (*VRE* 36). Leaving aside the questionable nature of this conversion, we can still wonder what a "total reaction to life" is, and how we would uncover one. He writes:

> Total reactions are different from casual reactions, and total attitudes are different from usual or professional attitudes. To get at them you must go behind the foreground of existence and reach down to that curious sense of the whole residual cosmos as an everlasting presence, intimate or alien, terrible or amusing, lovable or odious, which in some degree every one possesses. This sense of the world's presence, appealing as it does to our peculiar individual temperament, makes us either strenuous or careless, devout or blasphemous, gloomy or exultant, about life at large.... Non-religious as some of these reactions may be, in one sense of the word "religious," they yet belong to *the general*

sphere of the religious life, and so should generically be classed as religious reactions. (*VRE* 36–37)

For James, further, religion is a matter of seriousness rather than irony or pessimism. Here he criticizes both Arthur Schopenhauer and Friedrich Nietzsche for offering positions that combine "an ennobling sadness" with a "peevishness running away with the bit between its teeth." The writings of these two Germans remind James, "half the time, of the sick shriekings of two dying rats," and he continues that "they lack the purgatorial note which religious sadness gives forth." Religion as he conceives it, however, should be a matter of strict devotion. "There must be something solemn, serious, and tender about any attitude which we denominate religious." When we use the term "divine," it should "mean for us not merely the primal and enveloping and real." Rather, he has in mind the more narrow meaning of "the divine" as "only such a primal reality as the individual feels impelled to respond to solemnly and gravely, and neither by a curse nor a jest" (*VRE* 39).

When we examine religious experiences carefully, James notes, it becomes clear that the religious person is quite different from the philosophical. Within the latter class, he writes, the individual's focus is more "manly, stoical, moral." The philosopher's life is "less swayed by paltry personal considerations and more by objective ends that call for energy, even though that energy bring personal loss and pain" (*VRE* 45). The philosopher, operating by willpower, thus lacks an essential characteristic of the religious person who relies upon the power of the divine. James writes of a special "state of mind, known to religious men, but to no others," in which our will "to assert ourselves and hold our own has been displaced by a willingness to close our mouths and be as nothing in the floods and waterspouts of God." This particular mind-set—he calls it an "enchantment"—is either present in an individual or it is not, and individuals who do not have it "can no more become possessed by it than they can fall in love with a given women by mere word of command." This religious feeling is "an absolute addition to the Subject's range of life," giving him or her "a new sphere of power," a "new reach of freedom" and a "sort of happiness in the absolute and everlasting" that "we find nowhere but in religion." This feeling also enables the religious person to withdraw "when the outward battle is lost.... It redeems and vivifies an interior world which otherwise would be an empty waste" (*VRE* 46–47).

James notes that there seems to be an overriding sort of happiness that results from this type of helplessness or dependence. The human condition in an only partially welcoming world requires, he continues, that we admit "at least some amount of dependence on sheer mercy" and "practice some amount of renunciation, great or small." We are, as he writes, "in the end absolutely dependent on the universe." On the other hand, for those of a philosophical inclination—those with "states of mind which fall short of religion"—he indicates that "the surrender is submitted to as an imposition of necessity, and the sacrifice is undergone at the very best without complaint." For religious persons, however, "surrender and sacrifice are positively espoused." James continues that religious persons go further: "even unnecessary givings-up are added in order that the happiness may increase." In this way, religion is able to make "*easy and felicitous what in any case is necessary; and if it be the only agency that can accomplish this result, its vital importance as a human faculty stands vindicated beyond dispute.*" What sort of "vindication" this might be remains to be determined, of course, since the psychologist can only recognize the power of this feeling in those who have it. While it may be true that, for believers, religion "becomes an essential organ of our life, performing a function which no other portion of our nature can so successfully fulfill" (*VRE* 49), the psychologist must still admit that this feeling is open to other nonreligious interpretations by those who, unlike James, do not feel religion's "vital importance" and who reject the moral holidays that dependency would make possible.

We cannot explore here the remaining chapters of *The Varieties*, the hundreds of pages of the unseen and conversions and saints that helps to flesh out James's point about the difference between the philosophical and the religious mind. We must, however, glance at his distinction between the healthy-minded and the sick soul. Throughout the volume, he emphasizes the tremendous differences present in the spiritual lives of different individuals. "Their wants, their susceptibilities, and their capacities all vary and must be classed under different heads" (*VRE* 94). Still, he does believe that it is possible to sort these differences into two general groups. "The sanguine and healthy-minded live habitually on the sunny side of their misery-line," he writes, and "the depressed and melancholy live beyond it, in darkness and apprehension." Appealing to these different personalities are two kinds of religion, depending on which "side of the pain-threshold" individuals live (*VRE* 115). The members of the first group, including such individuals as

Emerson and Whitman, are able to appreciate nearly everything and to view nature overall as welcoming. Theirs is "the tendency which looks on all things and sees that they are good" (*VRE* 78). These individuals have, he notes, "a temperament organically weighted on the side of cheer and fatally forbidden to linger ... over the darker aspects of the universe." Whitman, for example, was able to expel "all contractile elements" from his work, and to express only "expansive" sentiments. While James suggests that in some extreme cases this optimism may be "quasi-pathological" or "a kind of congenital anaesthesia" (*VRE* 75–76), he still maintains that "the systematic cultivation of healthy-mindedness as a religious attitude is ... consonant with important currents in human nature, and is anything but absurd." All of us, he thinks, "divert our attention from disease and death as much as we can"; we try to keep "the slaughter-houses and indecencies without end on which our life is founded" somewhere out of sight and mind. This leaves us with a sanitized world that is "a poetic fiction far handsomer and cleaner and better than the world that really is" (*VRE* 80–81). He notes that in the more extreme versions of this "sky-blue optimistic gospel" (*VRE* 115), in the "mind-cure" and "new thought" of his day, individuals are directed to not recognize "the more evil aspects of the universe," to decline "to lay them to heart or make much of them," and even at times to deny "outright that they exist" (*VRE* 109). From this perspective, recognizing evil, and worse worrying about it, is a disease that will ruin our lives.

James contrasts such healthy-minded individuals with the sick souls for whom "the evil aspects of our life are of its very essence." For these individuals, "evil is an essential part of our being and the key to the interpretation of our life" (*VRE* 112). From their perspective, all the goods of our natural existence are perishable. "Riches take wings; fame is a breath; love is a cheat; youth and health and pleasure vanish," he writes, leading to the question "can things whose end is always dust and disappointment be the real goods which our souls require?" All life is haunted by "the great spectre of universal death, the all-encompassing blackness" and permeated by "the breath of the sepulchre [that] surrounds it" (*VRE* 118). These individuals find that evil penetrates their "essential nature," and resists "any superficial rearrangement of the inner self." Their realization of evil "requires a supernatural remedy" (*VRE* 114).

James notes the antagonism that develops between the healthy-minded and the "morbid-minded" views of life. For those in the latter group, "healthy-mindedness pure and simple seems unspeakably blind and shallow"; for those in the former, "the way of the sick soul seems unmanly and diseased," more concerned with "grubbing in rat-holes instead of living in the light" and preoccupied "with every unwholesome kind of misery" (*VRE* 136). He himself, no doubt in part because of his own depressive tendencies, considered in chapter 1, believed the healthy-minded approach inadequate for dealing with the darkness of life. While "averting one's attention from evil, and living simply in the light of good is splendid as long as it will work," he maintains that healthy-mindedness can survive only until "melancholy comes." He notes further that it is "inadequate as a philosophical doctrine, because the evil facts which it refuses positively to account for are a genuine portion of reality." More importantly, he continues, these evil facts "may after all be the best key to life's significance, and possibly the only openers of our eyes to the deepest levels of truth" (*VRE* 136). Because the evil facts are just as real aspects of nature as the good facts, we should assume, he writes, "that they have some rational significance, and that systematic healthy-mindedness, failing as it does to accord to sorrow, pain, and death, any positive and active attention whatever, is formally less complete than systems that try at least to include these elements in their scope" (*VRE* 138). Believing that a clearer recognition of "pity, pain, and fear, and the sentiment of human helplessness" (*VRE* 115–16) will offer us a clearer understanding of our complex situation, James concludes that the "completest religions" are the ones "in which the pessimistic elements are best developed." He suggests that Buddhism and Christianity are quite successful in this regard, because they are "essentially religions of deliverance: the man must die to an unreal life before he can be born into the real life" (*VRE* 138).

With this hinting at the question of an afterlife, we can consider James's ideas in the question of immortality. As we saw in chapter 2, in *The Principles* James expresses little use for the notion of a "soul." Focusing as he does in *The Varieties* on religious experience, he almost completely avoids the extra-experiential question of an afterlife. For him, the actuality of immortality is not a vital issue, even though he recognizes its centrality for others. Religion, he notes, "for the great majority of our own race *means* immortality, and nothing else. God is the producer of immortality; and whoever has doubts of immortality is written down as an atheist without further trial"

(*VRE* 412). James had taken up this topic a few years earlier in "Human Immortality." In this 1898 essay, while indicating that "immortality is one of the great spiritual needs of man," he again indicates his own general lack of interest in the topic. "I have to confess," he writes, "that my own personal feeling about immortality has never been of the keenest order, and that, among the problems that give my mind solicitude, this one does not take the very foremost place" (*ERM* 77–78). His real interest in this essay is to undermine two "supposed objections" (*ERM* 75) to immortality by attacking "difficulties which our modern culture finds in the old notion of a life hereafter,—difficulties that I am sure rob the notion of much of its old power to draw belief, in the scientifically cultivated circles to which this audience belong" (*ERM* 79).[24]

The first objection to immortality from science is based in the psychological assumption that the brain is the mind, an assumption that, as we have seen, James had made in *The Varieties* when he wrote of "the dependence of mental states upon bodily conditions" (*VRE* 20). Earlier, however, he had suggested that the connection between the two might be no more than accidental. While "the puritanism of science" defends the view that *"thought is a function of the brain"* (*ERM* 81), he writes that it is still possible that the brain only transmits rather than produces thought. As examples of the sort of transmission he has in mind, he offers refracting lenses and organ keys that produce neither light nor sound but simply transmit them. Similarly, he continues, while thought may be "a function of the brain," instead of being a "productive function" it might be a *"transmissive function."* He writes:

> Suppose, for example, that the whole universe of material things—the furniture of earth and choir of heaven—should turn out to be a mere surface-veil of phenomena, hiding and keeping back the world of genuine realities. Such a supposition is foreign neither to common sense nor to philosophy. Common sense believes in realities behind the veil even too superstitiously; and idealistic philosophy declares the whole world of natural experience, as we get it, to be but a time-mask, shattering or refracting the one infinite Thought which is the sole reality into those millions of finite streams of consciousness known to us as our private selves. (*ERM* 86)

Therefore, James concludes in "Human Immortality," in a fashion similar to Benjamin Franklin, that the soul's connection with the body may be accidental.[25]

The second objection to immortality that James attempts to undermine is based upon complaints that "the incredible and intolerable number of beings which, with our modern imagination, we must believe to be immortal, if immortality be true" (*ERM* 96). Some individuals are so overwhelmed with the sheer management of this possible throng, he continues, that they would forego immortality rather than "believe that all the hosts of Hottentots and Australians that have been, and shall ever be, should share it with us." While he notes that this position may represent an advance over the earlier belief that, since such people were "'heathen,' our forefathers felt a certain sort of joy in thinking that their Creator made them as so much mere fuel for the fires of hell" (*ERM* 98), he still believes that this objection constitutes no problem for immortality. He responds that "the tiresomeness of an over-peopled Heaven is a purely subjective and illusory notion, a sign of human incapacity, a remnant of the old narrow-hearted aristocratic creed." For James, on the contrary, "each new mind brings its own edition of the universe of space along with it, its own room to inhabit; and these spaces never crowd each other,—the space of my imagination, for example, in no way interferes with yours." In this pluralistic vision, there is no limit to the number of consciousnesses, nor to the amount of possible content as there might be in our familiar space-constrained material world. Theists, he continues, can say that God has "so inexhaustible a capacity for love that his call and need is for a literally endless accumulation of created lives. He can never faint or grow weary, as we should, under the increasing supply. His scale is infinite in all things. His sympathy can never know satiety or glut" (*ERM* 100–101).

Returning to *The Varieties*, we encounter again James's view that immortality is only "a secondary point." His concern is with the preservation of our values. "If only our ideals are cared for in 'eternity,' I do not see why we might not be willing to resign their care to other hands than ours" (*VRE* 412). He believes that the individual needs no guarantees: "For practical life at any rate, the *chance* of salvation is enough." Humans demonstrate a characteristic "willingness to live on a chance" (*VRE* 414). Throughout, James is concerned that hope remain possible and that resignation be unforced. In this regard, it is enough for him to have refuted the claim of some that immortality has been disproven by science.

The "More" and Mysticism

Given the level of generality and individual distinctness that has pervaded James's discussion thus far, he recognizes that his inquiry must proceed slowly. While he is dedicated to the appropriately rigorous inquiries of psychological science, he also recognizes that, at least with regard to the topic of religion, our language is not capable of sustaining such rigor. In "a field of experience where there is not a single conception that can be sharply drawn," he writes, to pretend "to be rigorously 'scientific' or 'exact' in our terms would only stamp us as lacking in understanding of our task." A far better stance, he continues, would be to suggest that "things are more or less divine, states of mind are more or less religious, reactions are more or less total, but the boundaries are always misty, and it is everywhere a question of amount and degree" (*VRE* 39–40). In this way, he attempts to study the individual reports of his various witnesses free from historical and sectarian blinders in an attempt to uncover continuities among their experiences.[26]

James's tentative distillation of individuals' religious "feelings, acts, and experiences" is in tune with this openness. He writes simply that "the life of religion in the broadest and most general terms possible . . . consists of the belief that there is an unseen order and that our supreme good lies in harmoniously adjusting ourselves thereto" (*VRE* 51; cf. 413). While he recognizes that various theologies contain different interpretations of this unseen order and of our proper method of adjustment to it, he emphasizes that to explore these theological differences would be to move away from the core aspect of religious experience. He writes: "When we survey the whole field of religion, we find a great variety in the thoughts that have prevailed there; but the feelings on the one hand and the conduct on the other are almost always the same, for Stoic, Christian, and Buddhist saints are practically indistinguishable in their lives. The theories which Religion generates, being thus variable, are secondary; and if you wish to grasp her essence, you must look to the feelings and the conduct as being the more constant elements" (*VRE* 397). Setting aside these feelings and conduct for the moment, we can focus on his notion of "a common nucleus" of "intellectual content" that all religions share. James writes that, after "the warring gods and formulas of the various religions" cancel each other out, there remains a "certain uniform deliverance in which religions all appear to meet" (*VRE* 399–400).[27]

James continues that religion has a "supernaturalist sense" that maintains "that the so-called order of nature, which constitutes this world's experience, is only one portion of the total universe, and that there stretches beyond this visible world an unseen world of which we now know nothing positive, but in its relation to which the true significance of our present mundane life consists." He maintains that, if we set aside the various aspects of doctrine, we will recognize that a person's faith consists in a belief "in the existence of an unseen order of some kind in which the riddles of the natural order may be found explained." In what he calls "the more developed religions," the world of nature functions as "the mere scaffolding or vestibule of a truer, more eternal world, and [is] affirmed to be a sphere of education, trial, or redemption" (*WB* 48). Given this split, the message of religion is thus in two parts: a feeling of uneasiness and of its resolution. The former part, "reduced to its simplest terms, is a sense that there is *something wrong about us* as we naturally stand"; the latter part is "a sense that *we are saved from the wrongness* by making proper connexion with the higher powers." This second stage—"the stage of solution or salvation"—brings individuals to identify their "real being" with "the germinal higher part" of themselves. In this attitude, the individual "*becomes conscious that this higher part is conterminous and continuous with a more of the same quality, which is operative in the universe outside of him, and which he can keep in working touch with, and in a fashion get on board of and save himself when all his lower being has gone to pieces in the wreck*" (*VRE* 400; cf. *ERM* 8; *TT* 129).

Two points should be made at this juncture. The first is a reminder that James the psychologist is simply reporting the content of these religious feelings distilled from the testimony of the many witnesses he has selected. Any claims about whether there *is* something "wrong" with us, or *how* we might be "saved," are a different matter. The second point is to reiterate his belief that this message enters human experience primarily by means of feeling or emotion. Reason or argumentation—"dogmatics"—plays a distinctly minor role in his understanding of religion.[28] He believes that religious persons do not have minds particularly attuned to appreciate proofs; they rather possess "a trustful sense of presence" (*VRE* 353) that orients their lives. Religion offers humans an "added dimension of emotion," and, since it provides relief from any uneasiness, it plays a positive role in human experience. Those who have come through the sorts of religious experiences that he describes often recognize a kind of salvation. There is, he writes, "new reach of freedom for us, with the struggle over, the keynote of the universe sounding in our ears, and everlasting possession spread before our eyes. This sort of happiness in the absolute and everlasting is what we find nowhere but in religion" (*VRE* 46–47). What we find in part, he writes, are feelings of two sorts: that there is more to existence than meets the senses, and that we can live in a comfortable dependence on its unseen powers.

After presenting us with these descriptions, James offers us some "theoretical and practical conclusions." He starts with five "characteristics" of the religious life, beginning with a series of three religious beliefs. The first is that "the visible world is part of a more spiritual universe from which it draws its chief significance." The second is that "union or harmonious relation with that higher universe is our true end." The third belief is that "prayer or inner communion with the spirit thereof—be that spirit 'God' or 'law'—is a process wherein work is really done, and spiritual energy flows in and produces effects, either psychological or material, within the phenomenal world." The final two characteristics of the religious life James calls "psychological." These are that the religious life offers us fourth, "a new zest which adds itself like a gift to life, and takes the form either of lyrical enchantment or of appeal to earnestness and heroism," and fifth, "an assurance of safety and a temper of peace, and, in relation to others, a preponderance of loving affections." So far, James is not defending these conclusions as true; he is just maintaining that they are "the characteristics of the religious life" (*VRE* 382–83) as drawn from the many "content" chapters of *The Varieties*.

James then continues on with a series of further conclusion-like points. The first is the pluralistic one that, since people are different, we should expect their level and mixture of religiosity to be different. He wonders whether individuals are "so like in their inner needs that, for hard and soft, for proud and humble, for strenuous and lazy, for healthy-minded and despairing, exactly the same religious incentives are required?" On the contrary, he maintains that "different functions in the organism of humanity [are] allotted to different types of man, so that some may really be the better for a religion of consolation and reassurance, whilst others are better for one of terror and reproof" (*VRE* 267–68). He thus rejects the view that "the lives of all men should show identical religious elements" and that "the existence of so many religious types and sects and creeds [is] regrettable," because he does not believe that "creatures in such different positions and with such different powers as human individuals are, should have exactly the same functions and the same duties" (*VRE* 384). Our problems are as different as our solutions, and we select "the gods we need and can use, the gods whose demands on us are reinforcements of our demands on ourselves and on one another" (*VRE* 266). As a kind of parallel, he notes that "if an Emerson were forced to be a [John] Wesley, or a [Dwight] Moody forced to be a Whitman, the total human consciousness of the divine would suffer." Consequently, the "divine" "must mean a group of qualities," that different individuals champion differently to fill out "human nature's total message." He continues that it is necessary to recognize "that we live in partial systems, and that parts are not interchangeable in the spiritual life." Thus, the "sick souls" need what he calls "a religion of deliverance," while the "healthy-minded" need something entirely different (*VRE* 384–85). Elsewhere he writes that what he calls "common-sense theism, the popular religion of our European race," demonstrates this kind of pluralism. "For the great mass of men," pluralism has been at the core of their religious life: and pressure from philosophers and theologians for "ultra-phenomenal unity" shows disdain for how religion is experienced (*ERM* 60).

James's second conclusion is that "the science of religions"—perhaps better, the anthropology of religion—is not itself a religion. Science is, as we saw in chapter 5, knowledge by acquaintance, knowledge from the outside, and "knowledge about a thing is not the thing itself." As a result, any attempt to develop a science of religions is no more likely to be a religious activity than understanding "the causes of drunkenness, as a physician understands them," is the same thing as being drunk (*VRE* 385).[29] He continues that, while the scientific approach might enable us "to understand everything about the causes and elements of religion, and might even decide which elements were qualified, by their general harmony with other branches of knowledge, to be considered true," still the greatest expert in this science might be unable "to be personally devout." Far more important for James than having a head full of religious information is that religion have an "effective occupation of a place in life," such that "its dynamic currents" would pass through an individual's being. Thus, the person "who lives the life" of religion, however narrowly, "is a better servant than he who merely knows about it, however much." This is why he maintains that it would be a mistake to assume that "the science of religions" is "an equivalent for living religion" (*VRE* 385–86).³⁰ He further believed that scientists were for the most part "so materialistic that one may well say that on the whole the influence of science goes against the notion that religion should be recognized at all," and that as a result there is an antipathy to religion that undermines its scientific study. He continues that the scientific inquirer into religion "has to become acquainted with so many groveling and horrible superstitions that a presumption easily arises in his mind that any belief that is religious probably is false. In the 'prayerful communion' of savages with such mumbo-jumbos of deities as they acknowledge, it is hard for us to see what genuine spiritual work—even though it were work relative only to their dark savage obligations—can possibly be done" (*VRE* 386–87; cf. *WB* 239).³¹ In consequence, he admits that "the conclusions of the science of religions are as likely to be adverse as they are to be favorable to the claim that the essence of religion is true" (*VRE* 387).

James does recognize, however, the possibility of a more critical approach, if philosophy were to "abandon metaphysics and deduction for criticism and induction, and frankly transform herself from theology into science of religions." What he calls "the spontaneous intellect of man" always understands matters in accordance with "its temporary intellectual prepossessions." By comparative study and criticism, however, philosophers are able to challenge what is merely "local" and "accidental." In this way they can "remove historic incrustations" from inherited dogmas and forms of worship and "eliminate doctrines that are now known to be scientifically absurd or incongruous." He writes that by winnowing away such "unworthy formulations," philosophy can discover "a residuum of conceptions that at least are possible." If philosophy treats them hypothetically, and if it "discriminates the common and essential from the individual and local elements of the religious beliefs," it should be able to mediate among the different faiths and develop a "consensus of opinion." From his own point of view, James indicates that "a critical Science of Religions of this sort" might over time be able to develop "as general a public adhesion as is commanded by a physical science" (*VRE* 359–60; cf. 342).

James's third conclusion is that we can never hope to omit the subjective in experience and live by some sort of pure science. He writes that it is "absurd" to try to suppress "the egoistic elements of experience," because what he calls "the axis of reality runs solely through the egoistic places—they are strung upon it like so many beads." To offer a description of the world that omitted "the various feelings of the individual pinch of destiny, all the various spiritual attitudes," strikes him as similar to "offering a printed bill of fare as the equivalent for a solid meal." Surely, religion as human practice does not makes this mistake. "The individual's religion may be egotistic," he admits, "and those private realities which it keeps in touch with may be narrow enough." Still, such a religion "always remains infinitely less hollow and abstract, as far as it goes, than a Science which prides itself on taking no account of anything private at all" (VRE 394). Individuality is based upon feeling, James continues, and "the recesses of feeling, the darker, blinder strata of character, are the only places in the world in which we catch real fact in the making, and directly perceive how events happen, and how work is actually done." As we saw in chapter 5, in contrast with this living world the world of concepts, "of generalized objects which the intellect contemplates," has no life. Using as an analogy pictures seen through stereoscopic or kinetoscopic devices, James writes that without the devices "the third dimension, the movement, the vital element," is not there (VRE 395; cf. PU 105–6).

Finally, James writes, religion is not something that we should hope to move beyond. "There is a notion in the air about us," he writes, "that religion is probably only an anachronism, a case of 'survival,' an atavistic relapse into a mode of thought which humanity in its more enlightened examples has outgrown; and this notion our religious anthropologists at present do little to counteract" (VRE 387). In the face of this view, he counters that even though "our ancestors made so many errors of fact and mixed them with their religion," it would be a mistake for us to "leave off being religious at all" (VRE 394). On the contrary, religion, because it occupies itself with "personal destinies" and thus keeps us "in contact with the only absolute realities which we know," must of necessity play "an eternal part in human history" (VRE 396).

Ultimately, what does religion reveal to us, James wonders, and what is its message? What can religion tell us about our personal destinies, if "indeed she reveals anything distinct enough to be considered a general message to mankind"? (VRE 396). One revelation, as we have already seen, is the primacy of feeling over thought, at least as regards matters spiritual. For example, there is his emphasis upon the similarities among the feelings and conduct of the various saints despite radically different doctrines. Second, James writes that the religious feelings are generally positive. "The resultant outcome of them is in any case what Kant calls a 'sthenic' affection, an excitement of the cheerful, expansive, 'dynamogenic' order which, like any tonic, freshens our vital powers." This emotion "overcomes temperamental melancholy and imparts endurance to the Subject, or a zest, or a meaning, or an enchantment and glory to the common objects of life." This aspect of the role of religious belief in human life is further evidence, James writes, why religion "cannot be a mere anachronism and survival, but must exert a permanent function, whether she be with or without intellectual content, and whether, if she have any, it be true or false" (VRE 397–99).

James writes in *The Varieties* that the various experiences that he has explored "prove the existence in our mental machinery of a sense of present reality more diffused and general than that which our special senses yield" (VRE 58–59). He posits of this "more" that we have "a *sense of reality, a feeling of objective presence, a perception* of what we may call '*something there*,' more deep and more general than any of the special and particular 'senses' by which the current psychology supposes existent realities to be originally revealed" (VRE 55). Earlier, he had written in a similar fashion that "the world of our present natural knowledge *is* enveloped in a larger world of *some* sort of whose residual properties we at present can frame no positive idea," and that "our whole physical life may lie soaking in a spiritual atmosphere, a dimension of being that we at present have no organ for apprehending" (WB 50, 52). For the religious person, the natural world is only partial, and beyond it stretches another reality about which nothing is known, even though it is assumed that the true meaning of our present life is only to be found in relation to that larger reality. Of course, these tentative formulations of a sense of a "more" do not guarantee that there is such a "more," they just recognize that many humans are confident that it exists. Similarly, when he writes that "psychology and religion . . . both admit that there are forces seemingly outside of the conscious individual that bring redemption to his life," he is not asserting any scientific proof of "redemption" but only reporting his witnesses' beliefs that redemption is real. As James makes explicit, in fact, psychology defines these forces as "subconscious" rather than supernatural, and suggests "that they do not transcend the individual's personality" (VRE 174).

Still, James suggests that minimally there appears to be a "more." He writes of his personal belief "that the world of our present consciousness is only one out of many worlds of consciousness that exist, and that those other worlds must contain experiences which have a meaning for our life also; and that although in the main their experiences and those of this world keep discrete, yet the two become continuous at certain points, and higher energies filter in." Continuing in this belief—or "over-belief"—helps him to stay "more sane and true." He admits that he could adopt "the sectarian scientist's attitude" and contract his reality to "the world of sensations and of scientific laws and objects," but what he calls "the total expression of human experience" pushes him beyond these "narrow 'scientific' bounds." For him, the world is "more intricately built than physical science allows" (*VRE* 408).[32] As a result, he writes elsewhere, "our fields of experience have no more definite boundaries than have our fields of view." Each is "fringed forever by a *more* that continuously developes," as our lives proceed (*ERE* 35/*MT* 68).[33]

James continues that "the expression 'field of consciousness' has but recently come into vogue in the psychology books." Each of these temporary fields "has its centre of interest," and around it "the objects of which we are less and less attentively conscious fade to a margin so faint that its limits are unassignable." He is especially interested to stress "indetermination of the margin." Within this "more" are to be found all of our memories and "the entire mass of residual powers, impulses, and knowledges that constitute our empirical self"; and the boundary "between what is actual and what is only potential at any moment of our conscious life" is difficult to say (*VRE* 188–90). The center of this "field of consciousness" is always the self. The human body is the self's "centre, centre of vision, centre of action, centre of interest. Where the body is is 'here'; when the body acts is 'now'; what the body touches is 'this'; all other things are 'there' and 'then' and 'that.' These words of emphasized position imply a systematization of things with reference to a focus of action and interest which lies in the body. . . . The body is the storm centre, the origin of co-ordinates, the constant place of stress in all that experience-train. Everything circles around it, and is felt from its point of view" (*ERE* 86 n.8).[34] How far this body stretches out into what is beyond, and how much of the "more" is relevant to human experience, are matters of ongoing development.

In *A Pluralistic Universe*, James attempts to move beyond the data presented in *The Varieties*. He notes that our "present field of consciousness is a centre surrounded by a fringe that shades insensibly into a subconscious more." Further, he writes that while he has used "three separate terms here to describe this fact," he could have used "three hundred, for the fact is all shades and no boundaries" (*PU* 130). He continues that "our natural experience, our strictly moralistic and prudential experience, may be only a fragment of real human experience." In particular, religious experiences "soften nature's outlines and open out the strangest possibilities and perspectives." Religious believers find that "the tenderer parts" of life are "continuous with a *more* of the same quality which is operative in the universe" beyond natural experience. Even if all of their "lower being has gone to pieces in the wreck," he writes, they will remain, at least in their own minds, continuous with "a wider self from which saving experiences flow in" (*PU* 138–39; cf. *VRE* 405).[35]

In this context, we can consider our beloved house pets. Our dogs, he writes, are "in our human life but not of it." They experience and "often play the cardinal part" in all sorts of events that they cannot in any way understand. When a dog bites a stranger and precipitates a lawsuit, for example, "the dog may be present at every step of the negotiations, and see the money paid, without an inkling of what it all means, without a suspicion that it has anything to do with *him*; and he never *can* know in his natural dog's life" (*WB* 52; cf. *EPs* 1). Taking the analogy in the other direction, he suggests the possibility of "some form of superhuman life with which we may, unknown to ourselves, be co-conscious" (*PU* 140). In other words, it is a mistake to assume that "our human experience is the highest form of experience extant in the universe." He continues that he believes, rather, that "we stand in much the same relation to the whole of the universe as our canine and feline pets do to the whole of human life. They inhabit our drawing-rooms and libraries. They take part in scenes of whose significance they have no inkling. They are merely tangent to curves of history the beginnings and ends and forms of which pass wholly beyond their ken. So we are tangents to the wider life of things" (*P* 143–44; cf. *TT* 132–33). In presenting this belief James claims no knowledge. Nor does he require that this account of the world be accepted as true—only that we allow that it *might* be true.[36]

Further discussing the notion of the subconscious, James notes that as a result of experiences under nitrous oxide intoxication he was forced to conclude that "our normal waking consciousness, rational consciousness as we call it, is but one special type of consciousness, whilst all about it, parted from it by the filmiest of screens, there lie potential forms of consciousness entirely different." He continues that many individuals, perhaps most, live their entire lives without suspecting the existence of these other forms of consciousness, but "apply the required stimulus, and at a touch" these other forms "are there in all their completeness, definite types of mentality which probably somewhere have their field of application and adaptation" (*VRE* 307–8). If we leave aside the chemical origin of his insight—an insight that is also possible with alcohol and other drugs[37]—James maintains that any adequate psychological account must incorporate the various reports of the similar religious experiences to which he has pointed in the course of *The Varieties*. "No account of the universe in its totality can be final which leaves these other forms of consciousness quite disregarded," he writes. "How to regard them is the question—for they are so discontinuous with ordinary consciousness" (*VRE* 308; cf. *ERM* 128). One obvious, and traditional, way to incorporate them is through supernaturalism. Under such an approach, "the level of full sunlit consciousness" becomes the smaller region of consciousness, surrounded or fringed by a much larger "transmarginal or subliminal region." This larger region is the region of supernatural meaning to which only some humans have easy access. "In persons deep in the religious life," he writes, "the door into this region seems unusually wide open; at any rate, experiences making their entrance through that door have had emphatic influence in shaping religious history" (*VRE* 381). The supernatural approach thus can incorporate the psychological explanation into its religious version of the data of the subconscious. "If the grace of God miraculously operates," he writes for example, "it probably operates through the subliminal door" (*VRE* 218).[38] Since James believes that any scientific attempt to understand religion must explore it "in connexion with the rest of Science," however, any religious descriptions of this "more" must be acceptable to psychology. In this regard, he writes that "the *subconscious self* is nowadays a well-accredited psychological entity. . . . Apart from all religious considerations, there is actually and literally more life in our total soul than we are at any time aware of." While he admits that much of this background context is insignificant—"imperfect memories, silly jingles, inhibitive timidities, 'dissolutive' phenomena of various sorts"—he maintains that there is more to the subconscious. Especially with regards to various high-points in the religious life, like conversions, mystical experiences, and prayers, he sees "invasions" from the subconscious region (*VRE* 402–3).

Within our broader consciousness, this vast well of memories and hopes, of ideals and expectations, is to be found more than is at any time actually present to consciousness. This well also functions as a reservoir of energies to which our normally tepid lives can gain access through proper efforts, as we saw in chapter 2. Drawing nearer to the religious interpretation of this subconscious, James is also willing to hypothesize "that whatever it may be on its *farther* side, the 'more' with which in religious experience we feel ourselves connected is on its *hither* side the subconscious continuation of our conscious life." Thus, he suggests that our interpretation of this feeling of a "more" can start with the "recognized psychological fact" of the subconscious and still embrace the religious interpretation, preserving for his psychological inquiry "a contact with 'science' which the ordinary theologian lacks" (VRE 403). It would still seem to be possible, however, to recognize this feeling of a "more"—the opacity and open-endedness of reality—without accepting his favored religious interpretation by emphasizing the possibility of delusion when we welcome as other "forms of consciousness" what might be simple misinterpretations of normal consciousness. The former suggests humility and care in our actions; the latter, dependency and wonderment in the face of the mystery of being.[39]

Although James floats the question of whether the "more" is "merely our own notion" (VRE 401), or a portion of larger reality, the answer seems clear to him.[40] In fact, he believes that the proper relation with this "more" can make us whole. "The farther limits of our being plunge," he writes, "into an altogether other dimension of existence from the sensible and merely 'understandable' world." Regardless of how we decide to name this "mystical" or "supernatural" region, we find there the source of most of our "ideal impulses," for whose origins we cannot offer articulate accounts. We belong to this region "in a more intimate sense than that in which we belong to the visible world, for we belong in the most intimate sense wherever our ideals belong." Further, because this "unseen region . . . produces effects in this world," its reality must be accepted. "When we commune with it, work is actually done upon our finite personality, for we are turned into new men, and consequences in the way of conduct follow in the natural world upon our regenerative change" (VRE 406). The various experiences that James considers real—"conversations with the unseen, voices and visions, responses to prayer, changes of heart, deliverances from fear, inflowings of help, assurances of support" (P 266)—produce real effects within our natural world. We call this emerging power "God," and "God is real since he produces real effects" (VRE 407). We find in God's existence guarantees and hope—

'God' means, he writes, "that 'you can dismiss certain kinds of fear'" (*SPP* 38)—and we find, in the struggle along with God to better the world, significance for our lives.

Closely related to James's discussion of the "more" is his consideration of mysticism. Despite the doubts of orthodox psychology and medicine,[41] he writes that "personal religious experience has its root and centre in mystical states of consciousness," and he carefully explores these states and their four "marks" (*VRE* 301–2): ineffability, noetic quality, transiency, and passivity. Briefly, ineffability refers to our inability adequately to express the meaning of the experience, noetic quality to our sense that such experiences contain insights into truth, transiency to the briefness of such states, and passivity to our inability to make them occur.[42] With regard to such mystical states, however, he admits, as we have seen, that he is able to speak of them, although very eloquently, only at second hand. In *The Will to Believe*, he writes: "All men know it at those rare moments when the soul sobers herself, and leaves off her chattering and protesting and insisting about this formula or that. In the silence of our theories we then seem to listen, and to hear something like the pulse of Being beat; and it is borne in upon us that the mere turning of the character, the dumb willingness to suffer and to serve this universe, is more than all theories about it put together" (*WB* 111). Still, given James's disparagement of second-hand religion, his personal admission of no access to mysticism might have suggested that he would avoid the topic. Yet he continues to defend strongly the evidentiary value of reports about experiences that he had not himself had. While initially puzzling, his position here does not contain a contradiction. Rather, he is maintaining that our inquiries into highly personal areas like religious experience are not likely to advance very far if we limit our considerations to only what is universally experienced. Proceeding from the general Jamesian premise that "to no one type of man whatsoever is the total fullness of truth immediately revealed," he reaches the clearly Jamesian conclusion that "each of us has to borrow from the other parts of truth seen better from the other's point of view." He continues that, "like the traveller, whose testimony about foreign countries we should be foolish not to believe," so too individuals' reports of religious experiences are "fit to be taken as *evidence*." Not all people see things the same way, but "each attitude being a syllable in human nature's total message, it takes the whole of us to spell the meaning out completely" (*VRE* 383–84). James thus calls for us to be "as objective and receptive" as we can to the testimony of others (*VRE* 301; cf. *EP* 173).⁴³ *The Varieties* is, except for its thin shell of theory, a display case of such testimonies, and admitting them into evidence is both good psychology and a way that we can try to broaden our perspectives on the meaning of life.⁴⁴ James, however, leaves behind his psychological stand and, in accordance with his interpretation of the "more" and of human dependency, comes down on the side of supernaturalism and answers in the affirmative.⁴⁵

In a related 1910 essay, "A Suggestion about Mysticism," James admits that much discussion of religious mysticism comes from the "outside," from people like himself who have no "direct authority of experience." The suggestion that he offers us is that we consider these presumed "states of mystical intuition" to be "only very sudden and great extensions of the ordinary 'field of consciousness,'" in which there is "an immense spreading of the margin of the field" of consciousness, such that "knowledge ordinarily transmarginal would become included, and the ordinary margin would grow more central" (*EP* 157). When the threshold lowers, "the field widens and the relations of its centre to matters usually subliminal come into view, the larger panorama perceived fills the mind with exhilaration and sense of mental power." With regard to "memories, concepts, and conational states," for example, there is ordinarily "no definite bound set between what is central and what is marginal in consciousness." James suggests that when the threshold moves downward, it brings "a mass of subconscious memories, conceptions, emotional feelings, and perceptions of relations, etc., into view all at once; and that if this enlargement of the nimbus that surrounds the sensational present is vast enough, while no one of the items it contains attracts our attention singly, we shall have the conditions fulfilled for a kind of consciousness in all essential respects like that termed mystical" (*EP* 158–59).

Religion and Truth

We have been considering James's presentation of the broad topic of religion and religious experience. In the course of this presentation, James-the-psychologist gives way to James-the-believer. We have seen several instances where he inclined his interpretation of the data toward the religious, attempting to show that nothing in the data would preclude such a possibility. He, of course, did not assert proof of the religious case, but he did assert that the religious interpretation had not been disproven, and that in this nondisproven stage religious belief is justifiable. As he had written in "Philosophical Conceptions and Practical Results," an experiential God "means something for us, and may be real" (*P* 264). Further, his broad survey of religious experience as a study of human behavior is designed to strengthen his case by demonstrating the breadth of religious interpretations.

In the "Conclusions" chapter of *The Varieties*, James increases his tilt toward religion. "Disregarding the over-beliefs, and confining ourselves to what is common and generic," he writes, "we have in *the fact that the conscious person is continuous with a wider self through which saving experiences come, a positive content of religious experience which, it seems to me, is literally and objectively true as far as it goes*" (*VRE* 405; cf. *PU* 138–39). There has surely been a gradual but complete shift here, from the prior stance of psychological inquirer to this current religious stance. Earlier in *The Varieties*, he spoke of an "unseen order" to which we should adjust as simply the message of religion. Now, he presents us with the claim that this message—that the conscious person is "continuous with a wider self through which saving experiences come"—is "literally and objectively true." Even if we try to take seriously his puzzling caveat "as far as it goes," he is no longer just reporting the experiences that his witnesses present and offering us their interpretations. Now he is telling us that the picture that his witnesses present is a true one. And, using the term "God" as our "natural appellation . . . for the supreme reality" or for "this higher part of the universe," he tells us that "we and God have business with each other; and in opening ourselves to his influence our deepest destiny is fulfilled." Surely, he has moved beyond the evidence present in his psychological inquiries. He has shifted from his exposition of what his witnesses believed to at least a hypothetical defense of the truth of their beliefs. The answer to the question of why James did this must be sought in his pragmatic justification of religion in terms of its effects in the lives of believers. As he writes, "that which produces effects within another reality must be termed a reality itself, so I feel as if we had no philosophic excuse for calling the unseen or mystical world unreal" (*VRE* 406; cf. 402, 412).

James offers us a sketch of his developing Pragmatism in the course of *The Varieties*. He is particularly interested in grounding theoretical discussions of religion in the practical differences that would "result from one alternative or the other being true" (*VRE* 350). Using this criterion, he maintains that God's familiar "metaphysical attributes"—aseity and necessariness and immateriality and indivisibility and so on—have no significance for human experience. As he puts it, "candidly speaking, how do such qualities as these make any definite connexion with our life?" Further, he wonders, "if they severally call for no distinctive adaptations of our conduct, what vital difference can it possibly make to a man's religion whether they be true or false?" (VRE 351–52). He continues that these "abstract general terms" become "in the theologians" hands... only a set of dictionary-adjectives, mechanically deduced," because in such instances "logic has stepped into the place of vision, professionalism into that of life." Religion, on the other hand, liberated from mismanagement by theological faculties and returned to the realm of experience, could face the pragmatic test. James's interest is thus in aspects of religion that make a difference in life, in religion as "a living practical affair" (P 265).[46] He writes that religion does not continue because of its "abstract definitions and systems of concatenated adjectives," nor its "faculties of theology and their professors." These are simply "aftereffects" and "secondary accretions" upon what he calls the "phenomena of vital conversation with the unseen divine" that renew themselves over the ages "in the lives of humble private men." If, however, we engage with what James calls God's "moral" attributes, like holiness, omnipotence, justice, and love, we find a vital function in life. "They positively determine fear and hope and expectation" (VRE 352–53).

Theism is related to the enduring and eternal. "The absolute things, the last things, the overlapping things, are the truly philosophic concern," James writes, "all superior minds feel seriously about them, and the mind with the shortest views is simply the mind of the more shallow man" (P 56/264). In addition, because Theism offers a better perspective on the future, it also favorably colors our present living. In a world with a God, he continues, "it is not likely that he is confined solely to making differences in the world's latter end; he probably makes differences all along its course." For James the pragmatic principle tells us that "the very meaning of the conception of God lies in those differences which must be made in our experience if the conception be true" (P 264). These experiences—"conversations with the unseen, voices and visions, responses to prayer, changes of heart, deliverances from fear, inflowings of help, assurances of support"—together "form the primary mass of direct religious experience on which all hearsay religion rests," and furnish "that notion of an ever-present God, out of which systematic theology thereupon proceeds to make capital in its own unreal pedantic way." Of course, these religious experiences "certainly share in the general liability to illusion and mistake" and "need not be infallible." At the same time, however, these experiences "are certainly the originals of the God-idea, and theology is the translation." It makes little difference beyond the use of "certain abstract words," he continues, whether "the God of systematic theology should exist or not exist," but it makes a great deal of difference whether "the God of these particular experiences" does. The loss of this personal God would be an "awful" blow to those "whose lives are stayed on such experiences" (*P* 266).

James writes that happiness is at the core of our being. "How to gain, how to keep, how to recover happiness, is in fact for most men at all times the secret motive of all they do, and of all they are willing to endure." He continues on with this descriptive account, noting that religion contributes to this pursuit, and that the happiness that religious belief offers us serves "as a proof of its truth." When such belief brings a person happiness, it "almost inevitably" is adopted. "Such a belief ought to be true," he writes of the believers' ideation, "therefore it is true" (*VRE* 71). Throughout *The Varieties*, James discusses the various religious experiences as possessing "enormous biological worth." Still, we may wonder whether there is any worth to the content claims of these revelations, and he himself asks "what is the objective 'truth' of their content?" (*VRE* 401; cf. 300). While he admits that "the natural propensity of man is to believe that whatever has great value for life is thereby certified as true," he still means for "truth" itself to be "taken to mean something additional to bare value for life" (*VRE* 401 n.23). Believers, of course, believe that religion is true. James—moving from chronicler to defender of religion—maintains that it is possible to present this religious material in a way that impartial science could accept.

The problem with pursuing this second line of inquiry, as we saw in the consideration of faith in chapter 3, is that our attempts to reach an answer here could drag on without resolution, and if we restrain beliefs, the lives of many potential believers would suffer in the meantime. Thus, James is drawn quickly back to a blending of the questions of usefulness and truth. This is the sense in which he writes "the uses of religion, its uses to the individual who has it, and the uses of the individual himself to the world, are the best arguments that truth is in it" (*VRE* 361). He had recognized all of this earlier in *The Varieties*, when he wrote that religious opinions, like any other respectable opinions, must be tested "by logic and by experiment" and not by "their author's neurological type." As we test our beliefs, our tests must be broad in nature, considering such criteria as *"immediate luminousness, ... philosophical reasonableness,* and *moral helpfulness"* (VRE 23). As he later writes in *Pragmatism*: "If theological ideas prove to have a value for concrete life, they will be true, for pragmatism, in the sense of being good for so much. For how much more they are true, will depend entirely on their relations to the other truths that also have to be acknowledged." Thus, for James, to the extent that "the Absolute of transcendental idealism" yields "religious comfort" to a set of believers, "it has that amount of value; it performs a concrete function." Although James admits to having problems with the Absolute, from a purely pragmatic point of view he realized that he "ought to call the Absolute true 'in so far forth,'" and as he writes, "I unhesitatingly now do so" (P 40–41).

It is necessary to consider more carefully the "theological ideas" of which James has just spoken. They seem to exist on at least three levels. Initially, there is the idea of an actual existing God. Second, there is the idea of a vibrant relationship with this God. Third, there is the idea of personal benefits that individuals derive from the feeling that they are living in a relationship with this God. Thus, individuals who accept religious ideas could be accepting the unproven existence of a God who is independent of their belief and of any contributions on their part, or the possibility of a relationship with an existing God that is in large part the result of their contributions, or the possibility of a personal feeling of support and salvation that could exist as the result of their contributions completely independently of any existing God.[47] The familiar recording approach would seem to demand a prioritization among these three levels, such that any relationship with God or any benefits derived from this relationship would be possible only if there were a God. For James, however, this is not a simple recording case, and we know that some individuals derive great personal comfort from a belief in the existence of a God even though they cannot prove that such a being exists.[48] In any case, the bottom line for James is simple: we may choose to believe, even when the available evidence is inadequate to convince everyone. At the same time, he claims no such right for what he calls, without clarification, "some patent superstition," nor for the acceptance of some belief "'that you know ain't true.'" He is proposing a freedom to believe covering only "living options which the intellect of the individual cannot by itself resolve," yet he admits that "living options never seem absurdities to him who has them to consider" (WB 32).

For James, "if the hypothesis of God works satisfactorily in the widest sense of the word, it is true." He maintains, moreover, that "whatever its residual difficulties may be, experience shows that it certainly does work" (P 143), at least for some. And, while he admits that believing in God might not "work" for everyone, he still maintains the right of those individuals for whom it does work to continue to believe at their own risk without interference from others. As a result, he is able to assert that he is not offering a "reckless faith." On the contrary, he writes, "I have preached the right of the individual to indulge his personal faith at his personal risk" (WB 8).

James's folding of the question of truth into the question of value is a further instance of his position that in the fullness of experience there is much that reason cannot prove. As he writes early in *The Varieties*, "if we look on man's whole mental life as it exists, on the life of men that lies in them apart from their learning and science, and that they inwardly and privately follow, we have to confess that the part of it of which rationalism can give an account is relatively superficial." There is much that we believe without "articulate reasons," and, while he admits that this rationalist component has great prestige "for it has the loquacity, it can challenge you for proofs, and chop logic, and put you down with words," he still maintains that reason is not of primary importance in the full life of the person. The rationalist part of your mental life, he writes, "will fail to convince or convert you all the same, if your dumb intuitions are opposed to its conclusions. If you have intuitions at all, they come from a deeper level of your nature than the loquacious level which rationalism inhabits.... Something in you absolutely *knows* that the result must be truer than any logic-chopping rationalistic talk, however clever, that may contradict it" (VRE 66–67; cf. WB 77–78). James admits that he is speaking here descriptively rather than prescriptively—as a psychologist rather than a logician—simply recognizing the fact people tend to follow their intuitions. "I do not yet say that it is *better* that the subconscious and non-rational should thus hold primacy in the religious realm," he writes. "I confine myself to simply pointing out that they do so hold it as a matter of fact" (VRE 68; cf. 340–42).

We have just seen how James works out the importance of results in his discussion of what he called the "metaphysical" and "moral" attributes of God. Rejecting the former as irrelevant to life, he concentrates on our intuitions about the latter. Continuing on in this vein, he writes that religious people believe "that not only they themselves, but the whole universe of beings to whom the God is present, are secure in his parental hands." In this comfortable state of dependence, they rest assured of a happy outcome: "There is a sense, a dimension, they are sure, in which we are *all* saved, in spite of the gates of hell and all adverse terrestrial appearances. God's existence is the guarantee of an ideal order that shall be permanently preserved. This world may indeed, as science assures us, some day burn up or freeze; but if it is part of his order, the old ideals are sure to be brought elsewhere to fruition, so that where God is, tragedy is only provisional and partial, and shipwreck and dissolution are not the absolutely final things" (*VRE* 407; cf. *P* 55/*P* 263–64). Although the actual existence of God would seem to provide the "guarantee" of this ideality, James is less concerned with what he sees as necessarily futile intellectual attempts to prove the existence of God than he is with recognizing the power that individuals are able to draw from the belief in God to order their lives. He thus treats the whole matter of our relation with a God as a contribution rather than a recording case. In a similar fashion, we can consider James's discussion of nonpetitional prayer, which he presents as "the very soul and essence of religion" or as "religion in act." What occurs in such prayer, he writes, is "the very movement itself of the soul, putting itself in a personal relation of contact with the mysterious power of which it feels the presence" (*VRE* 365–66). This formulation implies successful contact, although elsewhere in *The Varieties* he is more guarded (or psychological) in his formulations.

Earlier we saw that for James knowledge about religion does not necessarily correlate with devotion. He also notes that "relatively few medical men and scientific men" are able to pray. They seem unable to "carry on any living commerce with 'God,'" he continues, although he believes that many such individuals would feel "much freer and abler ... were such important forms of energizing not sealed up by the critical atmosphere in which we have been reared." While the religious path is potentially live for everyone, in some it is "shunted out from use" (*ERM* 160; cf. 132). In spite of their inability, however, others continue to pray, and he suggests that "the reason why we *do* pray ... is simply that we cannot *help* praying. It seems probable that, in spite of all that 'science' may do to the contrary, men will continue to pray to the end of time, unless their mental nature changes in a manner which nothing we know should lead us to expect. The impulse to pray is a necessary consequence of the fact that whilst the innermost of the empirical selves of a man is a Self of the *social* sort, it yet can find its only adequate

Socius [Companion] in an ideal world" (*PP* 1:301; cf. *WB* 93–94).⁴⁹ It may turn out, James continues, that "the sphere of influence in prayer is subjective exclusively, and that what is immediately changed is only the mind of the praying person." Still, he believes that religion "must stand or fall by the persuasion that effects of some sort genuinely do occur" (*VRE* 367).

James tells us, for example, that one of "the characteristics of the religious life" is the belief that "prayer or inner communion with the spirit thereof—be that spirit 'God' or 'law'—is a process wherein work is really done" (*VRE* 382). Ultimately, it seems that he does adopt the believer's position of contact through prayer. He writes, as we have seen, that there is an "unseen region" that produces "effects" in this world. By this, he means that when we interact by prayer with the "more" something positive happens to us: "work" is done upon us and "we are turned into new men." Here again, he is more concerned with the positive effects of our beliefs than with the reality of our religious objects. In both of these cases—the intuitions of dependency that give rise to feelings of comfort and the prayers that strengthen individuals in the troughs of life—his point is that some individuals find that religious interpretations work wonders, bringing comfort and power to their lives. Still, how are we to address the problem that the content of these interpretations—the caring God whom we contact through prayer—is a product of our fallibility. He explicitly denies that we "can attain on a given day to absolute incorrigible and unimprovable truth about such matters of fact as those with which religions deal" (*VRE* 268; cf. *C* 10:103).

Bertrand Russell further interprets James's statement "'if the hypothesis of God works satisfactorily in the widest sense of the word, it is true'" (*P* 143) to mean that James "simply omits as unimportant the question whether God really is in His heaven; if He is a useful hypothesis, that is enough." James, as we saw in chapter 3, requires that, before the aesthetic and practical criteria can be considered, the issue of God's existence must present itself as a logical stalemate, a situation that does not hold for the atheist Russell. For him, in James's mind "God the Architect of the Cosmos is forgotten; all that is remembered is belief in God, and its effects upon the creatures inhabiting our petty planet." Russell also misrepresents James's position on necessary truths that maintains, as we saw in chapter 4, that their necessity results from the fact that they are assumed mental comparisons. Russell suggests on the contrary that James is "certain that not even the multiplication table contains final and infallible truth"—to which he then complains that James has adopted "a dogma which, in philosophy, may be just as great a bar to open-mindedness as any other dogma."[50]

James as a religious thinker surely has problems, but he is not the cartoon figure with which we are all familiar thanks to those critics who are wont to talk about "the will to make believe." Russell, for example, maintains that there is "a fundamental difference" between James's position and the religious outlook of prior thinkers. James, he writes, is "interested in religion as a human phenomenon, but shows little interest in the objects which religion contemplates." The former point is surely true and important: James's interest in religion is as a human phenomenon. The latter point—that James has little interest in religion as a matter of recording objects of contemplation—is true but unimportant to James. Russell continues that James "wants people to be happy, and if belief in God makes them happy let them believe in Him." Russell is mostly correct here as well, but only if we include James's many careful qualifications that we have considered about the limited efficacy of the logical criteria and his focus on the possible positive function that God can play in people's lives. Russell continues on to his ultimate point: his belief that James's real interest is in "benevolence, not philosophy" and that James only becomes a philosopher—and bad philosopher at that—when he says that "if the belief makes them happy it is 'true.'" Russell's approach will only satisfy the person who views religion as a recording case dependent upon "an object of worship." For such a person, he believes, God is mistakenly seen as "an actual Being, not merely a human idea which has good effects," and it is this belief in an actual God "that has good effects, not James's emasculate substitute." Citing another recording case, Russell suggests that when "I say 'Hitler exists' I do not mean 'the effects of believing that Hitler exists are good.'" On the contrary, Russell means that there is a person named Hitler who is at work in the world. He concludes that for "genuine believer the same is true of God."[51] James responds to Russell's and others' charges as follow: "christian and nonchristian critics alike accuse me of summoning people to say 'God exists,' *even when he doesn't exist*, because forsooth in my philosophy the 'truth' of the saying doesn't really mean that he exists in any shape whatever, but only that to say so feels good" (*MT* 6). Any possible Jamesian resolution here must come through a rejection of Russell's position that only belief in a God beyond our contributions is genuine, and the allowance for belief in a finite God who produces vital effects in life.

We can apply James's criteria for evaluating mystical states to this larger issue to get a sense of the worth of religious experiences in general. In response to the question of whether "the mystic range of consciousness" furnishes "any *warrant for the truth* of the twice-bornness and supernaturality and pantheism which it favors," he offers a three-part reply. First, he tells us "mystical states, when well developed, usually are, and have the right to be, absolutely authoritative over the individuals to whom they come." Descriptively, "as a matter of psychological fact," these states are "usually authoritative over those who have them," those who "have been 'there,' and know." Moreover, he continues, when "the mystical truth" offers the power to reshape a life, "what mandate have we of the majority to order him to live in another way?" (*VRE* 334–35).[52] Second, he maintains that those who "stand outside" of these mystical states have no obligation "to accept their revelations uncritically" (*VRE* 335). Those who have not had similar experiences are not obliged to privilege them. "What comes must be sifted and tested, and run the gauntlet of confrontation with the total context of experience, just like what comes from the outer world of sense" (*VRE* 338). Third, James believes that mystical experiences "break down the authority of the non-mystical or rationalistic consciousness, based upon the understanding and the senses alone," and prove it "to be only one kind of consciousness." These mystical experiences open the door to "the possibility of other orders of truth, in which, so far as anything in us vitally responds to them, we may freely continue to have faith" (*VRE* 335). Thus, he writes that it must remain "an open question" whether these mystical states are "superior points of view, windows through which the mind looks out upon a more extensive and inclusive world" (*VRE* 338–39).

If we expand this approach beyond the issue of mystical states, we see James proposing that individuals whose religious propensities offer them a rich and working vision of life should be respected in their beliefs and practices. Because these beliefs and practices function positively in their lives, they are in some sense "true" for these individuals. For those who have no such propensities, however, religious beliefs and practices can claim no authority. While this clear and measured stance seems quite fine thus far, his third point is more problematic. He seems to be advocating the position that, because some individuals recognize a "more" that works in their lives, we must allow it a place in our overall vision. The "authority" of the "rationalistic consciousness" would be forced to make room for other forms of consciousness, and the demands of his third criterion would seem to undermine the protections of the second.[53] The impact of this conflict is moderated somewhat by the fact that James's interest is not in the conversion of nonbelievers, but in protecting believers who might otherwise feel intimidated into thinking that religion has been disproven by science. Thus, to critics of religion who say that we should not believe without proof, he responds, as we saw in chapter 3, that some kinds of evidence cannot come without prior belief. Those who find the religious perspective to be live—who believe that the logical criteria do not preclude religious belief, and who make use of the aesthetic and practical criteria to support it—have every right to continue to believe that the world has religious meaning and see if their belief proves true. The rest of us, it would seem, are required to make room for them and to suffer their interference with our lives—however minimal—in support of their beliefs.

James's understanding of possibility draws him back from the extremes of a tender-minded optimism or a tough-minded pessimism toward a pluralistic meliorism. He wonders what it would mean to say that "the salvation of the world" is possible. In response, he suggests that for the pragmatist it means that "some of the conditions of the world's deliverance do actually exist," and that the probability of salvation would rise as more of them are brought into existence. He continues that disinterest in the matter of the world's salvation "would contradict the very spirit of life." Neutrality here shows only that the individual does not understand the situation. "We all do wish to minimize the insecurity of the universe," he writes, "we are and ought to be unhappy when we regard it as exposed to every enemy and open to every life-destroying draft" (*P* 136–37).

While there are pessimists "who think the salvation of the world impossible," and optimists who think that the world's salvation is "inevitable," James advocates the midway position of meliorism. This view treats the world's salvation as neither guaranteed nor precluded, but as a possibility "which becomes more and more of a probability the more numerous the actual conditions of salvation become" (*P* 137). Although he admits that "shipwreck in detail, or even on the whole, is among the open possibilities," in his pluralistic, melioristic view, the world "*may be saved, on condition that its parts shall do their best*" (*SPP* 73). This would require us to accept the possibility that the world is growing "not integrally but piecemeal by the contributions of its several parts," and to live a life of contribution:

> Suppose that the world's author put the case to you before creation, saying: "I am going to make a world not certain to be saved, a world the perfection of which shall be conditional merely, the condition being that each several agent does its own 'level best.' I offer you the chance of taking part in such a world. Its safety, you see, is unwarranted. It is a real adventure, with real danger, yet it may win through. It is a social scheme of co-operative work genuinely to be done. Will you join the procession? Will you trust yourself and trust the other agents enough to face the risk?"

James believes that, facing such a choice, most of us would accept the challenge and "add our *fiat* to the *fiat* of the creator" (P 139–40). Thus, the powers available include both human and "superhuman forces." The latter include the familiar God of Monism, but also the possibility of that God "as but one helper, *primus inter pares* [first among equals], in the midst of all the shapers of the great world's fate" (P 143). Our world may thus grow better, if we cooperate with a finite but processive God and perhaps other superhuman forces.[54] James is thus not proposing a world that rejects the divine in order to make a place for the human.[55] Rather, he is offering an account of the world that gives humans a God and an intimate place within nature (cf. *PU* 143–44).

The world we live in might be such a world. We do not know, and based on what has transpired so far, we cannot expect to find out soon. But we need to decide, here and now, without waiting for a final answer because living a religious life requires our contributions. In such a case, James believes that we are justified in deciding to do so on aesthetic and practical grounds:

> In the end it is our faith and not our logic that decides such questions, and I deny the right of any pretended logic to veto my own faith. I find myself willing to take the universe to be really dangerous and adventurous, without therefore backing out and crying "no play." ... I am willing that there should be real losses and real losers, and no total preservation of all that is. I can believe in the ideal as an ultimate, not as an origin, and as an extract, not the whole. When the cup is poured off, the dregs are left behind forever, but the possibility of what is poured off is sweet enough to accept. (P 142)

In this justification of religious experience, however, James-the-believer moves too quickly. If a religious idea or belief seems to yield any measure of success in life, he would characterize it as partly verified. Our rich history of hasty generalizations and successful superstitions and seemingly undying prejudices should cause us to demand greater restraint from ourselves. While recognizing that some individuals claim that there is a "more," and that they derive personal benefits from living in accordance with this claim, neither of these admissions need commit us in any way to the reality of the "more." Democratic tolerance for others may require us to attend to their experiential reports, but it cannot require us to accept their interpretations of those experiences.[56] We can, in other words, admit their testimony without accepting all of its content. I have no doubt, for example, that there are many individuals who believe that their recovery from serious addiction would never have happened without God's help. While I may both accept their recovery and grant their interpretation of it, this surely does not prove that there is a God. To the stalwart psychologist, the successful recovery means two things: first, that humans, when challenged, are capable of remarkable responses; second, that the religious approach to living can provide powerful assistance here. It surely does not mean, however, that we should call the religious interpretation true.

I recognize that I live in a smaller and thinner world than do James and other people of religious convictions. Perhaps I am just spiritually myopic, unable to see the connections between the experiences that others report and their presumed supernatural interpretation, unable to accept the conclusions of religion, as he suggests, "much as blind persons now accept the facts of optics" (VRE 360). Or perhaps I am more concerned about the negative effects of some supernatural interpretations on those individuals and others. In *Pragmatism*, he offers an analogical argument that seems appropriate here. He writes there that human experience is not "the highest form of experience extant in the universe" (P 143). Further, as we have seen, he suggests that our relationship to the rest of the universe may resemble the relationship of our dogs and cats to the rest of human life. Just as they can take part in our lives only up to a certain level and no further, so too may I be able to recognize only part of what others can. I may be dumbly witnessing all sorts of religious mysteries that I cannot understand. James's clever analogy is, of course, indefeasible, but that makes his claim neither true nor false.

In *The Varieties*, James offers a similar comment. "The lustre of the present hour," he notes, "is always borrowed from the background of possibilities it goes with." Thus, when an individual's everyday experiences are "enveloped in an eternal moral order," life's sufferings have "an immortal significance" and one's "days pass by with zest; they stir with prospects, they thrill with remoter values." If, on the other hand, they are part of "the curdling cold and gloom and absence of all permanent meaning," found in his contemporary naturalism and evolutionism, the mystery of living "stops short, or turns rather to an anxious trembling" (*VRE* 119–20).[57] From my myopic depths I must admit that, for some people, this description continues to be true. Such individuals unfortunately find the natural interpretation of human existence a pale and inadequate shadow when compared to a supernatural perspective. This sad fact is as true about human nature today as it was when James was preparing *The Varieties* more than a century ago; it presumably will remain true as we move into the foreseeable future.

Afterword

This volume has been an attempt to assemble, contextualize, and evaluate the central aspects of James's philosophic work. Assembling James's ideas has been made easier by the magnificent critical editions of his writings and his correspondence that were published between 1975 and 2004. These thirty-one volumes present us with the richness of his philosophic ideas on embodiment, belief, rationality, problem solving, relations, pluralism, morality, social thought, and religious experience. Contextualizing his ideas has been made easier by the many dedicated earlier and contemporary commentators who have explored James's role in our intellectual history, offering their insights on the ideas and issues to which he was reacting, and indicating how James's insights could be of assistance in the future. A significant part of their work has been overturning the gross oversimplifications and selective presentations of his views that less careful critics had made prominent. Finally, evaluating James's ideas has been made easier by the broadened spirit of philosophical thinking over the last few decades that has abandoned many of the inherited assumptions about doing philosophy and advancing its development so that James's work can be given a fairer hearing.

As we have seen, James's philosophical style owes less to the scientist and more to the artist or poet. Unlike many philosophers who are overly enamored of the aesthetics of mathematics and physics, he does not rely on the rigidity of narrow argumentation or the rigor of scientific formulations to hammer his themes into a shape presumed proper for philosophic discourse. Rather, James, the physician and psychologist, explores his topics directly through an emphasis on individual experience, frequently using an especially clear example or a strikingly telling analogy as his key. His writing is always accessible because it carries a feel for the particular. Overall, careful readers find in James the sheer joy of working with a philosopher whose range of ideas and whose style of presentation make the next paragraph or chapter a greatly anticipated guest.

James's approach to the project of philosophy can be contrasted with much recent philosophizing that has become part of the professionalized dominion of academic insiders. By means of its narrowed focus and greater precision, this philosophy has made great technical progress, but this progress has come at significant cost. While we need not reject the valuable findings of these familiar logical, mathematical, and linguistic approaches, we can recognize that they are severely limited. Consequently, we are justified in maintaining that there is more to the search for the wisdom to direct our lives. Thus, we have a right to expect of adherents to this narrowed philosophy increased openness to such Jamesian values as a greater recognition of the importance of pluralism and a wholesome regard for the personal approaches and insights of others. Of ourselves we must require both a strong opposition to any and all claims to philosophic hegemony and a clear rejection of the easy answers that some readings of James would occasionally allow.

The legacy of James's thought is a powerful one. From among the many themes that we have considered above, we can revisit just a few strands. His combination of prescriptive philosophical positions with descriptive psychological positions helps us to grasp the complex operation of belief. In this way, we can better understand individuals in their needs and longings as they deal with a natural world of inadequate meaning where they consequently must live without guarantees. We must also make our life decisions without prior answers, in part because we modify our situations and our options through our actions. James also defends an open universe of possibility, spontaneity, and emergence, and he rejects the deadening effects of determinism. He rejects as well the blindness of a life glibly rooted in unjustified certainty, and calls upon us to adopt fallibilism as we move into the future. Another strand in his thought is an essential concern for individuals as they live their lives: with their fears and problems, with their hopes for the future, and with the tools that are available to them. Finally, James addresses the realm of religious experience as a component of life that requires us to avoid the tangles of doctrine while still recognizing the richness of existence that can present itself if we are open to it.

Afterword

James is essentially an American thinker. His pragmatic spirit, his sense of openness and possibility, and his ideals of democratic equality are all fundamentally American. Still, he is much more than just an American thinker, because the embodied life that he explores and the need for explanations that he recognizes are fundamental aspects of any adequate understanding of human existence. For James, we find ourselves in an open universe full of novelty and possibilities. Some of these possibilities are not favorable to us, and ultimately our end is certain. In the meantime, however, the process of our journey through life has to be constructed, largely by us, by means of the beliefs around which we fashion our reality. If we pay careful attention to the flow of experience and remain ever skeptical of the inherited doctrines that would restrain our choices, we can make for ourselves a welcoming home. If we do not attempt to enforce our systems of meaning on others but respect their uniqueness and champion the resultant pluralism, we can learn from their insights. If we remember that the search for wisdom to direct our lives on an ever-more integrating planet within an expanding cosmos is without guarantees or higher validation, we can live responsibility. It is my hope that readers will find within James's thought material that can inspire them to create more intelligent and satisfactory, if finite, lives.

Notes

1. PRELIMINARY CONSIDERATIONS

1. Royce, "William James," 3–4; Dewey, *Later Works*, 3:149; Whitehead, *Modes of Thought*, 3; Pollock, "James," 188–89. Jacques Barzun continues that he finds James "visibly and testably right—right in intuition, range of considerations, sequence of reasons, and fully rounded power of expression. He is for me the most inclusive mind I can listen to, the most concrete and the least hampered by trifles" (*Stroll*, 4).

2. J. J. McDermott, "Introduction" to *WWJ*, xi; *Streams of Experience*, 108; "Introduction" to Selections from William James, 140; "Introduction" to *WWJ*, xi–xii; "Foreword" to Seigfried, *Chaos and Context*, ix; *Culture of Experience*, 102.

3. Note on the death of William James, 694.

4. Peirce, *Collected Papers*, 6.182; cf. 184; Perry, *Thought and Character*, 2:436–37. James admits at one point to being "almost blind mathematically and logically" (*SPP* 93 n.16).

5. Holmes, "Holmes–Cohen Correspondence," 19, 43; cf. Holmes, *Holmes–Pollock Letters*, 1:78, 139.

6. Seth, review of *Pluralistic Universe*, 539, 536. Howard Vincente Knox further comments on the disdain that James sometimes stirs up among professional philosophers, who "conceive his philosophy as an attack upon their dignity and status, because it brings philosophy down from the clouds to earth, and places living above 'reflecting'—or, rather, regards reflecting as only one, rather queer, way of living, to be justified ultimately, if at all, only in the degree in which it unifies, not the 'universe,' but human interests and activities. The academic mind will always resent any doubt as to whether the academic life is its own justification, and the 'highest' that any mind can possibly conceive" (*Philosophy of William James*, 111; cf. Dewey, *Later Works*, 15:3).

7. Schiller, *Must Philosophers Disagree?*, 64–65, cf. 67, 96,182.

8. Bode, "William James in the American Tradition," 101; cf. 108–9. Cornell West notes that "James is not a traditional philosopher by either temperament or training. Rather he is a cultural critic trained in medicine, fascinated with the arts, imbued with a scientific conscience, and attracted to religion" (*American Evasion*, 54).

9. Williams, "William James and the Facts," 97; Hocking, *Types of Philosophy*, 427; cf. Jacks, "William James and His Message," 32.

10. Otto, "Distinctive Philosophy," 24, 10. Otto continues that James's "philosophic

intention was so unique, so different from the customary, that his method and output are sure to be misjudged unless a very special effort is made to determine exactly what he was about" (10–11).

11. Kallen, "Foreword," vi; Turner, *Examination*, 76; Mumford, *Golden Day*, 93; Bush, "Empiricism of James," 533; Earle, "William James," 776. See also Edward H. Madden: "James had an open, free, and breezy way of writing, and he refused to let the technical questions of philosophy cramp his literary style. The style reflected the personality; the freshness of the man was found in his original and pungent metaphors, examples, and epigrams" ("Introduction" to *WB*, xii).

12. Santayana, "William James," 593, 594; "Genteel Tradition," 535; "William James," 588; "Genteel Tradition," 535.

13. Royce, "William James," 36, 45, 7; Parkes, *American Experience*, 267–68. George Cotkin notes further that "what largely made James a successful public figure—someone to whom America turned to for guidance and inspiration in many matters—was his ability to universalize his private universe into public discourse, as well as the reality that his private turmoil was the common cultural property of other Americans" (*William James*, 21; cf. H. G. Townsend, *Philosophical Ideas*, 147–49).

14. Santayana, "William James," 584; Barzun, "William James," 905, 909; *Stroll*, 222; cf. Kallen, *William James and Henri Bergson*, 1.

15. D. S. Miller, "Some of the Tendencies," 654; Dewey, "William James," in *Middle Works*, 6:100; cf. Thayer, *Meaning and Action*, 133 n.1.

16. Carus, *Truth on Trial*, 23. Nicholas Lash similarly writes: "There is a great deal of sheer carelessness and imprecision in James's writings" (*Easter in Ordinary*, 23).

17. J. J. McDermott, "Introduction" to *EP*, xi; Williams, "William James and the Facts," 101. Joseph Warren Beach notes that James "wrote literature whatever his subject" (*Outlook*, 24).

18. Björkman, "William James," 48; Schiller, review of *Some Problems of Philosophy*, 571; review of *Will to Believe*, 547; cf. *Must Philosophers Disagree?*, 66, 81. Joseph Jastrow writes further that James's "popular writings made people think, because they so unpretentiously and engagingly showed what a deal of thinking lay behind those seemingly casual and really final phrases. He wrote in glimpses; but each glimpse, to a mind with helpful imagination, became a vista" ("American Academician," 27).

19. Brooks, *Confident Years*, 585. For the Jefferson passage, see Jefferson's letter to P. S. Dupont de Nemours (24 April 1816) (Jefferson, *Writings*, 1386–87).

20. For a study of Franklin as a pragmatist, see my volume, *Recovering Benjamin Franklin*.

21. See Richardson, *William James*, 17, 153–55; Simon, *Genuine Reality*, 18–20; R. W. B. Lewis, *Jameses*, 47–48, 64–65; Perry, *Thought and Character*, 1:39–103, 140–45, 247; Allen, *William James*, 13.

22. Emerson, *Nature*, in *Complete Works*, 1:3; "Divinity School Address," in *Complete Works*, 1:134; "American Scholar," in *Complete Works*, 1:105.

23. As he writes to his brother Henry at the time: "The reading of the divine Emerson, volume after volume, has done me a lot of good, and, strange to say has thrown a strong practical light on my own path. The incorruptible way in which he followed his own vocation, of seeing such truths as the Universal Soul vouchsafed to him from day to day and month to month, and reporting them in the right literary form, and thereafter kept his limits absolutely, refusing to be entangled with irrelevancies however urging and tempting, knowing both his strength and its limits, and clinging unchangeably to the rural environment which he once for all found to be most propitious, seems to me a moral lesson to all men who have any genius, however small, to foster" (C 3:234; cf. C 10:240).

24. John J. McDermott laments James's failure to engage, other than in this specific essay and in scattered references, the legacy of Emerson. "It is unfortunate that James never undertook a systematic study of Emerson," he writes, "especially one directed to his notions of experience, relations, and symbol." Had he done so, McDermott continues, "James would have found Emerson far more congenial and helpful than many of the other thinkers he chose to examine. More than James cared to admit, Emerson was his master" ("Introduction" to *ERM*, xxii). For other aspects of their relationship, see Carpenter, "William James and Emerson," 57; cf. "Points of Comparison," 470; H. G. Townsend, *Philosophical Ideas*, 133–34; Commager, *American Mind*, 91, 97–98.

25. Dewey, *Later Works*, 15:11; cf. 2:15–16; 5:157. For a similar evaluation by Santayana, see "William James," 585; "General Confession," 12–13.

26. James favorably reviewed the volume in 1904 (see *EP* 102–6).

27. Dewey, *Later Works*, 5:157–58; 15:11; 3:149; 2:10; 11:469, 473, 464. Daniel W. Bjork notes that "James stood between Emerson and Dewey, a pivot between the transcendentalism of the nineteenth century and the instrumentalism of the twentieth. He was a bridge between an age of waning idealism and an emerging one of professional science. James depicted passage from the intellectual perspective of one century to another. Janus-faced, he looked on two worlds, was a part of both and yet of neither" (*Compromised Scientist*, 2).

28. Pollock, "James," 187; J. J. McDermott, "Introduction" to Selections from William James, 140.

29. See R. W. B. Lewis, *Jameses*, 3–36; Habegger, *Father*, 9–29.

30. Kim Townsend notes that "the first William James, amassed a fortune in business and real estate holdings that made him the second-richest man in the country, after John Jacob Astor" (*Manhood*, 40).

31. See R. W. B. Lewis, *Jameses*, 37–70; Matthiessen, *James Family*, 3–135; Fisher, *House of Wits*; Habegger, *Father*; Perry, *Thought and Character*, 1:6–166.

32. The novelist Henry writes of his family's situation that "the rupture with my grandfather's tradition and attitude was complete; we were never in a single case, I think, for two generations, guilty of a stroke of business" (*Autobiographies*, 118; cf. 39).

33. For a summary of Henry's ideas, see William's 1884 "Introduction" to *Literary*

Remains of the Late Henry James (*ERM* 3–63; cf. Matthiessen, *James Family*, 136–205). See also William's farewell letter to his father (*C* 5:327–28).

34. John J. McDermott indicates that "we need to know more about the two younger brothers, Garth Wilkinson and Robertson, whose lives, from any perspective, were a series of crippling frustrations. Some of this can be traced to their participation in the Civil War, but much of it comes from sibling pressures and invidious comparisons with their spoiled but successful older brothers. And we must think more of Alice, who rejoiced at the discovery of her cancer, as it was a real disease at last and promised to take her from the neurasthenia and hypochondria that so dominated her life and that ran through the family as a whole" ("Introduction" to *WWJ*, xix).

35. Cf. Richardson, *William James*, 106–8; R. W. B. Lewis, *Jameses*, 53–57.

36. Allen, *William James*, 259.

37. See Allen, *Willliam James*; Simon, *Genuine Reality*; Richardson, *William James*; Matthiessen, *James Family*, 209–42; Perry, *Thought and Character*, 1:169–410.

38. James wrote to his brother Henry in 1872 that he "regretted extremely letting my drawing die out.... I have been of late so sickened & skeptical of philosophic activity as to regret much that I did not stick to painting, and to envy those like you to whom the aesthetic relations of things were the real world" (*C* 1:173). Any consideration of James's full career undermines this dichotomy, however; and his philosophical work is full of the deeply aesthetic appreciation of experience and the repeated use of vivid analogies. See Perry, *Thought and Character*, 1:190–201; Feinstein, *Becoming William James*.

39. On Lawrence, see Sharples, "Some Reminiscences," 532, 539; Perry, *Thought and Character*, 1:202–16.

40. On Brazil, see Perry, *Thought and Character*, 1:217–26; Machado, *Brazil through the Eyes of William James*.

41. James's final work consisted of a thesis—"Physiological Effects of Cold" (see *C* 4:378)—and a series of nine ten-minute oral exams. At least one of the examiners, Oliver Wendell Holmes Sr., was a close family friend. For the exam process, see *C* 4:383; *C* 10:271; von Kaltenborn, "William James at Harvard," 94.

42. See H. James, *Autobiographies*, 522–23. James apparently did treat a very small number of patients for mental disorders. See E. Taylor, *William James on Exceptional Mental States*, 3, 76, 186 n.4; *C* 8:275–76.

43. See Maher, *Biography of Broken Fortunes*, 27–76.

44. For more on James's thinking about, and possible flirtations with, suicide, see *WWJ* 7; *WB* 34–56; *C* 4:194, 248; *C* 8:157; Richardson, *William James*, 83, 108–22.

45. On his possible stay at the McLean Sanitarium, see Simon, *Genuine Reality*, 121–23; Menand, "William James."

46. *Essays, Comments, and Reviews* contains two reviews for 1865, one for 1867, and six reviews for 1868. During the worst period, however, James completed only one review for 1869, and none for 1870 or 1871. As his recovery advanced, James wrote two reviews for 1872, two for 1873, and eight for 1874 (*ECR* 197–288).

47. Henry James reports that what their father wanted of them was "just to *be* something, something unconnected with specific doing, something free and uncommitted, something finer in short than being *that*, whatever it was, might consist of" (*Autobiographies*, 286).

48. Neurasthenia was diagnosed by Dr. George Miller Beard, who wrote in 1881: "Nervousness is strictly deficiency or lack of nerve-force. This condition, together with all the symptoms of diseases that are evolved from it, has developed mainly within the nineteenth century, and is especially frequent and severe in the Northern and Eastern portions of the United States.... The chief and primary cause of this development and very rapid increase of nervousness is *modern civilization,* which is distinguished from the ancient by these five characteristics: steam-power, the periodical press, the telegraph, the sciences, and the mental activity of women" (*American Nervousness*, vi; cf. *Sexual Neurasthenia; Practical Treatise on Nervous Exhaustion*; Rosenberg, "Place of George M. Beard," 249–51).

49. John J. McDermott describes the impact of James's vastation not as crushing, but as liberating, noting that this experience "pressed upon him the need to generate, *de novo*, a promethean self worthy of the hidden but repressed possibilities of consciousness that all of us harbor but fail to energize" ("Introduction" to *ERM*, xiv).

50. I use a slash between citations to indicate instances where James reused his own materials. Some of these instances are to be expected, as when he edited down the two-volume *Principles of Psychology* to the one-volume *Psychology: Briefer Course*. Others are less obvious, such as his reuse of parts of "Philosophical Conceptions and Practical Results" (1898) in *Pragmatism* (1907). An awareness of these reuses is necessary to understand how James's thought developed and was presented over the years.

51. Cf. *WB* 112; *SPP* 84–87; *ECR* 115–17, 266.

52. Cf. *C* 1:167, 191, 215; Skrupskelis, "Introduction" to *ML*, xxii–xxiv.

53. The role of the Metaphysical Club will be considered in chapter 4.

54. Edward H. Madden notes that "James's marriage to Alice Gibbens was the turning point of his life; he never entirely recovered from occasional depressions, but he was finally able to live a fruitful life as a result of his wife's stability and strength of character" ("Introduction," *C* 8:xxix; cf. Madden and Madden, "Psychosomatic Illnesses of William James"; Kallen, "Introduction" to *Philosophy of William James*, 30).

55. James's Harvard colleague George Herbert Palmer saw his classroom work as "uneven, his lectures—somewhat dependent upon mood—often lacking continuity. If a student did not immediately 'catch on' he might go from one of them no richer than he came. But the same student next week was sure to be stirred by some passage so striking and searching that its truth became henceforth a veritable part of his mind and a way was opened to a whole new tract of formative thought" ("William James," 31).

56. James had originally refused to join the American Philosophical Association because he saw the work of the philosopher to be personal business that would not be advanced by social cooperation. As he wrote to the APA secretary in 1901, "I don't

foresee much good from a philosophical Society. Philosophical discussion proper only succeeds between intimates who have learned how to converse by months of weary trial & failure. The philosoph[er] is a lone beast dwelling in his individual burrow.—Count me *out!*" (C 9:558; cf. C 12:79). He nonetheless joined the association in 1904 and the next year was elected its sixth president.

57. Perry, *Thought and Character*, 1:128, 411; C 3:404.

58. There were frequent setbacks to James's medical condition brought on, he thought, by the pressures of the academic life. *The Correspondence* traces out a pattern of annual collapses. As he describes this pattern in 1891, "when the year's lecturing is done I always come tumbling down like a sail whose halyard is let go" (C 7:171).

59. For his reports on his disappointing experiments with mescal, see C 2:403; C 8:157–58.

60. For James's discussions of the various treatments, see C 3:385–86; C 9:476 (electrical); C 9:270–71; C 11:247; C 12:387 (mind-cure); C 3:125–26; C 9:261–67 (magnetic healing); C 3:261–62, 271, 275, 344; C 10:354; C 11:108–10, 439–40 (Fletcherizing); C 3:143, 146–47 192, 219, 226–27; C 9:277–78, 282, 296–97, 357, 365, 374–75, 382, 565; C 10:179, 205, 403; C 11:42, 49, 502; C 12:270 (injections). See also Fishbein, *New Medical Follies*, 98–101; Bjork, *William James*, 232–39.

61. The *Correspondence* contains reports of two serious mishaps, one in 1898 (see C 8:xxvi) and another in 1899 (see C 3:76–77; C 9:22; Richardson, *William James*, 375–76, 388).

62. See C 11:391, 502.

63. In September 1906 William writes to Henry: "Simplification of the field of duties I find more & more to be the summum bonum for me; & I live in apprehension lest the Avenger should cut me off before I get my message out. Not that the message is particularly needed by the human race, which can live along perfectly well without any one philosopher; but objectively I hate to leave the volumes I have already published without their logical complement. It is an esthetic tragedy to have a bridge begun, & stopt in the middle of an arch" (C 3:323; cf. C 9:526; C 10:71, 120, 334).

64. Horace Meyer Kallen, who prepared the volume for publication, agrees: "What William James thinks about man, and the world, and man's place in it, he has said in many books and many scattered papers. These do not present a complete system of philosophy, but rather special and intensive studies of problems Mr. James felt to be momentous and living at the time" ("Introduction," v).

65. Harold Chapman Brown notes that "James has drawn to himself the greatest reading public of all American philosophers . . . because in him each man can find the sanction for himself. Without dogmatism or pedantry, James is the voice of all individual human experiences. In him, each man can find a sympathetic auditor, and words vivid with the language of the street, encouraging his endeavours or at least pointing out the significance of his experiences for the great business of living" ("Philosophy," 172).

66. Arthur O. Lovejoy writes that "James's thought had a good deal more coherency, and the various parts of his reflection more of definite interconnectedness, than has commonly been recognized, more, indeed, than James himself ever paused to point out ... the truth is that James was by no means a good expounder of his own philosophy *as a whole*. ... [We need] to compare one passage with another, to put two partially contradictory utterances together and extract from them the residuum of positive affirmation, to take from one volume the clauses intended to qualify the propositions in another volume, to make explicit certain logical relations implied, but not fully drawn out" ("Present Philosophical Tendencies," 629–30).

67. John Dewey writes that "the problem of evil is a well-recognized problem, while we rarely or never hear of a problem of good. Goods we take for granted; they are as they should be; they are natural and proper ... it is difficult for the goods of existence to furnish as convincing evidence of the uncertain character of nature as do evils. It is the latter we term accidents, not the former, even when their adventitious character is as certain" (*Experience and Nature*, in *Later Works*, 1:45–46).

68. J. J. McDermott, "Introduction" to *EP*, xvi; *Culture of Experience*, 111; cf. "Introduction" to *WWJ*, xxiv.

69. J. J. McDermott, "Introduction" to *ERE*, xiii–xiv; "Introduction" to *EP*, xvii. George Herbert Palmer notes that "James had a delicate consideration of other, an observant tactfulness in putting all at ease. Few persons are habitually so kind. In consequence a troop of cranks attended him through life, in each of whom he found some merit and—more costly—some need.... What outlays of time and money he spent on half-baked philosophers!" ("William James, 30; cf. Chapman, "William James," 205).

70. See *ML* 270–73, 302–6; Peirce, *Collected Papers*, 6.201–2.

71. Charles Sanders Peirce, for example, wonders at one point who "could be of a nature so different from his as I? He is so concrete, so living; I a mere table of contents, so abstract, a very snarl of twine" (*Collected Papers*, 6.184).

72. George Herbert Palmer notes that "once, long before the days of spelling reform, he came to me with, 'Is n't it abominable that everybody is expected to spell in the same way? Let us get a dozen influential persons to agree each to spell after his own fashion and so break up this tyranny of the dictionary'" ("William James," 31; cf. *Letters*, 2:18–19; C 7:495; C 11:154).

73. Cf. *WB* 9, 239; *EPR* 134. In this vein, Charles Taylor writes that we should "credit James with an extraordinary insight into the spiritual needs of the modern world.... Like any sensitive intellectual of his time and place, James had to argue against the voices, within and without, that held that religion was a thing of the past, that one could no longer in conscience believe in this kind of thing in an age of science" (*Varieties*, 42–43).

74. Thomas Vernor Smith writes that James "not infrequently complains at the scientists ... because he feels that they have defined their method too narrowly or

overestimated their finished achievement.... Much of life is left without the cleansing and guiding influence of science because of this narrowness of men of science. James intended in the name of science to correct the insensitivity and narrowness of professional men of science" (*Philosophic Way of Life*, 78, 93–94; cf. E. Taylor, *William James on Exceptional Mental States*, 1).

75. For Paul K. Conkin, "the science which so often became the devil in his morality play was largely the insufferable product of arrogant and superficial scientists. James easily commended careful inquiry in every area and dared to bring careful techniques of inquiry into the field of religion. But he saw science, as sponsored and popularized in America, as a new church, rich in prestige, imperialistic in its claims, and intolerable in its intellectual pretensions. By unjustified metaphysical extrapolations, scientists had underwritten determinism, atheism, and cynicism, and had illegitimately cowed warm emotions, moral zeal, and religious aspiration" (*Puritans and Pragmatists*, 276–77; cf. D. S. Miller, "James's Doctrine," 545; Schiller, *Must Philosophers Disagree?*, 89).

76. Van Wyck Brooks suggests that before 1914 "there undoubtedly existed in the general mind a conscious belief in some variety of progress, and it was not till the nineteen-twenties that Henry Adams's point of view prevailed, for many writers, over William James's" (*Confident Years*, 587).

77. J. J. McDermott, "Introduction" to *WWJ*, xlii, xi, xliii, xli.

2. PSYCHOLOGY AND PHILOSOPHY

1. Ralph Barton Perry notes in 1907 that because James had "little respect for formal distinctions, he finds food for philosophy as well as food for psychology in the same experience. He was already a philosopher while he was a psychologist, and he is still a psychologist now that he is a philosopher" ("Professor James as a Philosopher," 96; cf. Brodbeck, "Philosophy in America," 11; J. J. McDermott, "Introduction" to *EP*, xii).

2. Gerald E. Myers writes that the ties between psychology and philosophy were so strong that "even after laboratory psychology was established as a curriculum area, it often remained in a university's philosophy department. However vigorous and promising it might seem, psychology was still viewed as a worldly fledgling of philosophy" ("Introduction" to *PP*, 1:xi; cf. Perry, "James the Psychologist," 122; Wilson, *Science, Community*, 97).

3. Josiah Royce notes in 1892 that "two philosophical branches are especially prospering to-day in our Universities, the study of Empirical Psychology, and the study of the History of Philosophy. I believe for my own part that these two pursuits ought to flourish and will flourish together, and that they will lead to very important constructive work. I see no just opposition of spirit between them" (*Spirit of Modern Philosophy*, viii).

4. For example, see J. MacBride Sterrett's 1909 assertion of philosophy's "well recognized position, not as one of the sciences; not as merely the unification of all the sciences, but as the science of the principles of all knowing and of the *absolute reality*

back of all that with which the natural sciences deal" ("Proper Affiliation of Psychology," 90).

5. For more on the initial development of American philosophy into a profession, see my study, *Thoughtful Profession*, 1–75.

6. Edward Wheeler Scripture writes in 1897 that "by the 'old psychology' I mean psychology before the introduction of experiment and measurement" (*New Psychology*, 452). In 1981, Gerald E. Myers posits that *The Principles* "signals the end of much armchair psychology, of psychological theorizing that never experimented, which had prevailed through the first half of the nineteenth century; it announces that future psychology belongs, not in the philosophical study, but in the laboratory" ("Introduction" to *PP*, 1:xv; cf. G. Murphy, *Historical Introduction to Modern Psychology*, xiii).

7. Soon to follow was John Broadus Watson's 1913 manifesto of Behaviorism: "Psychology as the behaviorist views it is a purely objective experimental branch of natural science. Its theoretical goal is the prediction and control of behavior. Introspection forms no essential part of its methods, nor is the scientific value of its data dependent upon the readiness with which they lend themselves to interpretation in terms of consciousness.... Psychology ... needs introspection as little as do the sciences of chemistry and physics" ("Psychology as the Behaviorist Views It," 158, 176).

8. Mace, "Editorial Foreword," 7.

9. Abraham Aaron Roback writes that "James colored psychology with a philosophical tinge. Without the healthy vitamin which he injected into it, psychology might have spent itself, in the early days, on sterile experimentation with chronoscope, mnemometers, and tachistoscopes" (*History of American Psychology*, 142).

10. George Santayana writes in 1891: "Even philosophy, which boasts to be eternal, and is reproached with being unprogressive, succumbs to the fashions; and of late she has made many attempts to dress at least parts of her person in the newest garments of science.... Especially in psychology is it legitimate to wish to be scientific, and to arrive at conclusions that shall be not merely speculative, but capable of verification and of compelling universal assent" ("James's Psychology," 552; cf. "William James," 586).

11. In his review of *The Principles*, Josiah Royce notes that "James shows us the value of the naturalist's point of view, which studies live creatures as if they were alive" ("New Study," 167)

12. Angell, "William James," 78; Kraushaar, "Lotze's Influence," 439; Perry, "James the Psychologist," 122–23; McDougall, "Works of William James," 314–15; Holt, "William James as Psychologist," 34; D. S. Miller, "William James, Man and Philosopher," 36; G. Murphy, *Historical Introduction*, 182–83.

13. Rand B. Evans notes that "the effect of William James and his *Principles of Psychology* has been such that there is a tendency in much of the literature on the history of psychology to portray James as the founder of American psychology. J. McKeen Cattell, a notable American psychologist and younger contemporary of James, wrote: 'A history of psychology in America prior to the last fifty years [before William James] would be

as short as a book on snakes in Ireland since the time of St. Patrick. In so far as psychologists are concerned, America was then like Heaven, for there was not a damned soul there.' Cattell's statement is incorrect, as the scholarship of the last few decades in the history of psychology makes clear" ("Introduction" to *PP*, 1:xliii; cf. Fay, *American Psychology before William James*; Boring, *History of Experimental Psychology*, 493–95).

14. In sharp opposition to this general appreciation of James and his work in psychology, Lightner Whitmer offers a fundamental—if overwrought—criticism in 1909. He writes that James is "temperamentally interested in mysticism, professionally engaged in philosophy, and temporarily assuming the role of a psychologist." Whitmer regards James as the "spoiled child of American psychology, exempt from all serious criticism," who, because of his excessive tolerance of others' beliefs, is "willing to exalt the value of systems which to the common-sense judgment contain but very few grains of truth." For Whitmer, this stance is far more appropriate to a "poet and prophet" than to a serious psychologist. He further describes James as "the leader of an antiscientific revolt," and as "a litterateur" who is gifted with "a charming literary style" and "a keen sense for the dramatic in presentation." Whitmer is particularly hostile to *The Principles*, noting that, while it is "the most popular text book in psychology" and "accepted by many as a standard work on the subject," the volume is "a book for the beginner, and not for the scholar" that owes its success to "the low level of scientific work in this country." Moreover, he is especially critical of what he sees as James's cavalier attitude toward the serious work of psychology present in that volume. He notes that as a result of James's dismissal of the contributions of some psychologists, "American students would naturally be unwilling to waste their time upon problems known to them only through the contemptuous remarks of an authority whom they consider competent, because he holds a professor's chair and has published the most popular text book in the science." Further, he writes, "James' attitude, even toward more general problems of psychology, is one of utter weariness at the difficult task of investigation on a scientific basis." For example, Whitmer writes, "for the work of these two men [Gustav Theodor Fechner and Ernst Heinrich Weber], James himself has nothing but half-humorous contempt. 'Those who desire this dreadful literature,' he says, 'can find it; it has a "disciplinary value"; but I will not even enumerate it in a foot note' [*PP* 1:518]" ("Mental Healing," 291, 295–97, 288, 294, 291, 293, 292; cf. Ladd, "Is Psychology a Science?," 395).

15. Rand B. Evans writes: "Within a decade after the publication of *The Principles of Psychology* James's type of 'introspection,' description of experience in a natural and uncontrolled way—the way empirical psychologists had used it for centuries—was replaced by the analytical introspection of the laboratory. The 'laboratory blackguards,' as James called them, were taking psychology in a direction he was unwilling to follow.... There were doubtless other factors that led James away from psychology as it developed into a discipline separate from philosophy. One... is that psychology became not only independent of philosophy but actually antagonistic to philosophical psychol-

ogy" ("Introduction" to *PP*, 1:lx; cf. Sterrett, "Proper Affiliation of Psychology," 99–100; E. Taylor, *William James on Consciousness*, xi–xii, 3, 183).

16. Dickinson Sergeant Miller notes that, when reading *The Principles*, "we soon note the difference wrought by what I may call the medical interest. You have from him not only a telling exposition of the state of theory on the functions of the brain, but you have a physiological interpretation of the association of ideas, a purely physiological interpretation of our so-called feeling of innervation.... He brings into psychology at every possible point the results of the study of abnormal cases, hysteria, insanity, double personality, automatic writing, hypnotism, etc.... The body is a constant presence and the abnormal is a source of light" ("Some of the Tendencies," 651; cf. Bakewell, "Introduction" to *Selected Papers*, viii).

17. As Gerald E. Myers writes, "as philosophy and psychology negotiated their divorce in the first years of the twentieth century, philosophers tended to focus upon James's metaphysics of radical empiricism, his pragmatism, and his philosophy of religion. *The Principles of Psychology* was more or less bequeathed to psychology" ("Introduction" to *PP*, 1:xxxviii).

18. Harvey Gates Townsend notes that James "is identified in the public mind with psychology, although after the publication of his *Principles* he had a declining interest in the 'nasty little subject.' It is apparent that James had at no time a competent and sustained interest in science.... The cast of his mind was speculative and subjective. He was ever fighting the battles of the inner life, of free will, human destiny, and religious phenomenology" (*Philosophical Ideas*, 136–37).

19. For example, James admits in *The Principles* that "the reader who found himself swamped with too much metaphysics in the last chapter ['The Automaton-Theory'] will have a still worse time of it in this one ['The Mind-Stuff Theory'], which is exclusively metaphysical" (*PP* 1:148; cf. 182; Ladd, "Psychology as So-Called 'Natural Science,'" 29–30).

20. Jacques Barzun notes that James and others showed "on the basis of science itself that science has limitations; and that this being so, mind (including art) overflows science on all sides" (*Energies of Art*, 341).

21. John E. Smith writes that for James "to be philosophical meant viewing every subject against the background of man and his place in the universe; it meant being aware that there is always more to your subject than you are able to capture at one time and from one perspective. Being philosophical on his terms was as much an attitude and a temper of mind as a standpoint or a position to be articulated in a particular system" (*Themes in American Philosophy*, 64).

22. James notes that the philosopher's occupation has been described by some as "'the art of endlessly disputing without coming to any conclusion,' or more contemptuously still as the 'systematische Missbrauch einer eben zu diesem Zwecke erfundenen Terminologie' [the systematic misuse of terminology specifically developed for this purpose]" (*SPP* 11–12).

23. For Henry Heath Bawden, "the subject-matter of philosophy, as ordinarily conceived, is the scientist's methodological scrapheap. All the residual problems which he shoves aside as unimportant or irrelevant are turned over to philosophy, which, as the various sciences successively split off from the parent stem, has thus to be satisfied with the vague chaos of general opinions which have not yet come under scientific scrutiny" (*Principles of Pragmatism*, 23–24).

24. Peirce writes that "fifty generations are nothing in the life of science" (*Collected Papers*, 5.60); and we shall see in chapter 4, the importance that James places in long-term investigation.

25. This theme returns in the discussion of rationality in chapter 3.

26. John Evan Turner maintains that "we find in this characterisation of philosophy the essential defect of James's whole general position—in always, that is, regarding philosophy as a '*sketch*,' a '*picture* of the world,' a '*bird's-eye view*'; for this surely is what philosophy, essentially as such, is not." He continues that "philosophy proper ... always and essentially deals not with facts and events merely as such, but with their underlying and determining principles; not, therefore, with 'a picture of the world in abridgement,' but with a rationale, however vague and inadequate that may prove to be, of the universe in its infinity." This flawed approach leaves James with a "very superficial view of the real nature of philosophy" (*Examination*, 31–32).

27. In 1895 James writes: "The besetting sin of philosophers has always been the absolutism of their intellects. We find an assumption that was the soul of Scholasticism, the assumption namely that anything that is necessary in the way of belief must be susceptible of articulate proof, as rampant as it ever was, in the irreligious agnosticism of to-day; and we find it moreover blossoming out into corollaries, as, for instance, that to believe anything without such proof is to be unscientific, and that to be unscientific is the lowest depth to which a thinking mind can fall. Now these assumptions necessarily make philosophy discontinuous with life, because biologically considered man's life consists for the most part in adjustments that are unscientific, and deals with probabilities and not with certainties ... no philosophy can be more that an hypothesis" (*EP* 93).

28. For George Santayana, "a system of philosophy is a personal work of art which gives a specious unity to some chance vista in the cosmic labyrinth. To confess this is to confess a notorious truth; yet it would be something novel if a philosopher should confess it, and should substitute the pursuit of sincerity for the pursuit of omniscience.... A philosopher setting forth his cognitive and moral experience in his own way would, therefore, not be more heterodox than a poet with an original vision, so long as he abstained from regarding so interesting an idiosyncracy as the measure of all things" ("Philosophical Heresy," 47; cf. Kallen, *William James and Henri Bergson*, 11–12).

29. As James writes in *The Principles*, "even divine Philosophy itself, which common mortals consider so 'sublime' an occupation, on account of the vastness of its data and outlook, is too apt to the practical philosopher himself to be but a sharpening and

tightening business, a matter of 'points,' of screwing down things, of splitting hairs, and of the 'intent' rather that the 'extent' of conceptions" (*PP* 2:1086).

30. James further explores this large problem of academic narrowness and isolation in "The Ph.D. Octopus" (*ECR* 67–74; cf. *C* 8:18, 30, 266–67; *C* 9:47; *C* 11:27–28, 193–94).

31. Charles Montague Bakewell complains to James that, while "in many ways I think that it [*PU*] is the best thing you have done," because it "best succeeds in bringing the reader to the angle of your vision," the book's anti-intellectualism forces readers "to regard your philosophy as a work of art, and of the impressionistic school" (*C* 12:328). Arthur Oncken Lovejoy writes to James in a similar fashion that "there is, after all . . . a difference between philosophy and lyric poetry; and virtually to tell the lay public that there isn't is to make philosophers, and one's own ostensibly coercive reasonings, appear ridiculous in men's eyes" (*C* 12:308). For other like-minded comments, see Kallen, "Introduction," 6–7; Frankel, "Introduction," 4; Blau, *Men and Movements*, 257).

32. James writes to Holt at that point that "no one could be more disgusted than I at the sight of the book. *No* subject is worth being treated of in 1000 pages! Had I ten years more, I could rewrite it in 500; but as it stands it is this or nothing—a loathsome, distended, tumefied, bloated, dropsical mass, testifying to nothing but two facts; *1st*, that there is no such thing as a *science* of psychology, and *2nd*, that W. J. is an incapable" (*C* 7:24).

33. John Dewey points to the mistake of taking *The Principles* "as a philosophical treatise rather than as a psychological one," or vice versa. For him the important fact was that "James began as a student of medicine and physiology, and was deeply concerned to point out the bearings of new knowledge in these subjects upon understanding the make-up and workings of human nature" (*Later Works*, 15:18; cf. 15:3; 3:149; Blau, *Men and Movements*, 252–53).

34. In his review of *The Principles*, G. Stanley Hall writes: "the author might be described an *impressionist* in psychology. His port-folio contains sketches old and new, ethical, literary, scientific and metaphysical, some exquisite and charming in detail and even color, others rough charcoal outlines, but all together stimulating and suggestive, and showing great industry and great versatility. . . . The author is a veritable storm-bird, fascinated by problems most impossible of solution, and surest where specialists and experts in his own field are most in doubt, and finding it very hard to get up interest in the most important matters, if settled and agreed to, even to state them well" (review of *The Principles*, 585, 589; cf. Santayana, "James's Psychology," 553; Boring, *History of Experimental Psychology*, 502).

35. The theme of human sexuality is perhaps better described as suppressed rather than ignored. As James writes to correspondent in 1888, some sexual themes are "hardly discussable in print" (*C* 6:421; cf. *C* 7:240; *C* 8:92–93). For his own part, he also seems to be committed to Victorian social values. Consider, for example, the following: "No one need be told how dependent all human social elevation is upon the prevalence of

chastity. Hardly any factor measures more than this the difference between civilization and barbarism. Physiologically interpreted, chastity means nothing more than the fact that present solicitations of sense are overpowered by suggestions of aesthetic and moral fitness which the circumstances awaken in the cerebrum; and that upon the inhibitory or permissive influence of these alone action directly depends" (*PP* 1:35/*PBC* 97; cf. Mace, "Editorial Foreword," 9).

36. Rand B. Evans writes that "The *Principles* is certainly James's masterpiece and probably the most significant psychological treatise ever written in America.... The *Principles* is also perhaps the best *entree* to any thorough understanding of James's thought" ("William James and His *Principles*," 11, 27). Margaret Knight continues that "no other textbook published in the 'nineties has much chance of being read to-day [1950] by anyone except a student of the history of psychology, but the *Principles* is still widely read for its own sake. One reason for this is that the book, though it is inevitably out of date on points of detail, is almost startlingly modern in its general approach" ("Introduction," 43; cf. Thayer, "Introduction" to *P*, xv; Sully, review of *Principles*, 395).

37. On the preparation of *Psychology: Briefer Course*, see *PBC* 466–91; *C* 7:181, 184; Sokal, "Introduction" to *PBC*, xi–xii.

38. Royce, "New Study of Psychology," 168. James later responds to various charges of formlessness by noting: "The order of composition is doubtless unshapely, or it would not be found so by so many. But planless it is not, for I deliberately followed what seemed to me a good pedagogic order, in proceeding from the more concrete mental aspects with which we are best acquainted to the so-called elements which we naturally come to know later by way of abstraction. The opposite order, of 'building-up' the mind out of its 'units of composition,' has the merit of expository elegance, and gives a neatly subdivided table of contents; but it often purchases these advantages at the cost of reality and truth" (*PBC* 2).

39. Peirce, review of *Principles*, in *Collected Papers*, 8.55–58, and in *Writings*, 8:231–32; cf. Ladd, "Psychology as So-Called 'Natural Science,'" 24–25.

40. Ladd, *Outlines of Physiological Psychology*, 3.

41. Gerald E. Myers writes of the split in James's thought between psychology and philosophy: "He had set out to write a book that introduced psychology as a natural science, reflecting its movement toward the laboratory and away from philosophy, a book that might become the definitive text in this new field. But the project forced him, he confessed, to operate from the outset with an assumption that the philosopher in him seriously mistrusted.... The assumption is dualism, the doctrine that there are *physical* things and there are *mental* things, and there is no way of 'reducing' one kind to the other.... The psychologist is forced to assume that one side of the dualism, the mental states of a person, can know the other side, things in a surrounding physical world; but he can neither explain nor justify this assumption. To try to do so is to leave psychology and enter philosophy" ("Introduction" to *PP*, 1:xiii–xiv; cf. Dewey, *Later Works*, 14:155–67; Perry, *Thought and Character*, 2:72–75).

42. That discussion takes place in "Does Consciousness Exist?," to be considered in chapter 5.

43. Gerald E. Myers notes that "the entire tradition of English philosophy, derived from Locke and Hume, and the whole German movement begun by Herbart, in his opinion, treated consciousness as if, like the physical environment for which we have a common descriptive language, it is constituted by units ('ideas') that are discrete, independent, substantive, and even recurrent. The main objective . . . in . . . 'The Stream of Thought,' is to refute this viewpoint and to replace it, largely on introspective grounds, with the picture of consciousness as a rapid continuous stream" ("Pragmatism and Introspective Psychology," 16–17; cf. Sully, review of *Principles*, 395).

44. Consider James's parallel presentation of human consciousness from 1880: "we have the most abrupt cross-cuts and transitions from one idea to another, the most rarefied abstractions and discriminations, the most unheard-of combinations of elements, the subtlest associations of analogy; in a word, we seem suddenly introduced into a seething caldron of ideas, where everything is fizzling and bobbing about in a state of bewildering activity, where partnerships can be joined or loosened in an instant, treadmill routine is unknown, and the unexpected seems the only law" (*WB* 185).

45. For Jacques Barzun, "vagueness is a mental fact in itself and not the debris of something clear and distinct. James was particularly proud of having restored vagueness to its rightful place in reality, and this achievement may be taken as a good example of his conquest over the rigid intellectualism of preceding psychologies. . . . Obviously, thinking by means of an assembly of bits and pieces, and under the waffle-iron of the categories, left no room for the whole range of nuances which we call vagueness and which forms so large a part—all unnamed—of our sentient existence" ("William James," 908; cf. Gavin, *William James*, 19–29).

46. J. J. McDermott, "Introduction" to *EP*, xxii. George Santayana writes that in James "the word experience is like a shrapnel shell, and bursts into a thousand meanings" ("William James," 586; cf. Earle, "William James," 776–77).

47. Working here as a psychologist, and not a metaphysician, James does not explore the question of whether introspection is trustworthy. On this matter, Gerald E. Myers writes: "Today, when philosophers visit the topic of introspection, they are usually preoccupied with the question, Do we possess an *infallible* faculty of self-scrutiny? Their inquiry concentrates less on what introspection is than on whether, as it sometimes claimed, its disclosures are indubitable" ("Pragmatism and Introspective Psychology," 12; cf. Earle, "William James," 778).

48. In the essay "Human Immortality," James considers the "metaphysical" question of whether bodies are necessary for thinking (see *ERM* 79–91). His views on the issue of immortality will be considered in chapter 7.

49. James notes further that "the *great* snare of the psychologist is the *confusion of his own standpoint with that of the mental fact* about which he is making his report. I shall hereafter call this the 'psychologist's fallacy' *par excellence*." Standing "outside of

the [subject's] mental state," psychologists tend to insert their own interpretation of the fact for what it means to the subject (*PP* 1:195; cf. Baldwin, *Dictionary*, 2:382; Dewey, *Art as Experience*, in *Later Works*, 10:128–29; J. E. Smith, *Themes in American Philosophy*, 69–70).

50. On this point, James writes that "the practically cognized present is no knife-edge, but a saddle-back, with a certain breadth of its own on which we sit perched, and from which we look in two directions into time. The unit of composition of our perception of time is a *duration*, with a bow and a stern, as it were—a rearward- and a forward-looking end. It is only as parts of this *duration-block* that the relation of *succession* of one end to the other is perceived. We do not first feel one end and then feel the other after it, and from the perception of the succession infer an interval of time between, but we seem to feel the interval of time as a whole, with its two ends embedded in it." After some discussion of the laboratory literature, he suggests that twelve seconds is "the *maximum filled duration* of which we can be both *distinctly and immediately* aware" (*PP* 1:574, 577; cf. *PBC* 245–46; Mead, *Mind, Self and Society*, 86). The question of the nature of time returns in chapter 5.

51. The German words, respectively, for "the father" in its nominative and dative forms, and combinations that yield "speed limit" and "weapons of mass destruction."

52. The problematic nature of concepts will return in chapter 5.

53. In a similarly metaphorical fashion, Peirce writes that philosophy's reasonings "should not form a chain which is no stronger than its weakest link, but a cable whose fibers may be ever so slender, provided they are sufficiently numerous and intimately connected" (*Collected Papers*, 5.265).

54. In addition to the transitive parts of experience, there are also other frequently unrecognized directional states of consciousness, as when we attempt to recall a forgotten name, or search for the proper word to complete a recalcitrant sentence. In these cases, we have "an acutely discriminitive sense," although "no definite sensorial image." James continues that these "sensorial images are stable psychic facts" that we can preserve in consciousness; but the "bare images of logical movement, on the contrary, are psychic transitions, always on the wing, so to speak, and not to be glimpsed except in flight" (*PP* 1:244; cf. 239).

55. For Ralph Barton Perry, James "agreed with the common and unfavorable verdict upon Hume. But those who had insisted most strenuously on Hume's failure had believed that its cause lay in his rigorous adherence to the principle of empiricism. Thus it fell out, according to James, that the needed corrections were administered by the alien school of Kant, which applied a remedy that was worse than the disease. James conceived it to be his role in philosophy to save empiricism through greater fidelity to its own tradition and standards, the fault of its later proponents lying not in the excess but in the timidity of their partisanship" (*Thought and Character*, 1:544; cf. Murray, *Pragmatism*, 19; Bixler, "William James as Religious Thinker," 124; Myers, "Introduction" to *PP*, 1:xxiii–xxiv).

56. This section was omitted in *PBC*.

57. Gustav Emil Müller writes that for James "the fundamental fact of spiritual life is thus not being a person but becoming one" ["ein Personwerden, nicht Personsein, darin besteht die Grundtatsache des Seelenlebens"] (*Amerikanische Philosophie*, 211).

58. In the background of much thinking on this topic in James's day is John Fiske's 1883 generalization about infancy. For Fiske, the great advantage to those creatures that live by learning over those that live by instinct is that their extended infancy makes for adaptability. He writes: "man's progressiveness and the length of his infancy are but two sides of one and the same fact ... it was the lengthening of infancy which ages ago gradually converted our forefathers from brute creatures into human creatures. It is babyhood that has made man what he is.... With such creatures as the codfish, the turtle, or the fly-catcher, there is accordingly nothing that can properly be called infancy. With them the sphere of education is extremely limited. They get their education before they are born.... But this steady increase of intelligence, as our forefathers began to become human, carried with it a steady prolongation of infancy. As mental life became more complex and various, as the things to be learned kept ever multiplying, less and less could be done before birth, more and more must be left to be done in the earlier years of life" ("Meaning of Infancy," 280, 283, 287).

59. James offers a series of physical examples of habits: "A scar anywhere is a *locus minoris resistentiae* [place of lesser resistance], more liable to be abraded, inflamed, to suffer pain and cold, than are the neighboring parts. A sprained ankle, a dislocated arm, are in danger of being sprained or dislocated again; joints that have once been attacked by rheumatism or gout, mucous membranes that have been the seat of catarrh, are with each fresh recurrence more prone to a relapse, until often the morbid state chronically substitutes itself for the sound one" (*PP* 1:111/*PBC* 127).

60. For most of us, there is also a resultant cost elsewhere: "We overlook misprints, imagining the right letters, though we see the wrong ones" (*TT* 96). George Herbert Mead notes that proofreaders pay a different price for their habituation: they "notice the words and letters and not the sense" (*Movements of Thought*, 397).

61. This is yet another reason why repeated experiences are not the same.

62. George Herbert Mead notes that "a trained body of troops exhibits a set of conditioned reflexes. A certain formation is brought about by means of certain orders. Its success lies in an automatic response when these orders are given. There, of course, one has action without thought. If the soldier thinks under the circumstances he very likely will not act; his action is dependent in a certain sense on the absence of thought" (*Mind, Self, and Society*, 102).

63. Walter Lippmann writes that "for the most part we do not first see, and then define, we define first and then see. In the great blooming, buzzing confusion [see *PP* 1:462; *PBC* 21] of the outer world, we pick out what our culture has already defined for us, and we tend to perceive that which we have picked out in the form stereotyped for us by our culture" (*Public Opinion*, 81; cf. Curti, *Social Ideas*, 448).

64. We will consider these questions more carefully in the context of James's social thought in chapter 6.

65. In *The Principles* James generally uses "self," whereas in *Psychology: Briefer Course* he uses "me."

66. For George Herbert Mead, "the 'I' is the response of the organism to the attitudes of the others; the 'me' is the organized set of attitudes of others which one himself assumes. The attitudes of the others constitute the organized 'me,' and then one reacts toward that as an 'I'" (*Mind, Self and Society*, 175).

67. Charles Horton Cooley expands on this point: "Self-feeling of a reflective and agreeable sort, an appropriative zest of contemplation, is strongly suggested by the word 'gloating.' To gloat, in this sense, is as much as to think 'mine, mine, mine,' with a pleasant warmth of feeling. Thus a boy gloats over something he has made with his scroll-saw, over the bird he has brought down with his gun, or over his collection of stamps or eggs; a girl gloats over her new clothes, and over the approving words or looks of others; a farmer over his fields and his stock; a business man over his trade and his bank-account; a mother over her child; the poet over a successful quatrain; the self-righteous man over the state of his soul; and in like manner everyone gloats over the prosperity of any cherished idea" (*Human Nature and the Social Order*, 143; cf. Royce, *Problem of Christianity*, 253–54).

68. As Josiah Royce writes: "I am not first self-conscious, and then secondarily conscious of my fellow. On the contrary, I am conscious of myself, on the whole, as in relation to some real or ideal fellow, and apart from my consciousness of my fellows I have only secondary and derived states and habits of self-consciousness" ("Self-Consciousness," 426).

69. Charles Horton Cooley further notes that "social consciousness, or awareness of society, is inseparable from self-consciousness, because we can hardly think of ourselves excepting with reference to a social group of some sort, or of the group except with reference to ourselves. . . . Self and society are twin-born, we know one as immediately as we know the other, and the notion of a separate and independent ego is an illusion" (*Social Organization*, 5).

70. For George Herbert Mead, "we are one thing to one man and another thing to another. . . . We divide ourselves up in all sorts of different selves with reference to our acquaintances. We discuss politics with one and religion with another. There are all sorts of different selves answering to all sorts of different social reactions" (*Mind, Self and Society*, 142).

71. Mary Whiton Calkins writes that "the child imitates his father's stride, because it is his father's, not from any intrinsic interest in the movement in itself, and he is fiercely Republican because his father belongs to the Republican party, not because he himself inclines toward these principles rather than toward others. The life of the child shows most clearly, indeed, the intense personal nature of imitation" (*Introduction to Psychology*, 341).

72. John Dewey notes that "to learn to be human is to develop through the give-and-take of communication an effective sense of being an individually distinctive member of a community" (*Public and Its Problems*, in *Later Works*, 2:332).

73. For George Herbert Mead, "self-criticism is essentially social criticism, and behavior controlled by self-criticism is essentially behavior controlled socially" (*Mind, Self, and Society*, 255).

74. W. E. B. Du Bois emphasizes these conflicts, especially as they are present in African Americans: "It is a peculiar sensation, this double-consciousness, this sense of always looking at one's self through the eyes of others, of measuring one's soul by the tape of a world that looks on in amused contempt and pity. One ever feels his twoness,—an American, a Negro; two souls, two thoughts, two unreconciled strivings; two warring ideals in one dark body, whose dogged strength alone keeps it from being torn asunder" (*Souls of Black Folk*, in *Writings*, 364).

75. He offers us such an interpretation in "The Dilemma of Determinism," to be considered in chapter 3.

76. Richard P. High and William R. Woodward write: "According to this doctrine, an idea—a sensory process—automatically expresses its motor effects unless it is inhibited by an antagonistic idea. Thus, for example, the idea of moving my hand results in that movement unless that idea is contradicted. For James, ideas are correlates of neural processes on their way to becoming manifest in action" ("William James and Gordon Allport," 64; cf. Myers, *William James*, 201).

77. Gerald E. Myers notes that all his life James "had problems of health, professional achievement, and personal motivation; to cope he had repeatedly to summon the support of an occasionally flagging willpower. Far from being a largely academic issue, the will was an extraordinarily poignant topic for him. Nowhere did he betray more zeal in harmonizing the disclosures of introspective psychology with the discoveries of physiology than in his search for an understanding of the will ... he tried to find practical ways to become a healthy rather than a sick soul" (*William James*, 198, 214).

78. In *Talks to Teachers*, James also considers children with what he calls a "balky will." Such children "are usually treated as sinful, and are punished; or else the teacher pits his or her will against the child's will, considering that the latter must be 'broken.' . . . Such will-breaking is always a scene with a great deal of nervous wear and tear on both sides, a bad state of feeling left behind it, and the victory not always with the would-be will-breaker" (*TT* 107).

79. Elsewhere, James considers "the case of an habitual drunkard under temptation": "He has made a resolve to reform, but he is now solicited again by the bottle. His moral triumph or failure literally consists in his finding the right *name* for the case. If he says that it is a case of not wasting good liquor already poured out, or a case of not being churlish and unsociable when in the midst of friends, or a case of learning something at last about a brand of whiskey which he never met before, or a case of celebrating a public holiday, or a case of stimulating himself to a more energetic resolve

in favor of abstinence than any he has ever yet made, then he is lost; his choice of the wrong name seals his doom. But if, in spite of all the plausible good names with which his thirsty fancy so copiously furnished him, he unwaveringly clings to the truer bad name, and apperceives the case as that of 'being a drunkard, being a drunkard, being a drunkard,' his feet are planted on the road to salvation; he saves himself by thinking rightly" (*TT* 110).

80. Bentham writes: "Nature has placed mankind under the governance of two sovereign masters, *pain* and *pleasure*. It is for them alone to point out what we ought to do, as well as to determine what we shall do" (*Introduction to the Principles of Morals and Legislation*, 827).

81. The theme of the moral prophet returns in chapter 5.

82. The issue of making productive use of our energies was explored in a different manner by Frederick Winslow Taylor in his studies of the "scientific" management of factories. See *Shop Management* and *Principles of Scientific Management*.

83. In *A Pluralistic Universe*, James writes of the recognition of "deeper reaches" by new thought: "There are resources in us that naturalism with its literal and legal virtues never recks of, possibilities that take our breath away, of another kind of happiness and power, based on giving up our own will and letting something higher work for us, and these seem to show a world wider than either physics or philistine ethics can imagine" (*PU* 138).

84. Fletcher notes: "I have coined the word '*fear-thought*' to stand for the unprofitable element of forethought, and have defined that variously-interpreted word 'worry' as *fearthought, in contradistinction to forethought*. I have also defined 'fearthought' as the *self-imposed* or *self-permitted* suggestion of *inferiority*" (*Happiness*, 24–25).

85. This topic is now being explored most carefully by the growing field of positive psychology. See Seligman and Csikszentmihalyi, "Positive Psychology"; Seligman, *Flourish*; Csikszentmihalyi, *Flow*.

86. The importance of the "more" in James's thought will be examined in chapter 7.

87. Elsewhere, James continues: "Ideality often clings to things only when they are taken thus abstractly. 'Causes,' as anti-slavery, democracy, etc., dwindle when realized in their sordid particulars. Abstractions will touch us when we are callous to the concrete instances in which they lie embodied. Loyal in our measure to particular ideals, we soon set up abstract Loyalty as something of a superior order to be infinitely loyal to; and Truth at large becomes a 'momentous issue,' compared with which truths in detail are poor scraps, 'mere crumbling successes.' So strongly do objects that come as universal and eternal arouse our sensibilities, so greatly do life's values deepen when we translate percepts into ideas! The translation appears as far more than the original's equivalent" (*SPP* 42–43).

88. The sense of power to which James is pointing has been recognized, for example, by Alcoholics Anonymous. In an appendix to the Blue Book entitled "Spiritual Experience," we find: "Though it was not our intention to create such an impression,

many alcoholics have nevertheless concluded that in order to recover they must acquire an immediate and overwhelming 'God-consciousness' followed at once by a vast change in feeling and outlook.... Quite often friends of the newcomer are aware of the difference long before he is himself. He finally realizes that he has undergone a profound alteration in his reaction to life; that such a change could hardly have been brought about by himself alone. What often takes place in a few months could seldom have been accomplished by years of self discipline. With few exceptions our members find that they have tapped an unsuspected inner resource which they presently identify with their own conception of a Power greater than themselves.... Most of us think this awareness of a Power greater than ourselves is the essence of spiritual experience. Our more religious members call it 'God-consciousness'" (Anonymous, *Alcoholics Anonymous*, 569–70. See also J. J. McDermott, "Jamesian Personscape").

89. Perry, *Thought and Character*, 2:155.

90. See, for example, *EPR* 14–19, 37–88, 119–66, 184–86; *EPs* 190–97, 200–203, 247–68, 322–24; *PU* 134–35.

91. Cf. *C* 8:364; Baum, "Attitude of William James," 599–600.

92. James continues that "at times I have been tempted to believe that the creator has eternally intended this department of nature to remain *baffling*, to prompt our curiosities and hopes and suspicion all in equal measure, so that although ghosts and clairvoyances, and raps and messages from spirits, are always seeming to exist and can never be fully explained away, they also can never be susceptible of full corroboration" (*EPR* 362).

93. Robert A. McDermott writes that "with all the founders of the Society for Psychical Research, James shared a double commitment: first, to investigate psychic phenomena according to the methods and criteria of science; and second, to enlarge the scope of science to include the study of phenomena that are random, unrepeatable, and dependent on unusual personal capacities and dispositions" ("Introduction" to *EPR*, xix).

94. See *EPR* 89–106, 361–75; *ML* 55–83; E. Taylor, *William James on Exceptional Mental States*.

95. Jacques Barzun notes that "James did not enjoy this kind of inquiry. He pursued it in part to maintain a critical pressure on what he called Scientific Sectarianism—the people who were sure beforehand. But the work itself James found tedious, undignified, often disgusting" (*Stroll*, 240).

96. For discussions of these two figures and related themes, see *EPR* 14–19, 79–88, 130–32, 184–91, 219, 253–360; R. A. McDermott, "Introduction" to *EPR*, xxi–xxvi; Münsterberg, *American Problems*, 117–48; Gardner, *Night Is Large*, 213–43.

97. James himself even admits to an instance of cheating during a demonstration: "I once had charge of a heart, on the physiology of which Prof. Newell Martin was giving a popular lecture. This heart, which belonged to a turtle, supported an index straw which threw a moving shadow, greatly enlarged, upon the screen, while the heart

pulsated. When certain nerves were stimulated, the lecturer said, the heart would act in certain ways which he described. But the poor heart was too far gone and, although it stopped duly when the nerve of arrest was excited, that was the final end of its life's tether. Presiding over the performance, I was terrified at the fiasco, and found myself suddenly acting like one of those military geniuses who on the field of battle convert disaster into victory. There was no time for deliberation; so, with my forefinger under a part of the straw that cast no shadow, I found myself impulsively and automatically imitating the rhythmical movements which my colleague had prophecied the heart would undergo. I kept the experiment from failing; and not only saved my colleague (and the turtle) from a humiliation that but for my presence of mind would have been their lot, but I established in the audience the true view of the subject.... I was acting for the *larger* truth, at any rate, however automatically; and my sense of this was probably what prevented the more pedantic and literal part of my conscience from checking the action of my sympathetic finger. To this day the memory of that critical emergency has made me feel charitable towards all mediums who make phenomena come in one way when they won't come easily in another" (*EPR* 364–65).

98. For Martin Gardner, "the strongest indictment that can be made against William James as a psychic researcher is that not once did he devise, or even consider devising, a sting operation. He was surely aware of how easily skeptics can set such traps. The psychologist G. Stanley Hall, for example, invented Bessie Beale, a fictitious person whose spirit Mrs. Piper had no difficulty reaching" (*Night Is Large*, 230; cf. Ewer, "Influence," 153).

99. Cf. *EPR* 20–21, 24–28, 192–202, 216–18. Robert A. McDermott notes that "in response to the skeptic, James offered a rather minimal claim—namely, that psychic phenomena are not impossible.... But he repeatedly noted, the scientific community is as capable of negative superstition as it is of demolishing the superstition of the believer" ("Introduction" to *EPR*, xxii).

100. Angell, "William James," 81; cf. T. V. Smith, *Philosophical Way of Life*, 109; Lippmann, "William James," 20–21.

101. Jastrow, *Fact and Fable*, 53–54, 75, 54–55, 76, vii–viii, 45, 39; cf. Scripture, *New Psychology*, 69.

102. Jastrow, "American Academician," 32; cf. Cattell, Note on the Society for Psychical Research, *EPR* 186; Coon, "Testing the Limits."

3. RATIONALITY AND BELIEF

1. James later admits that "'The Psychology of Philosophizing' would perhaps be a better title for this Essay than the one which it bears" (*EP* 359).

2. In *The Principles*, James suggests the value of using the terms "feeling" and "thought" interchangeably, although he admits that to do so may "use both words in a wider sense than usual, and alternately startle two classes of readers by their unusual sound" (*PP* 1:186).

3. A consideration of Peirce's call for a higher standard appears in chapter 4.

4. The theme of concepts as tools returns in chapter 5.

5. In *The Principles*, James writes that in many cases of rival scientific theories "that theory will be most generally believed which, besides offering us objects able to account satisfactorily for our sensible experience, also offers those which are most interesting, those which appeal most urgently to our aesthetic, emotional, and active needs" (PP 2:940; cf. PU 54–55).

6. Max Carl Otto writes that James's break with tradition "was perhaps his boldest heresy, and he was never forgiven for avowing it: for preferring the biological to the rationalistic approach; for believing that the senses, the creative imagination, the feelings, instead of being inevitable sources of error, might be authentic avenues to truth" ("Distinctive Philosophy," 16).

7. This passage marks the first of a number of James's casual anti-Catholic comments that will appear in this and later chapters.

8. Richard P. High and William R. Woodward write that "in spite of the irrational implications of his position, he argued that a person becomes free by choosing to believe in his freedom and acting on that belief. For James, the belief in human freedom energizes a person and thereby creates results in action that would not appear without that belief. In a sense, he argued that a person chooses to feel helpless or in control and that that decision affects his behavior" ("William James and Gordon Allport," 60).

9. As an example of this perspective, we may consider young Benjamin Franklin's 1725 *A Dissertation on Liberty and Necessity, Pleasure and Pain* (*Writings*, 57–71). See also my volume, *Recovering Benjamin Franklin*, 100–110.

10. James admits that this perspective does not appeal to everyone; for some this sort of universe seems "like the sight of the horrible motion of a mass of maggots in their carrion bed" (WB 136).

11. In a brief coda to this essay, James considers whether such indeterminism would preclude Divine Providence. His response is that the belief in free will "is not in the least incompatible with the belief in Providence, provided you do not restrict the Providence to fulminating nothing but *fatal* decrees." As long as God provides "possibilities as well as actualities to the universe," there is room for chance "uncontrolled even by him." As a result, "the course of the universe [may] be really ambiguous; and yet the end of all things may be just what he intended it to be from all eternity" (WB 138). Thus, for James, it is not necessary for God to control everything to be provident. This theme will return in chapter 7 with the consideration of a finite God.

12. Jacob Gould Schurman notes that "in the medium of logical minds, empiricism has developed into naturalism, with its apotheosis of the mechanical world, its paralysis of the free and real activity of the human ego, its forfeiture of the belief in the Divine existence and government, and its exchange of Christian hopefulness for the despairing heart-sickness to which it gives the speculative name of pessimism" (review of *Will to Believe*, 87).

13. In this regard, George Stuart Fullerton writes that "men generally find themselves born into some sort of a religious system of doctrine and practice. It serves and it has served as a scaffolding by the aid of which man builds up his moral and spiritual life ... if the system serves his purpose, and if he can profitably use it, it seems a more natural thing to accept it than to accept some other for which little more can be said.... Unless a man has good reason to move on, he would better stay where nature and the historical development of things have placed him" ("Right to Believe," 414–15).

14. James also describes the latter two criteria collectively as "my moral demand" (*WB* 115).

15. John Watson notes that "James does not mean that we are in all cases to take as true what it suits us personally to believe. It may, for example, suit a political leader to believe that every member of his party is scrupulously honest, but he is not justified in taking his wish as equivalent to fact. Again, it would be very pleasant if a man who is roaring with rheumatism in bed could by believing that he was well at once become well, or if a man who has only a dollar in his pocket could convert it by his wish into a hundred dollars; but it is obvious that in such cases the talk of believing by our volition is simply silly" (*Philosophical Basis of Religion*, 142).

16. David A. Hollinger writes: "The socially complacent American [James] worried about the damage a strict scientific conscience could do to the peace of mind of individuals, while the politically engaged Englishman of a generation before [Clifford] had worried about the damage religious authority could exact on a credulous population learning only gradually the liberating potential of a critical mind" ("James, Clifford, and the Scientific Conscience," 78).

17. Clifford, "Ethics of Belief," 177, 178, 182, 183, 184, 186.

18. Ellen Kappy Suckiel writes that "to fully appreciate the pragmatic magnitude of the meaning of God's existence, and thus to understand the pragmatic justification of religious belief, the subject must sincerely hold the religious option as a live one. But to hold the religious option as a live one is, of course, precisely what the scientific rationalist is unwilling to do" (*Heaven's Champion*, 34; cf. Madden, "Introduction" to *WB*, xiii–xiv).

19. For James's shift, see for example: C 8:476–77, 492–93; C 9:552; C 10:434, 449–50. Gail Kennedy notes that in "The Will to Believe," James "asserts two different propositions, not kept as distinct as they might have been either by him in that essay nor by his critics. The first is concerned with what should be called the 'right to believe': it is, that under certain conditions one is entitled to believe in the existence of a fact in advance of having complete evidence.... The second is concerned with what properly should be called the 'will to believe': it is, that there are certain cases where the belief in the future existence of a fact may itself help to produce that fact. As James puts it, there are 'cases where faith creates its own verification' [*WB* 80]" ("Pragmatism, Pragmaticism," 579–80).

20. Jacob Gould Schurman emphasizes that "in the field of action, doubt is as fatal

as downright rejection. You cannot, therefore, avoid taking sides. And where, as in living our lives, faith in a fact can help create the fact, it is surely absurd, as it is impossible, to have faith wait upon scientific evidence" (review of *Will to Believe*, 88).

21. George Stuart Fullerton writes that it is "too loosely generous to maintain that we have the right to believe any hypothesis that tempts us; some limiting clause is demanded.... We all know that there are certain things that I may do at my own risk, that I may not do at the risk of my neighbor.... I am inclined to think, therefore, that it is better to discard the words 'at our own risk,' and, recognizing the moral responsibility to ourselves and to the community under which we all stand, to discuss the right to believe with a full consciousness of such responsibility. Whether we accept this view of the universe or that, this system of practice or that, is not merely our own affair. It is also the concern of our neighbor. And as far as it is our own affair, it is too serious a matter to be classed with the things that we may do or leave undone at our own risk" ("Right to Believe," 410–12).

22. Edward H. Madden notes that "what annoyed James about Clifford and Huxley was their insistence that a man has the *duty* to be a religious agnostic since the evidence is inconclusive, a position James felt to be an intolerant one" ("Introduction" to WB, xv; cf. xxiii–xxiv; "Introduction" to C 8:xxxvii–xxxviii).

23. For F. C. S. Schiller, "every one has an inalienable right to his own opinion, to his personal reaction upon his world—until he can get a better. For the right to his opinion is the correlative of his duty to improve it" (*Must Philosophers Disagree?*, 105).

24. As James writes to L. T. Hobhouse, "*your* enemy is 'error,' while mine is the baleful social result, if 'Science' in the shape of abstraction, priggishness, and dessication, should lord it over all" (C 10:450).

25. Howard Vincente Knox notes that "to accuse James of irrationalism because he thus justifies acts of faith is as if one were to accuse a soldier of stupidity because, in performing some deed of valour, he could have had no guarantee that he would both succeed in his venture and come out of it alive" (*Philosophy of William James*, 80).

26. Josiah Royce writes that "man never merely finds, but also always cooperates in creating his world" ("William James," 37). In a similar fashion, Ralph Barton Perry notes: "The man who believes that he can win a race, or achieve a fortune, or win an election, or recover from illness, or overcome temptation, or renounce the devil and his works, is, owing to this belief, the more likely to succeed; provided, of course, the belief does not lead to a neglect of other causes.... The greater part of human action is theoretically premature. The individual must choose his occupation before the vocational experts have perfected the science of human aptitude, and without any complete evidence of future circumstance or development. The sick man must employ *some* remedy before the science of medicine is ideally complete. Men must erect some state, employ some economic policy, adopt some social program when the social sciences are notoriously inconclusive. Action cannot be postponed to await the leisurely completion of the theoretical processes" (*In the Spirit*, 192, 199).

27. Hocking, *Types of Philosophy*, 170; cf. *Meaning of God*, 140. Charles Taylor continues: "Clifford assumes that there is only one road to truth: we put the hypotheses that appeal to us under severe tests, and those that survive are worthy of adoption ... we can win the right to believe a hypothesis only by first treating it with maximum suspicion and hostility.... James holds, on the contrary, that there are some domains in which truths will be hidden from us unless we go at least halfway toward them" (*Varieties*, 46).

28. Singer, "Pragmatic Use of Language," 31; cf. 27–28; Durkheim, *Pragmatism and Sociology*, 393; E. C. Moore, *American Pragmatism*, 129. James writes to a correspondent at one point about "my 'W. to B,' of which the first Essay is called by some of my best friends 'the Will to Deceive,' 'the Will to make-Believe,' and other epigrammatic distortions" (C 11:257). Lewis Mumford continues in this vein that "the carefully limited area he left to religious belief in The Will-to-Believe was transformed by ever-so-witty colleagues into the Will-to-make-believe. His conscious philosophy of pragmatism, which sought to ease one of the mighty, recurrent dilemmas of his personal life, was translated into a belief in the supremacy of cash-values and practical results; and the man who was perhaps one of the most cosmopolitan and cultivated minds of his generation was treated at times as if he were a provincial writer of newspaper platitudes, full of the gospel of smile" (*Golden Day*, 97).

29. D. S. Miller, "James's Doctrine," 552–53; cf. "'Will to Believe,'" 173, 187–88; Cohen, *Reason and Nature*, 21; Meiklejohn, *What Does America Mean?*, 168–70.

30. G. E. Moore, "William James's 'Pragmatism,'" 141, 143. James's pragmatic understanding of truth will be considered in chapter 4.

31. We may wonder how large this "immense class" is; but surely James did not intend to include "nearly all" beliefs, as Moore maintains.

32. Marcus Singer notes that "it is an overstatement for James to say, as he does, 'Believe, and you shall be right, for you shall save yourself.' All he is strictly entitled to say is 'Believe, and you may be right, for you may save yourself.' But James's statement is itself an instance of the pragmatic use of language" ("Pragmatic Use of Language," 32–33).

33. For William Ernest Hocking, "there is a great region of the world which is unfinished and plastic, and where our action changes the facts. Treating a man as if he were an enemy may make him an enemy; treating him as a friend may make him such" (*Types of Philosophy*, 171).

34. Ralph Barton Perry notes that "all political managers and military chieftains claim the victory in advance, not from sheer fatuousness, nor because they are blind to the obstacles and difficulties, nor from childish boastfulness, but because they understand instinctively that collective self-confidence does in and of itself contribute to victory.... Distrust, on the other hand, is a serious and often fatal weakness" (*In the Spirit*, 193–94; cf. Hick, *Faith and Knowledge*, 36; Blau, *Men and Movements*, 258; Lee, "Two Pragmatisms," 450–51).

35. James does not explore the nature of this analogy; but for him—unlike for those who view religion as a recording case—the following comparison is possible: rejecting a religious life because its potential benefits come without guarantees is like a man's hesitating "indefinitely to ask a certain woman to marry him because he was not perfectly sure that she would prove an angel after he brought her home" (WB 30).

36. This theme returns in chapter 7.

37. David A. Hollinger praises James's "celebrated openness of mind over the arrogant, dogmatic closures we associate with the nineteenth-century scientific intelligentsia. The contemporaries of Darwin ascribed to the sciences a God's-eye view, and to the world a set of hard features discoverable by men and women bold enough to replace fantasy and superstition with facts. These Huxleys and Tyndalls and Cliffords thought themselves a new priesthood, and, while telling everyone what to believe, functioned as the thought-police of their age" ("James, Clifford," 69; cf. Pratt, "Religious Philosophy," 230; T. V. Smith, *Philosophic Way of Life*, 97–98; J. I. Miller, *Democratic Temperament*, 113).

38. An earlier version of this "intellectualist" position was offered by Thomas Jefferson in 1787: "Ignorance is preferable to error; and he is less remote from the truth who believes nothing, th[a]n he who believes what is wrong" (*Notes on the State of Virginia*, in *Writings*, 156).

39. Walter Lippmann writes that James's view "rests on the simplest of insights: that atheism and theisms are both dogmas, for there is scientific evidence for neither; that to withhold judgment is really to make a judgment, and act as if God didn't exist; that until the evidence is complete men have a right to believe what they most need" ("William James," 22).

40. Others would no doubt see this faith ladder as descending into delusion.

41. Cf. P 125; MT 72/ERE 99.

4. PRAGMATISM

1. Commager, *American Mind*, 97, 102; cf. A. W. Moore, *Pragmatism and Its Critics*, 10–11; S. Ratner, "Pragmatism in America," 193.

2. I am translating here from Carus's comments at the 1908 Heidelberg World Congress of Philosophy: "Der Pragmatismus komme zwar aus Amerika, aber, Gott sei Dank, hat die Bewegung noch nicht das ganze Land in Besitz genommen. Der Pragmatismus ist eine Krankheit hervorgegangen aus der Sucht etwas Neues und ganz Originelles zu schaffen. Was aber wahr daran ist, ist nicht neu und was neu ist, ist falsch" (Comments on Schiller and Armstrong, 737).

3. Carus, *Truth on Trial*, 44–45.

4. Mumford, *Golden Day*, 98; Brodbeck, "Philosophy in America," 22. Paul Elmer More continues in this vein that "it needs no profound study to see the weak joints in a logic which undertakes to determine the inmost nature of things by what we regard as pragmatically useful to our own lives, and to prove that truth is actually created by

what we think it expedient to believe" ("New Stage of Pragmatism," 457; cf. Schinz, *Anti-Pragmatism*, xv–xvii).

5. On this point, see my essays: "One Hundred Years of *Pragmatism*" and "History of Pragmatism."

6. Franklin, *Information to Those Who Would Remove to America*, in *Writings*, 977.

7. Addison Webster Moore writes in 1910 that "the present pragmatic movement is precisely an attempt to bring this 'old way of thinking' in science and practical social life into philosophy, and to this extent, therefore, is a new way of thinking—in philosophy" (*Pragmatism and Its Critics*, 2).

8. Ibid., 1; Perry, *Present Philosophical Tendencies*, 197.

9. George Boas notes in 1929 that there is a "miscellaneous group of philosophers known as 'pragmatists.' To reduce the teachings of this group to unity is next to impossible. They enter pragmatism with such a variety of preconceptions and preoccupations that the community of agreement between all of them is very slight." Unfortunately, Boas goes on mistakenly to assert that "Pragmatism in the words of its greatest popularizer, William James . . . was a method of attacking philosophy and not a philosophy itself" (*Major Traditions*, 410; cf. Lovejoy, "Thirteen Pragmatisms"; Woodbridge, "Pragmatism and Education," 227).

10. Peirce, *Collected Papers*, 5.412. John Dewey continues: "The term 'pragmatic,' contrary to the opinion of those who regard pragmatism as an exclusively American conception, was suggested to him [Peirce] by the study of Kant. In the *Metaphysic of Morals* Kant established a distinction between *pragmatic* and *practical*. The latter term applies to moral laws which Kant regards as *a priori*, whereas the former term applies to the rules of art and technique which are based on experience and are applicable to experience. Peirce . . . was interested in the art and technique of real thinking, and especially interested, as far as pragmatic method is concerned, in the art of making concepts clear, or of construing adequate and effective definitions in accord with the spirit of scientific method" (*Later Works*, 2:3–4; cf. S. Ratner, "Pragmatism in America," 195; Murphey, "Kant's Children," 9).

11. Peirce, *Collected Papers*, 5.11.

12. Dewey, *Later Works*, 2:18. In what he characterized as a "throughly pragmatic" volume, *Logic: The Theory of Inquiry*, Dewey writes that "so much misunderstanding and relatively futile controversy have gathered about the word ['Pragmatism'] that it seemed advisable to avoid its use" (*Later Works*, 12:4). Thus, we have his replacement of "Pragmatism" with "Instrumentalism."

13. The series, collectively entitled, *Illustrations of the Logic of Science*, contains the following essays by Peirce: "The Fixation of Belief," "How to Make Our Ideas Clear," "The Doctrine of Chances," "The Probability of Induction," "The Order of Nature," and "Deduction, Induction and Hypothesis" (*Writings*, 3:241–38). See Fisch's discussion in *Peirce, Semeiotic, and Pragmatism*, 283–91.

14. James, "Remarks on Spencer's *Definition of Mind as Correspondence*" (*EP* 7–22),

"Quelques Considérations sur la méthode subjective" ["Some Considerations regarding the Subjective Method"] (*EP* 23–31/331–38); "Reflex Action and Theism" (*WB* 90–113), and "The Function of Cognition" (*MT* 13–32).

15. See, for example: *EP* 94, 102–6, 123–39, 144–48; *VRE* 349–53, 408–14; *MT* 37–60.

16. Writing to his brother Henry just before the publication of *Pragmatism*, William notes that it is "from the point of view of ordinary philosophy-professional manners, a very unconventional utterance.... I shouldn't be su[r]prised if 10 years hence it should be rated as 'epoch-making,' for of the definitive triumph of that general way of thinking I can entertain no doubt whatever—I believe it to be something quite like the protestant reformation" (C 3:339; cf. C 11:350, 353). F. C. S. Schiller maintains that *Pragmatism* was "probably the best book ever written for the purpose of arousing interest in philosophic questions" (review of *Pragmatism*, 599).

17. H. S. Thayer writes that "*Pragmatism* more than any other book early in the present century distilled and defined for countless American and European readers this new and (so it was felt) peculiarly American philosophy." He notes further that "in the controversies over it and the clarifications James felt obliged to offer, the other philosophic work had to be set aside." Thus, James paid a high price for the success of *Pragmatism*: he "did not live to complete his philosophic system or write his more technical books" ("Introduction" to *P*, xi, xx; cf. Bakewell, review of *Pragmatism*, 624–25; Conkin, *Puritans and Pragmatists*, 278, 323).

18. In a 1907 letter to A. O. Lovejoy, James continues: "The book was never meant for a treatise, but for a sketch,—to make air and room for an empirical philosophy that might not necessarily be irreligious, to breathe in. Finer and more accurate work was reserved for the future. This was only to *win a platform* for more accurate discussion, and the single-word title of *Pragmatism* was chosen for tactical purposes (since it was already in use) to group my different tendencies together, and rally those who could sympathize, under one banner" (C 11:444).

19. James Rowland Angell continues in this theme: "To the man in the street (the back alley of philosophy) the attractiveness of pragmatism comes at least in part from its genial disrespect for the abstractions of philosophic thought and its hail-fellow-well-met attitude toward the lowliest yellow dog of a fact.... Indeed, we are never long deprived of the merry sound of the belligerent shillalah ringing lustily about the shoulders of the unfortunate rationalist, whom Professor James belabors at every turn with rare gusto" (review of *Pragmatism*, 227–28).

20. James writes to Hugo Münsterberg that "as Schiller, Dewey and I mean pragmatism, it is *toto coelo* [diametrically] opposed to either the original or the revived Kantism. What similarity can there possibly be between human laws imposed a priori on all experience as 'legislative,' and human ways of thinking that grow up piecemeal among the details of experience because on the whole they work best? It is this rationalistic part of Kant that pragmatism is expressly meant to overthrow" (C 11:328).

Charles Montague Bakewell, however, remarks that "the pragmatist's indebtedness to Kant seems quite obvious, and ... it is hardly generous of Professor James to speak of Kant as an old fossil, and to tell us, as he does in his California address, that philosophy's path should lie around Kant and not through him" (review of *Pragmatism*, 630; cf. Angell, review of *Pragmatism*, 229 n.1; Fisch, *Peirce, Semeiotic, and Pragmatism*, 288; J. J. McDermott, "Introduction" to *EP*, xxvii).

21. For Henry Heath Bawden, "the practical is what it is only by contrast with the theoretical, and ... the current pragmatism is the reaction from a speculative philosophy out of touch with the affairs of men" (*Principles of Pragmatism*, 6). In opposition to this view, Charles Montague Bakewell maintains that "the *Anhänger* [supporters] of pragmatism ... who are unacquainted, or but imperfectly acquainted, with the history of philosophy" fail to see that Pragmatism "does not solve the difficult problems of philosophy; it simply ignores them" (review of *Pragmatism*, 627).

22. For more on the Metaphysical Club, see Peirce, *Collected Papers*, 5.12–13; Wiener, *Evolution and the Founders of Pragmatism*, 18–30; Mills, *Sociology and Pragmatism*, 84–120; Kuklick, *Rise*, 47–54; Menand, *Metaphysical Club*.

23. Peirce, *Writings*, 3:261/*Collected Papers*, 5.394.

24. Peirce, *Writings*, 3:266/*Collected Papers*, 5.403. See also Peirce's discussion of the meaning of "lithium": "If you look into a textbook of chemistry for a definition of *lithium*, you may be told that it is that element whose atomic weight is 7 very nearly. But if the author has a more logical mind he will tell you that if you search among minerals that are vitreous, translucent, grey or white, very hard, brittle, and insoluble, for one which imparts a crimson tinge to an unluminous flame, this mineral being triturated with lime or witherite rats-bane, and then fused, can be partly dissolved in muriatic acid; and if this solution be evaporated, and the residue be extracted with sulphuric acid, and duly purified, it can be converted by ordinary methods into a chloride, which being obtained in the solid state, fused, and electrolyzed with half a dozen powerful cells, will yield a globule of a pinkish silvery metal that will float on gasoline; and the material of *that* is a specimen of lithium. The peculiarity of this definition—or rather this precept that is more serviceable than a definition—is that it tells you what the word lithium denotes by prescribing what you are to *do* in order to gain a perceptual acquaintance with the object of the word" (*Collected Papers*, 2.330).

25. Ralph Barton Perry maintains that "the modern movement known as pragmatism is largely the result of James's misunderstanding of Peirce" (*Thought and Character*, 2:409). H. S. Thayer's evaluation is more measured: "whether James is justly accused of misunderstanding and misapplying Peirce's ideas is a fine point of interpretation. We can regard James's pragmatism as a secondhand article or, because of its disparities with the original, as largely his own invention.... Recent tradition ... has represented the Jamesian doctrines as debased currency. The tendency has sometimes been encouraged by an ill-disguised if understandable attempt to 'save' pragmatism. However, the weight of tradition, as Peirce was fond of remarking, is no worthy arbiter of philosophic ideas"

(*Meaning and Action*, 135; cf. "Introduction" to P, xxi–xxvi; White, *Pragmatism and the American Mind*, 31).

26. For John Dewey, writing in 1907, "it lies in the nature of pragmatism that it should be applied as widely as possible; and to things as diverse as controversies, beliefs, truths, ideas, and objects" (*Middle Works*, 4:101). He continues in 1925 that "Peirce was above all a logician; whereas James was an educator and humanist and wished to force the general public to realize that certain problems, certain philosophical debates have a real importance for mankind, because the beliefs which they bring into play lead to very different modes of conduct" (*Later Works*, 2:7–8; cf. Kennedy, "Pragmatism, Pragmaticism," 582; Boodin, *Truth and Reality*, 184).

27. As H. S. Thayer notes, "there is evidently no reason why the term '*truth*' is not a fit subject for pragmatic analysis of meaning" (*Meaning and Action*, 135; cf. Murphey, "Kant's Children," 17).

28. James A. Gould writes that "although James drew heavily from Locke and the other British empiricists, it must always be remembered that their empiricism basically differs from pragmatic empiricism. The former is concerned with phenomena that have happened; the latter looks to future phenomena. Pragmatism uses ideas as tools for the exploration of the world, while Locke considered them to be in a sense copies of the world. James is interested in our reactions to phenomena, rather than our reception of them. We only understand the meaning of an idea after we have acted on it. Thus the pragmatist is characterized by activity; the British empiricists by passivity" ("R. B. Perry on the Origin of American and European Pragmatism," 443).

29. Cf. *ECR* 198–99, 381–82; *SPP* 24; *ML* 381–82; Dewey, *Middle Works*, 6:94–95.

30. Earlier James had described the tender-minded and the tough-minded approaches as "the feminine-mystical mind" and "the scientific-academic mind" respectively (*WB* 224).

31. In 1890 James had written that "the aspiration to be 'scientific' . . . was invented but a generation or two ago" (*PP* 2:1236 n.11).

32. Elizabeth Flower and Murray G. Murphey note that Pragmatism was "a movement which sought to create an empiricism rigorous enough to qualify as a philosophy of science but broad enough to embrace ethics and aesthetics, and even metaphysics and religion as well." As such, Pragmatism "was and has remained a synthetic philosophy designed to stop the war between science and religion and restore a unified world view" (*History of Philosophy in America*, 1:xvii).

33. Henry Heath Bawden notes in 1910 that "in these days, when the different branches of philosophy have become professions, and their language as unintelligible to the layman as the technicalities of the special sciences, the need of simplification is obvious. Pragmatism is an attempt to meet this need" (*Principles of Pragmatism*, vii–viii).

34. Peirce's formulation is as follows: "Consider what effects, which might conceivably have practical bearings, we conceive the object of our conception to have. Then,

our conception of these effects is the whole of our conception of the object" (*Writings*, 3:266/*Collected Papers*, 5.401).

35. Peirce writes that he, "finding his bantling 'pragmatism' so promoted, feels that it is time to kiss his child good-by and relinquish it to its higher destiny; while to serve the precise purpose of expressing the original definition, he begs to announce the birth of the word 'pragmaticism,' which is ugly enough to be safe from kidnappers" (*Collected Papers*, 5.414; cf. 5.3; 6.481–82; C 10:511–12; Perry, *Thought and Character*, 2:432–33, 436–37; Pollock, "James," 197–98).

36. Papini himself goes further: "pragmatism is really *less a philosophy than a method of doing without philosophy*. On the one hand, by striving against problems devoid of sense, such as metaphysics, monism and the like, it diminishes the field of action of that which, historically speaking, is called philosophy; and, on the other hand, by inciting men to act more than to talk, to alter things rather than to contemplate them, to force things actually to exist in a definite way, instead of asserting that they do so exist, it enlarges the field of action at the expense of pure speculation" ("What Pragmatism Is Like," 354).

37. The term "cash-value" has led to numerous misinterpretations of Pragmatism. As John Dewey writes: "William James said in a happy metaphor, that they ['the conceptions of reasoning'] must be 'cashed in,' by producing specific consequences. This expression means that they must be able to lead to concrete facts. But for those who are not familiar with American idioms, James' formula was taken to mean that the consequences themselves of our rational conceptions must be narrowly limited by their pecuniary value" (*Later Works*, 2:13 n.8; cf. Barzun, *Energies of Art*, 351; Royce, "William James," 33–35; Schiller, *Must Philosophers Disagree?*, 95–96).

38. John Grier Hibben disagrees. For him, "the mind which has not formed the habit of regarding the 'first things, principles, categories, supposed necessities,' will hardly be capable of entertaining any last things as 'fruits, consequences, facts,' which will be deemed worthy of any special value or significance whatsoever. To know the beginnings, the nature, and the ground of any set of phenomena under investigation, as well as the implications which are necessitated by them, is essential to any clear understanding of their worth, or of the possibilities of their practical application" ("Test of Pragmatism," 379).

39. James suggests that "the only pragmatic application of the substance-idea" is transubstantiation, an application that, he continues, "will only be treated seriously by those who already believe in the 'real presence' on independent grounds" (P 47; cf. Peirce, *Collected Papers*, 5.401/*Writings*, 3:265; *Collected Papers*, 5.541).

40. Cf. VRE 119–20, 407. John E. Smith writes that "James saw religion as the awareness on the part of the individual of the present incompleteness and broken character of his life; this awareness leads to the question of a higher power which can complete life and overcome the destructive forces in it" (*Spirit of American Philosophy*, 78).

41. The topic of Theism and hope will return in chapter 7.

42. In this regard, Frank Thilly notes that Pragmatism is technically "anti-intellectualistic in the sense that, in order to be true, a philosophy must satisfy other than logical demands" (*History of Philosophy*, 567).

43. With regard to this unfortunate term that appears frequently in James's writings, Benjamin Franklin presciently wrote in 1783: "Savages we call them, because their manners differ from ours, which we think the Perfection of Civility; they think the same of theirs" ("Remarks Concerning the Savages of North-America," in *Writings*, 969). We will encounter more instances of James's use of the term below.

44. We will encounter further examples of James's casual racism as we continue.

45. Cf. P 122–23; PP 1:274; SPP 32–33; C 11:411.

46. William Mackintire Salter notes that "it is well known that scientific men sometimes regard their theories as working hypotheses rather than as absolute truth. The atomic theory, the idea of an elastic ether, even the nebular hypothesis and Darwinism itself, are instances.... Theories are taken chiefly as more or less convenient instruments. They summarize the facts we know, putting them into handy, portable shape (like short-hand for words), and they lead us on to new facts. Scientific men without illusion do not so much believe them or disbelieve them as use them.... Anything that works, that helps, they hold to, until they find something that works better, helps more. What they hold to they may call true, for this from old usage is an honorific term—but they mean true to them; and what is true to-day may not be true to-morrow" ("Pragmatism," 657; cf. Thayer, "Introduction" to *MT*, xxvi).

47. Peirce, *Writings*, 3:273, 253–54/*Collected Papers*, 5.407, 5.384.

48. F. J. E. Woodbridge notes that "Pragmatism became a controversy about the nature of truth. Instead of encouraging analyses of the meaning of terms and ideas in the contexts wherein they occur, it encouraged a debate about the foundations of belief and the criteria of truth and falsity. How can we determine when our ideas are true, became a more important question than how can we determine what they mean.... The controversy diverted attention from what was fruitful to what was fruitless.... Pragmatism held out the promise of helping to clarify our ideas and that promise has been too much obscured by the controversy which made of pragmatism a debate about truth" ("Promise," 541–42, 552; cf. "Pragmatism and Education," 233–34; Jacks, "William James," 31).

49. H. S. Thayer writes that James's theory of truth was "never completely formulated, nor ... ever fully stated to anyone's satisfaction.... The 'theory' then is a sketch; the ideas that form it underwent different stages of development and organization with certain changes in James's outlook and interests. At different periods, different ideas or aspects of the theory received special expression or emphasis.... Taking his statements as a whole, there are difficulties in reconciling some with others" ("Introduction" to *P*, xxix).

50. In *The Principles*, James writes that "it is a familiar truth that some propositions are *necessary*. We *must* attach the predicate 'equal' to the subject 'opposite sides of a

parallelogram' if we think those terms together at all, whereas we need not in any such way attach the predicate 'rainy,' for example, to the subject 'tomorrow.' The dubious sort of coupling of terms is universally admitted to be due to 'experience'; the certain sort is ascribed to the 'organic structure' of the mind" (*PP* 2:1215). He informally refers to the results of experience as coming through the "front door" of our senses (*PP* 2:1225). The necessary truths, on the contrary, enter through the "back-door" (*PP* 2:1228), or use the "back stairs" (*PP* 2:1225), or are even "house-born" (*PP* 2:1237) or "brain-born" (*PP* 2:1235). James's analysis suggests that the various claims of necessity found in "classification, logic, and mathematics all result . . . from the mere play of the mind comparing its conceptions, no matter whence the latter may have come" (*PP* 2:1253). As such, all of these claims result from our accidentally evolved, but extremely useful, ability to make comparisons. See White, *Science and Sentiment*, 172–80; Santayana, review of *Principles*, 553–54; Brett, "Psychology of William James," 84–88; Myers, *William James*, 281–85.

51. Harry Norman Gardner writes to James, in what he thinks is disagreement, that "the supposal that the 100th decimal of π is a 5, is, even now, I hold, either true or false, and may be true. Its truth or falsity is determined, not by the verification-process by which we might arrive at a justified *acknowledgment* of its truth or falsity, but by the constitution of the ideal object we call a circle and the objective nature of our number-system" (*C* 11:513).

52. James Rowland Angell writes that "unquestionably, we get our truth from rough actual experience and equally, without question, we test it by its adequacy to experiential demands. But it is not so clear to the ordinary mind that the nature of truth is exhausted by any such account of it. There is a core of reality upon which our predications of truth and falsity must inevitably be grafted, and to which they are in part relative. In other writings, Professor James has more fully recognized this fact. There is, to use his own word, a 'grain' in things against which we cannot go if we would. To this stubborn grain in things his present exposition does scant justice. The world out of which we construct our truth is not wholly fluid" (review of *Pragmatism*, 231; cf. Bakewell, "On the Meaning of Truth," 582, 587).

53. Peirce, *Collected Papers*, 5.494, 5.60, 5.565; 2.173.

54. Ellen Kappy Suckiel writes that "the members of the community are progressively better able to account for and anticipate a greater number and variety of experiences. As such, they come to hold beliefs which are progressively more objective in that they increasingly transcend limited or partial points of view." Thus, James "postulates belief systems of ever-increasing degrees of truth, culminating in an ideal end-point that will not be superseded by a better set of beliefs (for there will be no confuting experiences). This James calls 'absolute truth'" (*Pragmatic Philosophy*, 109).

55. Both Clifford and Peirce accept action based upon probabilities in some cases. The former writes, for example, that "there are many cases in which it is our duty to act upon probabilities, although the evidence is not such as to justify present belief;

because it is precisely by such action, and by observation of its fruits, that evidence is got which may justify future belief." The latter notes that in "matters of real practical concern" some decision must be made in the present, not in "fifty generations" (Clifford, "Ethics of Belief," 189; Peirce, *Collected Papers*, 5.60; cf. Hollinger, "James, Clifford, and the Scientific Conscience," 71; Wernham, *James's Will-to-Believe Doctrine*, 72–74).

56. Josiah Royce's emphasis, like Peirce's, is elsewhere: "In seeking truth we do not seek the mere crumbling successes of the passing instants of human life. We seek a city out of sight. What we get of success within our passing experience is rationally as precious to us as it is, just because we believe that attainment to be a fragment of an essentially superhuman success, which is won in the form of a higher experience than ours,—a conspectus wherein our human experiences are unified.... We need unity of life. In recognizing that need my own pragmatism consists. Now, we never find unity present to our human experience in more than a fragmentary shape. We get hints of higher unity" (*Philosophy of Loyalty*, 340–41).

57. Dewey calls this process, which he develops in more prescriptive detail, "the pattern of inquiry" (*Logic*, in *Later Works*, 12:105–22; cf. my volume, *Understanding John Dewey*, 45–53).

58. David A. Hollinger points to Pragmatism's "sense of the role of scientific method in a universe of change and uncertainty. The pragmatists were more concerned than were many of their contemporaries with the integrity and durability of *inquiry*, on the one hand, and the tentativeness, fallibility, and incompleteness of knowledge on the other" ("Problem of Pragmatism," 93; cf. West, *American Evasion*, 67).

59. For Bruce Wilshire, "James believes that the correspondence-theory of truth, seemingly obvious, prompts us to ignore the evolving contexts in the world, mood-and-action-imbued, in which our lives have meaning—our probing, our bodily responses to our probing, our needs, suspecting, anticipatings, valuings, believings. Obvious and prosaic 'objective truth'—truth about 'what's out there'—bought at a price of an anorexic constriction of existence and meaning is bought too dear. Addictive, no quantity of it can ever satisfy. Hence James believes that truth in the fullest sense does not preexist its discovery" ("Breathtaking Intimacy," 116; cf. Thayer, "Introduction" to P, xxxviii; Bixler, "William James as Religious Thinker," 126; T. V. Smith, *Philosophic Way*, 88–89; Bergson, *Creative Mind*, 255–56).

60. In this spirit, A. E. Taylor writes as follows: "While all practice consists in *making* something, all truths are in the end *found* or *accepted*, not *made*. We may or may not formulate a certain proposition, but once formulated its truth means a right or claim to admission which is entirely independent of individual volition. Either it has the right or it has not, and individual choice can neither confer the right where it does not exist nor destroy it where it does. All that lies in our power is to grant or withhold our actual individual recognition, and thus the *right* to recognition inevitably remains unaffected by our action" ("Truth and Practice," 274; cf. Hibben, "Test of Pragmatism," 380–82).

61. Jacques Barzun develops James's point: "Truth is eternal only in the sense that

the shorthand, the symbols, the abstract record or prediction, may be filled out again with but small variations by a live experience. But the variation is there; the truth is the truth for a different being at a different time; he may modify it, reject it for another, turn it inside out. This is the history of art and philosophy and civilization, not to mention the moral evolution of every man this side the grave" (*Energies of Art*, 348–49).

62. Cf. *P* 102; *ERE* 38–42; *MT* 48–49, 51, 89. For Henry Heath Bawden, "the test of truth is whether or not it furnishes an adequate basis for action. Truth means control. That knowledge is true which gives order and direction to further experience. The test of truth is not in the judging itself as a thinking process, but in the act or in some other mode of experience which transcends thought" (*Principles of Pragmatism*, 211; cf. A. W. Moore, *Pragmatism and Its Critics*, 21).

63. F. C. S. Schiller notes in 1907 that James "has advanced beyond any other pragmatic writer up to date in illustrating and explaining how Pragmatism conceives the condition of *potential truth*, truth, that is, which is not in use, but merely stored up in the mind as a reserve wherewith to meet the situations which emerge in our life" (review of *Pragmatism*, 600). Henry Heath Bawden continues that "the significance of libraries, museums, laboratories, and all the machinery of civilization and culture" is that "they perpetuate for us the intellectual devices which have been worked out by our predecessors" (*Principles of Pragmatism*, 154).

64. Still, we encounter comments like the following by Ralph Barton Perry: "pragmatists have taught us to believe that an idea is true in so far as it works or satisfies *in any respect whatsoever*.... It would be correct to infer from such a supposition that an idea which was shown to be contrary to sensible fact, or contradictory to accredited truths, might yet be proved true by affording a surplus of sentimental or utilitarian value" (*Present Philosophical Tendencies*, 212; cf. review of *Pragmatism*, 371; Blanshard, "Ethics of Belief," 87; Knight, "Introduction" to *William James*, 53).

65. For John Henry Muirhead, "the belief that 'works' is true but it must work all around. It must satisfy our needs but it must satisfy them all, the needs of the reason not less than those of the will and emotions (if indeed they are different) our demand for harmony in our intellectual as well as for harmony in our moral world" ("Prof. William James's Philosophy of Religion," 245).

66. Michael Levin writes: "If the pragmatic maxim ... is taken in isolation, it appears to sanction believing whatever makes one happy. This widespread misunderstanding, reinforced by James's talk of 'the will to believe,' would make pragmatism a philosophy not for businessmen but for the village idiot" ("Why Not Pragmatism?," 43). Jacques Barzun expands upon this point, noting that "when James says that the pragmatic test is the discovery of what will succeed, what will produce efficient results, what will work, we shall not arbitrarily assume that he is suddenly and perversely taking as a model for his entire philosophy P. T. Barnum's success, or holding up as an example the impressive way a confidence man's idea 'works.' We shall know him to be thinking soberly and naturally of the exacting discipline by which a composer achieves

success in combining expressively all his voices, in which a mathematician revolves possible proofs of an intuited theorem until he finds one that will 'work'" (*Energies of Art*, 346–47).

67. Gardner, *Night Is Large*, 472, 469. He notes further: "Pragmatists believed, of course, that great benefits would flow from redefining truth as the meeting of tests for truth, but the actual results were decades of bewildering debate in which they wasted incredible amounts of time trying to explain to their opponents that they did not mean what their words, taken in the usual way, implied. They were guilty of violating what Peirce once called the 'ethics of terminology' [see *Collected Papers*, 2.219–26], the moral obligation to respect the traditional meanings of entrenched philosophical terms" (*Night Is Large*, 475–76).

68. In a similar fashion, John Stuart Mill writes in 1859 that "there is always need of persons ... to discover new truths, and point out when what were once truths are true no longer" (*On Liberty*, 999).

69. On this point, A. E. Taylor writes prescriptively: "Truth does not mean what is actually believed, but what ought to be believed, not what individuals accept, but what has a right to acceptance by all intelligences universally" ("Truth and Practice," 287; cf. J. Watson, *Philosophical Basis of Religion*, 159).

70. D. L. Murray notes that "Pragmatism appeals to the history of scientific truth, which has shown a continuous correction of 'truths,' which were re-valued as 'errors,' as better statements for them became available" (*Pragmatism*, 44).

71. Frederick Copleston writes that "Julius Caesar's existence at a certain period of history cannot properly be called true; but the statement that he existed is true, while the statement that he did not exist is false. At the same time the statement that Julius Caesar existed is not true in virtue of the meanings of the symbols or words employed in the statement. Hence we can say that it is true in virtue of a relation of correspondence with reality or fact" ("Pragmatism of James and Schiller," 92–93; cf. McTaggart, review of *Pragmatism*, 105; B. Russell, "William James's Conception of Truth," 117).

72. F. C. S. Schiller nicely paraphrases James's view as follows: "The most that can be claimed for a theory is that it is the *best and truest up to date*, and science never renounces the hope of finding one better and truer still. Hence scientific truth is essentially improvable and progressive. It progresses by the continuous correction of 'errors' (= truths of *inferior* value), and the continual augmentation of the value of the truths accepted. Thus no truth is eternal; every truth has its day ... scientific truths *are* improvable; the more progressive a science is, the more quickly do its 'truths' pass into 'errors,' and yield their title to superior successors. This interpretation of scientific procedure accounts, moreover, for the hopefulness of science; whereas, if we construe it as an (unavailing) pursuit of absolute truth, it is doomed to perpetual failure and disillusionment, as each successive truth is hailed as absolute, and then found to be erroneous. The history of science then becomes merely a passage from one error to another, and an argument for scepticism" ("Why Humanism?" 400–401).

73. For more examples of "truer," see *P* 93, 120, 269; *WB* 115; *SPP* 42. For "truest," see *MT* 40; *EP* 142; *C* 11:407. In *The Correspondence*, we find James using other idiosyncratic comparatives and superlatives like: "manyer" (*C* 6:121), "worser" (*C* 7:453), "gloriouser" (*C* 9:384), "righter" (*C* 9:528), "weller" (*C* 10:88), and "perfectest" (*C* 7:168).

74. H. S. Thayer writes that for James it was possible that certain beliefs could be "true (pragmatically) for some persons, and false for others." This does not mean that James was offering a subjective view. Rather, Thayer continues, for James "truth and meaning are objectively determined by certain relations. The relations in any case obtain among conditions that cause some human need and the emergence of purpose, and those that form the processes of belief and action by which resolutions and satisfactions are achieved. These conditions may vary, and profusely so, being relative to some specific situation of occurring need and point of view" ("Introduction" to *P*, xxxv–xxxvi; cf. Creighton, "Nature and Criterion of Truth," 592).

75. William Ernest Hocking is more comfortable with what he calls "negative pragmatism," the principle of which is, "'*That which does not work is not true.*' The corresponding positive principle, 'Whatever works is true,' I regard as neither valid nor useful. But invaluable as a guide do I find this negative test: if a theory has no consequences, or bad ones; if it makes no difference to men, or else undesirable differences; if it lowers the capacity of men to meet the stress of existence, or diminishes the worth to them of what existence they have; such a theory is somehow false, and we have no peace until it is remedied.... It is the function of the [negative] pragmatic test (as of pain and discomfort generally) to point out something wrong; the work of discovering what is right must be done by other means" (*Meaning of God*, xiii, xv).

76. John Elof Boodin notes that "the most important investigations in pure science, such as the beautiful researches in light and electricity, were carried on without reference to their utilitarian consequences by people inspired by a divine madness to discover the hidden harmony of things ... whether researches are useful or not, their usefulness does not make them true" (*Truth and Reality*, 191; cf. A. E. Taylor, "Truth and Practice," 284; Dewey, *Middle Works*, 4:108–9).

77. For example, we might consider here James's 1907 Cambridge phone number: 1028–2 (*C* 11:478).

78. As he writes, "no theory is absolutely a transcript of reality," and "most, perhaps all, of our laws are only approximations" (*P* 33). A. E. Taylor points to "the existence of propositions which are practically important and yet not strictly true. Thus π = 3.1416 is a statement which is frequently of practical significance, though we know it, strictly speaking, to be untrue.... Most, if not all, physical laws of nature, in the forms in which they are available for practical application to the control of events, involve the use of such rough approximations to truth" ("Truth and Practice," 285–86; cf. Caldwell, *Pragmatism and Idealism*, 129; Thayer, "Introduction" to *MT*, xxxix). Margaret Knight reminds us of other cases where falsity is helpful: "it is sometimes disadvantageous for

a patient to hold a true belief about the nature of his illness" ("Introduction" to *William James*, 54; cf. Lee, "Two Pragmatisms," 452).

79. Addison Webster Moore notes "that false ideas seem to be as industrious as true ones, that error gets up as early and stays up as late as truth, and often appears to work overtime" (*Pragmatism and Its Critics*, 87).

80. Royce, *Philosophy of Loyalty*, 331–32; cf. Bakewell, review of *Pragmatism*, 632; Pratt, "Truth and Ideas," 130.

81. B. Russell, *History of Western Philosophy*, 818; "Pragmatism," 107, 109.

82. B. Russell, *History of Western Philosophy*, 811; "Pragmatism," 96–97; "William James's Conception of Truth," 119–20; cf. 124–25; J. E. Russell, "Some Difficulties," 406–7.

83. Cf. *MT* 8, 299–310; *WB* 32; *P* 111. Frederick Copleston writes that "whether one agrees with James's thesis or not, one should not represent him as claiming that we are entitled to believe any proposition which affords us consolation or satisfaction, even if the balance of evidence goes to show that the proposition is false. It is true, for instance, that according to James we are entitled, other things being equal, to embrace a view of reality which satisfies the moral side of our nature better than another view. And it is by no means everyone who would agree with him. But this is no reason for disregarding the qualification 'other things being equal,' where 'other things' include, of course, already known truths and the conclusions deducible from them" ("Pragmatism of James and Schiller," 95).

84. Russell might be excused here for reading the passages from James that we have just seen as asserting that "it is useful because it is true" and "it is true because it is useful" mean exactly the same thing.

85. Ralph Barton Perry defends the pragmatic account here: "With pragmatists ... knowledge means *knowing*: a complex event, involving an individual knower, a something to be known, certain means of knowing it, and then, finally, the cognitive achievement or failure. Critics of pragmatism have attempted to dismiss this method of studying knowledge by calling it 'psychological,' rather than 'logical.' It is certainly not exclusively logical, because it takes into account the circumstances and agencies of knowledge, and not merely its grounds. But, on the other hand, it is not psychological in any limited or disparaging sense, because it seeks to distinguish the cases of *true* knowledge from the cases of *false* knowledge. In short, it is both psychological and logical; and for the reason that both psychological and logical factors enter into that particular complex which we call knowing" (*Present Philosophical Tendencies*, 199–200).

86. Thayer, "Introduction" to *MT*, xl; cf. J. E. Russell, review of *Meaning of Truth*, 24; Bakewell, "On the Meaning of Truth," 581.

87. A. J. Ayer, for example, writes: "For a proposition to be true it is not necessary that any one should believe, or even consider, it: there are countless facts that never will be known. No one knows, for example, how many fish there are in the North Sea

at this moment, or how many human beings have been born and died in the last four thousand years, but certainly there is in fact a definite number in each case" (*Metaphysics and Common Sense*, 92; cf. *Origins of Pragmatism*, 27). G. E. Moore continues in this vein: "I may have written a letter, and may believe that I used certain words in it. But my correspondent may believe that I did not. Can we always verify either of these ideas? . . . Suppose the letter has been destroyed; suppose there is no copy of it, nor any trustworthy record of what was said in it; suppose there is no other witness as to what was said in it, beside myself and my correspondent? . . . It seems to me quite plain that *very often indeed* we have two ideas, one or other of which is certainly true; and yet that, in all probability, it is no longer possible and never will be possible for any man to verify either. . . . We very often have true ideas which we cannot verify; true ideas, which, in all probability, no man ever will be able to verify" ("William James' 'Pragmatism,'" 101, 103; cf. 111, 122; Gardner, *Night Is Large*, 467, 470; A. E. Taylor, "Truth and Practice," 276–78).

88. Charles Sanders Peirce writes that "fallibilism is the doctrine that our knowledge is never absolute but always swims, as it were, in a continuum of uncertainty and of indeterminacy" (*Collected Papers*, 1.171).

89. Frederick Copleston notes that James admits "that there are truths which can or could be verified, but which have not yet been verified. Indeed, he is prepared to state that unverified truths 'form the overwhelmingly large number of the truths we live by,' and that truth lives 'for the most part on a credit system' [*P* 99–100]. If, however, truths are *made* true by verification or validation, it follows that unverified truths are potentially true, truths *in posse*. And this enables James to deal a blow at the philosophical rationalists or intellectualists who exalt static, timeless truths which are true prior to any verification. 'Intellectualist truth is [then] only pragmatist truth *in posse*' [*MT* 111]. And the total fabric of truth would collapse if it did not rest on some actually verified truths, that is, on some actual truths, just as a financial system would collapse if it possessed no solid basis in cash" ("Pragmatism of James and Schiller," 93–94).

90. Robert C. Pollock attributes much of James's problem here to "his fondness for the popular idiom and the broad stroke, and . . . his desire to communicate life and meaning to every type of audience" ("James," 195).

91. Josiah Royce offers a similar descriptive account: "we regard as true those ideas which we personally find it convenient, successful, expedient to treat as verifiable, even though we never verify them. The warrant of these unverifiable truths is, however, once more, the empirical usefulness of living as if they were verifiable. . . . The indirectly verifiable ideas, that is, the ideas which somebody else verifies, or even those which nobody yet verifies, but which agree sufficiently with verified ideas, we accept because it is advantageous to accept them" (*Philosophy of Loyalty*, 321–22).

92. See Peirce, "Fixation of Belief" (*Collected Papers*, 5.358–87/*Writings*, 3:242–57).

93. For F. C. S. Schiller, "it was an essential feature of 'pragmatism' to be recalcitrant to the scientific fiction which depersonalizes truth. If every 'truth' originates with an in-

dividual thinker facing an actual problem and choosing the best solution that presents itself to his mind, and framing the best judgment for containing it that he can conceive, and succeeding in winning the assent of others to the goodness of his judgment, it surely follows that its depersonalization is a fiction" (*Must Philosophers Disagree?*, 104).

94. Joseph Leon Blau notes that "whereas, in Peirce, the social dimension of thought led to a restriction of truth only to those ideas which would be agreed upon by an infinite community of laboratory scientists, James' 'large, loose way' of interpreting agreement (as agreeableness), made for an almost unlimited possibility of attributing truth-value to an idea. As long as an idea has agreeable consequences in the particular experience of some individual, somewhere, the idea has truth-value" (*Men and Movements*, 256).

95. See Dewey, *Logic*, in *Later Works*, 12:15–18; cf. Thayer, *Meaning and Action*, 193–94; Rorty, *Philosophy and Social Hope*, 32.

5. RADICAL EMPIRICISM AND PLURALISM

1. The eight articles, all reprinted in *ERE*, are "Does 'Consciousness' Exist?," "A World of Pure Experience," "The Thing and Its Relations," "How Two Minds Can Know One Thing," "The Place of Affectional Facts in a World of Pure Experience," "The Experience of Activity," "The Essence of Humanism," and "La Notion de Conscience" (in French). As James wrote at the time to F. J. E. Woodbridge, the editor of the *Journal of Philosophy*, where six of the articles appeared, "I appear to be growing into a graphomaniac. Truth boils over from my organism as muddy water from a yellowstone geyser" (*C* 10:542). John J. McDermott continues that "these essays formulate the long-simmering speculations of almost thirty years" ("Introduction" to *ERE*, xii; cf. xxvi–xxvii).

2. Ignas K. Skrupskelis notes that "James never worked out his version of radical empiricism systematically, and it still remains to be understood whether the failure is simply a failure of James's personality or is due to some fundamental flaw in his philosophical views. Whatever the reasons, James's radical empiricism never had an opportunity to prove its fruitfulness in philosophy. One can only speculate what American philosophy would have been like had James completed 'The Many and the One'" ("Introduction" to *MEN*, xx; cf. xxvi, xxx–xl; *MEN*, 330–31; Hare, "Introduction" to *SPP*, xxvii; Lowe, "James's Pluralistic Metaphysics," 158).

3. As we saw in chapter 4, James thought that he had had his say in *Pragmatism*, and he hoped to return to more "metaphysical" writings. He retired from Harvard at the end of the fall semester 1906–7, and, knowing that his heart was failing, he wanted to dedicate his remaining time to serious "scientific" work. Instead, he continued to be distracted by his felt need to revisit pragmatic themes. Much of this work eventually appeared in *The Meaning of Truth*.

4. It seems that even the relationship of Pragmatism to radical empiricism was unclear (or evolving) in James's mind. At times, he suggests that the two are the same:

"a certain systematic way of handling questions ... is ... known sometimes as the pragmatic method.... I have myself have given the name of 'radical empiricism' to that version of the tendency in question which I prefer" (*ERE* 79–80). At other times, however, he presents the two as independent, writing that "there is no logical connexion ... One may entirely reject it [radical empiricism] and still be a pragmatist" (*P* 6; cf. Copleston, "Pragmatism of James and Schiller," 97–99).

5. John J. McDermott writes that we can isolate "two persistent elements" in radical empiricism: "first, his claim that matter and mind are but functional distinctions; and second, his metaphysical version of the position previously taken in the *Principles*, in which he held we have feelings of the relations which exist between objects of our experience" ("Introduction" to *WWJ*, xxxvii; cf. Skrupskelis, "Introduction" to *MEN*, xxxii–xxxiii).

6. Cf. *PP* 1:268–69; *PBC* 176–77; *ECR* 462.

7. James writes elsewhere that "language in general, following its true logical instinct, distinguishes between these two applications of the notion of knowledge, the one being γνῶναι, *noscere*, *kennen*, *connaître*, the other being εἰδέναι, *scire*, *wissen*, *savoir*" (*MT* 18). This distinction appears in many places in his work (see, for example, *PP* 1:216–17, 249–50, 434, 553, 2:652; *PBC* 19; *WB* 72–73; *MT* 27–31; cf. Dewey, *How We Think*, in *Middle Works*, 6:273; *Later Works*, 8:227; E. C. Moore, *William James*, 116). James's point, of course, is not so much about the nature of these languages as it is about how we know the world.

8. Because of his focus on perception, James recommends laboratory and shop work for children. Such activities "engender a habit of observation, a knowledge of the difference between accuracy and vagueness, and an insight into nature's complexity and into the inadequacy of all abstract verbal accounts of real phenomena, which, once wrought into the mind, remain there as lifelong possession" (*TT* 31).

9. Arthur Oncken Lovejoy notes that James "came to each concrete bit of existence with an unspoiled power of *seeing* the thing as it was, in its unique differentness from other things. Man's ability to classify the objects of his experience is assuredly a convenient faculty; but it also makes for the blunting of his perceptions, since for most of us to recognize an object as belonging to a familiar class is forthwith to become more or less inattentive to all the characteristics of the object beyond those few flat, hackneyed, generalized ones which enable us to identify the class.... James's genius lay chiefly in ... an extraordinary immunity to the deadening influence of those intellectual processes of classification and generalization in which, in one form or another, scientific and philosophical reasoning largely consist. He kept an unweakened sense for the particularity of the particular—a sense which the occupations of the philosophical system-builder ordinarily tend to atrophy. Thus he was always prepared to see in each individual person, each separate fact, each immediately present aspect of experience, even in each distinct logical category, something unique, unshared, irreducible, ineffably individuated" ("William James as Philosopher," 92–93).

10. John J. McDermott writes that "in an effort to condemn as potentially dangerous a conceptual order not rooted in our actual experiencing, James overstresses the importance of the perceptual. Working from an acceptance of the still regnant dualism between thought and thing, he renders the conceptual as but a pale imitation" ("Introduction" to *ERE*, xxi–xxii; cf. J. E. Smith, "Introduction" to *VRE*, xxviii).

11. James puzzles at one point over "why we must translate experience from a more concrete or pure into a more intellectualized form." He suggests that "the rationalistic answer is that the theoretic life is absolute and its interests imperative; that to understand is simply the duty of man; and that who questions this need not be argued with, for by the fact of arguing he gives away his case." James, of course, favors "the naturalist answer . . . that the environment kills as well as sustains us, and that the tendency of raw experience to extinguish the experient himself is lessened just in the degree in which the elements in it that have a practical bearing upon life are analyzed out of the continuum and verbally fixed and coupled together, so that we may know what is in the wind for us and get ready to react in time" (*ERE* 47).

12. Ralph Barton Perry writes that it is "James's essential and characteristic contention that while both kinds of knowledge are indispensable, knowledge of acquaintance is completer and more conclusive than knowledge about, the latter being a substitute or adjunct which is required in order to overcome the limited range of the former. Knowledge is consummated when it coincides with reality, and that consummation occurs only in experience. . . . The tree of experience is the tree thus apprehended in its native terms—freshly, originally, intimately, personally, directly, contemporaneously, or presentatively; as distinguished from the tree as known absently, remotely, indirectly, or representatively" (*In the Spirit*, 45–46).

13. Wendell T. Bush wonders why an empiricist should "ever ask or seek to answer the question 'How can two minds know one thing?' This question arises in the context of epistemological subjectivism; it has a dialectical, not a natural foundation. You have to introduce one to the point of view of post-Kantian epistemology before he can even understand the question. An empiricist might just as properly ask, How can the souls of the unbaptized enter the Kingdom of Heaven? Taking each question in the content of its own presuppositions, the answer comes instantly; they can not. The question, 'Does consciousness exist?' is an empirical question, but if, empirically speaking, different minds are continually knowing the same things, it is hardly an empirical inquiry to ask whether the thing can possibly be done" ("Empiricism of James," 535).

14. In a similar fashion, John Dewey writes: "Philosophy, like all forms of reflective analysis, takes us away, for the time being, from the things had in primary experience as they directly act and are acted upon, used and enjoyed. Now the standing temptation of philosophy, as its course abundantly demonstrates, is to regard the results of reflection as having, in and of themselves, a reality superior to that of the material of any other mode of experience" (*Experience and Nature*, in *Later Works*, 1:26).

15. Joseph Leon Blau presents this view as follows: "The plain man, whose thought

has not been touched by philosophic considerations, is a realist. The world is there, outside himself. It contains physical things in a definite order of both space and time. He sees, hears, or otherwise perceives these physical things; he approaches them or retreats from them, manipulates them, uses them in whatever fashion he can. By and large, except for an occasional moment of wonder about the relation to things of men who lack one or more of the senses, he is convinced that the way in which he experiences things is typical, and that it is the normal human experience. He believes that the physical things were there before he perceived them and that they remain there afterwards. Their existence does not depend on him, nor have their properties any unique relation to his mind. When he calls something to the attention of another human being, that other perceives and handles the same thing. Things are both independent of men and common to men. Physical objects are considered as permanent and unchanging. Apparent variations in the object are explained as changes in the relation of the perceiver to the object, not changes in the object itself. Nor is there on this view anything special about the perceiver. He is a concrete individual, a particular kind of thing, as real as the things he perceives. Part of his nature as the kind of thing he is, is that he can perceive and be aware of other things as well as of himself. Knowledge is not a problem but a fact" (*Men and Movements*, 293–94).

16. See Holt, et al., *New Realism*; and Drake, et al., *Essays in Critical Realism*. See also my volume, *Thoughtful Profession*, 112–16.

17. James seems uninterested in the ontological status of the world before the development of consciousness, perhaps because the overlaying of consciousness on the natural word would tilt any discussion back toward dualism.

18. Frank Thilly presents James's view as follows: "we must take experience as it exists before it has been manipulated by conceptual thinking,—experience in its purity and primitive innocence,—if we would reach reality. We must go behind the conceptual function altogether and look to the more primitive flux of the sensational life for reality's true shape.... Reality is *pure* experience independent of human thinking; it is something very hard to find; it is what is just entering into experience and yet to be named, or else it is some imagined aboriginal presence in experience, before any belief about the presence has arisen, before any human conception has been applied. It is what is absolutely dumb and evanescent, the merely ideal limit of our minds. We may glimpse it, but we never grasp it; what we grasp is always some substitute for it which previous human thinking has peptonized and cooked for our consumption" (*History of Philosophy*, 568; cf. Copleston, "Pragmatism of James and Schiller," 89).

19. Under the headings of "*appreciations*" (*ERE* 18) and "affectional facts" (*ERE* 69), James describes the following situation: "Experiences of painful objects ... are usually also painful experiences; perceptions of loveliness, of ugliness, tend to pass muster as lovely or as ugly perceptions; intuitions of the morally lofty are lofty intuitions" (*ERE* 18). He notes that these facts were more ambiguous than most facts but, at the same time, they can function as good indicators of the fundamental ambiguity of all facts.

His point is that "subjectivity and objectivity are affairs not of what an experience is aboriginally made of, but of its classification," and that these classifications are the results of "our temporary purposes" (*ERE* 71). Further, he notes that the human animal has been forced to classify many things as "outer" to survive in the world, but no such need has arisen with the "affectional" facts that have been able to "lag" behind. "In practical life no urgent need has yet arisen for deciding whether to treat them as rigorously mental or as rigorously physical facts," he writes. "So they remain equivocal; and, as the world goes, their equivocality is one of their great conveniences" (*ERE* 73).

20. For George Herbert Mead, James is discussing "a cross-section of two histories. And the cross-section is identical. The room belongs to the history of the house. It has been there since the house was built. It is in that particular history. When the person comes into the room, that particular room with its furnishings becomes a fact of his history. He had been elsewhere yesterday. He comes into that particular room, and that room is now part of his experience; he goes out, and it is related to his former experiences. He had been in other houses, seen other furniture. He compares pictures. Each is related, you see, to his history. On the other hand, this room also belongs to the history of the house, of the architect, of the carpenter" (*Movements of Thought*, 394).

21. Edward Carter Moore presents these two types of relations as follows: "the doctrine of internal relations" maintains that "everything is related by its nature to everything else to form a unity such that any change in one part would mean a change in the other parts.... The opposite of this view was the doctrine of external relations. According to this view, some things may be related in such ways that they are—so to speak—not related, i.e., a change in one of them does not affect the others.... The monistic position is that everything is related to everything else by internal relations. Thus all in one—we have a genuine *universe*. Where we find only external relations we have not looked closely enough. Further examination will reveal internal relations" (*American Pragmatism*, 130–31).

22. The lectures were repeated at Harvard in November 1908. See *PU* 223–24; *C* 3:371; *C* 12:116–17.

23. As James wrote to F. C. S. Schiller in early 1908, "I accepted because I was ashamed to refuse a professional challenge of that importance, but I would it hadn't come to me. I actually *hate* lecturing; and this job condemns me to publish another book written in picturesque and popular style (when I was settling down to something whose manner would be more streng 'wissenschaftlich' [strongly 'scientific'], i.e. concise, dry, and impersonal). My free and easy style in 'Pragmatism' has made me so many enemies in academic & pedantic circles that I hate to go on increasing their number, and want to become tighter instead of looser. These new lectures will have to be even looser; for lectures *must* be prepared for audiences; and once prepared, I have neither the strength to re-write them, nor the self-abnegation to suppress them" (*C* 11:505–6; cf. 502; *C* 3:354). Ralph Barton Perry continues that "it is tempting to speculate on the contents of that 'Principles of Philosophy' which might have resulted from a decade

of rigorous and consecutive philosophizing, similar to that psychologizing of the '80s which resulted in the *Principles of Psychology*.... While he attained a vogue and influence almost unique among philosophical writers, he persisted in his 'squashy popular-lecture style,' and failed to produce that 'something serious, systematic and syllogistic' which he intended" (*Thought and Character*, 2:363–64).

24. In *Nature*, Ralph Waldo Emerson writes: "Our age is retrospective. It builds the sepulchres of the fathers. It writes biographies, histories, and criticism.... Why should not we have a poetry and philosophy of insight and not of tradition, and a religion by revelation to us, and not a history of theirs?" (*Complete Works*, 1:3).

25. For Isaac Woodbridge Riley, James's vision holds that "the universe is not a final *de luxe* edition, but a volume in the making,—it might well have been said a loose-leaf ledger" (*American Thought*, 315).

26. Jared Sparks Moore, writing in defense of Monism, notes that "pluralism, like pragmatism, is a confession of failure, a decision that if it is difficult to explain any given problem, that problem does not really exist at all—the fact must be accepted as a simple *datum* or 'gift,' but calls for no explanation. In direct application of the pragmatic method, pluralism is a plank to save from drowning the man who gets beyond his depth in the tumultuous stream of intellectual subtlety. In short, pluralism is no philosophy at all, but a denial of the need of any philosophy.... The very purpose of philosophy is to go deeper than either our ordinary knowledge or that of the sciences—to rationalize and intellectualize our various particular experiences in order to discover the unitary ground of them all" ("Religious Significance," 54).

27. We can consider, for example, John Evan Turner's almost ontological defense of Monism. He writes that James's "attempt to substitute Pluralism for Monism appears to defeat itself at the very outset.... The only way, *i.e.*, in which the problem itself can be stated is in terms of 'whole and part,' and then it appears to follow at once that some ultimate whole—*i.e.*, some type of Monism—is necessarily implied from the beginning by the very terms employed.... Since 'whole' is plainly a more ultimate idea than 'part'... it must be one object of philosophy to frame the conception of a whole of some kind or other; and while we may, *i.e.*, question the adequacy of any particular 'whole-idea' which may be offered as final, still we must admit as certainly necessary the idea of an ultimate whole of some kind—we must acquiesce in the search for the whole as being the true goal, even though we assay and reject any particular preferred wholes as being mere alloys, or even as worthless" (*Examination of William James's Philosophy*, 35–36).

28. For Joseph Leon Blau, "there are many varieties of metaphysical idealism... that... agree in the belief that what men experience, the constant flux of becoming, the confusion of sensation, instability, and change, is not real existence, not Reality. These are but appearance, the shadow of the real. A knowledge of Reality can not be derived from consideration of its counterpart in experience. Our only instrument for gaining a knowledge of Reality is the mind, man's spiritual part, for Reality is spiritual in its

fundamental character. The real universe is rational; it has an orderly, stable, permanent nature. Ultimately, in the real universe, existence, meaning, truth, and value are one" (*Men and Movements*, 188).

29. Cf. *PU* 52–53, 99–100; *MT* 83, 148–52; *ECR* 164, 515. Richard J. Bernstein writes: "Any description or analysis of what we see involves the use of concepts and categories that are selective and partial. It literally makes no sense to claim that we can exhaustively describe what we see; descriptions can be multifarious. What we take to be a description is intimately dependent on the aims, purposes, and concepts we employ. All vision has a horizontal character in which there is a foreground and background. The reason this is so important for James is that one of the major substantive doctrines he is arguing for in these lectures is that concrete reality and experience are richer, more dynamic, and thicker than can possibly be expressed by our concepts. This does not mean that our concepts *distort* reality; distortion enters only when we slip into thinking that reality itself is exhausted by our descriptions and conceptual analyses. This misguided tendency is what James labels '*vicious intellectualism*'" ("Introduction" to *PU*, xiii–xiv).

30. John J. McDermott notes that "the synthesis to which James is objecting derives from his rejection of what he takes to be the Hegelian penchant for taking the world as *All-einheit*, that is, from a single rather than from a multiple point of view. James's original opponent in this connection was his colleague Josiah Royce, for whom single ideas were but fragments unless they were grasped as part of an infinite system" ("Introduction" to *EP*, xviii).

31. James also points out that the Absolute, as "the all-knower," would seem to be burdened with knowing an "enormous mass of unprofitable information." For example, although "this table is not a chair, not a rhinoceros, not a logarithm, not a mile away from the door, not worth five hundred pounds sterling, not a thousand centuries old," it would seem that "the absolute must even now be articulately aware of all these negations. Along with what everything is it must also be conscious of everything which it is not" (*PU* 61–62).

32. Joseph Leon Blau notes that, "the monism which James describes is an exaggeration—we might almost call it a straw man. His exaggeration, however, is designed to aid in distinguishing two ways of thinking about reality, which he calls the 'each-form' and the 'all-form.' Any absolutistic philosophy, like that of Royce, for example, considers reality under its collective form. It regards the form of totality as the only rational way of thinking about reality" (*Men and Movements*, 260).

33. F. H. Bradley himself complains to James in late 1904 that it is unfortunate "that you say so much about the neo-Kantian Absolute. I should say myself that there are very few persons indeed who believe in it & who understand it as you understand it. Most of us understand it in an opposite sense.... It seems to me a pity that you should run the risk of getting your views ignored or rejected summarily, by making assertions or assumptions about what many of us hold which leave us to wonder" (*C* 10:504; cf.

Seth, review of *Pluralistic Universe*, 540–41; A. E. Taylor, review of *Pluralistic Universe*, 576; Bakewell, review of *Pragmatism*, 626).

34. In this regard, George Stuart Fullerton writes that "no one is merely a philosopher; he is also a man, with the usual endowment that makes man something more than a rational animal. He has read the history of philosophy to little profit who has not seen in the succession of systems unrolled before him plain traces of the education and training, the passions and prejudices, the hopes and fears, of their very human authors" ("Right to Believe," 418).

35. It is not necessary to take his association of Hegel's thought with "the effects of nitrous-oxide-gas-intoxication" to be a criticism. Rather, it seems that when James writes that in intoxication and in Hegel "the mind sees all the logical relations of being with an apparent subtlety and instantaneity to which its normal consciousness offers no parallel" and that, with the return of sobriety, these mystical insights disappear (*WB* 217–18; cf. *VRE* 307–8), he is attempting to portray the similarities in sensation that can arise from the two.

36. See *PP* 1:192, 503–4, 516–18; *PBC* 25–26.

37. Ralph Barton Perry writes: "There were for James, as there were in fact, two Fechners. When James was writing the *Principles*, Fechner's *Psychophysik* was already a recognized classic in modern experimental psychology. . . . The second Fechner was the metaphysical Fechner, who conceived the universe as a series of overlapping souls from God down through the earth-soul to man, and from man to the unobservable psychic states that lie below the threshold of his consciousness. This daring speculation excited James's imagination, and at the same time satisfied two motives in his thought: he had always been tempted by the panpsychistic view of physical nature, and his religious thought had steadily moved towards the hypothesis of superhuman consciousness" (*Thought and Character*, 2:586–87; cf. Titchener, *Experimental Psychology*, 2:xx–cxvi).

38. James perhaps saw similarities between Fechner's condition and his own earlier depression that we considered in chapter 1.

39. The title of one of Fechner's volumes is *Die Tagesansicht gegenüber der Nachtansicht* [The daylight view in contrast with the night view] (see *PU* 78 n.3; cf. Zweig, "Gustav Theodor Fechner," 556).

40. Benjamin Franklin had developed a similar position in his 1728 "Articles of Belief and Acts of Religion" (*Writings*, 83–90). More recently, Eugene Fontinell writes: "If we are here and now constituted in part by and partly constituting a consciousness of immeasurably wider, perhaps everlasting, life, then a postdeath continuing relation with such a consciousness cannot be immediately and with certainty ruled out. We may, unknown to us, be already living 'within' this larger life, and certain of those fields now constituting the individual self may already be playing a role in and in a sense constituting this larger life" (*Self, God, and Immortality*, 125).

41. F. H. Bradley writes to James in 1909 that "I, to be frank, do not think that Fechner's arguments as to the earth soul are worth anything. But as to the unlimited pos-

sibility of non-human organic life I found him conclusive & you will, I think, see that I have used him, as well as referred to him. I do not see how we are to show that there are beings higher than men, & I could not urge this positively. But as to the indefinite possibility of such beings I think I was clear. Fechner's arguments ... helped to take me back to a wider form of pantheism. I don't see *any* connection in principle between Absolute Idealism & the giving the highest place to human beings. That strikes me as a onesidedness which came historically but is not logical at all" (C 12:154–55).

42. F. C. S. Schiller notes that "James *always* overstated his intellectual debts. I shall never forget a confidential little lunch in my rooms at Oxford, to which I invited my friend, H. V. Knox, to meet James, in order that we might both ask him what precisely he had owed to Bergson. He told us. When he had done, we both cried out, spontaneously and simultaneously, 'But these are the very things which *we* have learnt from *you!*'" (*Must Philosophers Disagree?*, 103).

43. Bergson, *Introduction to Metaphysics*, 1.

44. Cf. *SPP* 49–50; *PP* 1:237; *PBC* 147.

45. In a similar fashion, Bergson writes: "Were all the photographs of a town, taken from all possible points of view, to go on indefinitely completing one another, they would never be equivalent to the solid town in which we walk about. Were all the translations of a poem into all possible languages to add together their various shades of meaning and, correcting each other by a kind of mutual retouching, to give a more and more faithful image of the poem they translate, they would yet never succeed in rendering the inner meaning of the original. A representation taken from a certain point of view, a translation made with certain symbols, will always remain imperfect in comparison with the object of which a view has been taken, or which the symbols seek to express" (*Introduction to Metaphysics*, 3).

46. While James finds little value in "intellectualistic logic," because "reality, life, experience, concreteness, immediacy, use what word you will, exceeds our logic, overflows and surrounds it," and he finally decides "to *give up the logic*" (*PU* 95–96; cf. 129–31; *ERE* 137), I would not characterize his position as irrationalism. Morris Raphael Cohen responds more critically that "James' hostility to logic was not necessitated by any of his psychological observations. To see the motives which led him to espouse Bergson's extreme anti-intellectualism, we must reflect on the peculiar fascination and repulsion which the neo-Hegelian, and especially the Bradleyan argument for the absolute, had for him. There is very little difference in content between Bradley's absolute as experience and Bergson's absolute intuition, which James identifies with pure experience. They all postulate the fusion of unity and plurality in an experience that passes logical understanding or discursive reason. But James, having no taste or aptitude for rigorous logic, wished to defend his theism or vitalistic view of the world by the empirical evidence of abnormal psychology. Against such efforts the pitiless scepticism of Bradley's logic is radically destructive.... So James is driven to extreme anti-rationalism, not by rank outsiders who reject the idealistic or vitalistic universe, but by those who would

establish it by cold and seemingly lifeless logic" (*Reason and Nature*, 42–44; cf. Turner, *Examination of James's Philosophy*, 51; J. Watson, "Some Remarks on Radical Empiricism," 116–17; J. E. Russell, "Some Difficulties," 411; Lovejoy, "William James as Philosopher," 109–10; C 12:309–10, 317).

47. Discussing the term "income," Oliver Wendell Holmes Jr. notes in a similar vein that "a word is not a crystal, transparent and unchanged, it is the skin of a living thought and may vary greatly in color and content according to the circumstances and the time in which it is used" (*Towne v. Eisner*, 425).

48. John Elof Boodin writes: "Is not philosophy, and must it not always be, in the experimental stage?... Truth is at best experimental, and nothing can be more fatal than stopping the experiment.... Why should we insist so persistently on fitting human nature into one arbitrary mold for the sake of conventional consistency? Why should we not have recourse to different forms of religion and different systems of philosophy, different universes of appreciation, according th the varying moods and needs of the soul?... The history of philosophy is a picture gallery in which we can study not only the history of thought, but the history of ourselves, and through sympathy with the past become conscious of our own meaning in our various moods.... The race, in its historic experience, will eventually pass upon the individual insight, and reject or incorporate into its institutional network, according as it explains or simplifies life" (*Truth and Reality*, 4–6, 10, 14).

49. John Evan Turner, for example, wonders whether there can be "a *universe* which is pluralistic... Would not such a world be a multiverse, and no true universe at all? 'Universe' surely means, essentially, oneness somewhere, however that unity may be hidden from our finite spiritual vision behind the veil of independent existences which it appears impossible to comprehend within any coherent monistic scheme" (*Examination of William James's Philosophy*, 30).

6. ETHICS AND SOCIAL THOUGHT

1. The question of the nature of human well-being has other answers as well. William Ernest Hocking, for example, maintains that we cannot determine well-being without first determining what is right: "In ethics... pragmatism attempts to judge what is right by what works well, as making for 'the greatest good for the greatest number,' or some other measure of welfare.... But we cannot judge what is right by what promotes welfare or survival or happiness, because we can only determine what promotes welfare, etc., by first enquiring what is right" (*Types of Philosophy*, 165).

2. Charles Augustus Strong responds to James's position: "I cannot see why a *demand*, as such, is sacred. I should rather say that what is primarily sacred is people's *well-being*, not what it enters into their poor benighted heads to demand. I cannot believe that the child's demand for the moon, or the debauchee's for sensual pleasure are, originally & in themselves, just as sacred as the mother[']s good wishes for her child, or the saint's aspiration for holiness. I cannot consider that the sacrifice of the former is a

'butchery.' I should say that the sacredness of demands does not exist at this stage, but only appears when the demand is considered in its reference to the *lasting well-being* of all concerned" (C 7:153).

3. The extent to which James attempted to listen to others may be indicated by Dickinson Sergeant Miller's comment: "Consider the range of his reference to literature, the extraordinarily serious attention he gives to obscure authors, and young authors, and authors out of repute, and provincial authors, and uneducated authors, and eccentric authors, and insane authors" ("Some of the Tendencies," 663).

4. Arthur E. Murphy notes that "this distinctively moral individualism is not much argued by James. It is presupposed in his theory and exemplified in his practice. All that is needed to justify the assumption is a world of individuals as genial and generous as William James" ("Philosophical Scholarship," 180).

5. For more instances of James's emphasis on "brain-born" moral values, see *PP* 2:988, 1265–66; *MT* 59/*ERE* 136; *VRE* 211–15.

6. Thomas Jefferson writes of this "taste" as a moral sense: "Man was destined for society. His morality therefore was to be formed to this object. He was endowed with a sense of right & wrong merely relative to this. This sense is as much a part of his nature as the sense of hearing, seeing, feeling. . . . The moral sense, or conscience, is as much a part of man as his leg or arm. . . . State a moral case to a ploughman & a professor. The former will decide it as well, & often better than the latter, because he has not been led astray by artificial rules" (*Writings*, 901–2).

7. Dickinson Sergeant Miller writes that "the most impressive thing" in James was "his sense of mystery, of the more beyond, of what the world and life may contain, of what the individual he speaks with may contain, which perhaps even the man himself does not know but which may yet come forth; which is there in all likelihood whether it come forth or not. No one had a deeper feeling for *other life than his own* or a more unaffected respect for its possibilities" ("William James, Man and Philosopher," 41).

8. For James's position on the ability of dogs to use signs, see *PP* 2:980.

9. For another instance of James's blindness, see his sister Alice's report on his attitude toward the eviction of farmers in Ireland. She notes that he could make fun of the evictions because he believed that "the horror" of the evictions "entirely vanishes when you see the nature of the cabins,—existence without being so much preferable to existence within" (Matthiessen, *James Family*, 649).

10. Consider the following related passage as James's possible commentary on Henry David Thoreau's life at Walden Pond: "Among us English-speaking peoples especially do the praises of poverty need once more to be boldly sung. We have grown literally afraid to be poor. We despise anyone who elects to be poor in order to simplify and save his inner life. If he does not join the general scramble and pant with the money-making street, we deem him spiritless and lacking in ambition. We have lost the power even of imagining what the ancient idealization of poverty could have meant: the liberation from material attachments, the unbribed soul, the manlier indifference,

the paying our way by what we are or do and not by what we have, the right to fling away our life at any moment irresponsibly—the more athletic trim, in short, the moral fighting shape" (*VRE* 293; cf. 222).

11. Cf. *TT* 4; *WB* 144. A particularly telling example of how difficult it is to live according to this principle can be found in James's problems with the plan of his in-laws, William and Mary Salter, to adopt a child. As he writes to his mother-in-law, Eliza Putnam Gibbens, in June 1900, "the plan seems to me fraught with terrible risks for the remoter future and with a present inconvenience which I should think would fairly be disastrous. If they were younger, securer in health, and if they dwelt in the country or in a rural town it would be different. And it would be different if, being as they are, they were richer" (*C* 9:233–34). After the adoption had been arranged, however, James saw the light; and he wrote again in July: "Since hearing of the adoption as an accomplished fact I feel tremendously ashamed of my recent remarks to you about it, wh. of course the Salters won't have seen. It has been as striking a case of 'a certain blindness' as I ever knew, I taking the external mercenary mechanical view of an act which, as livingly entered upon by the Salters, was evidently one of passionate faith and impulse" (*C* 9:244).

12. A few years later, James offers a related example to his Gifford audience in Edinburgh: "No American can ever attain to understanding the loyalty of a Briton towards his king, of a German towards his emperor; nor can a Briton or German ever understand the peace of heart of an American in having no king, no Kaiser, no spurious nonsense, between him and the common God of all" (*VRE* 260).

13. Robert Coles writes that "James wants to show how self-centered any of us, from whatever background or society, can get." James points, he notes, to "our ability to mouth pieties, then go on to climb over our neighbors and friends, in pursuit of money, power, prestige, whatever—and in so doing let ourselves off the hook by calling all sorts of other people a variety of unfriendly names, thereby clearing our own slates quite thoroughly" (review of *Varieties*, 29).

14. The tastelessness of this comment is perhaps mitigated somewhat by the fact that James was referring to the slaughters of 1894–96, not the genocide of 1915–16 (see *C* 8:107–8, 177, 351, 583; *VRE* 271).

15. Howard Vincente Knox writes that "the importance of individuals is evidently a very democratic principle, and James was a true American in holding fast to it. But his democratic faith rests, not on the figment of a natural equality of all men, but on a deep psychological insight into their infinite variety and personal uniqueness. He perceived that the community has an interest in allowing wide scope for experiments in living that may lead to salutary innovations" (*Philosophy of William James*, 5; cf. 77–78).

16. For a further consideration of this theme, see my essay: "Systems of Justice and the Role of the Moral Prophet."

17. Max Carl Otto writes that for James "social institutions endangered the purity of individuality. Even organizations formed to combat economic injustice and to win for

deprived men and women a better chance at the basic requisites of a satisfying life were likely, by encroaching upon 'the sacredness of private integrity,' to be a greater evil than the evil they were intended to remedy" ("On a Certain Blindness," 189).

18. For some of James's comments on women, see *ECR* 246–56, 402–7; *PP* 2:991, 1055–57; *ERM* 152; *VRE* 212. Of James's overall view, Charlene Haddock Seigfried writes that his "explicit support of the ideology of separate spheres, which restricts women to the privacy of the home and reserves the public sphere for men, mires him in sentimentality rather than in the sympathetic understanding so characteristic of his interactions with others whose way of life differs dramatically from his own." She continues that James "consistently viewed" women "from a masculinist, or ideologically patriarchal angle of vision; that is, one which equates humanness with maleness and believes that women's proper role is to serve men's interests" (*Pragmatism and Feminism*, 111; cf. 111–41; Garrison and Madden, "William James," 217–19; J. I. Miller, *Democratic Temperament*, 33–53; Myers, *William James*, 424–29).

19. Cf. C 10:303–4; C 12:249–50, 259–60, 435–37; Myers, *William James*, 432–34.

20. In 1893 James had written to Hugo Münsterberg that the problem with homeopathic physicians "is that they are men of one idea; and what with their narrowness, and the gross ignorance on the part of orthodox doctors of things that *they* know, there is no such thing as an all-round *physician* to be had—only sectarians" (C 7:398; cf. 496).

21. Cf. *ECR* 567; C 7:496; C 8:348–49, 351.

22. Beers, *Mind That Found Itself*.

23. Merle Eugene Curti writes that "the fact that James had no direct experience with poverty did not keep him from saying a good deal about it. In explaining the sanctity of poverty as an adornment to a good life, he made much of the opposition between the men who *have* and the men who *are*. The gentleman had been cherished, not because he possessed land and riches but because of his personal superiority in courage, pride, and generosity" (*Social Ideas*, 434; cf. Conkin, *Puritans and Pragmatists*, 335–36).

24. Edward H. Madden notes that James's position on the status of black Americans was not in any way progressive: "After the Civil War there were a number of crucially important events in the struggle against racism: the Civil Rights Act of 1875; the debate between emigration or assimilation of American blacks, with Frederick Douglass fighting for assimilation; the Supreme Court decision (of 1883) declaring the 1875 act unconstitutional; the *Plessy v. Ferguson* decision (1896) that established the separate-but-equal doctrine; the Niagara Movement and the subsequent emergence of the National Association for the Advancement of Colored People (of which a student of James's, W. E. B. Du Bois, was one of the organizers). It is a measure of James's involvement in the struggle against racism that he did not even mention these events, let alone do anything relevant to them, nor was he engaged in the work of any of the above named organizations" ("Introduction" to C 8:xxxv).

25. Edward H. Madden suggests that "why James was asked to speak remains unclear, as it was apparently to James himself. What is clear is that he had mixed feelings

about being chosen.... In being someone who avoided serving in the Civil War ... James was an odd choice" ("Introduction" to C 8:xxxv; cf. 263; C 3:9; Simon, *Genuine Reality*, xiv, 313–14; J. J. McDermott, "Introduction" to *ERM*, xxi).

26. At this same battle, James's brother Garth Wilkinson, the adjutant of the 54th, was severely wounded.

27. One of the other speakers at this ceremony was Booker T. Washington, who noted that "that which for three centuries had bound master and slave, yea, North and South, to a body of death, could not be blotted out by four years of war" ("Address at the Unveiling," 28). Afterward, William writes to his brother Henry: "Read the darkey Washington's speech, a model of elevation and brevity. The thing that struck me most in the day was the faces of the old 54th soldiers, of which there were perhaps about thirty or forty present, with such respectable old darkey faces, the heavy animal look entirely absent, and in its place the wrinkled, patient, good old darkey citizen" (C 3:9; cf. C 2:89; C 8:260, 262, 266). For an attempt to contextualize James's use of the term "darkey," see Myers, *William James*, 596 n.99.

28. See also: *EPs* 16, 32; *ECR* 82, 348.

29. *VRE* 69; *ERM* 170; cf. Perry, *Thought and Character*, 2:308. For a series of less tasteful comments, see *EPR* 268–69; *WB* 192, 239/*EPR* 135; *ERM* 173.

30. Cf. C 3:39; C 4:474; C 6:269; C 7:282; C 11:263.

31. For Edward H. Madden, "James was less the culture hero than some have argued and more the man *in* and very much *of* his time and class: that his attitudes were those of the late nineteenth-century northern liberal, *ambivalent*; that with his jostling and conflicting private and public views, he was neither crusader nor racist" ("Introduction" to C 8:xxxvi).

32. See, for example, Perry, *Thought and Character*, 2:280–322; Myers, *William James*, 429–30.

33. George R. Garrison and Edward H. Madden note that James "was not much of a reformer even in the areas where he extended himself. Moreover, he showed unexpected blind spots on the issues of racism, women's rights, British oppression of the Irish, and British imperialism in general.... His individualism kept him from acting in concert with others through effective organizations to bring to bear cumulative pressure." Rather than considering James to be "a significant reformer," they continue, we should view him "as a person who, in some instances, had what looked like good ideas to us today, and who implemented them occasionally in something less than a striking fashion" ("William James," 207, 211; cf. Mills, *Sociology and Pragmatism*, 260–74).

34. Curti, *Social Ideas*, 441; West, *American Evasion*, 61; Conkin, *Puritans and Pragmatists*, 275. Conkin continues that "except for the issue of imperialism, James remained largely aloof from national politics.... He held back from espousing political and economic reform and preached his own gospel of individualism" (*Puritans and Pragmatists*, 335; cf. Schneider, *History of American Philosophy*, 486; Williams, "William James and the Facts," 96).

35. J. J. McDermott, review of Barzun's *Stroll with William James*, 128; "Introduction" to *ERM*, xxi.

36. Merle Eugene Curti writes that James's position was "incompatible with the full development of the very individuality of the masses of Americans for which in principle James sincerely stood" (*Social Ideas*, 458; cf. *Growth of American Thought*, 563; Cohen, *Reason and Nature*, 45–46).

37. Edward Carter Moore suggests that James offers the idea of a moral holiday to indicate that "the belief of the meliorist (or any other theist) has different consequences in terms of action than does the belief of the materialist." If we believe that "the control of the universe is, at least partly, in higher hands than ours," then we need not "fight ceaselessly against evil, but may on occasion rest from the struggle and take a holiday from moral strife, confident that the ills of the world are still being combatted by other powers" (*American Pragmatism*, 122).

38. Max Carl Otto writes that James "had an uncanny aptness for catching the luster of a life wherever and however it was lived ... but it was in his case the correlative of a tendency to slight the environmental circumstances in response to which, or in spite of which, the better potentialities of human beings are realized, or, because of which ... they are thwarted, twisted, or entirely crushed out.... James treated certain important social facts as he might have brushed against strangers in a crowd" ("On a Certain Blindness in William James," 187–88; cf. 190).

39. As George Santayana notes, "William James enjoyed in his youth what are called advantages: he lived among cultivated people, travelled, had teachers of various nationalities" ("William James," 584).

40. For Vivian J. McGill, "James gave no direct attention to economics. He made withering attacks upon the Absolutes of Bradley and Royce and upon other impostures in the realm of philosophy but he had nothing to say against the basic tyrannies and prejudices in the economic world; yet these were surely more dangerous to the zest and rich variety of life he desired than the poor dragons of Bradley and Royce which he slew so gaily" ("Pragmatism Reconsidered," 291).

41. John Dewey wonders whether an ethics of reform reduces our moral lives "to the futile toil of a Sisyphus who is forever rolling a stone uphill only to have it roll back so that he has to repeat his old task?" He agrees that it does, "judged from progress made in a control of conditions which shall stay put and which excludes the necessity of future deliberations and reconsiderations." Still, he continues that pessimism is not justified because "continual search and experimentation to discover the meaning of changing activity, keeps activity alive, growing in significance" (*Human Nature and Conduct*, in *Middle Works*, 14:144–45).

42. For the original passage, see Emerson, *Journals and Miscellaneous Notebooks*, 13:80.

43. Morris Raphael Cohen similarly notes that philosophy must be interested in more than social reform: "the real importance of philosophy lies in its very indepen-

dence from the petty actualities of daily life" (*Dreamer's Journey*, 165–66). He writes elsewhere about "the need of men to maintain even in war the things that make the country worth defending. Purely theoretic studies seem to me to be of those fine flowers which relieve the drabness of our existence and help to make the human scene worth while" (*Faith of a Liberal*, 86). In another place, he notes that "in seeing human fate as part of a great cosmic drama, men arise above their petty limitations and learn to look upon their passions and achievements with that measure of aloofness which is essential to any vision that can be called philosophic and to any civilization that can be called liberal" (*American Thought*, 297; cf. *Preface to Logic*, 201).

44. George Santayana writes that James "felt that he had lost his country. Intervention in Cuba might be defended, on account of the perpetual bad government there and the sufferings of the natives. But the annexation of the Philippines, what could excuse that? What could be a more shameless betrayal of American principles? What could be a plainer symptom of greed, ambition, corruption, and imperialism?" (*Persons and Places*, 402; cf. Coon, "One Moment," 72–74).

45. In *The Principles*, James had offered this similar passage: "In many respects man is the most ruthlessly ferocious of beasts.... Constrained to be a member of a tribe, he still has a right to decide, as far as in him lies, of which other members the tribe shall consist. Killing off a few obnoxious ones may often better the chances of those that remain. And killing off a neighboring tribe from whom no good thing comes, but only competition, may materially better the lot of the whole tribe. Hence the gory cradle, the *bellum omnium contra omnes* [war of all against all], in which our race was reared; hence the fickleness of human ties, the ease with which the foe of yesterday becomes the ally of to-day, the friend of to-day the enemy of tomorrow; hence the fact that we, the lineal representatives of the successful enactors of one scene of slaughter after another, must, whatever more pacific virtues we may also possess, still carry about with us, ready at any moment to burst into flame, the smouldering and sinister traits of character by means of which they lived through so many massacres, harming others, but themselves unharmed" (*PP* 2:1028–29).

46. In the midst of World War I, James Hayden Tufts writes in a Jamesian fashion that "the lover of paradox can find no richer field than that of the ethics of states. On the one hand no institution has commanded nobler devotion or inspired loftier art; on the other, none has lent itself so ruthlessly to the destruction of every human interest and value, or has practiced so consistently what in common life we would call crime.... It has been convicted by history of organizing hatred more effectively than love; of organizing oppression more resolutely than safeguards of liberty; and of bending its energies and using its resources more unsparingly to destroy life than to save it" ("Ethics of States," 186).

47. Consider Ralph Waldo Emerson's similar position: "Every thing is beautiful seen from the point of the intellect, or as truth. But all is sour if seen as experience.

Details are melancholy; the plan is seemly and noble" ("Love," *Complete Works*, 2:171; cf. *SPP* 43 n.16).

48. Oliver Wendell Holmes Jr. writes in 1895: "Now, at least, and perhaps as long as man dwells upon the globe, his destiny is battle, and he has to take the chances of war. If it is our business to fight, the book for the army is a war-song, not a hospital-sketch. It is not well for soldiers to think much about wounds. Sooner or later we shall fall; but meantime it is for us to fix our eyes upon the point to be stormed, and to get there if we can.... The faith is true and adorable which leads a soldier to throw away his life in obedience to a blindly accepted duty, in a cause which he little understands, in a plan of campaign of which he has no notion, under tactics of which he does not see the use" ("Soldier's Faith," 487).

49. James asks in 1902 whether "the worship of material luxury and wealth, which constitutes so large a portion of the 'spirit' of our age, make[s] somewhat for effeminacy and unmanliness?... War and adventure assuredly keep all who engage in them from treating themselves too tenderly. They demand such incredible efforts, depth beyond depth of exertion, both in degree and in duration, that the whole scale of motivation alters. Discomfort and annoyance, hunger and wet, pain and cold, squalor and filth, cease to have any deterrent operation whatever. Death turns into a commonplace matter, and its usual power to check our action vanishes. With the annulling of these customary inhibitions, ranges of new energy are set free, and life seems cast upon a higher plane of power. The beauty of war in this respect is that it is so congruous with ordinary human nature. Ancestral evolution has made us all potential warriors; so the most insignificant individual, when thrown into an army in the field, is weaned from whatever excess of tenderness towards his precious person he may bring with him, and may easily develop into a monster of insensibility" (*VRE* 291).

50. Consider, for example, the following passage from Roosevelt's pen: "I wish to preach, not the doctrine of ignoble ease, but the doctrine of the strenuous life, the life of toil and effort, of labor and strife.... The man must be glad to do a man's work, to dare and endure and to labor; to keep himself, and to keep those dependent upon him. The woman must be the housewife, the helpmeet of the homemaker, the wise and fearless mother of many healthy children.... When men fear work or fear righteous war, when women fear motherhood, they tremble on the brink of doom; and well it is that they should vanish from the earth, where they are fit subjects for the scorn of all men and women who are themselves strong and brave and high-minded" (*Strenuous Life*, 1, 3–4). For James's comments of Roosevelt's worship of war, see *ECR* 152–53, 162–66. See also Frederick Douglass's 1863 call for black enlistments: "You owe it to yourself and your race to rise from your social debasement and take your place among the soldiers of your country, a man among men. Depend on it, the subjective effect of this one act of enlisting will be immense and highly beneficial. You will stand more erect, walk more assured, feel more at ease, and be less liable to insult than you ever were before. He who

fights the battles of America may claim America as his country—and have that claim respected" ("Why Should a Colored Man Enlist?," 529–30; cf. 536).

51. John Dewey believed that most people's lives were tough enough already. He writes to a correspondent in 1915 that James's war essay showed that "his sympathies were limited by his experience; the idea that most people need any substitute for fighting for life, or that they have to have life made artificially hard for them in order to keep up their battling nerve, could come only from a man who was brought up an aristocrat and who had lived a sheltered existence" (Myers, *William James*, 602 n.151; cf. J. J. McDermott, "Introduction" to *EP*, xxv; "Introduction" to *ERM*, xxvi–xxvii). James's developing sense of social justice, to which we now turn, would seem to mitigate this criticism somewhat.

52. In 1891, James had written: "Listlessness, apathy, dawdling, sauntering, the smoking of cigarettes and living on small sarcasms, the 'Harvard indifference,' in short, of which outsiders have so frequently complained, are the direct fruit of keeping these men too long from contact with that world of affairs to which they rightly belong.... These excellent fellows need contact of some sort with the fighting side of life, with the world in which men and women earn their bread and butter and live and die" (*ECR* 37).

53. Consider James's remark from 1902: "One hears of the mechanical equivalent of heat. What we now need to discover in the social realm is the moral equivalent of war: something heroic that will speak to men as universally as war does, and yet will be as compatible with their spiritual selves as war has proved itself to be incompatible. I have often thought that in the old monkish poverty-worship, in spite of the pedantry which infested it, there might be something like that moral equivalent of war which we are seeking. May not voluntary accepted poverty be 'the strenuous life,' without the need of crushing weaker peoples?" (*VRE* 292).

54. See also: James's comments on the value of summer forestry work for toughening his sons (*C* 8:516, 525; *C* 9:23, 261), and his suggestion that "pride and pugnacity" can play a role in education by developing in students "a general unwillingness to be beaten by any kind of difficulty" (*TT* 41).

55. Addams, *Newer Ideals of Peace*, 9, 118, 122; cf. Schott, "Jane Addams," 248–49; Deegan, *Self, War and Society*, 26–28, 36–37.

56. Hall, "Practical Relations," 12.

57. Calkins, "Militant Pacifism," 70, 75, 74, 79, 75–76, 79, 76, 79, 75; cf. Stratton, "Control of the Fighting Instinct," 12; Bixler, "Two Questions," 67–68.

58. Dewey, *Human Nature and Conduct*, in *Middle Works*, 14:80, 78.

59. Mead, "National-Mindedness and International-Mindedness," 357, 363, 367, 363, 366.

60. Anonymous, "Military Spirit and Pragmatism," 178.

7. RELIGION

1. I have detailed the transition from what philosophy had been in America around 1875 to what it was becoming early in the twentieth century in *Thoughtful Profession*, 1–37.

2. James describes this experience from 1898 to his wife Alice as follows: "the night turned out one of the most memorable of all my memorable experiences.... The guide had got a magnificent provision of firewood, the sky swept itself clear of every trace of cloud or vapor, the wind entirely ceased so that the fire-smoke rose straight up to heaven. The temperature was perfect either inside or outside the cabin, the moon rose and hung above the scene before midnight, leaving only a few of the larger stars visible, and I got into a state of spiritual alertness of the most vital description. The influences of Nature, the wholesomeness of the people round me, especially the good Pauline [Goldmark], the thought of you and the children, dear Harry on the wave, the problem of the Edinburgh lectures, all fermented within me till it became a regular Walpurgis Nacht. I spent a good deal of it in the woods, where the streaming moonlight lit up things in a magical checkered play, and it seemed as if the gods of all the nature-mythologies were holding an indescribable meeting in my breast with the moral gods of the inner life.... It was one of the happiest lonesome nights of my existence, and I understand now what a poet is. He is a person who can feel the immense complexity of influences that I felt, and make some partial tracks in them for verbal statement. In point of fact, I can't find a single word for all that significance, & don't know what it was significant of, so there it remains, a mere boulder of *impression*" (C 8:390–91; cf. *PU* 15; Richardson, *William James*, 372–76). For James's other possible religious experiences, see *EP* 159–64; C 5:127–29; Richardson, *William James*, 209–10, 470–71.

3. Josiah Royce continues in this theme in 1902 that "Religion, in its higher sense, constitutes the most important business of the human being.... Man's present and worldly life, as experience shows it to us, is, even in the most fortunate cases, a comparatively petty affair, whose passing joys and sorrows can be viewed as of serious and permanent importance only in case this life means what it at present never empirically presents to us, namely a task and a destiny that have, from some higher point of view, an absolute value" ("What Should Be the Attitude," 280–81).

4. *Letters*, 2:211; cf. C 10:395–97; C 8:228.

5. Gordon W. Allport writes in 1950 that "during the past fifty years religion and sex seem to have reversed their positions. Writing in the Victorian age William James could bring himself to devote barely two pages [of *PP*] to the role of sex in human life which he labeled euphemistically the 'instinct of love.' Yet no taboos held him back from directing the torrent of his genius into the *Varieties of Religious Experience*. On religion he spoke freely and with unexcelled brilliance.... Scarcely any modern textbook writers in psychology devote as much as two shamefaced pages to the subject—even though religion, like sex, is an almost universal interest of the human race" (*Individual and His Religion*, 1–2; cf. J. Ratner, "Introduction" to *Varieties*, xii).

6. See Gifford, "Ralph Waldo Emerson."

7. Gifford's will is reprinted in Jaki, *Lord Gifford and His Lectures*, 66–76. The cited passages appear on p. 74.

8. James describes his overall project to a correspondent in April 1900 as follows: "The problem I have set myself is a hard one: 1st to defend (against all the prejudices of my 'class,') 'experience' against 'philosophy' as being the real backbone of the world's religious life—I means prayer, guidance, and all that sort of thing immediately and privately felt, as against high and noble general views of our destiny and the world's meaning; and second, to make the hearer or reader believe what I myself invincibly do believe, that altho all the special manifestations of religion may have been absurd (I mean its creeds and theories) yet the life of it as a whole is mankind's most important function. A task well nigh impossible, I fear, and in which I shall fail; but to attempt it is *my* religious act" (C 9:185–86).

9. This is perhaps why James writes to F. C. S. Schiller that his Gifford lectures "are all facts and no philosophy" (C 10:27).

10. Martin E. Marty writes that *The Varieties* is "a classic that is too psychological to have shaped most religious inquiry and too religious to have influenced much psychological research" ("Introduction" to *Varieties*, vii; cf. Ewer, "Influence," 152–53).

11. Writing in Baldwin's *Dictionary*, Joseph Jastrow similarly emphasizes the continuity between normal and abnormal: "The broadest and in many respects most scientific and suggestive use of the term pathology regards it as coextensive with normal in biology; the latter applies to normal life in all its variety and complexity, the former to that of the morbid, the diseased, and the abnormal in no less extensive and comprehensive a sense" ("Pathology," 267; cf. Perry, *Thought and Character*, 2:325).

12. John E. Smith points to a number of James's supporters who "criticized the prominence he gave to extreme and exaggerated cases. This led, in their view, to an undue restriction of religious experience to eccentric encounters and episodes bordering on the abnormal" ("Introduction" to *VRE*, xvii–xviii; cf. J. Ratner, "Introduction" to *Varieties*, vi–vii; Edie, "William James and the Phenomenology," 255).

13. Edwin Diller Starbuck denies that these "specialists in religion" are the powerful forces that James believed them to be. For him, "the great and solid results of human attainment are wrought out within the everyday life of the compact mass of humanity," and "it is there we are to go if we are to get the truest picture at last of what religion really is." Starbuck further suggests that "this mass of living, acting, striving persons, with its varying shades of experience, and its fine feel each for the other . . . has done more, not only in refining and fixing our modes of religious life, but in discovering and shaping them in beliefs, than have the 'revelations' of all mystics combined" ("Varieties of Religious Experience," 103–4; cf. C 10:458–59).

14. Frank Sewall notes that "we see good old John Bunyan, and the preacher Whitefield, and Saint Theresa, and Cotton Mather, Channing, Tolstoi, and Thoreau, Billy Bray, Madame de Guyon, Sister Seraphique, Saint Francis and Saint Xavier, William

Penn and John Woolman, and many others led out by the magic of this master to dance, so to speak, to the measures of the modern psychology of religion" ("Professor James," 244).

15. As David A. Hollinger writes, "James managed in *Varieties* to articulate more vividly than ever before his loyalty to modern science's principles of intersubjective testability and professional consensus, and his loyalty to a worldview in which supernatural power of the sort posited by his own cultural tradition was an authentic presence and agent of undetermined scope" ("'Damned for God's Glory,'" 18).

16. Stevens, review of *Varieties*, 114–15; Coe, review of *Varieties*, 66; Sewall, "Professor James," 246, 250; Berle, "Psychology of Christian Experience," 19, 14; Hibben, review of *Varieties*, 184; cf. Santayana, "William James," 589–90; Hall, *Adolescence*, 2:292–93 n.8; Caldecott, "Work of William James," 312.

17. In Baldwin's *Dictionary*, Alexander Thomas Ormond offers a representative contemporary definition of "religion" as "Subjectively, the experience which arises out of man's conscious relation to some transcendent agent or agents, upon whose attitude towards him his welfare is believed in some measure to depend; objectively, the body of beliefs and practices which arise in connection with this experience, and which are ordinarily associated with some form of institutional life" ("Religion," 452).

18. Edwin Diller Starbuck notes that the focus of James's inquiry is on such questions as "what does this particular religious experience feel like from the *inside*, and how does the world look viewed from this standpoint?" ("Varieties of Religious Experience," 101).

19. For John E. Smith, "James saw religion as the awareness on the part of the individual of the present incompleteness and broken character of his life; this awareness leads to the question of a higher power which can complete life and overcome the destructive forces in it" (*Spirit of American Philosophy*, 78).

20. In the "Divinity School Address," Emerson proclaims: "Historical Christianity has fallen into the error that corrupts all attempts to communicate religion. As it appears to us, and as it has appeared for ages, it is not the doctrine of the soul, but an exaggeration of the personal, the positive, the ritual.... Whilst the doors of the temple stand open, night and day, before every man, and the oracles of this truth cease never, it is guarded by one stern condition; this, namely; it is an intuition. It cannot be received at second hand. Truly speaking, it is not instruction, but provocation, that I can receive from another soul" (*Complete Works*, 1:130, 126–27).

21. Hibben, review of *Varieties*, 184–85; Royce, *Problem of Christianity*, 40–41. John E. Smith notes that James never offered a distinction "between religious community and 'organized religion,' with the result that the latter was made to stand in total contrast to religion as it exists in the individual soul; organized religion was for him something 'second-hand'" ("Introduction" to *VRE*, xix; cf. *Spirit of American Philosophy*, 78–79; C. Taylor, *Varieties*, 20–29; Lash, *Easter in Ordinary*, 57–58).

22. John E. Smith writes that for James religious intolerance is "due entirely to an

ecclesiastical spirit filled with the desire for dominion, both political and intellectual, over the hearts and minds of human beings." Thus, in James's mind, "religion as first-hand individual experience is innocent, having no place on the negative side of the ledger in which are recorded the disasters of religious wars and the bitter conflicts among differing sects and denominations" ("Introduction" to *VRE*, xxxix).

23. John Watson responds to the notion of a finite God as follows: "if the being who is by an abuse of language called God is finite, either in knowledge or in power—and the one is not really separable from the other—how can we possibly worship or trust him? We may be worshipping and trusting the wrong being; or He may be too much occupied with his own affairs, or He may not be able to help us, either because He is not wise enough, or because He is too weak" ("Some Remarks on Radical Empiricism," 118–19).

24. John J. McDermott writes that James's position on immortality "is more a hope than a belief." James, he continues, "was struck by two aspects of the possibility of human immortality: first, that it is such a deep and pervasive concern of human life and, second, the possibility that we can communicate with the dead." Moreover, this interest in immortality "was to occupy much of his time in the later years of his life, when he was concerned with psychical research" ("Introduction" to *ERM*, xvii; cf. Fontinell, *Self, God, and Immortality*).

25. In his *Dissertation on Liberty and Necessity, Pleasure and Pain* of 1725, Franklin writes: "upon *Death*, and the Destruction of the Body, the Ideas contain'd in the Brain, (which are alone the Subjects of the Soul's Action) being then likewise necessarily destroy'd, the Soul, tho' incapable of Destruction itself, must then necessarily *cease to think* or *act*, having nothing left to think or act upon. It is reduc'd to its first inconscious State before it receiv'd any Ideas. And to cease to *think* is but little different from *ceasing to be*" (*Writings*, 69).

26. Wayne Proudfoot suggests, however, that our greatest obstacle in appreciating *The Varieties* after a century "is likely to be James's lack of attention to historical context. He juxtaposes material from biographies of Counter-Reformation saints with quotations from Tolstoy, Ramakrishna, and contemporary proponents of mind-cure.... He wants to construct a composite portrait of types of religious experience that he takes to be the same across different historical and cultural settings" ("Pragmatism," 43; cf. Barnard, "Varieties of Religious Experience," 58).

27. David A. Hollinger writes that "James's ostensibly specieswide account of religious experience is deeply Protestant in structure, tone, and implicit theology.... *Varieties* is constructed to foreground certain religious sensibilities and not others, and to present the core of religion in general as having been most attractively manifest in exactly the cultural tradition to which James's listeners and readers were directly heir" ("'Damned for God's Glory,'" 11, 14; cf. Levinson, *Religious Investigations*, 23; C. Taylor, *Varieties*, 22–23; Proudfoot, "Pragmatism," 41).

28. For Hastings Rashdall, "Prof. James's preoccupation with the marvellous and

the abnormal almost inevitably conducts him to, if indeed it is not inspired by, a determination to find the essence of religion in feeling and emotion, and to belittle its rational or intellectual side.... He is prepared apparently to base religion entirely upon the evidence afforded by these abnormal experiences to the few who have gone through them. The rest of us must apparently depend entirely upon the external testimony of those who have experienced such things.... Prof. James's position can only be described as a deliberate abandonment of the search for truth and a handing over of Religion and Morality (and why not Science?) to the sway of wilful caprice. To me at least to believe that my Religion or Philosophy was only true for me would be exactly the same thing as not believing it at all" (review of *Varieties*, 247–49; cf. J. Watson, *Philosophical Basis*, 153–54).

29. Cf. *VRE* 319–22; Suckiel, *Heaven's Champion*, 43.

30. Consider James's analogous claim: "The science of logic never made a man reason rightly, and the science of ethics (if there be such a thing) never made a man behave rightly. The most such sciences can do is to help us to catch ourselves up and check ourselves, if we start to reason or to behave wrongly; and to criticise ourselves more articulately after we have made mistakes" (*TT* 15).

31. As we saw in chapter 6, James at his best is far more tolerant of others' values.

32. F. C. S. Schiller notes that for James, "our continuity with something wider, in which our ideal impulses originate, seems indisputable. But what is the source of these infiltrations from the subliminal, remains a matter for 'over-beliefs,' as to which men naturally differ. He himself claims to share the 'piecemeal supernaturalism' [*VRE* 409] of the plain man, and holds it meaningless to call 'God' an absolute Whole" (review of *Varieties*, 155).

33. Clarence Irving Lewis writes that "*it is only because we are active beings that our world is bigger than the content of our actual experience*.... All that 'more' which belongs to the objects presented to him [the active being], over and above what is immediately given, and all the rest of reality, as it stands related to his object but not presented with it, resides in this potency of possible experience. For the passive being, the *only possible* passage of experience is the actual one: the only continuities of reality ... would be the actual flux of experience" (*Mind and the World Order*, 140–41).

34. Cf. Brett, "Psychology of William James," 82; J. J. McDermott, *Culture of Experience*, 106–7.

35. Henry Samuel Levinson notes that "religious originals believed not so much in *another* world as in a *wider* world than the ones that most naturalists, positivists, moralists, and materialists affirmed. They perceived real things that the irreligious did not perceive" (*Religious Investigations*, 99; cf. Gavin, *William James*, 45).

36. His "faith ladder" was considered in chapter 3.

37. James describes alcohol as "the great exciter of the *Yes* function in man" (*VRE* 307).

38. Frederick Courtney French notes that the psychologist can use "the sublimi-

nal self" to "explain sudden conversions, celestial visions and mystic ecstasies." Because these experiences came "from the hidden region of the subconscious," it was very natural—although he believes mistaken—to ascribe them to "a supernatural source." James, however, "departs from the standpoint of science when he suggests that the phenomena of the religious consciousness may be doorways into the spiritual world. Whatever metaphysics or epistemology may say of such a view, psychology as a science must regard these religious experiences as purely phenomenal. It does not find in them any manifestation of the transcendent, although their possessors often so interpret them. Science is as rigorously phenomenalistic in the mental sphere as in the physical sphere" (abstract of "Relation of Psychology," 380).

39. Ellen Kappy Suckiel prefers the religious interpretation: "if James were asked the question 'What is the seemingly higher power with which the subject is in communion in religious experience?' his initial and conservative reply would be that it may be nothing more than the subject's own subconscious mind.... It is hard to imagine a more disappointing answer. To suggest that it may be no more than the deeper regions of the individual's own mind which provide the source and sufficient explanation of our religious sensibility is to abandon entirely the religious point of view. If this were all there were to James's proposal, we would have to conclude that he has paid an impossibly high price in his attempt to mediate between science and religion.... He hopes to use the subconscious mind not as the final word in his philosophy of religion, but rather as a secure starting point from which to generate a more ambitious, if more tentative, hypothesis" (*Heaven's Champion*, 120–21).

40. John Grier Hibben, however, maintains that "in the subconscious region there may be the open door through which divine influences operate . . . but it may be also the region of chimeras and delusion" (review of *Varieties*, 185; cf. Taves, "Fragmentation of Consciousness," 62).

41. James notes that "the mass of phenomena generally called *mystical*" continue to be treated with contempt, even though "the phenomena are there, lying broadcast over the surface of history. No matter where you open its pages, you find things recorded under the name of divinations, inspirations, demoniacal possessions, apparitions, trances, ecstacies, miraculous healings and productions of disease, and occult powers possessed by peculiar individuals over persons and things in their neighborhood.... There never was a time when these things were not reported just as abundantly as now" (*WB* 223/*EPs* 248; cf. *EP* 165).

42. See *VRE* 302–23; cf. J. E. Smith, "William James's Account of Mysticism," 250–51.

43. John E. Smith writes of James's capacity for entering into the lives of others: "It was this virtue that enabled James to fulfill his obligation as an accurate observer of personal experience and to grasp this experience sympathetically without having to live through all of it himself" ("Introduction" to *VRE*, xvi).

44. Adolf Augustus Berle urges us to be more skeptical. James, he writes, "exhibits

here a credulity which is hardly accordant with the demands of the enlightened intellect of our age.... We cannot swallow in this reckless fashion, as evidence of things unseen, the testimonies which if made at the time would be defective, because few men can accurately make a self-diagnosis under the very best conditions, and which, made after years of increment of religious activity, instruction, and discipline, are undoubtedly of some scientific worth, but for the particular purposes to which they are applied, in our judgment, scientifically worthless or nearly so.... Most of these data have absolutely no means of verification. They can be subjected to no test at all, but the subjective test of the investigator's own mind" ("Psychology of Christian Experience," 10–12; cf. "Professor James on Religious Experience," 933).

45. For James Henry Leuba, James's position is "that the mystical experience points to, or signifies, a union of the individual with Someone or Something else. Now, that is just as much an interpretation of immediate experience as the affirmation of the Salvation Army lassie that she has met Christ face to face. Before it can be accepted as true the alleged 'immediate' experience in both instances must be tested according to the canons of scientific evidence, for the 'perceptual' quality of the experience no more justifies the mystic in placing credence in it than the absence of certain organic sensations authorizes the asylum patient to believe that the doctors have removed his viscera" (*Psychology of Religious Mysticism*, 309–10).

46. William James Earle notes that "the older dogmatists attempted to justify religion once and for all by pointing to its privileged origin in some kind of revelation; newer dogmatists—the 'medical materialists'—attempted to discredit religion once and for all by pointing to its disreputable origin in some curious bodily state. Neither approach is acceptable. Religion must be judged in the same way that everything else is judged, by proving itself useful (in specifiable ways) in some possible future" ("William James," 780).

47. As Etienne Gilson writes, "it is psychologically interesting to know that it does one good to *believe* there is a God; but that is not at all what the believer believes; what he actually believes is, that there *is* a God. The problem of religion requires that there is some being to which we must be bound; and the problem of Revelation requires that there is some divinely made statement to which we must bow. I am not at all denying the intrinsic validity of the other attitudes, but I beg to stress the fact that, useful and instructive as they may prove to be, they finally leave out the religious problem itself. Indeed, they cannot even ask it. After reading W. James, I still want to know if my religious experience is an experience of God, or an experience of myself. For in both cases there can be a psychological religious experience, but in the first case only can there be a religion" (*Reason and Revelation*, 96–97; cf. McTaggart, review of *Pragmatism*, 106–7; Singer, "Pragmatic Use of Language," 30–31; Henle, "Introduction," 125; Lovejoy to James, C 11: 424–25).

48. For Bertrand Russell, "the advantage of the pragmatic method is that it decides the question of the truth of the existence of God by purely mundane arguments,

namely, by the effects of belief in His existence upon our life in this world. But unfortunately this gives a merely mundane conclusion, namely, that belief in God is true, i.e. useful, whereas what religion desires is the conclusion that God exists, which pragmatism never even approaches" ("William James's Conception of Truth," 125; cf. Thayer, "Introduction" to P, xxxiii–xxxiv).

49. Frank Thilly writes that for James "Theism is the only conception of God that will satisfy our emotional and volitional nature. God is a part of the universe, a sympathetic and powerful helper, the great Companion, a conscious, personal, and moral being of the same nature as ourselves, with whom we can come into communion, as certain experiences (sudden conversions, faith-cures) show. To be sure, this theistic hypothesis cannot be completely proved, but neither can any system of philosophy be proved; every one of them is rooted in the will to believe. The essence of faith is not feeling or intelligence, but will, the will to believe what cannot be scientifically demonstrated or refuted" (*History of Philosophy*, 570; cf. Coe, review of *Varieties*, 65).

50. B. Russell, *History of Western Philosophy*, 818; "Philosophy of William James," 289; cf. "William James's Conception of Truth," 116.

51. B. Russell, *History of Western Philosophy*, 818.

52. Philip Kitcher writes that James is offering us "an unobjectionable psychological generalization: people who have had what they characterize as mystical experiences will typically conceive those experiences to be indicators of transcendent reality. The epistemological sting comes with James's claim that they have the right to do so. How do they come to have this right? . . . It would . . . seem reasonable for them to wonder if the voices they hear or the visions they see are different from the hallucinations of the drug taker or the delusions of the mentally ill" ("Pragmatist's Progress," 101).

53. This is one of the practical results of James's defense of such notions as "true for me" (SPP 113) that we encountered in chapter 4.

54. Edward H. Madden writes that "James's rejection of a block universe and his concept of pluralism entail the concept of a finite god . . . a deity not capable of wholly preventing or overthrowing evil but one who is actively and practically fighting against it." For James, such a god was preferable to an infinite one: "It is a god in the making and not one totally made in advance," a god that needs "not glorification but the cooperation of men in a mutual onslaught on the practical evils of life" ("Introduction" to WB, xxv–xxvi; cf. Mayer, *History of American Thought*, 287; J. S. Moore "Religious Significance," 53; E. C. Moore, *American Pragmatism*, 133–34; A. E. Taylor, review of *Pluralistic Universe*, 585).

55. Bertrand Russell would seem to be doing so when he writes: "That Man is the product of causes which had no prevision of the end they were achieving; that his origin, his growth, his hopes and fears, his loves and his beliefs, are but the outcome of accidental collocations of atoms; that no fire, no heroism, no intensity of thought and feeling, can preserve an individual life beyond the grave; that all the labours of the ages, all the devotion, all the inspiration, all the noonday brightness of human genius, are

destined to extinction in the vast death of the solar system, and that the whole temple of Man's achievement must inevitably be buried beneath the debris of a universe in ruins—all these things, if not quite beyond dispute, are yet so nearly certain, that no philosophy which rejects them can hope to stand. Only within the scaffolding of these truths, only on the firm foundation of unyielding despair, can the soul's habitation henceforth be safely built" ("Free Man's Worship," 67).

56. Richard Rorty writes that "we do not mock a mother who believes in her sociopathic child's essential goodness, even when that goodness is visible to no one else. James urges us not to mock those who accept what he calls 'the religious hypothesis'—the hypothesis that says 'the best things are the more eternal things' [WB 29]—merely because we see no evidence for this hypothesis, and a lot of evidence against it" ("Religious Faith," 94).

57. For thinkers like John Dewey, of course, "religious" is an adjective that applies more naturalistically to "attitudes that lend deep and enduring support to the processes of living" in the face of the admission that there is no permanent meaning (*Common Faith*, in *Later Works*, 9:12; cf. my *Understanding John Dewey*, 268–82).

Works Cited

Addams, Jane. *Newer Ideals of Peace*. Urbana: University of Illinois Press, [1906] 2007.
Allen, Gay Wilson. *William James: A Biography*. London: Rupert Hart-Davis, 1967.
Allport, Gordon W. *The Individual and His Religion: A Psychological Interpretation*. New York: Macmillan, 1950.
Angell, James Roland. Review of James, *Pragmatism*. International Journal of Ethics 18, no. 22 (January 1908): 226–35.
———. "William James." *The Psychological Review* 18, no. 1 (January 1911): 78–82.
Anonymous. *Alcoholics Anonymous: The Story of How Many Thousands of Men and Women Have Recovered from Alcoholism*. 3rd ed. New York: Alcoholics Anonymous World Services, 1976.
———. "The Military Spirit and Pragmatism." *Living Age* 69, no. 3458 (15 October 1910): 177–79.
Ayer, Alfred Jules. *Metaphysics and Common Sense*. San Francisco: Freeman, Cooper, 1970.
———. *The Origins of Pragmatism: Studies in the Philosophy of Charles Sanders Peirce and William James*. San Francisco: Freeman, Cooper, 1968.
Bakewell, Charles Montague. "Introduction" to *Selected Papers on Philosophy* by William James, v–x. New York: Dutton, 1917.
———. "On the Meaning of Truth." *Philosophical Review* 17, no. 6 (November 1908): 579–91.
———. Review of James, *Pragmatism*. *Philosophical Review* 16, no. 6 (November 1907): 624–34.
Baldwin, James Mark, editor. *Dictionary of Philosophy and Psychology*. 3 vols. New York: Macmillan, 1901–5.
Barnard, G. William. "*The Varieties of Religious Experience*: Reflections on Its Enduring Value." *Journal of Consciousness Studies* 9, nos. 9–10 (September–October 2002): 57–77.
Barzun, Jacques. *The Energies of Art: Studies of Authors, Classic and Modern*. New York: Harper and Bros, 1956.
———. *A Stroll with William James*. Cambridge: Harper and Row, 1983.
———. "William James: The Mind as Artist." *A Century of Psychology as Science*, edited by S. Koch and D. E. Leary, 904–10. Washington, D.C.: American Psychological Association, 1992.

Works Cited

Baum, Maurice. "The Attitude of William James toward Science." *Monist* 42, no. 4 (October 1932): 585–604.
Bawden, Henry Heath. *The Principles of Pragmatism: A Philosophical Interpretation of Experience*. Boston: Houghton Mifflin, 1910.
Beach, Joseph Warren. *The Outlook for American Prose*. Chicago: University of Chicago Press, 1926.
Beard, George Miller. *American Nervousness: Its Causes and Consequences*. New York: Putnam's, 1881.
———. *A Practical Treatise of Nervous Exhaustion (Neurasthenia): Its Systems, Nature, Sequences, Treatment*. New York: Treat, 1888.
———. *Sexual Neurasthenia: Its Hygiene, Causes, Symptoms and Treatment*. New York: Treat, 1884.
Beers, Clifford Whittingham. *A Mind That Found Itself: An Autobiography*. New York: Longmans, Green, 1908.
Bentham, Jeremy. Selection from *An Introduction to the Principles of Morals and Legislation* [1789]. *The English Philosophers from Bacon to Mill*, edited by E. A. Burtt, 827–91. New York: Modern Library, 1939.
Bergson, Henri. *The Creative Mind*, translated by Mabelle L. Andison. New York: Philosophical Library, 1946.
———. *An Introduction to Metaphysics*, translated by T. E. Hulme. New York: Putnam, 1912.
Berle, Adolf Augustus. "Professor James on Religious Experience." *Congregationalist and Christian World* 87, no. 51 (20 December 1902): 933.
———. "The Psychology of Christian Experience." *Bibliotheca Sacra* 60 (January 1903): 1–27.
Bernstein, Richard J. "Introduction" to James, *A Pluralistic Universe*, xi–xxix.
Bixler, Julius Seelye. "Two Questions Raised by 'The Moral Equivalent of War.'" Kallen, *In Commemoration of William James, 1842–1942*, 58–71.
———. "William James as Religious Thinker." Sellery and Dykstra, *William James: The Man and the Thinker*, 119–41.
Bjork, Daniel W. *The Compromised Scientist: William James in the Development of American Psychology*. New York: Columbia University Press, 1983.
———. *William James: The Center of His Vision*. New York: Columbia University Press, 1988.
Björkman, Edwin. "William James, the Man and the Thinker." *American Review of Reviews* 37 (January 1908): 45–48.
Blanshard, Brand. "The Ethics of Belief." *Philosophic Exchange* 1 (1971): 81–93.
Blau, Joseph Leon. *Men and Movements in American Philosophy*. Englewood Cliffs, NJ: Prentice-Hall, 1952.
Boas, George. *The Major Traditions of European Philosophy*. New York: Harper, 1929.

Works Cited

Bode, Boyd Henry. "William James in the American Tradition." Sellery and Dykstra, *William James: The Man and the Thinker*, 101–16.

Boodin, John Elof. *Truth and Reality: An Introduction to the Theory of Knowledge*. New York: Macmillan, 1911.

Boring, Edwin G. *A History of Experimental Psychology*. New York: Century, 1929.

Brett, George S. "The Psychology of William James in Relation to Philosophy." Kallen, *In Commemoration of William James, 1842–1942*, 81–94.

Brodbeck, May. "Philosophy in America, 1900–1950." *American Non-Fiction, 1900–1950*, edited by Brodbeck, James Gray, and Walter Metzger, 3–94. Chicago: Regnery, 1952.

Brooks, Van Wyck. *The Confident Years: 1885–1915*. New York: E. P. Dutton, 1952.

Brown, Harold Chapman. "Philosophy." *Civilization in the United States: An Inquiry by Thirty Americans*, edited by H. E. Stearns, 163–77. New York: Harcourt, Brace, 1922.

Bush, Wendell T. "The Empiricism of James." *Journal of Philosophy* 10, no. 20 (25 September 1913): 533–41.

Caldecott, A. "The Work of William James: I—As Pragmatist." *Sociological Review* 3, no. 4 (October 1910): 310–14.

Caldwell, William. *Pragmatism and Idealism*. London: Adam and Charles Black, 1913.

Calkins, Mary Whiton. *An Introduction to Psychology*. New York: Macmillan, 1901.

———. "Militant Pacifism." *International Journal of Ethics* 28, no. 1 (October 1917): 70–79.

Campbell, James. "Ayer and Pragmatism." *The Philosophy of A. J. Ayer*, edited by L. E. Hahn, 83–104. Library of Living Philosophers 21. Chicago: Open Court, 1992.

———. "A History of Pragmatism." *The Continuum Companion to Pragmatism*, edited by Sami Pihlström, 69–80. New York: Continuum International, 2011.

———. "One Hundred Years of *Pragmatism*: *Transactions of the Charles S. Peirce Society* 43, no. 1 (Winter 2007): 1–15.

———. *Recovering Benjamin Franklin: An Exploration of a Life of Science and Service*. Chicago: Open Court, 1999.

———. "A Study of Human Nature Entitled *The Varieties of Religious Experience*." *Journal of Speculative Philosophy* 17, no. 1 (2003): 14–29.

———. "Systems of Justice and the Role of the Moral Prophet." *Justice through Diversity? A Philosophical and Theological Debate*, edited by M. A. Sweeney, 81–97. Lanham, MD: Rowman and Littlefield, 2016.

———. *A Thoughtful Profession: The Early Years of the American Philosophical Association*. Chicago: Open Court, 2006.

———. *Understanding John Dewey: Nature and Cooperative Intelligence*. Chicago: Open Court, 1995.

———. "William James and the Ethics of Fulfillment." *Transactions of the Charles S. Peirce Society* 17, no. 3 (Summer 1981): 224–40.

Carpenter, Frederic Ives. "Points of Comparison between Emerson and William James." *New England Quarterly* 2, no. 3 (July 1929): 458–74.
———. "William James and Emerson." *American Literature* 11, no. 1 (March 1939): 39–57.
Carus, Paul. Comments on Schiller and Armstrong. *Bericht über den III. Internationalen Kongress für Philosophie*, edited by Theodor Elsenhans, 737. Heidelberg: Carl Winter's Universitätbuchhandlung, 1909.
———. *Truth on Trial: An Exposition of the Nature of Truth*. Chicago: Open Court, 1911.
Cattell, James McKeen. Note on the Society for Psychical Research [1898]. James, *Essays in Psychical Research*, 186.
Chapman, John Jay. "William James." *Selected Writings of John Jay Chapman*, edited by Jacques Barzun, 203–7. New York: Farrar, Straus, & Cudahy, 1957.
Clifford, William Kingdon. "The Ethics of Belief" [1877]. *Lectures and Essays*, edited by Leslie Stephen and Frederick Pollock, 2:177–211. 2 vols. London: Macmillan, 1879.
Coe, George Albert. Review of James, *The Varieties of Religious Experience*. *Philosophical Review* 12, no. 1 (January 1903): 62–67.
Cohen, Morris Raphael. *American Thought: A Critical Sketch*. Glencoe, IL: Free Press, 1954.
———. *A Dreamer's Journey: The Autobiography of Morris Raphael Cohen*. Glencoe, IL: Free Press, 1949.
———. *The Faith of a Liberal*. New York: Henry Holt, 1946.
———. *A Preface to Logic*. New York: Henry Holt, 1944.
———. *Reason and Nature: An Essay on the Meaning of Scientific Method*. Glencoe, IL: Free Press, [1931]; rev. ed. 1953.
Coles, Robert. Review of James, *The Varieties of Religious Experience*. *New Republic* (2 October 1971): 28–31.
Commager, Henry Steele. *The American Mind: An Interpretation of American Thought and Character since the 1880s*. New Haven: Yale University Press, 1950.
Conkin, Paul K. *Puritans and Pragmatists: Eight Eminent American Thinkers*. Bloomington: Indiana University Press, 1968.
Cooley, Charles Horton. *Human Nature and the Social Order*. New York: Scribners, 1912.
———. *Social Organization: A Study of the Larger Mind*. New York: Scribners, 1916.
Coon, Deborah J. "Testing the Limits of Sense and Science: American Experimental Psychologists Combat Spiritualism, 1880–1920." *American Psychologist* 47, no. 2 (February 1992): 143–51.
Copleston, Frederick Charles. "The Pragmatism of James and Schiller." *A History of Philosophy*. Vol. 8, pt. 2, 86–108. Garden City, NY: Doubleday, 1966.

Cotkin, George. *William James: Public Philosopher*. Baltimore: Johns Hopkins University Press, 1990.
Creighton, James Edwin. "The Nature and Criterion of Truth." *Philosophical Review* 17, no. 6 (November 1908): 592–605.
Csikszentmihalyi, Mihaly. *Flow: The Psychology of Optimal Experience*. New York: Harper and Row, 1990.
Curti, Merle Eugene. *The Growth of American Thought*. New York: Harper and Bros. 1943.
———. *The Social Ideas of American Educators*. Paterson, NJ: Littlefield, Adams, [1935] 1959.
Deegan, Mary Jo. *Self, War, and Society: George Herbert Mead's Macrosociology*. New Brunswick, NJ: Transaction, 2008.
Dewey, John. *The Later Works of John Dewey, 1925–1953*, edited by J. A. Boydston. 17 vols. Carbondale: Southern Illinois University Press, 1981–90.
———. *The Middle Works of John Dewey, 1899–1924*, edited by J. A. Boydston. 15 vols. Carbondale: Southern Illinois University Press, 1976–83.
Douglass, Frederick. "Why Should a Colored Man Enlist?" [1863]. *Frederick Douglass: Selected Speeches and Writings*, edited by P. S. Foner and Y. Taylor, 528–31. New York: Lawrence Hill Books, 1999.
Drake, Durant, Arthur O. Lovejoy, James Bissett Pratt, Arthur K. Rogers, George Santayana, Roy Wood Sellers, and Charles A. Strong. *Essays in Critical Realism: A Co-operative Study of the Problem of Knowledge*. London: Macmillan, 1920.
Du Bois, W. E. B. *Writings*, edited by Nathan Huggins. New York: Library of America, 1986.
Durkheim, Emile. *Pragmatism and Sociology* [1913–1914]. *Emil Durkheim, 1858–1917*, edited by Kurt H. Wolff, 386–436. Columbus: Ohio State University Press, 1960.
Earle, William James. "William James (1842–1910)." *Encyclopedia of Philosophy*, edited by D. M. Borchert, 4:774–86. 10 vols. Detroit: Thomson Gale, [1967]; 2nd ed. 2006.
Edie, James M. "William James and the Phenomenology of Religious Experience." *American Philosophy and the Future*, edited by Michael Novak, 247–69. New York: Scribners, 1968.
Emerson, Ralph Waldo. *The Complete Works of Ralph Waldo Emerson*, edited by E. W. Emerson. 12 vols. Boston: Houghton, Mifflin, 1904.
———. *The Journals and Miscellaneous Notebooks of Ralph Waldo Emerson*, edited by W. H. Gilman, R. H. Orth, and A. R. Ferguson. 16 vols. Cambridge: Harvard University Press, 1960–82.
Evans, Rand B. "Introduction: The Historical Context" to James, *The Principles of Psychology*, 1:xli–lxviii.
———. "William James and His *Principles*." *Reflections on "The Principles of Psychol-*

ogy": *William James after a Century*, edited by M. G. Johnson and T. B. Henley, 11–31. Hillsdale, NJ: Lawrence Erlbaum, 1990.

Ewer, Bernard C. "The Influence of William James upon Psychology." *Personalist* 23 (Spring 1942): 150–58.

Fay, Jay Wharton. *American Psychology before William James*. New Brunswick, NJ: Rutgers University Press, 1939.

Fechner, Gustav Theodor. *Die Tagesansicht gegenüber der Nachtansicht*. Leipzig: Breitkopf und Härtel, 1879.

Feinstein, Howard M. *Becoming William James*. Ithaca: Cornell University Press, 1984.

Fisch, Max Harold. *Peirce, Semeiotic and Pragmatism: Essays by Max H. Fisch*, edited by K. L. Ketner and C. J. W. Kloesel. Bloomington: Indiana University Press, 1986.

Fishbein, Morris. *The New Medical Follies*. New York: Boni and Liveright, 1927.

Fisher, Paul. *House of Wits: An Intimate Portrait of the James Family*. New York: Henry Holt, 2008.

Fiske, John. "The Meaning of Infancy" [1883]. *Miscellaneous Writings of John Fiske*, 7:279–91. 12 vols. Boston: Houghton-Mifflin, 1902.

Fletcher, Horace. *Happiness as Found in Forethought minus Fearthought*. Chicago: Stone, 1897.

Flower, Elizabeth, and Murray G. Murphey. *A History of Philosophy in America*. 2 vols. New York: Putnam, 1977.

Fontinell, Eugene. *Self, God, and Immortality: A Jamesian Investigation*. Philadelphia: Temple University Press, 1986.

Frankel, Charles. "Introduction" to *The Golden Age of American Philosophy*, edited by Frankel, 1–17. New York: Braziller, 1960.

Franklin, Benjamin. *Writings*, edited by J. A. Leo Lemay. New York: Library of America, 1987.

French, Frederick Courtney. Abstract of "The Relation of Psychology to the Philosophy of Religion." *Journal of Philosophy* 2 (1905): 380–81.

Fullerton, George Stuart. "The Right to Believe at One's Own Risk." *Philosophical Review* 16, no. 4 (July 1907): 408–18.

Gardner, Martin. *The Night Is Large: Collected Essays, 1938–1995*. New York: St. Martin's Press, 1996.

Garrison, George R. and Edward H. Madden. "William James—Warts and All." *American Quarterly* 29, no. 2 (Summer 1977): 207–21.

Gavin, William Joseph. *William James and the Reinstatement of the Vague*. Philadelphia: Temple University Press, 1992.

Gifford, Adam. "Ralph Waldo Emerson" [1872]. *Lectures Delivered on Various Occasions*, 3–37. N.p.: N.p. 1899.

Gilson, Etienne. *Reason and Revelation in the Middle Ages*. New York: Scribners, 1938.

Works Cited

Gould, James A. "R. B. Perry on the Origin of American and European Pragmatism." *Journal of the History of Philosophy* 8 (1970): 431–50.
Habegger, Alfred. *The Father: A Life of Henry James, Sr.* New York: Farrar, Straus and Giroux, 1994.
Hall, Granville Stanley. *Adolescence: Its Psychology and Its Relations to Physiology, Anthropology, Sociology, Sex, Crime, Religion and Education.* 2 vols. New York: Appleton: 1907.
———. "Practical Relations between Psychology and the War." *Journal of Applied Psychology* 1, no.1 (March 1917): 9–16.
———. Review of James, *The Principles of Psychology*. *American Journal of Psychology* 3, no. 4 (February 1891): 578–91.
Hare, Peter H. "Introduction" to James, *Some Problems of Philosophy*, xiii–xli.
Henle, Paul. "Introduction" to Selections from William James. *Classic American Philosophers*, edited by M. H. Fisch, 115–27. Englewood Cliffs, NJ: Prentice-Hall, 1951.
Hibben, John Grier. Review of James, *The Varieties of Religious Experience*. *Psychological Review* 10, no. 2 (March 1903): 180–86.
———. "The Test of Pragmatism." *Philosophical Review* 17, no. 4 (July 1908): 365–82.
Hick, John. *Faith and Knowledge*. Ithaca: Cornell University Press, [1957]; 2nd ed. 1966.
High, Richard P. and William R. Woodward. "William James and Gordon Allport: Parallels in Their Maturing Conceptions of Self and Personality." *Psychology: Theoretical-Historical Perspectives*, edited by R. W. Rieber and K. Salzinger, 57–79. New York: Academic Press, 1980.
Hocking, William Ernest. *The Meaning of God in Human Experience: A Philosophic Study of Religion*. New Haven: Yale University Press, 1912.
———. *Types of Philosophy*. New York: Scribners, 1929.
Hollinger, David A. "'Damned for God's Glory': William James and the Scientific Vindication of Protestant Culture." Proudfoot, *William James and a Science of Religions*, 9–31.
———. "James, Clifford, and the Scientific Conscience." *The Cambridge Companion to William James*, edited by R. A. Putnam, 69–83. Cambridge: Cambridge University Press, 1997.
———. "The Problem of Pragmatism in American History." *Journal of American History* 67, no. 1 (June 1980): 88–107.
Holmes, Oliver Wendell. "The Holmes–Cohen Correspondence," edited by F. S. Cohen. *Journal of the History of Ideas* 9, no. 1 (January 1948): 3–52.
———. *Holmes–Pollock Letters: The Correspondence of Mr. Justice Holmes and Sir Frederick Pollock, 1874–1932*, edited by M. D. Howe. 2 vols. Cambridge: Harvard University Press, 1941.
———. "The Soldier's Faith" [1895]. *The Collected Works of Justice Holmes: Complete*

Works Cited

Published Writings and Selected Judicial Opinions of Oliver Wendell Holmes, edited by S. M. Novak, 3:486–91. 5 vols. Chicago: University of Chicago Press, 1995.
———. *Towne v. Eisner*, 245 US 418–27 (1917), *United States Reports*. New York: Banks Law Publishing, 1918.
Holt, Edwin Bissell. "William James as Psychologist." Kallen, *In Commemoration of William James, 1842–1942*, 34–47.
Holt, Edwin Bissell, Walter Taylor Marvin, William Pepperell Montague, Ralph Barton Perry, Walter B. Pitkin, and Edward Gleason Spaulding. *The New Realism: Cooperative Studies in Philosophy*. New York: Macmillan, 1912.
Jacks, Lawrence Pearsall. "William James and His Message." *Contemporary Review* 99 (1911): 20–33.
Jaki, Stanley L. *Lord Gifford and His Lectures: A Centenary Retrospect*. Macon, GA: Mercer University Press, 1986.
James, Henry. *Autobiographies*, edited by Philip Horne. New York: Library of America, 2016.
James, William. *The Correspondence of William James*, edited by Ignaz K. Skrupskelis and Elizabeth M. Berkeley. 12 vols. Charlottesville: University Press of Virginia, 1992–2004.
———. *Essays, Comments, and Reviews*. Cambridge: Harvard University Press, 1987.
———. *Essays in Philosophy*. Cambridge: Harvard University Press, 1978.
———. *Essays in Psychical Research*. Cambridge: Harvard University Press, 1986.
———. *Essays in Psychology*. Cambridge: Harvard University Press, 1983.
———. *Essays in Radical Empiricism*. Cambridge: Harvard University Press, [1912] 1976.
———. *Essays in Religion and Morality*. Cambridge: Harvard University Press, 1982.
———. *The Letters of William James*, edited by his son Henry James. 2 vols. Boston: Atlantic Monthly Press, 1920.
———. *Manuscript Essays and Notes*. Cambridge: Harvard University Press, 1988.
———. *Manuscript Lectures*. Cambridge: Harvard University Press, 1988.
———. *The Meaning of Truth*. Cambridge: Harvard University Press, [1909] 1975.
———. *A Pluralistic Universe*. Cambridge: Harvard University Press, [1909] 1977.
———. *Pragmatism: A New Name for Some Old Ways of Thinking*. Cambridge: Harvard University Press, [1907] 1975.
———. *The Principles of Psychology*. 3 vols. Cambridge: Harvard University Press, [1890] 1981.
———. *Psychology: Briefer Course*. Cambridge: Harvard University Press, [1892] 1984.
———. *Some Problems of Philosophy*. Cambridge: Harvard University Press, [1911] 1979.
———. *Talks to Teachers on Psychology and to Students on Some of Life's Ideals*. Cambridge: Harvard University Press, [1899] 1983.

———. *The Varieties of Religious Experience: A Study in Human Nature*. Cambridge: Harvard University Press, [1902] 1985.

———. *The Will to Believe and Other Essays in Popular Philosophy*. Cambridge: Harvard University Press, [1897] 1979.

———. *The Writings of William James: A Comprehensive Edition*, edited by J. J. McDermott. New York: Random House, 1967.

Jastrow, Joseph. "An American Academician." *Educational Review* 41, no. 1 (January 1911): 27–33.

———. *Fact and Fable in Psychology*. Boston: Houghton, Mifflin, 1900.

———. "Pathology." *Dictionary of Philosophy and Psychology*, edited by J. M. Baldwin, 2:267–68. 3 vols. New York: Macmillan, 1902.

Jefferson, Thomas. *Writings*, edited by M. D. Peterson. New York: Library of America, 1984.

Kallen, Horace Meyer. "Foreword" to Kallen, *In Commemoration of William James, 1842–1942*, v–x.

———. "Introduction: The Meaning of William James for 'Us Moderns,'" 1–55. *The Philosophy of William James: Selected from His Chief Works*. New York: Modern Library, 1925.

———. *William James and Henri Bergson: A Study in Contrasting Theories of Life*. Chicago: University of Chicago Press, 1914.

———, ed. *In Commemoration of William James, 1842–1942*. New York: Columbia University Press, 1942.

Kaltenborn, Hans von. "William James at Harvard." *Harvard Illustrated Magazine* 8, no. 5 (February 1907): 93–95.

Kennedy, Gail. "Pragmatism, Pragmaticism, and the Will to Believe—A Reconsideration." *Journal of Philosophy* 55, no. 14 (3 July 1958): 578–88.

Kitcher, Philip. "A Pragmatist's Progress: The Varieties of James's Strategies for Defending Religion." Proudfoot, *William James and a Science of Religions*, 98–138.

Knight, Margaret. "Introduction" to *William James: A Selection from His Writings on Psychology*, ed. Knight, 13–62. Baltimore: Penguin, 1954.

Knox, Howard Vincente. *The Philosophy of William James*. London: Constable, 1914.

Kraushaar, Otto F. "Lotze's Influence on the Pragmatism and Practical Philosophy of William James." *Journal of the History of Ideas* 1, no. 4 (October 1940): 439–58.

Kuklick, Bruce. *The Rise of American Philosophy: Cambridge, Massachusetts, 1860–1930*. New Haven: Yale University Press, 1977.

Ladd, George Trumbull. "Is Psychology a Science?" *Psychological Review* 1, no. 4 (July 1894): 392–95.

———. *Outlines of Physiological Psychology*. New York: Scribners, 1891.

———. "Psychology as So-Called 'Natural Science.'" *Philosophical Review* 1, no. 1 (January 1892): 24–53.

Works Cited

Lash, Nicholas. *Easter in Ordinary: Reflections on Human Experience and the Knowledge of God*. Notre Dame: University of Notre Dame Press, 1988.
Lee, Vernon (Violet Paget). "The Two Pragmatisms." *North American Review* 192 (October 1910): 449–63.
Leuba, James Henry. *The Psychology of Religious Mysticism*. New York: Harcourt, Brace, 1925.
Levin, Michael. "Why Not Pragmatism?" *Commentary* 75, no. 1 (January 1983): 43–47.
Levinson, Henry Samuel. *The Religious Investigations of William James*. Chapel Hill: University of North Carolina Press, 1981.
Lewis, Clarence Irving. *Mind and the World Order: Outline of a Theory of Knowledge*. New York: Scribners, 1929.
Lewis, R. W. B. *The Jameses: A Family Narrative*. New York: Farrar, Straus and Giroux, 1991.
Lippmann, Walter. *Public Opinion*. New York: Macmillan, [1921] 1960.
———. "William James" [1910]. *Public Persons*, edited by G. A. Harrison, 20–23. New York: Liveright, 1976.
Lovejoy, Arthur Oncken. "Present Philosophical Tendencies." *Journal of Philosophy* 9, no. 23 (7 November 1912): 627–40.
———. "The Thirteen Pragmatisms" [1908]. *The Thirteen Pragmatisms, and Other Essays*. Baltimore: Johns Hopkins Press, 1963, 1–29.
———. "William James as Philosopher" [1911]. *The Thirteen Pragmatisms, and Other Essays*, 79–112.
Lowe, Victor. "William James's Pluralistic Metaphysics of Experience." Kallen, *In Commemoration of William James, 1842–1942*, 157–77.
Mace, C. A. "Editorial Foreword" to *William James: A Selection from His Writings on Psychology*, edited by Margaret Knight, 7–10. London: Penguin, 1954.
Machado, Maria Helena P. T. editor. *Brazil through the Eyes of William James*. Cambridge: Harvard University Press, 2006.
Madden, Edward H. "Introduction" to *The Correspondence of William James*, vol. 8. C 8:xxiii–xlvii.
———. "Introduction" to James, *The Will to Believe*, xi–xxxviii.
Madden, Marian C. and Edward H. Madden. "The Psychosomatic Illnesses of William James." *Thought* 54 (December 1979): 376–91.
Maher, Jane. *Biography of Broken Fortunes: Wilkie and Bob, Brothers of William, Henry, and Alice James*. Hamden, CT: Archon, 1986.
Marty, Martin E. "Introduction" to James, *The Varieties of Religious Experience*, vii–xxvii. New York: Penguin, 1982.
Matthiessen, Francis Otto. *The James Family*. New York: Knopf, 1947.
Mayer, Frederick. *A History of American Thought: An Introduction*. Dubuque, IA: William C. Brown, 1951.

McDermott, John Joseph. *The Culture of Experience: Philosophical Essays in the American Grain*. New York: New York University Press, 1977.
———. "Foreword" to Charlene Haddock Seigfried, *Chaos and Context: A Study in William James*, ix–xiii. Athens: Ohio University Press, 1978.
———. "Introduction" to James, *Essays in Philosophy*, xi–xxxv.
———. "Introduction" to James, *Essays in Radical Empiricism*, xi–xlviii.
———. "Introduction" to James, *Essays in Religion and Morality*, xi–xxvii.
———. "Introduction" to James, *The Writings of William James*, xiii–xliv.
———. "Introduction" to Selections from William James, *Pragmatism and Classical American Philosophy: Readings and Interpretive Essays*, edited by J. J. Stuhr, 140–51. New York: Oxford University Press, 2000.
———. "A Jamesian Personscape: The Fringe as Messaging to the 'Sick Soul.'" *Harvard Divinity Bulletin* 39, nos. 3–4 (Summer/Autumn 2011): http://bulletin.hds.harvard.edu/articles/summerautumn2011/jamesian-personscape.
———. *Streams of Experience: Reflections on the History and Philosophy of American Culture*. Amherst: University of Massachusetts Press, 1986.
McDermott, Robert A. "Introduction" to James, *Essays in Psychical Research*, xiii–xxxvi.
McDougall, William. "The Works of William James: II—as Psychologist." *Sociological Review* 3, no. 4 (October 1910): 314–15.
McGill, Vivian J. "Pragmatism Reconsidered: An Aspect of John Dewey's Philosophy." *Science and Society* 3, no. 3 (Summer 1939): 289–322.
McTaggart, John McTaggart Ellis. Review of *Pragmatism*. *Mind*, n.s. 17, no. 65 (January 1908): 104–9.
Mead, George Herbert. *Mind, Self and Society from the Standpoint of a Social Behaviorist*, edited by C. W. Morris. Chicago: University of Chicago Press, 1934.
———. *Movements of Thought in the Nineteenth Century*, edited by M. H. Moore. Chicago: University of Chicago Press, 1936.
———. "National-Mindedness and International-Mindedness" [1929]. *Selected Writings*, edited by A. J. Reck, 355–70. Chicago: University of Chicago Press, 1981.
Meiklejohn, Alexander. *What Does America Mean?* New York: Norton, [1935] 1972.
Menand, Louis. *The Metaphysical Club: A Story of Ideas in America*. New York: Farrar, Straus and Giroux, 2001.
———. "William James and the Case of the Epileptic Patient." *New York Review of Books* (17 December 1998): 81–93.
Mill, John Stuart. *On Liberty* [1859]. *The English Philosophers from Bacon to Mill*, edited by E. A. Burtt, 949–1041. New York: Modern Library, 1939.
Miller, Dickinson Sergeant. "James's Doctrine of 'The Right to Believe.'" *Philosophical Review* 51, no. 6 (November 1942): 541–58.
———. "Some of the Tendencies of Professor James's Work." *Journal of Philosophy* 7, no. 24 (24 November 1910): 645–64.

———. "'The Will to Believe' and the Duty to Doubt." *International Journal of Ethics* 9, no. 2 (January 1899): 169–95.

———. "William James, Man and Philosopher." Sellery and Dykstra, *William James: The Man and the Thinker*, 31–52.

Miller, Joshua I. *Democratic Temperament: The Legacy of William James*. Lawrence: University Press of Kansas, 1997.

Mills, C. Wright. *Sociology and Pragmatism: The Higher Learning in America*, edited by I. L. Horowitz. New York: Oxford University Press, 1966.

Moore, Addison Webster. *Pragmatism and Its Critics*. Chicago: University of Chicago Press, 1910.

Moore, Edward Carter. *American Pragmatism: Peirce, James, and Dewey*. New York: Columbia University Press, 1961.

———. *William James*. New York: Washington Square Press, 1965.

Moore, George Edward. "William James' 'Pragmatism'" [1908]. *Philosophical Studies*, 97–146. London: Routledge and Keegan Paul, 1922.

Moore, Jared Sparks. "The Religious Significance of the Philosophy of William James." *Sewanee Review* 21 (January 1913): 41–58.

More, Paul Elmer. "The New Stage of Pragmatism." *The Nation* 88 (6 May 1909): 456–59.

Müller, Gustav Emil. *Amerikanische Philosophie*. Stuttgart: Fr. Frommanns Verlag, [1936]; 2nd ed. 1950.

Muirhead, John Henry. "Professor William James's Philosophy of Religion." *International Journal of Ethics* 13, no. 2 (January 1903): 236–46.

Mumford, Lewis. *The Golden Day: A Study in American Literature and Culture*. Boston: Beacon, [1926]; rev. ed. 1957.

Münsterberg, Hugo. *American Problems from the Point of View of a Psychologist*. New York: Moffatt, Yard, 1910.

Murphey, Murray G. "Kant's Children: The Cambridge Pragmatists." *Transactions of the Charles S. Peirce Society* 4, no. 1 (Winter 1968): 3–33.

Murphy, Arthur Edward. "Philosophical Scholarship." *American Scholarship in the Twentieth Century*, edited by M. E. Curti, 168–206. Cambridge: Harvard University Press, 1953.

Murphy, Gardner. *An Historical Introduction to Modern Psychology*. Rev. ed. New York, Harcourt, Brace, 1930.

Murray, David Leslie. *Pragmatism*. London: Constable, 1912.

Myers, Gerald E. "Introduction: The Intellectual Context" to James, *The Principles of Psychology*, 1:xi–xl.

———. "Introduction" to James, *Talks to Teachers*, xi–xxvii.

———. "Pragmatism and Introspective Psychology." *The Cambridge Companion to William James*, edited by R. A. Putnam, 11–24. Cambridge: Cambridge University Press, 1997.

Works Cited

———. *William James: His Life and Thought.* New Haven: Yale University Press, 1986.

Note on the death of William James. *Psychological Review.* 19, no. 6 (November 1910): 694.

Ormond, Alexander Thomas. "Religion." *Dictionary of Philosophy and Psychology,* edited by J. M. Baldwin, 2:452. 3 vols. New York: Macmillan, 1902.

Otto, Max Carl. "The Distinctive Philosophy of William James." Sellery and Dykstra, *William James: The Man and the Thinker,* 7–27.

———. "On a Certain Blindness in William James." *Ethics* 53, no. 3 (April 1943): 184–91.

Palmer, George Herbert. "William James." *Harvard Graduates' Magazine* 29 (September 1920): 29–34.

Papini, Giovanni. "What Pragmatism Is Like." *Popular Science Monthly* 71 (October 1907): 351–58.

Parkes, Henry Bamford. *The American Experience: An Interpretation of the History and Civilization of the American People.* New York: Knopf, 1947.

Peirce, Charles Sanders. *Collected Papers of Charles Sanders Peirce,* edited by C. Hartshorne, P. Weiss, and A. W. Burks. 8 vols. Cambridge: Harvard University Press, 1931–60.

———. *Writings of Charles S. Peirce: A Chronological Edition,* edited by M. H. Fisch, et al. Bloomington: Indiana University Press, 1982–.

Perry, Ralph Barton. *In the Spirit of William James.* New Haven: Yale University Press, 1938.

———. "James the Psychologist—As a Philosopher Sees Him." *Psychological Review* 50, no. 1 (January 1943): 122–24.

———. *Present Philosophical Tendencies: A Critical Survey of Naturalism, Idealism, Pragmatism and Realism, together with a Synopsis of the Philosophy of William James.* New York: Longmans Green, 1912.

———. "Professor James as a Philosopher." *Harvard Illustrated Magazine* 8, no. 5 (February 1907): 96–97.

———. "A Review of Pragmatism as a Theory of Knowledge." Pts. 1 and 2. *Journal of Philosophy* 4, no. 14 (4 July 1907), 365–74; 4, no. 16 (1 August 1907), 421–28.

———. *The Thought and Character of William James.* 2 vols. Boston: Little, Brown, 1935.

Pollock, Robert Channon. "James: Pragmatism." *The Great Books: A Christian Appraisal,* edited by H. C. Gardiner, 4:187–98. 4 vols. New York: Devin-Adair, 1949–1953.

Pratt, James Bissett. "The Religious Philosophy of William James." *Hibbert Journal* 10, no. 1 (October 1911): 225–34.

———. "Truth and Ideas." *Journal of Philosophy* 5, no. 5 (27 February 1908): 122–31.

Proudfoot, Wayne. "Pragmatism and 'an Unseen Order' in *Varieties.*" Proudfoot, *William James and a Science of Religions,* 31–47.

———. ed. *William James and a Science of Religions: Reexperiencing "The Varieties of Religious Experience."* New York: Columbia University Press, 2004.
Rashdall, Hastings. Review of James, *The Varieties of Religious Experience. Mind*, n.s. 12, no. 46 (April 1903): 245–50.
Ratner, Joseph. "Introduction" to William James, *The Varieties of Religious Experience*, v–xxxiv. New Hyde Park, NY: University Books, 1963.
Ratner, Sidney. "Pragmatism in America." *Essays in American Historiography*, edited by D. Sheehan and H. C. Syrett, 193–216. New York: Columbia University Press, 1960.
Richardson, Robert D. *William James: In the Maelstrom of American Modernism*. Boston: Houghton Mifflin, 2006.
Riley, Isaac Woodbridge. *American Thought: From Puritanism to Pragmatism and Beyond*. New York: Henry Holt, 1915.
Roback, Abraham Aaron. *History of American Psychology*. New York: Library Publishers, 1952.
Roosevelt, Theodore. *The Strenuous Life: Essays and Addresses*. New York: Century, [1900] 1918.
Rorty, Richard. *Philosophy and Social Hope*. London: Penguin Books, 1999.
———. "Religious Faith, Intellectual Responsibility, and Romance." *The Cambridge Companion to William James*, edited by R. A. Putnam, 84–102. Cambridge: Cambridge University Press, 1997.
Rosenberg, Charles E. "The Place of George M. Beard in Nineteenth-Century Psychiatry." *Bulletin of the History of Medicine* 36 (1962): 245–59.
Royce, Josiah. "A New Study of Psychology." *International Journal of Ethics* 1, no. 2 (January 1891): 143–69.
———. *The Philosophy of Loyalty*. New York: Macmillan, 1908.
———. *The Problem of Christianity*. Chicago: University of Chicago Press, [1918] 1968.
———. "Self-Consciousness, Social Consciousness and Nature" [1898]. *The Basic Writings of Josiah Royce*, edited by J. J. McDermott, 1:423–61. 2 vols. Chicago: University of Chicago Press, 1969.
———. *The Spirit of Modern Philosophy: An Essay in the Form of Lectures*. Boston: Houghton, Mifflin, 1892.
———. "What Should Be the Attitude of Teachers of Philosophy towards Religion?" *International Journal of Ethics* 13, no. 3 (April 1903): 280–85.
———. "William James and the Philosophy of Life." *William James and Other Essays on the Philosophy of Life*. New York: Macmillan, 1912, 3–45.
Russell, Bertrand. "A Free Man's Worship" [1903]. *The Basic Writings of Bertrand Russell, 1903–1959*, edited by R. E. Egner and L. E. Denonn, 66–72. New York: Clarion, 1961.
———. *A History of Western Philosophy and Its Connection with Political and Social*

Circumstances from the Earliest Times to the Present Day. New York: Simon and Schuster, 1945.
———. "The Philosophy of William James" [1910]. *Logical and Philosophical Papers, 1909–1913*, edited by J. G. Slater, 286–89. New York: Routledge, 1992.
———. "Pragmatism" [1909]. *Philosophical Essays*, 79–111. New York: Simon and Schuster, 1966.
———. "William James's Conception of Truth" [1908]. *Philosophical Essays*, 112–30. New York: Simon and Schuster, 1966.
Russell, John Edward. Review of James, *The Meaning of Truth*. *Journal of Philosophy* 7, no. 1 (6 January 1910): 22–24.
———. "Some Difficulties with the Epistemology of Pragmatism and Radical Empiricism." *Philosophical Review* 15, no. 4 (July 1906): 406–13.
Salter, William Mackintire. "Pragmatism: A New Philosophy." *Atlantic Monthly* 101, no. 5 (May 1908): 657–63.
Santayana, George. "A General Confession" [1940]. *The Essential Santayana: Selected Writings*, 4–22. Bloomington: Indiana University Press, 2009.
———. "The Genteel Tradition in American Philosophy" [1911]. *The Essential Santayana*, 526–40.
———. "James's Psychology." *Atlantic Monthly* 67 (April 1891): 552–56.
———. *Persons and Places: Fragments of an Autobiography*, edited by W. G. Holzberger and H. J. Saatkamp Jr. Cambridge: MIT Press, [1944] 1986.
———. "Philosophical Heresy" [1915]. *The Essential Santayana*, 44–50.
———. "William James" [1920]. *The Essential Santayana*, 584–94.
Schiller, Ferdinand Canning Scott. *Must Philosophers Disagree? and Other Essays in Popular Philosophy*. London: Macmillan, 1934.
———. Review of James, *Pragmatism*. *Mind*, n.s. 16, no. 64 (October 1907): 598–604.
———. Review of James, *Some Problems of Philosophy*. *Mind*, n.s. 20, no. 80 (October 1911): 571–73.
———. Review of James, *The Varieties of Religious Experience*. *The Nation* 75 (21 August 1902): 155.
———. Review of James, *The Will to Believe*. *Mind*, n.s. 6, no. 24 (October 1897): 547–54.
———. "Why Humanism?" *Contemporary British Philosophy: Personal Statements*, edited by J. H. Muirhead, 387–410. London: Allen & Unwin, 1924.
Schinz, Albert. *Anti-Pragmatism: An Examination into the Respective Rights of Intellectual Aristocracy and Social Democracy*. Boston: Small, Maynard, 1909.
Schneider, Herbert Wallace. *A History of American Philosophy*. New York: Columbia University Press, [1946] 2nd edition 1963.
Schott, Linda. "Jane Addams and William James on Alternatives to War." *Journal of the History of Ideas* 54, no. 2 (April 1993): 241–54.

Works Cited

Schurman, Jacob Gould. Review of James, *The Will to Believe*. *Philosophical Review* 7, no. 1 (January 1898): 86–88.
Scripture, Edward Wheeler. *The New Psychology*. New York: Scribners, 1897.
Seigfried, Charlene Haddock. *Pragmatism and Feminism: Reweaving the Social Fabric*. Chicago: University of Chicago Press, 1996.
Seligman, Martin E. P. *Flourish: A Visionary New Understanding of Happiness and Well-Being*. New York: Free Press, 2011.
Seligman, Martin E. P. and Mihaly Csikszentmihalyi. "Positive Psychology: An Introduction." *American Psychologist* 55, no. 1 (January 2000): 5–14.
Sellery, George C. and Clarence A. Dykstra, eds. *William James: The Man and the Thinker*. Madison: University of Wisconsin Press, 1942.
Seth, James. Review of James, *A Pluralistic Universe*. *Philosophical Review* 18, no. 5 (September 1909): 536–42.
Sewall, Frank. "Professor James on Religious Experience." *New-Church Review* 10 (April 1903): 243–64.
Sharples, S. P. "Some Reminiscences of the Lawrence Scientific School." *Harvard Graduates' Magazine* 26, no. 4 (June 1918): 532–40.
Simon, Linda. *Genuine Reality: A Life of William James*. New York: Harcourt Brace, 1998.
Singer, Marcus G. "The Pragmatic Use of Language and the Will to Believe." *American Philosophical Quarterly* 8, no. 1 (January 1971): 24–34.
Skrupskelis, Ignaz K. "Introduction" to James, *Essays, Comments, and Reviews*, xxi–xxxix.
———. "Introduction" to James, *Manuscript Essays and Notes*, xiii–xlviii.
———. "Introduction" to James, *Manuscript Lectures*, xvii–lxiii.
Smith, John Edwin. "Introduction" to James, *The Varieties of Religious Experience*, xi–li.
———. *The Spirit of American Philosophy*. Albany: SUNY Press, [1963]; rev. ed. 1983.
———. *Themes in American Philosophy: Purpose, Experience and Community*. New York: Harper Torchbooks, 1970.
———. "William James's Account of Mysticism: A Critical Appraisal." *Mysticism and Religious Traditions*, edited by S. T. Katz, 247–79. Oxford: Oxford University Press, 1983.
Smith, Thomas Vernor. *The Philosophic Way of Life*. Chicago: University of Chicago Press, 1929.
Sokal, Michael M. "Introduction" to James, *Psychology: Briefer Course*, xi–xli.
Starbuck, Edwin D. "The Varieties of Religious Experience." *Biblical World* 24 (1904): 100–111.
Sterrett, J. MacBride. "The Proper Affiliation of Psychology—with Philosophy or with the Natural Sciences?" *Psychological Review* 16, no. 2 (March 1909): 85–106.

Works Cited

Stevens, George B. Review of James, *The Varieties of Religious Experience*. *American Journal of Theology* 7, no. 1 (January 1903): 114–17.
Stratton, George Malcolm. "The Control of the Fighting Instinct." New York: American Association for International Conciliation, December 1913, pamphlet no. 73.
Suckiel, Ellen Kappy. *Heaven's Champion: William James's Philosophy of Religion*. Notre Dame: University of Notre Dame Press, 1996.
———. *The Pragmatic Philosophy of William James*. Notre Dame: University of Notre Dame Press, 1982.
Sully, James. Review of James, *The Principles of Psychology*. *Mind* o.s. 16, no. 63 (July 1891): 393–404.
Taves, Ann. "The Fragmentation of Consciousness and *The Varieties of Religious Experience*: William James's Contribution to a Theory of Religion." Proudfoot, *William James and a Science of Religions*, 48–72.
Taylor, Alfred Edward. Review of James, *A Pluralistic Universe*. *Mind*, n.s. 18, no. 72 (October 1909): 576–88.
———. "Truth and Practice." *Philosophical Review* 14, no. 3 (May 1905): 265–89.
Taylor, Charles. *Varieties of Religion Today: William James Revisited*. Cambridge: Harvard University Press, 2002.
Taylor, Eugene. *William James on Consciousness beyond the Margin*. Princeton: Princeton University Press, 1996.
———. *William James on Exceptional Mental States: The 1896 Lowell Lectures*. Amherst: University of Massachusetts Press, 1984.
Taylor, Frederick Winslow. *Principles of Scientific Management*. New York: Harper and Bros. 1911.
———. *Shop Management*. New York: American Society of Mechanical Engineers, 1903.
Thayer, Horace Standish. "Introduction" to James, *The Meaning of Truth*, xi–xlvi.
———. "Introduction" to James, *Pragmatism*, xi–xxxviii.
———. *Meaning and Action: A Critical History of Pragmatism*. Indianapolis: Hackett, [1968]; 2nd ed. 1981.
Thilly, Frank. *A History of Philosophy*. New York: Henry Holt, 1914.
Titchener, Edward Bradford. *Experimental Psychology: A Manual of Laboratory Practice*. 2 vols. New York: Macmillan, 1901, 1905.
Townsend, Harvey Gates. *Philosophical Ideas in the United States*. New York: American Book, 1934.
Townsend, Kim. *Manhood at Harvard: William James and Others*. New York: Norton, 1996.
Tufts, James Hayden. "Ethics of States" [1915]. *Selected Writings of James Hayden Tufts*, edited by James Campbell, 186–202. Carbondale: Southern Illinois University Press, 1992.

Works Cited

Turner, John Evan. *An Examination of William James's Philosophy: A Critical Essay for the General Reader.* Oxford: Blackwell, 1919.

Washington, Booker T. "Address at the Unveiling of the Monument to Robert Gould Shaw" [31 May 1897]. *African American Political Thought, 1890–1930: Washington, Du Bois, Garvey, and Randolph,* edited by C. D. Wintz, 27–29. Armonk, NY: M. E. Scharpe, 1996.

Watson, John. *The Philosophical Basis of Religion.* Glasgow: MacLehose, 1907.

———. "Some Remarks on Radical Empiricism." *Queen's Quarterly* 18, no. 2 (October–December, 1910): 111–19.

Watson, John Broadus. "Psychology as the Behaviorist Views It." *Psychological Review* 20, no. 3 (May 1913): 158–77.

Wernham, James C. S. *James's Will-to-Believe Doctrine: A Heretical View.* Kingston: McGill-Queen's University Press, 1987.

West, Cornell. *The American Evasion of Philosophy: A Genealogy of Pragmatism.* Madison: University of Wisconsin Press, 1989.

White, Morton Gabriel. *Pragmatism and the American Mind: Essays and Reviews in Philosophy and Intellectual History.* New York: Oxford University Press, 1973.

———. *Science and Sentiment in America: Philosophical Thought from Jonathan Edwards to John Dewey.* New York: Oxford University Press, 1972.

Whitehead, Alfred North. *Modes of Thought.* New York: Free Press, [1938] 1968.

Whitmer, Lightner. "Mental Healing and the Emmanuel Movement," part 4. *Psychological Clinic,* 2 (15 February 1909): 282–300.

Wiener, Philip Paul. *Evolution and the Founders of Pragmatism.* Cambridge: Harvard University Press, 1949.

Williams, Donald Cary. "William James and the Facts of Knowledge." Kallen, *In Commemoration of William James, 1842–1942,* 95–126.

Wilshire, Bruce. "The Breathtaking Intimacy of the Material World: William James's Last Thoughts." *The Cambridge Companion to William James,* edited by R. A. Putnam, 103–24. Cambridge: Cambridge University Press, 1997.

Wilson, Daniel J. *Science, Community, and the Transformation of American Philosophy, 1860–1930.* Chicago: University of Chicago Press, 1990.

Woodbridge, Frederick J. E. "Pragmatism and Education." *Educational Review* 34, no. 3 (October 1907): 227–40.

———. "The Promise of Pragmatism." *Journal of Philosophy* 26, no. 20 (26 September 1929): 541–52.

Zweig, Arnulf. "Gustav Theodor Fechner (1801–1887)." *Encyclopedia of Philosophy,* edited by D. M. Borchert, 3:555–58. 10 vols. Detroit: Thomson Gale, [1967]; 2nd ed. 2006.

Index

Absolute, the: as all of reality, 21, 123, 181, 182–88, 196; as form of consciousness, 55, 76, 179, 275; Emerson and, 9–10. *See also* Idealism

Absolutism. *See* Idealism

action, as contribution or recording, 65, 69, 101–10, 138, 144, 146, 153–56, 275, 279

Adams, Henry, and pessimism, 23, 296n76

Addams, Jane, on war, 236

Aggasiz, Louis, 14, 213

Alcoholics Anonymous, and spiritual power, 308n88

Allport, Gordon W., on religion and sex, 347n5

Angell, James Roland: on WJ and psychical research, 76–77; on WJ and truth, 322n52; on Pragmatism, 317n19

American Philosophical Association, 17, 26, 293n56

American Psychological Association, 17, 26, 29

animals: and levels of consciousness, 208, 267, 283; and signs, 339n8; and vivisection, 216–17

Aristotle: as philosopher, 2; as pragmatist, 114

Ayer, Alfred Jules, on truth, 327n87

Bakewell, Charles Montague: on *Pluralistic Universe*, 301n31; on Pragmatism, 317n20, 318n21

Barzun, Jacques: on WJ and psychical research, 309n95; on WJ and truth, 323n61, 324n66; on WJ as artist, 7, 299n20; on WJ as philosopher, 289n1; on vagueness, 303n45

Bawden, Henry Heath: on philosophy, 300n23; on Pragmatism, 318n21, 319n33; on truth, 324nn62–63

Beach, Joseph Warren, on WJ as writer, 290n17

Beard, George Miller, on nervousness, 293n48

Beers, Clifford Whittingham, 219

behaviorism, 297n7

Bentham, Jeremy, on pleasure and pain, 67, 308n80

Bergson, Henri: on percepts and concepts, 195–98; as philosopher, 192; on time, 193–95; on ways of knowing, 192–93

Berkeley, George: as empiricist, 45, 119, 135; as idealist, 173; as philosopher, 4; as pragmatist, 114

Berle, Adolf Augustus, on religious experience, 247, 352n44

Bernstein, Richard J., on vicious intellectualism, 335n29

Björkman, Edwin, on WJ as writer, 8

Bjork, Daniel W., on WJ as bridge, 291n27

Blau, Joseph Leon: on Absolutism, 335n32; on Idealism, 334n28; on WJ and Peirce, 329n94; on Realism, 331n15

"block universe" (WJ), 145, 156, 160, 185, 354n54

Boas, George, on Pragmatism, 316n9

Bode, Boyd Henry, on WJ as philosopher, 4

Boodin, John Elof: on the history of philosophy, 338n48; on pure science, 326n76

Bradley, Francis Herbert: on the Absolute, 335n33; on Fechner, 336n41

Brodbeck, May, on Pragmatism, 112

Brooks, Van Wyck: on WJ, 8; on progress, 296n76

Brown, Harold Chapman, on WJ as individualist, 294n65

Bush, Wendell T.: on Empiricism, 331n13; on WJ, 5

Calkins, Mary Whiton: on imitation, 306n71; on war, 236–37
Carus, Paul: on Pragmatism, 112, 315n2; on WJ as writer, 8
"cash value" (WJ), 126–27, 189, 314n28, 320n37
Cattell, James McKeen, on American psychology, 297n13
Chautauqua, New York, 210–12
Chesterton, Gilbert Keith, 120
Chicago Pragmatism, 10
Civil War, American, WJ and, 14, 221–22, 224, 231
Clifford, William Kingdon, and the justification of belief, 88, 97–102, 103, 107, 122, 157–58, 322n55
Coe, George Albert, on *The Varieties*, 247
Cohen, Morris Raphael: on WJ and logic, 337n46; on philosophy, 343n43
Coles, Robert, on selfishness, 340n13
Commager, Henry Steele, on Pragmatism, 111–12
Common Sense Realism, 132–35, 172–73. See also Realism
Comte August, as pragmatist, 114
Conkin, Paul K.: on WJ and science, 296n75; on WJ as social thinker, 342n34
consciousness. See self
Cooley, Charles Horton, on sense of self, 306n67, 306n69
Copernicus, 23–24
Copleston, Frederick Charles, on truth, 325n71, 327n83, 328n89
"cosmic consciousness" (WJ). See Absolute, the
Cotkin, George: on WJ as public philosopher, 290n13; on WJ as social reformer, 224
Curti, Merle Eugene, on WJ as social reformer, 224, 341n23, 343n36

Dalton, John, 135
Darwinism, 81, 82, 129, 213
Descartes, Rene, as philosopher, 4, 37
determinism, 21–23, 37, 66–67, 88–93. See also free will
Dewey, John: as American philosopher, 6; as Hegelian, 186; on institutional reconstruction, 225–29; on WJ and Peirce, 319n26; on WJ as artist, 7–8; on WJ as pragmatist, 2;

on WJ as social reformer, 346n51; on WJ's influence, 10–11; on philosophy, 331n14; on Pragmatism, 114, 316n10, 316n12, 319n26, 320n37; on *The Principles*, 301n33; on problem of evil, 295n67; as religious thinker, 355n57; as social reformer, 225–26; on the self, 307n72; on social reform, 343n41; on warfare, 237; on warranted assertability, 158–59
divine, the, 250–51
Divine Providence, 311n11
Douglass, Frederick, on black enlistments in the Civil War, 345n50
Du Bois, W. E. B.: on double-consciousness, 307n74; WJ on, 223–24

Earle, William James: on WJ as philosopher, 5; on religion, 353n46
Edwards, Jonathan, as American philosopher, 1
Eliot, Charles William, as president of Harvard, 16, 27
Emerson, Ralph Waldo: as American philosopher, 1, 6; on Christianity, 349n20; as friend of the James family, 12; WJ on, 9–10, 18, 86, 228, 250–51, 254–55, 291nn23–24; on nature, 334n24, 344n47
Empiricism, and fallibilism, 100; radical, 161–70, 179–80, 182–83, 304n55, 319n28; traditional, 45, 54, 57–58, 121–24, 126, 131, 196, 205–6
Evans, Rand B., on WJ as psychologist, 297n13, 298n15, 302n36
evil, problem of, 20, 188, 295n67
evolution. See Darwinism

faith, religious, 87–88, 241–42
faith ladder, 108–9, 267, 274
fallibilism, 21–22, 77, 98–99, 100, 155, 328n88
Faraday, Michael, 135
Fechner, Gustav Theodor: and analogy, 191; and consciousness, 191–92; as philosopher, 190–91
Fiske, John, on infancy, 305n58
Fletcher, Horace, on fearthought, 70, 308n84
Flower, Elizabeth, and Murray G. Murphey, on Pragmatism, 319n32

376

Index

Fontinell, Eugene, on immortality, 336n40
Franklin, Benjamin: as American philosopher, 6; on human freedom, 311n9; on immortality, 258, 350n25; on polytheism, 336n40; as pragmatist, 9, 111, 113; as Puritan, 9; on "savages," 321n43; WJ on, 8–9
free will, 16, 61–62, 130–31, 311n8. *See also* will
French, Frederick Courtney, on religious experience, 351n38
Fresnels, Augustin-Jean, 72
Fullerton, George Stuart: on philosophy, 336n34; on religious belief, 312n13, 313n21

Galileo Galilei, 27, 72, 135
Galvini, Luigi, 72
Gardner, Harry Norman, on truth, 322n51
Gardner, Martin: on WJ as psychical researcher, 310n98; on truth, 148, 325n67
Garrison, George R., on WJ as social reformer, 342n33
Gifford, Adam, 242
Gilson, Etienne, on WJ and God, 353n47
gnosticism, 92–93
God: and believers, 96; as finite, 251–52, 354n54; WJ on, 269–70, 274–78
Gould, James A., on empiricism, 319n28
"Great Companion" (WJ), 55, 77–78
Green, Thomas Hill, 181

habit: human plasticity and, 48–51; in relation to custom, 49–50; religion as, 245–46; war and, 230–36
Hall, Granville Stanley: on WJ as psychologist, 301n34; as psychic researcher, 310n98; on warfare, 236
"healthy-minded" (WJ), 254–56, 262
Hegel, Georg Wilhelm Friedrich: and dialectical method, 186–87; as idealist, 107, 181, 186, 189, 335n30; as obscure writer, 44, 336n35; as philosopher, 186, 187
Hibben, John Grier: on first things, 320n38; on religious experience, 247, 249; on subconscious, 352n40
High, Richard P., and William R. Woodward: on action, 307n76; on free will, 311n8
Hobhouse, Leonard Trelawny, 313n24
Hocking, William Ernest: on WJ as philosopher, 5; on moral action, 338n1; on need for action, 102, 314n33; on negative pragmatism, 326n75
Hollinger, David A.: on Pragmatism, 323n58; on scientific dogmatism, 312n16, 315n37; on *The Varieties*, 349n15, 350n27
Holmes, Oliver Wendell, Jr.: on concepts, 338n47; on WJ as philosopher, 3; as member of the Metaphysical Club, 16, 116; on soldiering, 345n48
Holmes, Oliver Wendell, Sr., 292n41
Holt, Edwin Bissell, on WJ as philosopher, 29
Hume, David: as empiricist, 34, 51, 83, 96, 119, 135, 173, 179, 303n43; as inadequate empiricist, 45, 304n55; as pragmatist, 114
Hunt, William Morris, 13
Husserl, Edmund, 26

Idealism, 119, 145, 156, 180–89, 257, 300n27. *See also* Absolute, the
immortality, 256–59, 260, 303n48, 336n40, 350n24
imperialism, 229–30
infancy, importance of, 305n58

James, Alice (sister): on WJ, 17, 339n9; and illness, 292n34; and siblings, 12
James, Alice Howe Gibbens (wife): and family, 16–17; marriage to WJ, 293n54
James, Garth Wilkinson (brother): and Civil War, 14, 292n34, 342n26; and siblings, 12
James, Henry, the Elder (father): ideas, 13, 291n33, 293n47; life, 12–13; as religious mystic, 240
James, Henry (brother): and Civil War, 14; on James family, 291n32, 293n47; on WJ's philosophy, 17; and siblings, 12
James, Mary Robertson Walsh (mother), 12
James, Robertson (brother): and Civil War, 14, 292n34; and siblings, 12
James, William, of Albany (grandfather), 11–12
James, William (WJ): on abstract ideas, 71, 232; as artist, 7, 10, 13, 285, 292n38, 301n34; and Brazil, 14, 16; as cheater, 309n97; on common sense, 132–35, 163; on consciousness, 40–48, 172–80, 266, 267–71; as

377

James, William (WJ) (*continued*)
Darwinian, 25, 85, 129, 185; on death, 17–18, 20, 294n63; on Emerson, 9–10, 18, 86, 228, 250–51, 254–55, 291nn23–24; on ethics, 200–239; on evil, 20, 123, 188; on experience, 5, 21, 41, 174–76, 240, 269–71, 303n46, 331n13, 347n2; and fallibilism, 21–22, 77, 98–100, 155; on faith, 87–88, 241–42; on faith ladder, 108–9, 267, 274; on freedom, 7–8, 18, 93; on "front door" and "back door" of the mind, 205–6, 321n50, 339n5; on habit, 48–52; and Harvard Medical School, 14, 16; as Harvard professor 1, 16–17, 25–27, 240, 329n3; on human plasticity, 48–49; ill health and depressions, 14–16, 17, 69–70; on individualism, 7, 10, 18, 100, 206–15, 226–29, 342n34; on inner ideals, 212–13; on institutions, 215, 225–29, 248–50; as irrationalist, 196, 313n25, 337n46; on "knowing" as ambiguous, 163–72, 330n7; on life of luxury and wealth, 345n49, 346n54; and logic, 3, 289n4, 337n46; on the "more," 71, 73, 76, 133, 190, 199, 265–71, 278, 280–81, 283; as opponent of science, 22, 296n75; on percepts and concepts, 164–72, 176–79, 195, 241–42, 259–64; and psychical research, 71–78; as philosopher, 2, 3–6, 11, 16, 19, 21, 290n13, 291n27, 296n1; on philosophy, 19, 20, 32–38, 37–38, 198–99; as physician, 7, 21, 285, 292n42; as pluralist, 21, 47, 76, 85, 161, 258, 354n54; on Pragmatism, 113–59, 272; as pragmatist, 3, 317n19; prejudices of, 66, 208–9, 211–12, 339n9, 340n11; as psychologist, 16, 25–30, 152, 243, 285, 299n18; on radical empiricism, 3, 21, 161–70, 179–80, 182–83; on rationality, 79–88, 281; on relations, 3, 45, 162, 179–80, 186, 199; on the self, 52–60; on social justice, 220–21, 234–35; as social reformer, 224–29, 341nn23–24, 342n33, 343n36; on temperament, 120–21; on tender- and tough-minded thinkers, 33, 87, 121–24; on time, 42, 133, 135, 193–95; on truth, 136–48, 150–53, 153–58, 271–84, 321n50; as tolerant, 20, 78, 295n69, 340n13; on vagueness, 41, 45, 309n92; vastation of, 15–16, 240, 293n49; on vicious intellectualism, 160, 184–85, 335n29; on vivisection, 216–17; on will to believe, 16, 94–110; on women, 341n18; as writer, 7–8, 19
—, works: "Does Consciousness Exist?," 172–74; *Essays in Radical Empiricism*, 161, 329n2; *The Many and the One*, 161, 329n2; "The Moral Equivalent of War," 230–36; "The Moral Philosopher and the Moral Life," 200–206; "On a Certain Blindness," 206–10; "Philosophical Conceptions and Practical Results," 114–20; *Pragmatism*, 114–15, 161; *The Principles of Psychology*, 29–31, 38–40; *Psychology: Briefer Course*, 38, 40; *A Pluralistic Universe*, 35, 180–81; "The Sentiment of Rationality," 80–88, 91, 95; *Some Problems of Philosophy*, 18; "The Stream of Thought/Consciousness," 40–48; *Talks to Teachers*, 38; *The Varieties of Religious Experience*, 242; "What Makes a Life Significant," 210–13, 220–21; *The Will to Believe*, 30, 94; "The Will to Believe," 94–106; "A World of Pure Experience," 179–80
Jastrow, Joseph: on WJ as psychologist, 77–78; on WJ as writer, 290n18; on pathology, 348n11
Jefferson, Thomas: on intellectual error, 315n38; on moral sense, 8, 339n6

Kallen, Horace Meyer, on WJ as writer, 5, 294n64
Kant, Immanuel: overestimation of, 34, 115–16, 119–20, 133, 304n55, 317n20; as pragmatist, 114, 316n10; as rationalist, 40, 45–46, 51, 173, 181, 185; on religious experience, 265
Kennedy, Gail, on the will to believe, 312n19
Kitcher, Philip, on WJ and mystical experience, 354n52
Knight, Margaret: on belief, 326n78; on *The Principles*, 302n36
Knox, Howard Vincente: on WJ and individualism, 340n15; on WJ and rationality, 313n25; on WJ as philosopher, 289n6
Kraushaar, Otto F., on *The Principles*, 29

labor issues, 220–21
Ladd, George Trumbull, on the definition of psychology, 39

Index

Lash, Nicholas, on WJ as writer, 290n16
Lavoisier, Antoine, 27
Lawrence Scientific School 14, 16
Leibniz, Gottfried Wilhelm, 2, 21–22
Leuba, James Henry, on WJ and mystical experience, 353n45
Levin, Michael, on Pragmatism, 324n66
Levinson, Henry Samuel, on religious belief, 351n35
Lewis, Clarence Irving, on active creatures, 351n33
Lincoln, Abraham, 14, 95
Lippmann, Walter: on experience, 305n63; on religious belief, 315n39
Locke, John: as empiricist, 20, 34, 40, 119, 135, 173; as inadequate empiricist, 42, 303n43, 319n28; as philosopher, 26; as pragmatist, 114
Lovejoy, Arthur Oncken, on WJ's philosophy, 295n66, 301n31, 330n9
lynching, 222–23

Madden, Edward H.: on belief, 313n22; on WJ as social reformer, 341nn24–25, 342n31, 342n33; on WJ as writer, 290n11; on WJ's marriage, 293n54; on pluralism, 354n54
Marty, Martin E., on *The Varieties*, 348n10
Materialism. *See* theism
McDermott, John Joseph: on idealism, 335n30; on importance of biographical information, 11; on WJ and belief, 20; on WJ and Emerson, 291n24; on WJ and experience, 40–41; on WJ and immortality, 350n24; on WJ as historian of philosophy, 20; on WJ as philosopher, 2–3, 23–24; on WJ as social reformer, 224; on WJ as writer, 8; on WJ's radical empiricism, 329n1, 330n5, 331n10; on WJ's siblings, 292n34; on WJ's vastation, 293n49
McDermott, Robert A., on psychical research, 309n93, 310n99
McDougall, William, on WJ as psychologist, 29
McGill, Vivian J., on WJ as social reformer, 343n40
Mead, George Herbert: on habitual action, 305n60, 305n62; on I/me, 306n66; on national- and international-mindedness, 238; on radical empiricism, 333n20; on social self, 306n70, 307n73
medicine, practice of, 217–18
meliorism, 22–23, 109–10, 113, 123, 131, 281–82
mental health, 219–20
Metaphysical Club, 16, 116
metaphysics: definition of, 31, 88; pragmatism and, 124–25, 127–32; psychology and, 299n19; in *The Varieties*, 242
Mill, John Stuart: on abilities of women, 70; as philosopher, 4; as pragmatist, 114; on truth, 325n68
Miller, Dickinson Sergeant: on WJ and belief, 299n16; on WJ and openness to others, 339n3, 339n7; on WJ as artist, 7; on WJ as philosopher, 29, 102
mind-cure. *See* "New Thought"
monism. *See* pluralism
Moody, Dwight, 262
Moore, Addison Webster: on Pragmatism, 113, 316n7; on truth, 327n79
Moore, Edward Carter: on moral holidays, 343n37; on relations, 333n21
Moore, George Edward, on truth, 102–3, 327n87
Moore, Jared Sparks, on pluralism, 334n26
moral holidays, 225, 228, 343n37
More, Paul Elmer, on Pragmatism, 315n4
Müller, Gustav Emil, on WJ and personhood, 305n57
Münsterberg, Hugo, 21, 317n20, 341n20
Muirhead, John Henry, on Pragmatism, 324n65
Mumford, Lewis: on philosophy, 5; on Pragmatism, 112; on WJ and belief, 314n28
Murphy, Arthur Edward, on WJ, 339n4
Murphy, Gardner, on WJ as philosopher, 29
Murray, David Leslie, on truth, 325n70
Myers, Gerald E.: on introspection, 303n47; on philosophy and psychology, 296n2, 299n17, 302n41; on *The Principles*, 297n6; on stream of thought, 303n43; on will, 307n77
mysticism, 241, 270–71, 280

neurasthenia, 15, 293n48
"New Thought," 70, 308n83
Nietzsche, Friedrich, 253

optimism. *See* meliorism
Ormond, Alexander Thomas, on religion, 349n17
Otto, Max Carl: on WJ as philosopher, 5, 289n10, 311n6; on WJ as social reformer, 340n17, 343n38

Palmer, George Herbert: on WJ and spelling reform, 295n72; on WJ and tolerance, 295n69; on WJ as teacher, 293n55
Papini, Giovanni: on Pragmatism, 320n36; as pragmatist, 126
Parkes, Henry Bamford, on WJ as thinker, 6–7
Pascal's Wager, 96, 109
Pasteur, Louis, 158
pathology, 244–45, 348n11
Peirce, Charles Sanders: and ethics of terminology, 325n67; on fallibilism, 328n88; on WJ as thinker, 3, 295n71; and justification of belief, 322n55; and Metaphysical Club, 16; as pragmaticist, 82, 97, 125–27, 157; as pragmatist, 30, 111, 114, 116–18, 137, 141, 319n34, 329n94; on *The Principles*, 39, 300n24, 304n53; as tychist, 21
Perry, Ralph Barton: on belief and action, 313n26, 314n34; on Hume, 304n55; on WJ and Fechner, 336n37; on WJ and Peirce, 318n25; on WJ and psychic research, 71; on percepts and concepts, 331n12; on philosophy and psychology, 296n1; on Pragmatism, 113, 324n64, 327n85; on *The Principles*, 29
pessimism. *See* meliorism
philosophy: academic or professional, 4–6, 11, 19, 21, 33, 36–37, 116, 120, 122, 127, 145, 173, 286, 293n56; nature of, 5, 32–38, 331n14, 336n34, 338n48
Plato, 2, 26, 37, 184
pluralism, 93, 98–100, 126, 160–99, 261–62, 286–87
Pollock, Robert Channon: on WJ as philosopher, 2; on WJ as writer, 328n90; on philosophy, 11
positive psychology, 308n85
Pragmaticism (Peirce), 125–27, 157, 320n35
Pragmatism, 111–59; negative pragmatism (Hocking), 326n75; origin of the term, 113–14
prophets, moral, 69, 209
Proudfoot, Wayne, on *The Varieties*, 350n26
"psychologist's fallacy" (WJ), 303n49
psychical research, 71–78
psychology: fringes of, 71–78; and logic, 152–54; "new" or physiological psychology, 25, 26–28, 31–32, 244; and religion, 242–47
psycholophy, 25–32, 38–41

Quine, Willard Van Orman, 9, 30

racial issues, 221–24, 230
Rashdall, Hastings, on belief, 350n28
Rationalism, 54, 121, 131, 143, 169–70, 179–80, 196
rationality: criteria of, 82–87, 89–90, 95; importance of, 77, 79–82
Realism, 26, 172. *See also* Common Sense Realism
relations: as both conjunctive and disjunctive, 180; as experienced, 3, 45, 120, 162; as external or internal, 179, 186, 199, 333n21
religion: as conduct or theology, 259–60, 262–64, 273, 276–77, 286, 348n8; definition of, 247–50, 347n3, 349n17; as habit or fever, 245–46; for healthy-minded or sick soul, 254–56; as personal or institutional, 248–50; and sexuality, 347n5; and subconscious, 351n38; and truth, 271–84
Renouvier, Charles, 16
Riley, Isaac Woodbridge, on WJ and change, 334n25
Roback, Abraham Aaron, on WJ as psychologist, 297n9
Rockefeller, John D., 219–20
Roosevelt, Theodore, on hardihood, 232, 345n50
Rorty, Richard: on WJ and tolerance, 355n56; as philosopher, 9

Index

Royce, Josiah: on action, 313n26; on WJ as philosopher, 1–2; on WJ as American philosopher, 6; WJ on, 185; as idealist, 107, 123, 173, 186, 335n30, 343n40; on philosophy and psychology, 296n3; on Pragmatism, 151, 323n56, 328n91; on *The Principles*, 38–39, 297n11; on religion, 347n3; on religious experience, 249–50; on self-consciousness, 306n68

Russell, Bertrand: on religious belief, 278–79, 354n55; on truth, 151–53, 353n48

Salter, William Mackintire, on working hypotheses, 321n45

Santayana, George: on WJ and experience, 303n46; on WJ and Spanish-American War, 344n44; on WJ as artist, 7; on WJ as philosopher, 6; on WJ's youth, 343n39; on philosophy, 300n28; on philosophy and psychology, 297n10

Schiller, Ferdinand Canning Scott: on belief, 313n23; on *Pragmatism*, 103, 317n16; on WJ and intellectual debt, 337n42; on WJ and the "more," 351n32; on WJ as philosopher, 4, 8; on truth, 324n63, 325n72, 328n93

Schopenhauer, Arthur: as pessimist, 214, 253; as philosopher, 4

science, 62, 326n76

Schurman, Jacob Gould, on religious belief, 311n12, 312n20

Scripture, Edward Wheeler, on psychology, 297n6

Seigfried, Charlene Haddock, on WJ's ideas on women, 341n18

self, 26, 52–60. *See also* soul

Seth, James, on WJ as philosopher, 3–4

Sewall, Frank, on *The Varieties*, 247, 348n14

sexuality, 38, 301n35, 347n5

Shaw, Robert Gould, 222

"sick souls" (WJ). *See* "healthy-minded"

Singer, Marcus G.: on belief, 314n32; on truth, 102

Skrupskelis, Ignaz K., on radical empiricism, 329n2

slavery, 221–22, 224, 228, 239

Smith, John Edwin: on WJ and empathy, 352n43; on WJ and religion, 320n40, 348n12, 349n19, 349nn21–22; on WJ as philosopher, 299n21

Smith, Thomas Vernor, on WJ and science, 295n74

Society for Psychical Research, 73, 74, 77, 309n93

"Socius." *See* "Great Companion"

Socrates, as pragmatist, 114

soul, as substance, 51–52, 256. *See also* self

Spencer, Herbert, 4, 181, 213

Spanish-American War, 115, 229–30, 344n44

Spinoza, Baruch: as philosopher, 37; as pragmatist, 114; as rationalist, 83

Starbuck, Edwin Diller, on *The Varieties*, 348n13, 349n18

Sterrett, J. MacBride, on philosophy as a science, 296n4

Stevens, George B., on *The Varieties*, 246–47

St. Louis Hegelians, 116

Strong, Charles Augustus, on moral demands, 338n2

Suckiel, Ellen Kappy, on religious belief, 312n18, 322n54, 352n39

Swedenborg, Emanuel, 12

Taylor, Alfred Edward, on truth, 323n60, 325n69, 326n78

Taylor, Charles: on Clifford, 314n27; on WJ as religious thinker, 295n73

Taylor, Frederick Winslow, 308n82

Thayer, Horace Standish: on WJ and Peirce, 318n25; on *Pragmatism*, 317n17; on truth, 154, 319n27, 321n49, 326n74

theism, 87–88, 118–19, 128, 181–82, 273–74, 354n49

Thilly, Frank: on Pragmatism, 321n42; on pure experience, 332n18; on Theism, 354n49

Thoreau, Henry David, on the life of poverty, 339n10

time, problem of, 42, 133, 135, 193–95

tolerance, 100, 203–6, 210, 283

Townsend, Harvey Gates, on WJ as psychologist, 299n18

Index

Townsend, Kim, on William James of Albany, 291n30
Transcendentalism, 9–10, 116
transubstantiation, 320n39
truth: necessary, 321n50; Pragmatism and, 136–59; religion and, 271–84
Tufts, James Hayden, on war, 344n46
Turner, John Evan: on Monism, 334n27, 338n49; on WJ as philosopher, 5, 300n26
tychism, 21

vastation, 12–13, 15–16, 69, 293n49
vivisection, 216–17

war and peace, 80, 229–39
Washington, Booker T., 223–24, 342n27
Watson, John: on belief, 312n15; on finite God, 350n23
Watson, John Broadus, on Behaviorism, 297n7

Wesley, John, 86, 262
West, Cornell, on WJ as philosopher, 289n8
Whitehead, Alfred North, 2
Whitman, Walt: as healthy-minded, 254–55, 262; as moral prophet, 209
Whitmer, Lightner, on WJ as psychologist, 298n14
will, 60–69, 88–89, 307n78; and action, 61–70; and attention, 57–58, 61–70. *See also* free will
Williams, Donald Cary, on WJ as philosopher, 4–5
"will to believe, the" (WJ), 94–110
Wilshire, Bruce, on WJ and truth, 323n59
Wilson, Woodrow, 239
Woodbridge, Frederick J. E., on Pragmatism, 321n48
Wright, Chauncey, and the Metaphysical Club, 16, 116

www.ingramcontent.com/pod-product-compliance
Lightning Source LLC
Chambersburg PA
CBHW021815300426
44114CB00009BA/183